A Candid Look
at How the
News Is Made

Behind the Front Page

DAVID S. BRODER

SIMON AND SCHUSTER
New York

SIMON AND SCHUSTER and colophon are registered trademarks of Simon & Schuster, Inc.
Designed by Karolina Harris
Manufactured in the United States of America
10   9   8   7   6   5   4   3   2   1
Library of Congress Cataloging in Publication Data

Broder, David S.
  Behind the front page.

  Bibliography: p.
  1. Journalism—Political aspects—United States.
2. Reporters and reporting—Washington (D.C.)
3. Government and the press—United States.
4. Journalists—United States.   I. Title.
PN4888.P6B7   1987   071'.3   86-31630
ISBN: 0-671-44943-5

Contents

Introduction:
Clique Journalism

I *HAVE* a friend—in California, naturally—who does not read a newspaper. He does not take any magazines. He does not own a television set. And he says he does not turn on the radio except to get the weather forecast when the evidence before his eyes is ambiguous.

If you ask him how he keeps up with what is going on, he says conversations tell him what he needs to know. He rides the bus to and from work—he is an odd Californian in that respect, too—and hears people talk about the news that has attracted their interest. His friends keep him up to date on the fortunes or vicissitudes of those he cares about, and they let him know if there are movies or plays or sports events he might be interested in attending. As for the rest, he does not figure he is missing much.

By recreating the conditions of an earlier era, when rural and village folk depended on conversations at church or tavern or marketplace for all they knew, he has built his own cocoon. He lives a full, happy life, as far as I can judge from our occasional visits, and has time to work in his garden, take long walks, read good novels, and sit and reflect—time that we news junkies squander on our addiction.

I am one of those. I wake up in the morning to an all-news public radio station, watch a morning news show on television at breakfast, read anywhere from four to six papers in the course of the day, and usually watch more than one television news show in the evening. I subscribe to more magazines and buy more books than I can read. My garage—I hope the fire department is not listening—is full of old newspapers and magazines that I may someday find the time to sort, clip, and file.

As if that were not bad enough, I have been writing for newspapers since the fifth grade in Chicago Heights, Illinois, when my friend Jimmy Davis (now a distinguished sociologist at Harvard) was given a hectograph—a primitive mimeograph machine—for Christmas. With our pal, Joe Poerio, we started a neighborhood "newspaper" which we peddled for a penny a copy. I continued on high school, college, and Army papers, on the *Pantagraph* in Bloomington, Illinois, my first daily newspaper job, and for the last thirty years in Washington, where I am part of the largest concentration of reporters in the world.

While my addiction is real, I think I am closer to the norm than my California friend. Most Americans live in an environment that is saturated with news. Newspaper circulations are at an all-time high. Millions more read weekly news magazines and specialized journals. Television stations broadcast up to six hours of local and network news and public affairs programs a day. All-news radio stations and cable television channels bring their versions of reality into the home or office.

In a society saturated with news, its purveyors have become prominent figures. Television anchormen and reporters are some of the most familiar, trusted, and (sometimes) controversial people in the land. Investigative reporters are celebrities, praised for the evils they expose, condemned for their methods. Films are made about journalists; enrollments in journalism schools grow.

And yet this news-conscious, news-addicted society is often critical of those who work in the news media. People curse the messengers, even as they hungrily consume the message. Journalists have been made painfully conscious of the polls showing that our business suffers from its own credibility gap, that even as we give each other awards for excellence, there is substantial distrust from those we serve.

The polls are confirmed by daily experience. We are challenged on performance, on prejudices, and on the very position we occupy in society. That position is unique. The American press is a private business performing a vital public function under a specially protected constitutional status, exempt from regulation by government, immunized against many of the forms of pressure and persuasion to which other institutions are subject in our system of checks and balances. The way the press has used its special position is viewed critically by many of those we purport to serve. Some of that skepticism is inevitable. The more important a commodity or a service becomes to people, the more critical they become about its quality.

Some of the criticisms that come our way are unwarranted. For example, the notion that we are trying to supplant the elected government in running the country or steering its direction is far off base in my opinion. But we have earned some of the criticism by sins of commission, by errors of reporting and of judgment, by invasions of privacy and insensitivity to people's feelings. We have earned it also by sins of omission, missing or coming late to important stories.

Most important, we have earned some distrust by being vague, murky, and occasionally misleading about the nature of our work, or by not pausing to explain what we are about. We show our arrogance again in our response to criticism. We are as thin-skinned a bunch as you would ever want to meet. We can dish it out but most of us have a hard time taking it. When I was a student at the University of Chicago forty years ago, its president, Robert Maynard Hutchins, suggested that the press form a council from its own ranks to monitor and evaluate the performance of newspapers. He was told to buzz off. A quarter-century later, such a council was formed, but it starved for funds and respect and died.

The flame of internal criticism is kept flickering by a few journalism reviews and seminars, but it is only in the last fifteen years or so—in response to public debate about the role of the mass media—that some news organizations have developed a mechanism for evaluating and acting on complaints and criticisms from readers and viewers. In 1986, only three dozen newspapers employed ombudsmen or readers' representatives, and the broadcast media are even more laggard. The absence of a method to make corrections on most television and radio news shows suggests either belief in a superhuman degree of perfection among their correspondents or an institutional reluctance to go back and straighten out mistakes.

Most of all, we resist admitting that—reporters, broadcasters, editors, or producers—we do exercise great influence in this society, preferring to see ourselves as simple scribes, recording the words and actions of others. It is so much easier that way. But it is an act of self-deception—and not our only one, either.

The consumer fraud, if you will, begins right at the top, with the flagship of our business, the *New York Times,* and its famous slogan, "All the News That's Fit to Print." I talked about that slogan in a speech I gave honoring the 1979 winners of the Pulitzer Prize—the most prestigious award in journalism—at the National Press Club in Washington. Some editors liked the speech well enough to reprint it; others criticized it for telling tales out of school and giving ammunition to our critics. What I said that stirred the controversy was this:

It ["All the News That's Fit to Print"] is a great slogan, but it is also a fraud. Neither the *Times* nor the *Washington Post* nor any other newspaper —let alone the nightly network news shows—has space or time to deal with all the actions taken and the words uttered in the city of Washington with significance for some of its readers or viewers. And that says nothing of what is happening every day in the rest of the country and the world.

All of us know as journalists that what we are mainly engaged in deciding is not what to put in but what to leave out. A reporter returning to the office from a congressional hearing may have a thick stack of statements and pages of notes, but he learns he has 14 column-inches to tell what has taken hours to unfold. An editor may have two columns to convey the substance of a strategic-arms agreement seven years in the negotiation.

For television, the selection process is even more cruel. . . .

If we treated our audience with the respect its members deserve, and gave them an accurate understanding of the pressures of time and space under which we work, we could acknowledge the inherent limitations and imperfections in our work—instead of reacting defensively when they are pointed out. We could say plainly what we all know to be the case, that the process of selecting what the reader reads involves not just objective facts but subjective judgments, personal values and, yes, prejudices. Instead of promising All the News That's Fit to Print, I would like to see us say— over and over, until the point has been made—that the newspaper that drops on your doorstep is a partial, hasty, incomplete, inevitably somewhat flawed and inaccurate rendering of some of the things we have heard about in the past 24 hours—distorted, despite our best efforts to eliminate gross bias, by the very process of compression that makes it possible for you to lift it from the doorstep and read it in about an hour. If we labeled the product accurately, then we could immediately add: But it's the best we could do under the circumstances, and we will be back tomorrow with a corrected and updated version.

If we did that, I suspect, not only would we feel less inhibited about correcting and updating our own stories, we might even encourage the readers to contribute their own information and understanding to the process. We might even find ourselves acknowledging something most of us find hard to accept: that they have something to tell us, as well as to hear from us. And if those readers felt that they were part of a communications process in which they were participants and not just passive consumers, then they might more easily understand that their freedoms—and not just ours—are endangered when the search warrants and subpoenas are visited on the press.

This book had its beginning in that speech and the controversy it provoked. My purpose is to try to remove some of the myths about delivering the news, to look realistically and critically at contemporary journalism. Not all of it, obviously. But at a vital part for the reputation and credibility of the press and for the public's knowledge and understanding: the reporting of national politics and government from Washington, D.C.

As a reporter in Washington since 1956, the last twenty years as the national political correspondent and columnist for the *Washington Post,* I have had a firsthand look at many controversies, from the Watergate case, which banished the President from government, to the Janet Cooke case, which tarnished the reputation of journalism's highest prize and of my own newspaper.

My perspective is that of a newspaperman; that's been my job for almost all my adult life. But I have had chances to look inside the other major segments of what has been called our six-tier communications system: radio, television, weekly and monthly magazines, and books. I have done radio commentaries for Westinghouse Broadcasting System, TV news and commentary programs for NBC and the other commercial networks and for public television. I have contributed to *Newsweek,* the *New Republic, Harper's, The Atlantic,* and several other magazines, and I have written three books on politics before this one.

For the most part, I write about things I know firsthand. In many of the cautionary tales that follow, the person who screwed up was the person who stares back sleepily from the mirror when I shave. But I have tried to deal with other mass media to the extent my experience permits, especially with television, which has changed journalism and politics and the public's perception of both.

AT the outset, I want to call attention to a problem I will be discussing throughout the book. It is a form of journalistic corruption to which the current crop of Washington reporters—I include myself—is particularly susceptible. I call it clique journalism.

Even in the first generation of modern Washington correspondents, those at the top—columnists such as Walter Lippmann, Joseph and Stewart Alsop, Drew Pearson, Marquis Childs, Thomas L. Stokes, David Lawrence, Roscoe Drummond, Arthur Krock, and James Reston—enjoyed intimate friendships with Presidents, secretaries of state, leading senators and representatives. In addition to the weight of their printed words, many of their memoirs make it clear that they often served as influential private counselors to the men in power. *Washington Post* Executive Editor Benjamin C. Bradlee, who likes to warn reporters that coziness with government officials is "a pact with the devil," was a close friend of John F. Kennedy. As he makes clear in his book, *Conversations with Kennedy,* the friendship that developed spontaneously between an ambitious young senator and an ambitious young journalist in the 1950s was cultivated by both, during the early 1960s, for their mutual advantage.

In the capital today, there are many more journalists who have incomes, educations, and influence that put them on a par with the men and women they cover. Not surprisingly, there is much more mixing between the two groups than occurs between mayors and city hall reporters. Describing "the socialite journalist" in a 1985 *Washington Monthly* article, Charlotte Hays and Jonathan Rowe said that "in a city where the elected powers come and go, the press has become a part of the permanent social establishment. . . . Socializing with the Washington media becomes a priority, even for the very highest. President Jimmy Carter, for example, showed up for the 1980 opening of the L.A. *Times*'s new bureau on I Street. [Bureau chief Jack] Nelson, who knew Carter when he was a reporter with the *Atlanta Constitution,* sees nothing extraordinary about the President of the United States stopping by a newspaper party. 'I don't see any reason why we shouldn't consider ourselves on equal footing with those we cover,' he says."

In a 1984 issue of *The Nieman Reports,* Murray Seeger, a veteran reporter who has become the chief publicist for the AFL-CIO, took many of his former colleagues (including me) to task for our reporting of labor's role in the 1984 campaign. Seeger said he had "the feeling that newspapers are becoming a class media, edited and written by upper-class individuals for an audience that is largely upper-middle-class or higher."

Some critics have taken this argument a long step further by arguing that the press and government are really one. In 1982, William L. Rivers, a former Washington correspondent who had become a journalism professor at Stanford, published a book on the Washington press called *The Other Government*. He argued that Washington reporters "have acquired the authority and sometimes even the power of a shadow government." Noting the perquisites, privileges, and access provided reporters in Congress and the executive departments, and the importance officials attach to what they see in the media, Rivers wrote, "In a sense the two governments—the official government and the national news media—increasingly form part of a single, symbiotic unit... a double-mirror effect, in which each side responds to what the other is doing, while at the same time adjusting itself to the other side's anticipated needs."

Harper's magazine writer Tom Bethell wrote in 1977, "The news media have now become a part of the government in all but formal constitutional ratification of the fact. For all intents and purposes, the *New York Times* and CBS News can best be understood as departments of the federal bureaucracy."

When the argument is carried that far, it is nonsense. Most reporters would make rotten politicians or public officials. We are not organizers; we are, in fact, chronically disorganized. We are not consensus-seekers; we tend to be naysayers. We do not work well with other people; it is not accidental that we have chosen work—writing—that we must do by ourselves. Most important of all, we are voyeurs. We would rather watch than do. Tom Wicker of the *New York Times* had it right when he wrote, in *On Press*, "I have never known a reporter who actively sought real political power for himself.... Reporters want *journalistic* power and eminence, all right.... Reporters love to be heeded by powerful personages, but most wouldn't know what to do with *actual* power (outside their news organizations) if they had it.... The monitoring of power, to a reporter, is more important and exciting by far—and a lot more gratifying—than the exercise of power."

There are exceptions: reporters and writers like the late Richard L. Neuberger and Blair Moody became senators, as did ex-broadcaster

Jesse Helms. The late Tom McCall moved from Portland television to the Oregon governorship and Seattle Mayor Charles Royer also has a TV background.

But the idea of the press as government will not stand scrutiny. A government is a group of people bonded by certain common aims, programs, or interests who share the exercise of power through the writing and administration of law. The press cannot function as a government, because it cannot organize to do anything. Even if you assume that each individual reporter, editor, producer, or anchorman is seething with policy ideas, which they aren't, no three of those individuals can be organized to do anything in common.

The press is an institutional anarchy—and prefers to keep it that way. Each news organization is a law unto itself, and within each organization, individual, autonomous judgments tend to subvert, overthrow, or simply ignore the established norms. When the press has to organize something, we generally fail. Periodically efforts will be made to "structure" the questioning in the President's news conference. They invariably founder on the insistence that every reporter should be free to do his own thing. Let a thousand flowers bloom. Let several hundred reporters crowd the East Room, jostling and shouting and competing for the President's attention; let every question be given the same priority—none—whether trivial or cosmic, parochial or of universal interest. The mess you see on the press's side of a presidential news conference is an exact measurement of our capacity to function as a part of government.

Nonetheless, the close working relationships between journalists and public officials have led to what I call clique journalism. In recent years our reporting of government and national politics has narrowed to coverage of the insiders, by the insiders, and for the insiders. I dwell on the dangers of such coverage because I think it corrupts our character. It diverts us from our main function of serving the broad public and it alienates us from that public, whose support is ultimately the only safeguard of the professional freedom we require to do our jobs.

Our jobs are tough enough, even if we are not diverted by external pressures or subverted by our own status and success. What journalism can produce for a society always falls short of the society's needs, and even further short of historical or philosophical truth.

The way we cover the news is to dig for facts, in hopes that they will yield an approximation of truth. They rarely do. It was Lippmann, the greatest American journalist of this century, who wrote more than sixty years ago in *Public Opinion* that "There is a very small body of exact knowledge, which it requires no outstanding ability or training to deal with. The rest is in the journalist's own discretion. Once he departs from the region where it is definitely recorded at the County Clerk's office that John Smith has gone into bankruptcy, all fixed standards disappear. The story of why John Smith failed, his human frailties, the analysis of the economic conditions on which he was shipwrecked, all of this can be told in a hundred different ways."

My experience suggests that we often have a hard time finding our way through the maze of facts—visible and concealed—in any story. We often misjudge character, mistake plot lines. And even when the facts seem most evident to our senses, we go astray by our misunderstanding or misjudgment of the context in which they belong.

This last source of error arises often in campaign coverage, and so I start this effort to illustrate the limits of journalism in that graveyard of so many presidential hopes—the New Hampshire primary.

1
Missing
the Story

CHAPTER ONE
Taken Out
of Context

*T*HE snow was cascading down that Saturday morning in Manchester, New Hampshire, when Senator Edmund S. Muskie headed toward the offices of the *Manchester Union Leader* for the first scheduled event of the day. Like much in modern campaigning, this "event" was designed more for the press and the cameras than for the citizenry. Fewer than a hundred hardy campaign workers and casual passersby, stamping their feet in the snow, would join the newspaper's employees watching from windows.

Ed Muskie was the front-runner in the New Hampshire presidential primary, so when his press aides alerted the reporters living at the Sheraton-Wayfarer in nearby Bedford that Muskie would go to the *Union Leader* Saturday morning to reply to attacks from publisher William Loeb, they were guaranteed that this was one media event that would draw heavy coverage.

As he walked through the snow, hands jammed into his overcoat pockets and his head bent against the snow, Muskie looked as if he might be having second thoughts. But for the reporters trailing him, the setting and the timing were perfect. It was early in the day; we would have plenty of time to file for the early Sunday deadlines. The event would be a natural lead-in to our Sunday wrap-up pieces, summarizing the New Hampshire situation nine days before the primary. In confronting Loeb, who had been giving Muskie the same brutal front-page editorial treatment he had given other moderates and liberals in both parties who appeared to threaten the publisher's favored right-wing candidates, the senator from Maine was symbolically confronting the frustrations which had turned New Hampshire from an expected easy triumph into an exhausting, embittering struggle. The story looked to have some potential.

It proved to have much more than that.

The human factor is always the least predictable element in covering politics. That is why the beat is so fascinating. Under the pressure of campaigns for high office, people react in ways that are always revealing and often unexpected. In this case, Muskie's strategists wanted him to show indignation and righteous wrath and regain the offensive in what they saw as an eroding effort to hold off the challenge of his major rival, Senator George McGovern of South Dakota. The concerns focused on the impact of two *Union Leader* editorials: one concerned an alleged derogatory comment by Muskie about the important French-Canadian voting bloc; the other impugned the behavior and character of the candidate's wife, Jane.

What actually happened there in the snowstorm, as Muskie stood on the flatbed truck drawn up before the *Union Leader* building, was more unexpected and dramatic. By noon, back in the warmth of the Wayfarer, I wrote about it in an unrestrained fashion:

> With tears streaming down his face and his voice choked with emotion, Senator Edmund S. Muskie (D-Maine) stood in the snow outside the *Manchester Union Leader* this morning and accused its publisher of making vicious attacks on him and his wife, Jane.
>
> The Democratic presidential candidate called publisher William Loeb "a gutless coward" for involving Mrs. Muskie in the campaign and said four times that Loeb had lied in charging that Muskie had condoned a slur on Americans of French-Canadian descent.
>
> In defending his wife, Muskie broke down three times in as many minutes—uttering a few words and then standing silent in the near blizzard, rubbing at his face, his shoulders heaving, while he attempted to regain his composure sufficiently to speak.

The story—accompanied by a photo—ran under a four-column headline as the off-lead of the Sunday *Washington Post* and continued for twenty-three paragraphs inside. David Nyhan's story, which described Muskie as "weeping silently," was played even more prominently on the front page of the *Boston Globe*. The *New York Times* ran a photograph on page 1, but relegated the story to page 54, perhaps because reporter James M. Naughton cast his story around Muskie's denunciation of Loeb and mentioned the tears and broken speech only once, in the sixth paragraph. The *Washington Star* used a UPI story on page 2 which noted in the eighth paragraph that Muskie was "visibly shaken" but offered no further details.

That Saturday night, CBS News had an arresting clip of the event, which Roger Mudd introduced by saying that Muskie, after denouncing Loeb, "suddenly became emotional and found it difficult to continue." The screen was filled with Muskie's face, the features contorted.

As Theodore H. White later wrote in *The Making of the President 1972*, "Rarely has the instrument of television been able, without any preconceived political intent, to frame perspectives more strikingly." CBS opened its news show with a brief report on a West Virginia flood, then shifted to a long segment on President Nixon's trip to China, where, as White wrote, "in this context of beauty and majesty there were Richard Nixon and Chou En-lai feeding goldfish from the moon bridge in smiles and amity." Then, with only a commercial break, the scene shifted to Manchester, with "Ed Muskie on the flatbed truck crying, or choking up, but obviously in great distress as his voice broke in a denunciation of the man who had attacked his wife. The contrast between the President's management of great events in Asia and the Democratic candidate's disturbance over an unexplained slander in Manchester, New Hampshire, was sharp."

Watching it on a weekend visit home in Washington, the crack political reporter Jack W. Germond, then with the Gannett newspapers' Washington bureau, instantly decided to fly back to New Hampshire, because, he said, "I knew something was happening."

Indeed it was. Within twenty-four hours, Muskie's weeping became the focus of political talk, not just in New Hampshire, but wherever in America or the world the pattern of the developing presidential race was discussed. His tears would be generally described as one of the contributing causes to his disappointing showing in the March 7 primary. Muskie beat McGovern by a margin of 46 to 37 percent, but his managers had publicized their goal of winning at least 50 percent of the New Hampshire Democratic vote. Underdog McGovern was able to claim that the results showed Muskie's weakness and his own growing strength. Muskie never recovered from that Saturday in the snow.

At the time, controversy centered on Muskie's insistence he never shed the tears we thought we saw. Melting snow from his hatless head filled his eyes, he said, and had him wiping his face. While admitting that exhaustion and emotion got the better of him that morning, the senator believed that he was damaged more by the press and television coverage of the event than by his own actions.

In retrospect, it is clear that Muskie was victimized neither by himself nor by the press, but by a classic dirty trick that had been engineered by agents of the distant and detached President Nixon. The Loeb editorial that had brought Muskie out in the snowstorm had been based on a letter forged by a White House staff member, intent on destroying Muskie's credibility. But we did not know that.

EIGHT years later, another dramatic event took place during another New Hampshire primary, and once again the press was directly involved in both its creation and its impact. This one was in Nashua, and the weather was no problem, for it was held inside the Nashua High School gym. There was a huge press corps in attendance for the debate between George Bush and Ronald Reagan sponsored by the *Nashua Telegraph*. It was the last Saturday night before the 1980 primary. With all published polls showing the Reagan-Bush race too close to call, every reporter in the state thought the primary and very possibly the Republican nomination would be settled by the debate, and before the first word had been uttered, the press corps reached a verdict that Reagan had wiped Bush out.

Reagan had shown up with four other Republican contenders, Senators Howard H. Baker, Jr., of Tennessee and Bob Dole of Kansas, and Illinois Representatives John B. Anderson and Philip M. Crane. They had been excluded by the sponsor because they were trailing in the polls. He had walked on stage with them, asserting that "fair play" required they be allowed to join in. When the newspaper editor—forgetting that the Reagan campaign had underwritten the costs of the evening—ordered a technician to cut off his microphone, Reagan bellowed, "I'm paying for this microphone, Mr. Green." (In his excitement, Reagan mispronounced the name of editor Jon Breen. It was the only line he blew all night.)

Throughout, Bush played into Reagan's hands by acting the rigid, uncomfortable heavy, so disdainful of his rivals that he did not even acknowledge their presence.

This time, there was no disagreement in the reports of what occurred—or its significance. The *Post* account, which Lou Cannon and I wrote, said:

> The polite Republican presidential race exploded in anger tonight against presumed front-runner George Bush about the issue of who had the right to debate him three days before the New Hampshire primary.
>
> Four other GOP contenders of various ideological stripes joined Ronald Reagan in condemning Bush and the *Nashua Telegraph* for insisting that Reagan alone be allowed to debate Bush before an excited audience of 2,000 in the Nashua High School gymnasium.

Germond and Jules Witcover, in the *Star*, called it "an angry brawl" in which "four candidates walked off a debate stage and castigated George Bush in harsh terms." On the front page of the *Times*, Hedrick Smith said, "Four Republican presidential candidates angrily attacked George Bush tonight for what Senator Howard H. Baker, Jr., called an effort 'to reinstitute closed door politics' after the four were excluded from participation in a debate between Mr. Bush and Ronald Reagan." The page-one story in the *Globe* by David Nyhan and Robert Healy said the debate "erupted into a bitter disagreement."

As in the Muskie incident eight years earlier, it was the behavior of the front-runner that attracted press attention. All of the stories referred to Bush's refusal to meet with Reagan and the four other candidates. The stories also noted that Bush had looked rigidly ahead and said nothing when Reagan led the four on stage.

The impression was of a stiff-necked, arrogant front-runner violating the rules of fair play. Although the Nashua newspaper tried in a Monday afternoon story to exonerate Bush, the impression persisted right up to primary day that Bush had blown it.

When Reagan clobbered Bush 50 to 23 percent, Nashua was seen as Bush's downfall. The man who had been crowned "front-runner" after upsetting Reagan in the January Iowa caucuses was knocked back into an also-ran status from which he would not recover.

But, as eight years earlier in Manchester, there were two problems with the story. The first, of which there were hints at the time, was that

Nashua was a carefully laid trap. Reagan campaign manager John P. Sears had successfully involved the other four Republicans in a plot to embarrass the favorite.

The second problem was that, unbeknown to us, our readers, and apparently the other contenders, the Reagan managers had polls at least a day earlier which convinced them that Bush was no longer in front. Nashua was simply the *coup de grâce* for George Bush.

Had we known those things, we might have written our Nashua stories in a way that might have suggested that Ronald Reagan, who has always played the nice-guy role in politics and often has gained sympathy as the underdog, was on this occasion a manipulative politician, using slippery tactics to spring a surprise coup on a weakened challenger and on his newspaper hosts. As in Manchester, what we didn't know hurt us—and those who depend on us for their news.

To understand how such slipups happen, one should understand something of the work habits and psychology of reporters. It is not an accident that we refer to "news stories" as the basic ingredient of the news. Reporters are essentially storytellers, heirs to a narrative tradition as old as mankind. Stories have settings and characters and plot lines. Whether we acknowledge it or not, we are constantly devising the scripts we think appropriate for the events we are covering.

Explicitly in my mind and, I think, implicitly in the *Post* story I wrote from Manchester, there was a specific context or scenario into which the Muskie performance fit: it was the unraveling of a presidential front-runner's campaign.

The fourth paragraph of my story said Muskie's appearance at the *Union Leader* "was designed to counter a threat to his support in the March 7 presidential primary from readers who had read the *Union Leader*'s charge Thursday that Muskie was unsympathetic to Franco-Americans."

But that was only part of the threat. For weeks, the *Post*'s coverage had emphasized that the senator, who was running even with President Nixon in the polls and well ahead of any opponent for the nomination, had chosen a high-risk, early-knockout strategy. He would run in all the early primaries and hope to collapse the opposition and nail down the nomination by April 25, when Massachusetts and Pennsylvania completed the run of the first six contests.

In a January 5 story describing that strategy, with quotations from Muskie aides, I set out what became the standard context for viewing the New Hampshire primary:

> To Muskie's benefit, three of the first seven primaries are in his native New England and two others are in Midwestern states where Polish Catholics— Muskie himself is a Polish Catholic—provide a significant element of the Democratic primary vote.
>
> Nonetheless, Muskie faces a real problem in those early primaries. He alone of the Democratic contenders is committed to running in all seven; his opponents can pick their spots, concentrate their campaigning there, and hope to whipsaw Muskie, who will be forced to divide his own time and resources seven ways.
>
> On paper, the leadoff primary in New Hampshire figures to be fairly easy for Muskie, with only George McGovern, Vance Hartke and Sam Yorty providing the opposition in his back yard. [Later, Wilbur Mills joined the field.] But the smaller a Muskie majority in the neighboring state, the less impressive his win would be, so the Maine senator is forced to take time to campaign extensively in New Hampshire to avoid the possibility of getting less than 50 percent of the total vote.

The same theme was reiterated—this time with a note of increased tension—in a long analytical piece I wrote for the February 14 *Post*. "Senator Edmund S. Muskie has abandoned New Hampshire for the next two weeks," I began, "leaving his local backers nervously calculating how to protect his apparently healthy lead in the Democratic presidential primary against a pair of major threats." After telling how Muskie had overridden the pleas of local supporters and skipped out on that Saturday night's state Democratic committee fund-raising dinner in order to celebrate his wife's birthday with friends in Washington, I said:

> His backers here make no effort to conceal their concern that by the time Muskie returns for a final "blitz" of the state, his lead may have been shaved from two sides.
>
> Sen. George McGovern's steadily accelerating, campus-fed canvassing operation is attempting to undercut Muskie's support among the issue-

oriented suburban and small-town Democrats.

And backers of Sen. Vance Hartke, Los Angeles Mayor Sam Yorty and write-in candidate Wilbur Mills are prying—and in some instances, buying—their way into Muskie's strength among the Democratic ward heelers of this industrial town [Manchester].

The threat is not to Muskie's victory in the first primary of the year—that is conceded by everyone. What is at stake is whether he wins in his neighbor state by an impressive enough margin to gain any momentum for the more important primaries in Florida, a week later, and in Illinois and in Wisconsin.

The story went on to detail the canvassing and advertising efforts that the Muskie campaign would make while he was in Florida, Wisconsin, and several western states, then added:

But in a primary as small as New Hampshire's, where only 60,000 to 80,000 are expected to vote and 10,000 votes can spell the difference between an impressive win and an embarrassing squeaker, there is no substitute for a candidate's talking person-to-person to the voters.

So the notion that the front-runner's position was fragile and that he was spread too thin for his own backers' comfort was now part of the context, established both in reporters' minds and in the thoughts of perceptive readers.

There was a second theme that was probably clearer in the conversations of the journalists on the scene than in the copy we were filing. That was the possibility that Muskie might crack under the strain of his schedule and the tension of the most important election of his career.

Deep down in the February 14 story, I alluded to it: "If sensitivity is the measure of insecurity, there is plenty of evidence that the Muskie camp feels some pressure from McGovern's campaign. . . . Several times this week, Muskie reacted with anger to questions from high school students he charged were 'planted' by the McGovern camp."

The scenes were uglier than that bland paragraph suggested. At one school, the senator had interrogated a teenager who had asked an uncomfortable question as if he were a prosecutor trying to shake the alibi of an accused wife-killer.

Lou Cannon witnessed those high school blowups and gained a further insight into the state of Muskie's temper when he was invited to join in a friendly poker game aboard a Muskie charter. As Cannon described it in his book, *Reporting: An Inside View*, "On the first hand Muskie was dealt four cards to an inside straight and threw down his hand with an oath when he failed to make the straight on the fifth card. I like Muskie just fine but I made a personal decision right then that he seemed a little temperamental to be President of the United States."

In his book, Cannon asked the right question:

What does a political reporter do with this kind of insight? As in this instance, it is rarely written as a hard news story the first time the thought arises. Most reporters have a healthy reluctance to play amateur psychiatrist. Often, the incidents are trivial in themselves. Sometimes, as with the poker game, they occur in semi-private settings which many reporters— myself included—feel uncomfortable in exploiting directly for journalistic purposes.

So what we reporters tend to do is to store away in our minds such incidents and then use them to interpret—to set a context—for major incidents when they occur.

Such was the case with Muskie's emotional display in Manchester. One reason that Jack Germond reacted as swiftly and surely as he did to the television pictures of the scene was that he had been present— as I was—at an off-the-record session almost a year before, where a group of political reporters had dinner and a long evening of discussion with Muskie. What all of us present remembered about the evening was that much of the time Muskie was in a bellowing rage, brought on by persistent efforts to draw him forth on the Vietnam War.

All of us suspected that under the calm, placid, reflective face that Muskie liked to show the world, there was a volcano waiting to erupt. And so we treated Manchester as a political Mt. St. Helens explosion, and, in our perception, an event that would permanently alter the shape of "Mt. Muskie."

So it was not an accident that in the fifth paragraph of the February 27 story, I wrote: "The 60 to 70 newsmen and supporters huddled in the snowstorm to hear the senator's speech watched with surprise as the normally disciplined Muskie let his anger and his frustration show."

And it was not an accident that after clearly identifying Loeb as a harsh critic of the senator's and the chief supporter of his rival, Sam

Yorty, I still gave front-page prominence to the publisher's response: "I think Sen. Muskie's excited and near-hysterical performance this morning again indicates he's not the man that many of us want to have his finger on the nuclear button."

It was the temper tantrum theme that Muskie's political foes, such as Senator Bob Dole, then the Republican National Chairman, used in their second-day comments that built the momentum for the story and kept it bubbling in the press.

WITH the advantage of hindsight, I think I was correct to treat the Manchester incident as a major event and to put it in the context of both a high-risk, go-for-broke campaign strategy and an exhausted, emotional candidate who was unable to sustain the pace. Muskie himself said as much after the campaign in an interview for *The Making of the President 1972*:

> That previous week, I'd been down to Florida, then I flew to Idaho, then I flew to California, then I flew back to Washington to vote in the Senate, and I flew back to California, and then I flew into Manchester and I was hit with this "Canuck" story. I'm tough physically, but no one could do that—it was a bitch of a day. The staff thought I should go down to the *Union Leader* to reply to that story. If I was going to do it again, I'd look for a campaign manager, a genius, a schedule-maker who has veto power over a candidate's own decisions. You got to have a czar. For Christ's sake, you got to pace yourself. I was just goddamned mad and choked up over my anger.

The key was the "Canuck letter" Muskie mentioned in the interview with White. It was a curious document, which had appeared two days earlier along with a front-page editorial, signed by Loeb and head-lined, "Sen. Muskie Insults Franco-Americans." With bold-faced type and capital letters Loeb hammered home his message. The editorial concluded:

> We have always *known* that Senator Muskie was a hypocrite. But we never expected to have it so clearly *revealed* as in this letter sent to us from Florida.

•   •   •

Along with the editorial was a photocopy of a hand-printed letter with many misspellings, in an almost childlike hand, sent to Loeb by a Paul Morrison and postmarked Deerfield Beach, Florida. It told how the writer had encountered Muskie and his party in Florida. According to his tale, Muskie was asked how he could know much about the problems of blacks, since there were so few of them in Maine, and "a man with the Senator said, 'No, not blacks, but we have Cannocks.'" Muskie, the writer said, laughed at the remark and invited the questioner to "'come to New England and see.'"

Loeb's editorial comment was that if Morrison "hadn't taken the trouble to write about his experience ... no one in New Hampshire would know of the derogatory remarks emanating from the Muskie camp about the Franco-Americans in New Hampshire and Maine—remarks which the senator found amusing."

Since French Canadians are a major Democratic voting bloc in New Hampshire, particularly in Manchester, and since "Canuck" (as it is usually spelled) is an offensive epithet to them, it was not surprising that Muskie's phone canvassers instantly found a negative reaction to the senator and pressed him strongly to denounce the *Union Leader* editorial as a lie.

Muskie did not need much urging. Like many other Democrats, he regarded the *Union Leader* and its publisher William Loeb (who died in September 1981) as one of the most flagrantly biased opinion-mongers in the business. Among other things, Loeb and his paper had labeled the senior senator from Maine and 1968 Democratic vice presidential candidate "Moscow Muskie," "Flip-Flop Muskie," and "a phony."

Far worse, in Muskie's eyes, was Loeb's decision to reprint as another front-page editorial a bitchy, caustic portrayal of his wife, Jane, which had originally appeared in *Women's Wear Daily* and was picked up in edited form in *Newsweek*. The article depicted her smoking, drinking, cussing, and generally behaving in a way conservative New Hampshire voters might not think becoming for a prospective First Lady. So Muskie decided to hit back at Loeb.

AT that point, some of the internal dynamics of the press took over the operation. Consider, for a moment, one of the central paradoxes in any journalist's life: we crave novelty but live in a world where routine is vital. Freshness and surprise are built into the definition of news; the unusual, the unexpected, and, best of all, the unprecedented are what we seek. But we know the world is full of repetition, because the daily routine of our own organizations is rigid and unvarying: deadlines must be met, so that presses may roll and papers be delivered on time.

Hence, the requirement for those who are seeking to "make news" is itself paradoxical: they must, ideally, do something unusual, unexpected, or unprecedented. But they must do it in a time, place, and manner that fit the unvarying routine of the news organizations.

The Muskie appearance at the *Union Leader* was of this character. It is unusual for a candidate to denounce the publisher of a leading newspaper in a state where he is campaigning. The normal rule in political campaigns is to ignore such attacks or to deal with their instigators at arm's length, through a letter to the editor or a rebuttal from the press secretary.

John F. Kennedy had ignored the rule in the case of the *Union Leader*, declaring at a rally in downtown Manchester, "I believe there is probably a more irresponsible newspaper in the United States, but I can't think of it. I believe that there is a publisher who has less regard for the truth than William Loeb, but I can't think of his name." But Kennedy had saved his blast for the last night of the 1960 general election campaign, when, knowing that he would lose the state to Richard Nixon, he indulged his anger at Loeb and warmed the hearts of local Democrats.

The conventional rule in politics is that "you don't get into a fight with anyone who buys ink by the barrel." Muskie's denunciation came at a time when Loeb had more than a week before the primary to reply. And the picture of a major presidential candidate delivering his denunciation on the doorstep of the newspaper—rather than from a distance—was also unusual enough to guarantee attention. (I remember one Nixon aide saying incredulously, "What was he doing there? Even if he hadn't broken down and cried, it was not the place for him to be. It was—*unpresidential*." That comment may have reflected as much about the buttoned-up quality of the Nixon operation as it did about Muskie.)

Still, the question is, Did we see what we thought we saw? Years later, I asked some of the Muskie aides and Muskie himself what had happened on the flatbed truck. Muskie told me, "I arrived in Manchester tired, nearly exhausted. The staff said that I had an opportunity to make a point about Loeb, who was personally unpopular with Democrats in the state. So I yielded.

"I did not cry. I know it is not easy to distinguish between anger on the verge of tears and crying, but there was no flow of tears. . . . There was melting snow. But I choked up in my anger, and it was a bad scene, whatever it was. Interestingly, the first reaction I heard that day was positive, that I had confronted Loeb and told him what I thought. Only later did I hear the reaction that it was a sign of weakness on my part, that it was disturbing people. Eventually, the reaction was devastating."

Richard Stewart, then Muskie's press secretary and now with the *Boston Globe*, remembered seeing "a metamorphosis" in Muskie's mood. When he was shown the Loeb editorial criticizing his wife when he arrived in Manchester that Friday night, going to the *Union Leader* "changed from a political tactic to a personal confrontation, and that changed the whole tone of the event," Stewart said.

"I was standing on the sidewalk with George Mitchell [then Muskie's campaign manager and now senator from Maine], and he said, 'That's going to hurt.' I said, 'Every woman in America will say, "I wish my husband would stand up for me that way."' But he was right and I was wrong. . . . Talking to Muskie later, he did not think he had lost control of the situation or command of himself. But at an inappropriate moment, after his voice broke, he took a handkerchief out of his pocket and wiped at his eyes. I don't know whether he was wiping tears or melting snow, but he [Muskie] subscribes to the latter version."

Jim Naughton, who covered the story for the *Times*, told me in 1985 that he was standing at Muskie's feet, "looking up directly into his face . . . and I swear to this moment I'm not sure if he was in tears." Neither then nor later did I have much doubt about what I wrote. Circumstances gave me an unusually complete record of the event.

When we arrived in front of the newspaper office and Muskie and the other speakers were on the flatbed truck, waiting to begin, I pulled out my notebook and began to jot down a description of the scene. In an instant, the notes were being washed away and the paper turned to mush by the wet snow. So I put the notebook back in my pocket and instead turned on the tape recorder and described the scene to the recorder, spelling out the names of the others on the platform. When Muskie began speaking, I just kept the tape running.

Back at the Wayfarer, I played the key passages on the tape over and over again, making sure I transcribed the muffled phrases accurately and measuring the gaps with my watch. I typed out my visual images of the scene. I put it all into the account:

> Muskie's voice broke for the first time as he read the title of the editorial [containing the material unflattering to his wife; it was called "Big Daddy's Jane"]. He recovered and said of Loeb: "This man doesn't walk. He crawls."
>
> Muskie fought to regain his composure while the small band of sup-porters applauded for about 15 seconds. Then he said in a loud voice, "He's talking about my wife. . . ."
>
> Again, he wept, and 20 seconds later, said in a husky tone, "Maybe I've said all I should. . . . It's fortunate for him he's not on this platform beside me. . . ."
>
> Muskie's shoulders shook, and he rubbed his face hard. "A good woman . . . ," he managed to say, and then the tears, mingled with the melting snow on his head, stopped him again. For 20 seconds the crowd stood silent, as Muskie seemed unable to go on. At that point, Louis Jol-bert, a friend from Maine, shouted out, "Who's with Muskie?" and the crowd cheered long enough for the Senator to compose himself.

Did I check with Muskie to ask if he had wept? I am certain that I did not. I did follow him to a nearby hotel, where he filmed a brief interview with a Boston television station. Standing in the improvised hotel room–studio, watching the interview, I remember thinking that I had never seen Muskie look so ravaged and worn. I certainly had the opportunity there to ask him. But whether from sympathy or timidity, I did not walk over to him and say, "Well, Senator, what the hell happened up there? Have you flipped out—or what?" Instead, I included in my story the next day a comment Muskie made in his interview:

> Muskie told an interviewer after his speech that he felt that in reprinting the item [from *Women's Wear Daily* and *Newsweek*] Loeb was "just delib-

erately slurring ... a good woman ... deliberately cutting down her character just to get to me. I guess the full realization of what he'd done just hit me this morning, suddenly, and I couldn't go on."

The other circumstance that should be noted is that I wrote the story in unusual isolation. When Muskie left Manchester, he headed north to visit a dogsled race and do other New Hampshire–type campaign activities, taking along his press secretary and many reporters. I stayed in Manchester.

The reporters who accompanied Muskie were, as Naughton said later, "at a fundamental disadvantage. ... We had to write on typewriters perched on our knees and then dictate from pay phones along the way, [while] those of you who had either the wit or the luck to be in the warmth of the Wayfarer were able to learn of the impact of the event. ...."

I wrote with no other reporters to kibitz with about what we had seen and no Muskie aides around to "reinterpret" the morning's events. And the story was edited by people in Washington who had no reference point for comparison other than the wire service accounts, which described Muskie as "tearful" or "shaken" but did not by any means dramatize the scene. As far as I can recall, there was no internal questioning of the accuracy of the story then, or later, at the *Post*. Still, it nags at me as do few other stories I have ever written.

WHAT Muskie did not know and what I certainly did not know at the time I wrote the Manchester story was that there was another set of facts which would have put the incident into a very different context. Those facts related to a series of actions, ordered and coordinated by the Nixon White House and designed to harass, to vex, and to embarrass the front-running Democrat, who was judged as a serious threat to Nixon's reelection. The "Canuck letter" was part of that plot.

Had those facts been know, I might have described Muskie in different terms: not as a victim of his own overambitious campaign strategy and his own too-human temperament but as the victim of a fraud, managed by operatives of a frightened and unscrupulous President. That story surely would have had a different impact.

Given Loeb's history, there was ample reason for skepticism about the origins of the "Canuck letter." Indeed, in my story about the Manchester incident, I devoted seven paragraphs to that subject, noting that "the Deerfield Beach telephone company does not list a Paul Morrison among the 15 Morrisons in its directory," and noting that Loeb, while promising "a very interesting follow-up" on the letter, had not yet produced the author.

The story also quoted at length the denials of the senator himself and others who were with him in Florida that any such thing had happened.

But it was not until seven months later, when Nixon was sailing toward a landslide victory over McGovern and Muskie was back tending to his Senate business, that the mystery began to unravel. Marilyn Berger, then a colleague at the *Post*, told me one evening that Ken W. Clawson, a former *Post* reporter who had gone to work at the White House earlier as deputy director of information, had told her that he was the author of the "Canuck letter."

I urged Berger to tell her story to Carl Bernstein and Bob Woodward and on October 10 they described the "Canuck letter" as part of a "massive campaign of political spying and sabotage conducted on behalf" of the reelection effort by White House and Nixon campaign officials. As Woodward and Bernstein spelled it out in that and later stories and in their book *All the President's Men*, there was a trail of incidents going back to mid-1971 that suggested, in Muskie's words, that "somebody was out to ambush us." Letters attacking other Democrats were sent out on facsimiles of Muskie's Senate stationery. Sensitive polling data disappeared from his headquarters. Phony campaign flyers were distributed in his name. Harassing phone calls were made to voters by people purporting to be Muskie campaign workers. On and on the list went, making it clear that Muskie was the victim of a systematic sabotage effort.

Had Muskie made such charges the previous winter, without proof, he would likely have been judged paranoid or a crybaby by most of us reporters. Had he been able at the time to provide the proof, the political history of the year would undoubtedly have been very different.

What the incident shows, for journalistic purposes, is the risk of misleading the reader when the reporter's information is incomplete. I put the Manchester speech into one context—accurately, I believe— of a campaign and a personality that were accessible to journalistic view. I did not put it into another context—of campaign sabotage—because that was covert and, at the time, unknown. Unwittingly, I did my part in the work of the Nixon operatives in helping destroy the credibility of the Muskie candidacy.

THE incident in Nashua eight years later was less melodramatic and more equivocal, and for those reasons, its lessons I think are more broadly applicable.

Again there was no questioning of the basic facts. This time, we had so many reporters on the scene that we couldn't have missed the story if we had tried. As it turned out, the clustering was as lucky a happenstance as my turning on the tape recorder had been in Manchester eight years earlier.

The Bush-Reagan debate had been on the campaign schedule for a couple of weeks. Several days before it was slated, Lou Cannon, with his unrivaled sources in the Reagan camp, was telling me that he had "a feeling" that Reagan was going to make something special of it. Circumstances played into Reagan's hands when the Federal Election Commission, a few days before the event, suggested that the *Nashua Telegraph* might be guilty of an illegal campaign contribution if it paid for the gym rental and other expenses of a debate in which Reagan and Bush were the only participants. When the Bush organization demurred, Reagan's camp—eager for the confrontation—said they would pay the bill.

As the day of the debate drew nearer, the demands from the other five candidates—Baker, Dole, Anderson, and Crane and ex-Governor John B. Connally of Texas—grew louder. Reagan had indicated his sympathy with their position, but it was not until Cannon and I got to the high school that we learned there was an active effort under way to change the rules. An agitated Jon Breen, the editor of the *Telegraph*, was telling anyone who would listen that if the Reagan camp tried to force him to revise the format, he was prepared to pull his paper out of the sponsorship and announce that Reagan had reneged on his commitment.

I left the high school for forty-five minutes to make a pizza run, and came back to find the place awash with rumors that several of the other candidates were arriving to try to get into the act and that meetings were taking place out of our sight. I also discovered that three other *Post* reporters—Martin Schram, Myra MacPherson, and Art Harris—who had been covering other phases of the New Hampshire action, had joined us and a horde of other reporters. It seemed like wretched excess to the accountants and editors back in Washington, but as it turned out, having all the reporters on the scene saved our neck.

We had a short huddle of the *Post* brigade, and Cannon and I agreed to go into the gym and secure good seats for the debate, while the other three watched the offstage arguments.

Cannon and I split the note taking during the debate, while Mac-Pherson, Schram, and Harris talked with the campaign managers in the cafeteria about the backstage fighting and were there when the four excluded candidates (all but Connally, who was campaigning out of state) came off the gym stage and exploded in anger against Bush.

As a result, even though it was about 9:30 on a Saturday night when the debate finished, we were able—by feeding five sets of notes through two typewriters and an improvised editing and dictating relay system—to get two complete, detailed, and fairly coherent stories, totaling sixty-four paragraphs, into Washington in time for the main edition deadline of 11 P.M. for the Sunday paper.

We went back to the Wayfarer warmed by the glow that reporters get—even before the first of several drinks takes effect—when they know they've got a hell of a story and think that they've handled it well under deadline pressures. This one was especially sweet because the lateness of the event and the scarcity of Saturday night television network news broadcasts meant that most readers would get their first inkling of the story from the morning papers.

As we bragged of our prowess as reporters in the Wayfarer bar, reliving over and over the sheer wonderfulness of the evening as a political and journalistic happening, the thought came again and again, "Boy, there is no place like New Hampshire." And many of the veterans proclaimed it "the best story up here since Muskie in Manchester."

The possibility that there might be another comparison to Manchester did not cross our minds—that once again we had been manipulated. This time the manipulator was not the unseen and unknown author of the "Canuck letter" but Reagan's campaign manager, John P.

Sears, who was very visibly on the scene. We put the events into one context, the one Sears designed, and reported them in that fashion. Then, belatedly, we learned there might have been another context that would give them quite a different meaning.

EVEN before the Nashua debate, the political context—or story line—for New Hampshire 1980 was less clear, at least in my mind, than the 1972 one had been. George Bush had upset the favored Ronald Reagan in Iowa the month before, but Reagan had made that easy by barely bothering to campaign in the state. In New Hampshire, both Reagan and Bush were campaigning hard and well, drawing good crowds, and both appeared to have effective organizations backing them. What seemed to be happening was that the focus on their rivalry was leaving little room for the other five Republicans in the race. So it was no surprise to reporters that the other five were clamoring for admission to the Reagan-Bush debate; for them, exclusion would further certify their status as fringe players and discourage voters from "throwing away" a vote on any of them.

What was a surprise was the presence of all but Connally in the Nashua gym and Reagan's ardent championing of their cause. While Reagan had indicated his sympathy for their plight, the plan to have them confront Bush was a last-minute stratagem by John Sears. (One of the ironies of this story is that Sears was summarily fired from his post on the day of the New Hampshire primary, because of internal conflicts essentially unrelated to his successful Nashua ploy.) There was enough of a sniff of ambush around the operation that Cannon and I included, as the third paragraph of our story, this language: "Bush's campaign manager, James A. Baker III, said the extraordinary protest was 'a setup' and showed that 'it's stop–George Bush time' in the GOP contest."

But the theme was not developed in the main story, except for the quotations from Bush and Baker pointing out that Bush had accepted Reagan's challenge to a two-man debate and was "playing by the rules" set by the Nashua newspaper.

The sidebar story, written by Martin Schram and Myra MacPherson, delved a bit more fully but did not resolve the mystery. "The controversy," they wrote, "began in the early afternoon, when Reagan decided—according to his staff—to broaden the debate to include all challengers, since he had agreed to pay for the event and it was he who had borne the brunt of the criticism from the candidates who were left out.

"Bush's advisers tell it differently. They say that Reagan telephoned the *Nashua Telegraph*, the newspaper that had originally scheduled the two-man debate, and that Reagan told the *Telegraph* he was going to pull out of the debate if it would not be broadened to include all candidates."

Both the *Post* and the *Star* stories noted Sears's pleasure with the evening's events, but neither of the Washington papers nor the *New York Times* nor the *Boston Globe* conveyed accurately the machinations of the Reagan campaign manager.

That failure emerges clearly when you read the retrospective accounts in Jack Germond and Jules Witcover's book about the 1980 campaign, *Blue Smoke and Mirrors*, in the *Washington Post* staff's book, *The Pursuit of the Presidency 1980*, and in Cannon's 1982 political biography, *Reagan*. Those books describe how John Sears and campaign press secretary Jim Lake concocted the Nashua plot. They called the other Republicans one by one and urged them to come to Nashua. Then they dropped the word to *Telegraph* editor Jon Breen and the Bush camp that Reagan would not abide by the original rules. But they omitted the information that the other candidates had been asked to show up, thus creating the impression that Reagan might withdraw from the debate.

"The motivation," Germond and Witcover wrote, "was largely defensive, but Sears was also beguiled by the notion of stirring the pot a little. He considered Bush both arrogant and personally uncertain, and he relished the idea of putting added pressure on him by changing the rules." Cannon and Bill Peterson, in the *Post*'s book, said, "Sears had opened negotiations with the other candidates, inviting them to the debate without telling Bush." And, apparently, without telling Reagan either, for Germond and Witcover revealed in their book that "Lake told him [Reagan] of the change as they drove toward Nashua less than an hour before the debate was scheduled to begin."

If the behind-the-scenes machinations were murky to the reporters in Nashua, most of us carried stereotypes of the candidates' characters in our heads, just as we always do. In the case of George Bush, that stereotype could be summed up in one word: preppy. It was his label long before his fellow Eli, Doonesbury cartoonist Garry Trudeau, caricatured him that winter as the ultimate preppy. It derived from Bush's Greenwich, Connecticut, upbringing, his Houston oil equipment wealth, his too-young-for-his-years, Arrow-shirt-ad good looks, his athleticism, his excess enthusiasm (embodied in the awful campaign slogan that Bush was "Up for the '80s"), and his bonhomie.

The corollary belief in most of our minds was that Bush was somewhat out of place and ill at ease in the rough-and-tumble world of politics, uncertain how to protect himself and how to touch up an opponent in the clinches.

Loeb described him with cruel accuracy when he wrote that Bush came on stage in Nashua "looking like a small boy who had been dropped off at the wrong birthday party." Backstage, as the others were soon to complain, he had refused to meet with Reagan and the other four candidates or to join their appeal to Breen. While Reagan and Breen were continuing to debate the ground rules before the audience, and while the other four stood behind them, mugging and waving to their fans in the gym, Bush sat stony-faced, staring straight ahead.

As Germond and Witcover wrote, "There were many things Bush might have done . . . to avoid disaster. His refusal to meet with the other four, all of them Republican officeholders of some prominence, was an unnecessary insult. . . . Even once the others were on stage, Bush might have saved the situation by making some good-humored fun of Reagan's stratagem and explaining the virtues of keeping his commitments to the *Nashua Telegraph*. He might even have gotten away with kidding Reagan about being afraid to meet him alone. Instead he simply froze, and no one mistook it. 'What can I say?' an adviser shrugged. 'He choked up.'"

And because that was what we reporters were expecting of George Bush, that is what we wrote. It was the theme of the stories that night and of the second-day reaction pieces—in all of which Sears and Lake indignantly denied Bush's complaint that he had been "sandbagged."

That view came through clearly in a satirical song columnist Jerry terHorst and I wrote for the Bush press corps a few days later—a song which, like many other press corps campaign ballads, made explicit what was only implicit in our newspaper copy. Written to the tune of "Joshua Fit the Battle of Jericho," it said:

> Nashua was the battle that lost the war
> > To Reagan and the Gang of Four.

Another stanza explained the source of Bush's fatal error:

> Bush was such a stickler for games with rules,
> > The kind they play in better schools.
> He thought the interlopers would just look like fools,
> > If he kept his word and cool.

So the incident was treated as a big hoo-ha in which Reagan had turned the tables on Bush. Our stories gave due credit to the man who played the trick, John Sears. MacPherson and Schram ended their color piece this way:

> Down the corridor and around the corner from the bandroom where the also-rans were lambasting Bush, leaning against a wall outside the gymnasium where Reagan was debating Bush, Reagan campaign manager John Sears was leaning against the lockers. He was smiling. Reagan aide Charles Black came up and shook Sears' hand. "Another day on the campaign trail," Sears said, smiling at the end of what he obviously felt had been a day well spent.

Germond and Witcover also used Sears as the kicker on their piece in the *Star*: "Accepting thanks from the spurned candidates after they walked out, Sears smiled and said, 'We're just party unifiers.'"

BUT it was not just Bush that Sears had duped into playing his game that night. It was us as well. While Reagan was arguing with Breen, I had whispered to Cannon, "Reagan is winning this nomination right here." But a few days later, I was confronted with evidence suggesting I was flat wrong. In the view of some of his key strategists, Reagan had already won New Hampshire—and the nomination. He was just putting the frosting on the cake. I did not find that out until the day after the primary, when I bumped into Richard B. Wirthlin, Reagan's pollster, at Boston's Logan Airport and slid in next to him on the flight back to Washington.

He opened his New Hampshire polling book and replayed the primary for me in a way that knocked my theories about the dynamics of that contest into a cocked hat—and surprised almost everyone else when I reported them in the *Post* the next day. His data showed that in a highly volatile electorate, where one third of the voters changed their minds in the last week, "the critical event in the Reagan surge was not the widely publicized confrontation with Bush in Nashua last Saturday night but the League of Women Voters' debate in Manchester three nights earlier. That was widely, but mistakenly, viewed as a rather boring, no-win affair."

As I summarized the data in the *Post*:

> Wirthlin found that 37 percent of the Republican voters had seen or heard about it [the League of Women Voters' all-candidate debate] and 86 percent of them thought there had been a clear-cut winner. Reagan was named as the winner by 33 percent, Bush by 17 percent, Anderson by 14 percent and Baker by 12 percent. Among those who had followed the debate, Reagan soared 15 points against Bush, and overall in the GOP electorate, he closed the gap to 2 points.
>
> "I knew at that point we would win it," Wirthlin said.

To say that I was shocked by his analysis would be an understatement. (And to this day, there are skeptics among the Reagan advisers and the reporters who were in New Hampshire.) The importance of the earlier League of Women Voters' debate had escaped me. Cannon and I had come perilously close to blowing the assignment of reporting that Wednesday night debate, let alone of analyzing it clearly. We had been worried about deadlines, so I suggested that we watch it on television at our motel, as we had done with a similar debate in Iowa. Only minutes before the debate was to begin did I discover my mistake: the debate was being televised on a delayed basis, not live, in Manchester. We scrambled around and found a radio, but not before the debate was under way. Dan Balz, our political editor, covered the first ten minutes off the tube in Washington (where it was televised live) and eventually we caught up. But neither of us had any idea who had won or lost.

The Reagan campaign did a good job of keeping to itself the knowledge that Wednesday night's League of Women Voters' debate had shattered Bush's front-runner status. The conspiracy of silence was aided by a bit of luck, of which I learned only when I was writing this chapter, five years after the events. David Nyhan of the *Boston Globe*, who reported both Muskie in Manchester and Reagan-Bush in Nashua, informed me that he in fact had gotten wind of Wirthlin's findings before the Nashua debate and, indeed, had referred to them in a story he wrote early that Saturday. The story appeared in the tiny first edition of the Sunday *Globe*, seen by none of us in New Hampshire, an edition that was actually on the presses before the debate began. When he wrote it, Nyhan knew that Reagan had asked the other candidates to join the debate, but he did not know what would happen. High up in the story, he wrote:

> What apparently prompted Reagan's decision to invite other candidates at virtually the last minute was the result of some New Hampshire polling the former California governor has conducted all week.
>
> At the beginning of the week, a Reagan campaign source said, Bush had passed Reagan in the Californian's own polling. The Reagan polling operation turned up some interesting aspects when it tried to gauge the impact of Wednesday night's debate, where all seven candidates participated for the first time this year.
>
> According to the Reagan camp, the polling showed that just over one-third of the viewers of the debate thought Reagan came off best, and one-sixth thought Bush looked best.

Nyhan told me in 1985 that he believed that material would be saved by the editors in Boston for later editions of the paper, but instead it was "killed out" to make room for the later developments in the dramatic evening. That happenstance is typical of the frantic decision making and lack of communication between reporters and editors under the pressures of deadlines and space limitations.

Had Nyhan's information appeared in the main edition of the *Globe*, read in New Hampshire as well as in Massachusetts, I would have lost my Wirthlin polling scoop of the following Thursday. And had the polling results been known to other candidates and to the press, it would have cast a different light on Reagan's sudden attack of conscience about excluding the other candidates from the Nashua debate.

If Reagan had been seen as the fellow backing out of a one-on-one debate with Bush immediately after Bush had fallen from his throne, then other stories would have suggested a rather opportunistic motive on Reagan's part, as Nyhan's story did for the one edition.

The stories on Reagan might have resembled the stories about President Jimmy Carter a couple of months earlier. Carter had accepted a debate with his challenger for the Democratic nomination, Edward M. Kennedy, in Iowa, when the Massachusetts senator was ahead of him in the polls. But when the Iranian hostage situation and Kennedy's early campaign blunders reversed their standing, Carter said he could not leave the White House long enough to go to Iowa, nor could he arrange to debate Kennedy in Washington. He said it was because of the hostage crisis, but most reporters strongly suggested in their stories that the polls had something to do with it, too.

The skeptical stories did not keep Carter from defeating Kennedy in the Iowa caucuses or from winning the nomination. Most of the reporters I interviewed for this chapter believe, in retrospect, that Reagan would have defeated Bush in the Republican battle, no matter how we had portrayed the maneuvers surrounding the Nashua debate. That is the way John Sears sees it, too. Looking back at Nashua five years later, he insisted that he had been straightforward in his dealings with the newspaper, with Bush, and with the other Republican candidates and had not manipulated any of them. "I don't feel badly about it at all," he said. "I don't think we did anything wrong."

Sears also said that despite the gains for Reagan and the setback to Bush in the earlier League of Women Voters' debate, he was uncertain coming into Nashua whether Reagan would actually win New Hampshire. Be that as it may, at the time Reagan's own managers displayed great concern that no skepticism about motives should prevent the press from playing its assigned part in the scheme. Someone in the Reagan camp, in fact, supplied a little of what the CIA calls disinformation to Germond and Witcover. Their story the night of the Nashua debate included these paragraphs:

> The Reagan scheme to change the format was hatched by campaign manager John Sears after polling data showed that Bush had gained ground after the debate last Wednesday in which all the candidates appeared.
> What he devised was a situation in which Reagan might profit if all the

candidates appeared and interest in the debate was defused or, alternatively, a situation in which Bush would be the villain in preventing the others from being heard.

It is conceivable, of course, that neither the Manchester incident in 1972 nor the Nashua debate in 1980 really changed history as much as the candidates or journalists thought at the time. In discussing this chapter with several reporters who covered those campaigns, I found some who thought that McGovern's surge—powered by the emotion of the anti–Vietnam War cause—was sure to overtake Muskie in some primary, if not in New Hampshire. Others who covered Muskie believe he was an emotional bomb just waiting to explode, that if Loeb's editorial had not triggered his temper or tears, something else would have.

In a similar vein, there are those who say that the stiffness Bush showed on stage in Nashua would inevitably have undone his candidacy, especially when it was contrasted with Reagan's presence and quick-wittedness before an audience. Bush, they say, was riding for a fall.

These fundamental character traits, my colleagues argue, far outweigh any spin we in the press and television may give to a story because of the preconceptions we bring to it or the imperfect information available when we write or broadcast. They may be right, but history does not allow us to go back and replay these contests with various events deleted. What I do know is that, in the early stages of a presidential nomination campaign, when voters are beginning to make up their minds about the contenders, a single negative incident can assume gigantic proportions. Lacking very much in the way of long-term, deeply held, accumulated impressions of these candidates, voters reasonably assume that any event on which the press and television focus their attention must be significant and revealing. Certainly Muskie and Bush are not the only ones who believe that the journalistic treatment of that morning in Manchester and that evening in Nashua—those two media events—proved to be critical in influencing the New Hampshire primary and the choice of the presidential nominee.

With the advantage of hindsight, I think there is a warning for both reporters and readers in the Manchester and Nashua incidents. Even the simplest, most dramatic, and seemingly most obvious stories are subject to distortion. Even when we are accurate, as for the most part we were in our reporting from Manchester and Nashua, even when we are fairly detailed in our descriptions, even when we are fairly sophisticated in putting the event in context, the news we deliver can fall short of the truth. Recognizing that reality does not mean that readers should discard the news as a mere fiction, of no use or value to them. Even a flawed story can provide important hints of the deeper reality the reporter does not know or cannot probe. But these tales should point up the importance of maintaining a critical or skeptical attitude. Both readers and reporters should be alert to warning signs that the reality may be other than it seems.

Such warning signs were there in both Manchester and Nashua: Where did that "Canuck letter" come from? Was it real or a fiction designed to bait the trap for Muskie? What explained Reagan's turnabout on inviting the other candidates? Was it just fair play or did his campaign know something about the race that others did not know?

What these incidents show is that even when the story is happening before our eyes, even when our access to the event is unimpeded, we can unwittingly distort its meaning by being unaware of the full context. By the same token, as we will see in the next chapter, journalists can make terrible mistakes about the characters even of people we have come to know very well over a long period of years. Like Richard M. Nixon, for example.

CHAPTER TWO
Misjudged Characters

R *EPORTERS* meet such interesting people. Indeed we do. But we have the devil's own time deciphering them, figuring out what makes them tick. That is a part of our job we cannot duck, however, for the definition—or, as some would say, the creation—of a public personality is bedrock journalism, and especially political reporting.

Some people arrive in the political or governmental arena already well known. Dwight D. Eisenhower was the commanding general of the Allied armies that liberated Europe. Robert and Edward Kennedy were the younger brothers of the late President. John Glenn was a national hero as the first American to orbit the earth, and Ronald Reagan started his political career with a highly flattering image of his personality, created in dozens of movies and hundreds of television appearances.

But even in the cases of such well-known figures, the characters they had assumed or been given in their previous lives were not sufficient to define them as political personalities for the broad public. "Dollar Bill" Bradley, the Princeton University and New York Knicks basketball star, had a well-earned reputation as a clutch player, a team man who was at his best when the stakes were highest. But when he ran for the Senate in 1978, the voters of New Jersey wanted to know what had impelled the unusual leap from athletics to politics and what notions of himself and the world he brought with him.

It falls to the press to describe and define the character of the candidate or the public official. Sometimes we must arbitrate between conflicting versions. Men and women give out dissonant signals at different times. When that static forms, it falls to the press to try to clear it: What was the true character of Wilbur Mills? Was he the "influential chairman of the powerful House Ways and Means Committee," as he was routinely described for years, a subtle legislative craftsman with a sophisticated understanding of the tax code and its policy ramifications? Or was he a foolish, drunken man, cavorting with sleazy stripteasers and winding up being fished by police from a wrecked car in Washington's Tidal Basin?

How do we handle the responsibility? None of us are trained psychologists or psychoanalysts, and we are barred from creating fictional characters on the news pages. Yet our work forces us to be creators of characters, so we are constantly in over our heads.

Our colleagues who draw editorial page cartoons deal with the problem in straightforward fashion. They caricature people, and they admit they are doing so. Often, without admitting it, we do the same thing. We select, we compress, and we may exaggerate particular features of the people we are writing about, and in doing so, we create caricatures. If you doubt that, consider this abridged journalistic history of the presidential contests, running backwards from 1984 through 1968: The Blah Liberal (Mondale) lost to the Great Communicator (Reagan), who when he was known as the Grade-B Actor had defeated the Fussy Moralizer (Carter), who had defeated the Awkward Lineman (Ford), who had succeeded Tricky Dick (Nixon), two years after Tricky Dick had swamped the Prairie Populist (McGovern). Four years before that, of course, the New Nixon (Tricky Dick in disguise) had gotten to the White House by edging out the Happy Warrior (Humphrey), in a contest in which the Fiery Segregationist (Wallace) had finished third.

When we resort to that kind of simplification, reducing complex personalities to two-word labels, we ought to give ourselves a two-word warning: dig deeper. Often we do not, but there are enough examples around to show that it is not impossible. Given all the problems that are built into these character studies, it is remarkable how good some of them turn out to be. Way back on January 16, 1976, when Jimmy Carter was hardly a blip on the horizon of presidential politics, Don Oberdorfer wrote a sketch of him for the *Washington Post* that anticipated so many of the later discoveries about Carter that it is almost eerie to read in retrospect:

> The image of Carter is that of an easygoing Southern farmer with a home-spun manner and a ready grin, so much the candidate of the common man that his nickname, Jimmy, is on all his campaign literature and will be submitted on all ballots.
>
> Beneath the surface there is another set of attributes—a keen, disciplined intellect which propelled him close to the top of his class at the U.S. Naval Academy, a fierce determination and unshakable certitude about his own decisions.
>
> "He's one of the kindest people I know, but he's stubborn," said his mother, "Miss Lillian," describing her son in terms of paradox often used by those who know him well. "He's like a beautiful cat with sharp claws."

Oberdorfer traced back to their origins the forces that shaped Carter's complex character: a relentless ambition, bred into the boy by his strong-minded mother; an antipolitician strain, rooted in the bitter experience of attempted vote fraud against him in his first try for the state senate; a certainty about his own destiny and his own views, linked to his "absolute confidence in his relationship to God" and his deep religious faith; a willingness to campaign unstintingly for years at a time and to give his opponents no quarter, evident in his two races (the first unsuccessful) for governor; a workaholic but isolated approach to the task of governing, marked by long hours in the office, copious reading and briefings, but "with few close peer relationships," and heavy reliance "on a few young aides."

In what turned out to be almost a prophetic judgment on the failings that would cripple Carter in Washington, Oberdorfer wrote:

> Because of his highly independent ways and tendency for public confrontation to bring pressure on the legislature, Carter was unpopular with many fellow politicians.
>
> "Jimmy never learned the three guiding rules of politics—reward your friends, punish your enemies, and then make up with enemies," said a former legislative supporter who wishes him well.

•   •   •

Oberdorfer concluded with what seemed to be a minor anecdote—but one that was designed to raise some basic questions in the reader's mind. Noting Carter's reiterated promise that, "I will never tell a lie, make a misleading statement, betray a trust, or avoid a controversial issue," Oberdorfer told how he had encountered in Carter not just a typical politician's tendency to "shade his recollections to best advantage," but a case in which "his retentive memory somehow blacked out a disadvantageous fact."

Carter had courted Alabama Governor George Wallace and Wallace's supporters in Georgia during his 1970 race for governor. But two years later, he rejected Wallace's request that he make a seconding speech for his nomination at the Democratic national convention. The incident was confirmed for Oberdorfer by Carter's press secretary, Jody Powell, and his top political assistant, Hamilton Jordan, "but when Carter was asked on two occasions recently, he flatly denied he'd ever been asked to make a convention speech for Wallace," Oberdorfer wrote.

"Although his two closest aides insisted otherwise, Carter said he could not recall the Wallace bid until they produced documentary evidence of its existence from his files. At that point, he telephoned this reporter to apologize. 'Jody was right and I was wrong...I was just completely wrong,' Carter said. Later, he sent a letter stating that he had been in error."

EIGHT years later, another *Post* reporter, George Lardner, Jr., had a similarly disquieting experience with another about-to-be-discovered Democratic presidential contender, Gary Hart. Down in a long profile datelined Ottawa, Kansas, Lardner wrote:

Hart was born here on Nov. 28, 1936. His biographies give the date as Nov. 28, 1937, but official records in Kansas and a family birthbook kept by Uncle George Hartpence reportedly say 1936. Asked several times about the discrepancy, Hart said last week that he would "check into it."

Yesterday in Nashua, N.H., he tacitly acknowledged getting his age wrong, telling a reporter, "It's whatever the records say. It's not a big deal." Asked how the mistake was made, he shrugged and replied, "I don't know."

Lardner reported another peculiar set of circumstances surrounding the change in the family name from Hartpence to Hart. It came about in 1961, when the future senator had switched from Yale Divinity School to law school and was thinking about a governmental career. As Lardner wrote:

> Gary Hartpence came home in 1961 and went to court to change the family name. According to Hart, his father had talked about it for years because he claimed the original family name had been Hart. And both parents, "particularly my mother, had always wanted to revert to the original name."
>
> "I had no objection to it," he said. "I was still in school. I don't think I went to court."
>
> Court records show he made the main presentation.

Though Lardner had placed the question about Hart's name and date of birth in the context of a detailed examination of his life and career and had gone out of his way to avoid sensationalizing them, there was some eyebrow raising when his piece appeared on January 17, 1984, as part of the *Post* series on the Democratic contenders. But it was not until six weeks later, when Hart exploded to prominence with his New Hampshire victory, that both issues became major news stories. Lardner rewrote and expanded his earlier report, realizing that many people had missed the first reference. When television took up the issues, also showing Hart to have changed his signature style at various points in his career, doubts were planted that caused some voters to take a second look.

THE profiles Oberdorfer and Lardner wrote demonstrate that tenacious, talented reporters, alert to the small details that convey large meaning and with adequate time to work, can get beyond the clichés of character. When editors make these assignments, they know there is a risk that reporters less skillful than Lardner and Oberdorfer may go seriously awry when trying to sketch the character of a complex politician. But the greater risk is to repeat the conventional wisdom or the cliché of the moment. To my mind, the press treatment of President Gerald R. Ford was a prime example of falling into that trap.

Ford was a familiar and popular figure in Washington long before he was picked by Richard Nixon to replace Spiro Agnew as Vice President and then elevated into the presidency by Nixon's resignation. Reporters knew him as an amiable and open longtime congressman, with a conventional Midwest Republican conservative's view of the world; as a man who did his homework on the issues before the Congress but had never shown any great flair or imagination; and as a partisan who tempered his shafts with an obvious affection for political opponents and a sense that some questions had an importance that transcended partisanship. In a rather emotional moment, at the end of a luncheon with reporters and editors of the *Washington Post*, as the Nixon impeachment process was nearing its end, Ford said, "I don't know what the future may hold for me—or for any of us. But I want you to know that I am a man who likes having critics who are not enemies." That was the essence of Jerry Ford: a man who was personally secure and comfortable with his own views, abilities, and limitations, who had acquired the skills of his profession as a politician and the tolerance that characterizes most of the political world, but who would never, under ordinary circumstances, have been considered "presidential."

Ford was largely unknown to the public when he became President. And he was a new subject for the editorial cartoonists, whose livelihood depends on their ability to caricature. As *Newsweek* said a month after he assumed the presidency in 1974, the problem was "the 38th President's relative lack of the distinctive physical features that the cartoonists love to distort" and his smooth takeover of the office made his "on-the-job persona . . . too amorphous to inspire a sharply defined caricature."

In their hour of necessity, the cartoonists fell back on one aspect of the new President that was unusual: his athleticism. Ford had played football for the University of Michigan, had coached football at Yale while attending law school there, and at sixty-one, was an avid golfer, skier, and tennis player who swam laps in his pool to stay in shape. So the cartoonists hopped on that angle. In a sampling used by *Newsweek* to illustrate its article, Ford was shown as a football player, a wrestler, a golfer, a boxer, a swimmer, and a jogger—usually matched against an intimidating opponent labeled "Inflation," which was the biggest domestic problem he inherited.

It was not long before the metaphor began to turn against Ford. Indeed, the seeds of destruction had been planted before he was President. In an October 1973 profile, the *New York Times* quoted Lyndon B. Johnson's remark that Ford was so dumb "he can't chew gum and walk at the same time." The origins of the line are something of a mystery. Ford and Johnson often clashed when Johnson was President and Ford the House minority leader. But the archivists and scholars at the Johnson and Ford presidential libraries have no record of Johnson ever making the comment, and such former staff aides as George Reedy, George Christian, Bill Moyers, and Liz Carpenter said they had never heard it from Johnson's lips. Political writer Richard Reeves quoted a cruder version of it in his book, *A Ford, Not a Lincoln*, attributing to Johnson the assertion that "Ford is so dumb he can't fart and chew gum at the same time." There are even more scatalogical versions around, but Reedy, a former Johnson press secretary, claimed they are "apocryphal."

Once put in circulation by the *Times*, however, the line was indelible. Less than a month into the Ford presidency, George F. Will wrote a column for the *National Review* that said, "Either Gerald Ford is a lot abler than he has hitherto been given credit for being, or being President is easier than recent Presidents have contrived to convince us that it is. . . . In any case, Mr. Ford has not made a significant misstep yet during this difficult transition period, as he has coped with tasks that are more difficult than walking and chewing gum at the same time."

But soon the missteps began—both physical and verbal—and they fed the metaphor with which reporters characterized a "bumbling presidency," under a leader who was not only an accidental but an accident-prone President.

Ford's immunity from criticism ended a month after he took over, when he pardoned Nixon. His reputation for policy turnabouts began when he canceled his ill-fated "WIN button" campaign to "Whip Inflation Now" to focus on an unexpectedly severe recession. But what fixed the image of Ford as Bumbler were not these substantive questions but trivial gaffes that built into a journalistic thunderclap.

At first they were treated tolerantly and not overemphasized. When Ford went to the Far East and Vladivostok at the end of 1974, *Time* magazine's Hugh Sidey wrote that "the big, comfortable American galumphed over the red carpets as if he were out rabbit hunting, unconcerned about his too-short pants, searching the eyes of those he met for a human connection. . . . When a Japanese Scout gave Ford a neckerchief, the President tried to put it on. The scarf got hung up on Ford's big dome, and for a second the little guy did not know just what to do. Ford finally got the neckerchief in place and leaned down and took the boy's hand; that 'Thank you' from one Scout to another would have melted steel."

Sidey made it sound human and appealing. And Ford's verbal slips were treated the same way. Reporters who had covered Ford during his years in the House, when he was an indefatigable campaigner, and his months in the vice presidency, when he was also on the road a lot, knew that he was usually a pedestrian speaker. When he spoke as President in January 1975 at a Washington awards luncheon of the National Collegiate Athletic Association, there was no great surprise when he mangled a key line in his prepared address and turned it into a knock on himself. Telling the coaches and athletic directors that he felt a great bond with them, Ford said, "We both buy aspirin by the six-pack—and we both have a certain lack of performance in our jobs." The word he meant, of course, was "permanence." The *New York Times* ran a short Associated Press story on the fluff on page 46.

Those gaffes were seen then as evidence of a naturalness that journalists found appealing in contrast to Richard Nixon's contrivance. In February 1975, Alan L. Otten, the *Wall Street Journal*'s Washington bureau chief, commented in a column that the attractive "aspect of the Ford presidency [is] that so far he's managed to remain an honest, open, decent human being. And with the public's unprecedented distrust of government and politicians, that's not an insignificant contribution.

"Mr. Ford is not only a lot smarter than his critics suggest, but he's also an unusually honest and straightforward man, of considerable personal and professional integrity. He tends to say what he thinks and mean what he says—an occasionally unsettling change from his immediate predecessors."

Meg Greenfield, then deputy editor of the *Post*'s editorial page, praised Ford about the same time, in her *Newsweek* column. "What I find so distinctive about Mr. Ford," she said, "is that he seems to have guarded against the insidious encroachments of personal fantasy on life as it is, and to have no gift for living in or projecting a heroic third-person account of himself."

Greenfield said the quality she admired was not necessarily an unmixed blessing:

> Here and there in the White House you will find some consternation over all this and not just on the part of image makers either. It's not that the President's evident lack of "side" is thought to undermine his assertion of authority in the White House or even (as some mutters go) that his plain-old-Jerry approach to public appearances lacks dignity. Rather, it represents an anxiety that Mr. Ford's lack of talent and appetite for creating an illusion of mystery and larger-than-life purpose and strength play havoc with his ability to fulfill the symbolic function of the presidency or even to manage and exploit—as Presidents in some degree must—the public perception of what he is doing. Not to put too fine a point on it, Gerald Ford is not Charles de Gaulle. But then, he is not Richard Nixon either.

The incident that took all this out of the atmosphere of affectionate concern for the ordinariness of the President occurred on June 1, 1975. Arriving in Salzburg, Austria, for a meeting with Egyptian President Anwar Sadat, Ford stumbled coming down the ramp of his plane, catching his heel near the bottom of the flight of stairs and slipping down the last five rain-slicked steps onto the tarmac. Twice more that day Ford stumbled, and once Sadat took his arm to steady him.

The *Post* played the story under a four-column headline on page 8, but ran two three-column pictures on page 1. The *Times* gave it a two-column head on page 1, under a three-column picture of the President being assisted to his feet by the Austrian chancellor, Bruno Kreisky, and a military aide.

It was an awkward moment, but the accompanying stories attributed the incidents to fatigue and a "football knee," which had been reported previously in stories about Ford's athleticism but never given much attention. I asked reporters who traveled with Ford on the trip whether there was any suspicion that Ford was drunk. The President's liking for a martini was well known to reporters, and all of them had seen Ford at moments when he was relaxed, if not high. But there was no implication of drunkenness in any of their accounts or in their later recollections of the incident.

The *Post* followed up with a pair of stories, one reporting that he had given his "football knee" a workout with nine holes of golf in Salzburg, with no apparent ill effects, and another tracing the history of the injuries to both knees and the treatments Ford had received for them.

It took a few days for the columnists to get to the incident, and when they did, they were not benign. Nicholas von Hoffman, for example, in the *Post*: "Our Presidents tend to look their worst when they sally forth abroad, but this voyage is more embarrassing than most. When Mr. Ford's old football knee gave way under him and he spilled down the last couple of steps on the plane ramp at Salzburg, the fall summarized the journey. Stumble, fumble, tumble and jumble."

Von Hoffman's piece was exceptionally harsh, but it was part of a pattern, fed by new incidents of verbal and physical missteps. Twice in September of 1975, there were unsuccessful attempts on Ford's life by demented women—once in Sacramento, where the pistol was wrestled away before a shot was fired, and later in San Francisco, where the bullets missed. On October 14, a car driven by joyriding youths collided with the presidential limousine in Hartford, Connecticut, and while Ford escaped uninjured, he did seem accident-prone. Two weeks later, when he was host at a White House state dinner for President Sadat, Ford toasted "the great people and government of Israel . . . Egypt, excuse me." Six days later, as he and Sadat continued their talks in Florida, Ford bumped his head against the side of a swimming pool, bruising his forehead.

It all seemed to climax at the end of 1975. As *Time* magazine summarized it:

Gerald Ford left Washington last week in his distinctive way. After a convivial evening at the White House, he wished guests "a merry Christmas and a merry—uh—a happy New Year." Then, as he was walking toward his helicopter, his legs got tangled up in his dogs' leashes. A day later, he was waiting on the ski-lift line at Vail, Colo., when one of the chairs swung around and almost knocked him over. Two days later, he took a spill on the slopes. Many skiers do the same, of course, but Ford's spill was duly recorded by the cameras and splashed across TV screens and front pages.

Once again, von Hoffman weighed in, ridiculing "President Klutz falling down stairs and tripping over old ladies in wheelchairs." Elsewhere, in the same essay, Ford was "the blunderous leader . . . Mr. Ten Thumbs . . . The Great Flub-Dub . . . catastrophically close to making himself into the national clown . . . a lovable, unpretentious hick who can't pronounce the word judgment and says 'gummermint' without noticing it . . . Nixon's Revenge . . . Old Bungle Foot," and a few other things.

More damaging than the newspaper columns was the ridicule Ford was getting from television comedians on programs with massive audiences. Chevy Chase, on NBC's *Saturday Night Live*, did a series of impressions of prominent politicians. When he came to Ford, all he did was back up a half dozen steps, start forward, and then stumble into the microphone, winding up on his knees. It brought down the house.

But no one at the White House was laughing. After the extensive photo and television coverage of Ford's slip on the slopes in Vail, presidential press secretary Ron Nessen lashed out at the incident as "the most unconscionable misrepresentation" in history. "It would be a mistake if that impression cost him votes," he said. "This President is healthy, he is graceful, and he is by far the most athletic President in memory."

Predictably, Nessen's outburst—probably the most defensive statement from the White House since Richard Nixon's declaration that "I am not a crook"—fed a story which had taken on a life of its own. *The Wall Street Journal*, in an editorial called "Bumbling on a Bum Rap," said Nessen "has taken what is essentially a joke and turned it into a serious matter, and moreover, a serious matter on which he cannot hope to win. To sensible people, the whole idea of a presidential press secretary bragging about his boss's gracefulness makes the whole team look comic. A free suggestion to Mr. Nessen—let the jokers make jokes and encourage Mr. Ford to show us he can stand up on the real issues."

Nessen said in his memoir, *It Sure Looks Different from the Inside*, that he thought he was talking informally with reporters in the Vail press room on that Sunday morning, but conceded he had not put the comments off the record. He said it illustrated the wisdom of the advice he had been given: "Don't screw up on a slow news day." But the more serious problem was that Ford's physical "tumbles and stumbles" had come to be a metaphor for the way he was dealing with "the real issues." In very much the same way that cartoonists focus on one feature—like Nixon's ski-jump nose or five o'clock shadow—the pundits were using Ford's slips to describe his political position.

Both *Time* and *Newsweek* dealt with the "ridicule problem" in late 1975. In its cover story, *Newsweek* linked it to a series of upheavals in the Ford campaign organization, policy turnabouts in the White House, and a precipitous decline in the polls, which, for the first time, showed Ford trailing challenger Ronald Reagan: "The bad news took Ford by surprise and engendered a palpable sense of dismay around the White House—a sourish feeling that the President might have tied his shoelaces together a bit too often for his own political good. Ford, conceded one troubled counselor, 'is coming across as Bozo the President.'"

Ford tried to defuse the ridicule by saying it did not bother him. In an interview with Lou Cannon and myself aboard Air Force One, Ford said, "I feel very strongly [that the stumblebum caricature] is an inaccurate depiction. Most of the critics... have never played in a ball game, have never skied. I don't know whether it's a self-defense mechanism in themselves or what, but I'm kind of amused at that." He insisted that he was physically fit and said the jibes were just part of a long tradition of caricaturing and ridiculing Presidents. "It's just part of the American sense of humor," he said, "and I guess you have to live with it. The main thing is that you don't have to believe it, and I don't."

Nessen, for his part, acted on the advice given tongue-in-cheek by humorist Art Buchwald in a January 1976 column, on how "to turn an act of clumsiness into one of skill and dexterity." According to Buchwald, when Nessen was asked about the fall on the ski slopes, he should have said:

Yes, the President fell as planned this afternoon in six inches of snow near a large Aspen tree.... Before he left Washington, the President made plans to fall just once so all the photographers would get the only picture they had made the trip for.... It took great skill to fall exactly where the photographers were stationed....

Q—Ron, are you trying to tell us that every time the President stumbles, it is thought out in advance?

A—Let's say it's discussed beforehand. As you know, Mr. Ford is the most coordinated President we've ever had, so we don't want him to stumble too often. But when the occasion arises where we think a slip or a fall will help his image, we urge him to do it.

Q—Whose idea was it for the President to fall down the steps getting off the plane in Salzburg last June?

A—Henry Kissinger's. He wanted to show President Sadat that we weren't putting pressure on him.

Q—So you feel President Ford's fall at Salzburg turned President Sadat around?

A—Well, the Suez Canal is now open, isn't it?

In time, Nessen went on NBC's *Saturday Night Live* and showed he could be a good sport, as his boss—among others—was subjected to the usual mockery. An even odder scene occurred in March 1976, when Ford was the guest of honor at the annual Radio-Television Correspondents Association dinner, where Chevy Chase was the featured entertainer. Ford laughed good-naturedly as the comic went through his standard stumbling routine, winding up with his announcing the new Ford campaign slogan: "If I'm so dumb, how come I'm President?"

"Mr. Chevy Chase," Ford said when he got to the microphone, "You are a very, very funny suburb." Ford faked a stumble of his own, for laughs, but then committed a genuine gaffe when he referred to his prospective Democratic challenger as "Jimmy Connors" (the tennis star).

The stumblebum issue never disappeared, despite Ford's efforts to laugh it off. It came up at a campaign stop at Butler University in Indianapolis, before the April Indiana primary, when Ford told a questioner that the *Saturday Night Live* satire bothered him no more than "water off a duck's back." It arose in early May, when he bumped his head entering a helicopter on the White House lawn. It came up at the end of May, when he bumped his head on the top of the doorway of a stagecoach, while campaigning in Pendleton, Oregon.

An image had been fixed in the minds of the reporters covering Ford and it was sustained by them with whatever material came to hand.

Edward Walsh, who joined the White House press corps for the *Post* after Ford had been President for seventeen months, found that the insiders' affectionate nickname for Ford was the Bonz, a clown. Any reporter crossing Ford's path during the campaign was sure to hear the latest verbal gaffe within the hour: whether Ford was praising Ohio State while talking to the students at Iowa State or calling Senator S. I. Hayakawa of California "Hayacomma." One of Ford's malapropisms was so popular that the reporters' tapes of it were virtually erased through replaying. Ford was supposed to ridicule Carter's foreign policy ideas as amounting to a prescription that the United States "speak softly and carry a flyswatter." But it came out, improbably, at the end of a long day of whistle-stop campaigning in Illinois as "flywasher," and the laughter was at Ford's expense, not Carter's.

All of this conditioned the press's reaction to Ford's most consequential gaffe of the fall campaign, the "liberation" of Poland in his second debate with Carter. In defending the record of his administration's dealing with the Soviet Union, Ford made the exaggerated claim that "there is no Soviet domination of Eastern Europe, and there never will be under a Ford administration." When Max Frankel of the *New York Times*, who had asked the question, phrased a follow-up that gave Ford an opportunity to extricate himself, the President plunged on: "I don't believe, Mr. Frankel, that the Yugoslavians consider themselves dominated by the Soviet Union. I don't believe that the Rumanians consider themselves dominated by the Soviet Union. I don't believe that the Poles consider themselves dominated by the Soviet Union. Each of those countries is independent, autonomous. It has its own territorial integrity, and the United States does not concede that those countries are under the domination of the Soviet Union. As a matter of fact, I visited Poland, Yugoslavia, and Rumania to make certain that the people of those countries understood that the President of the United States and the people of the United States are dedicated to their independence, their autonomy, and their freedom."

Carter responded that he "would like to see Mr. Ford convince the Polish-Americans and the Czech-Americans and the Hungarian-Americans in this country that those countries don't live under the domination and supervision of the Soviet Union behind the Iron Curtain." But it took some time for the significance of Ford's gaffe to sink in. Robert Teeter, the Ford pollster, found that between 11 P.M. and 1 A.M. Eastern time the night of the debate, Ford led Carter 44 to 43 percent on which candidate had done a better job.

But the analyses for the next morning's papers and the excerpts from the debate on the next day's morning and evening television news shows all emphasized Ford's blunder. By evening it was Carter by 62 to 17. As Teeter said at a postelection conference at Harvard, "Reports of the debate had reemphasized the President as a mistake-prone, inept bumbler, exactly what we had spent six or seven weeks trying to get away from."

The problem was compounded by Ford's stubbornness in resisting a clarification. It took four days before he conceded at a specially arranged meeting with leaders of Eastern European ethnic organizations that "the original mistake was mine. I did not express myself clearly. I admit it."

Clearly from the beginning, Ford was trying to reiterate the traditional American view that the United States will not concede permanent Soviet domination of Eastern Europe. But by the time Ford admitted his error and moved to correct it, the incident had broken the momentum of the Ford campaign, which had been closing ground steadily for the previous six weeks, and had given a shot in the arm to Carter's faltering effort a month before the election. Given the closeness of the outcome, it could well have been decisive.

WAS the press unfair to Ford? As far back as January 1976, the question had become a matter of public debate. Max Lerner, a liberal columnist, said "the ordeal of ridicule" on television and in the press was damaging Ford, not just as a candidate but as President, in both national and international affairs. The press, he said, "can afford to distinguish between hard slugging on policy decisions and unfair attacks of a personal character."

John Chancellor, NBC's fair-minded anchorman, told *Time* magazine he disagreed. When the President falls on the ski slope at a spot where photographers have been invited to be present, he said, "that's news, and we're going to cover it."

Indeed it is. But as Chancellor would agree, I think, there is not only Walter Lippmann's distinction between news and truth, but a simpler distinction between news and caricature. The original decision to portray Ford in an athletic metaphor was made by cartoonists who were grasping for a singular feature to focus the new and largely unknown President. Under the influence of the prevailing psychology, those of us who were writing about Ford fell too easily into the same temptation. I remember that it took a conscious effort on my part to go beyond the stereotype in a column written on the eve of the 1976 election:

If the Lord of Charity had seen fit to rescue this nation from being engulfed by the evils of an imperial presidency, he would have sent us, not an ark, but a Gerald R. Ford. Actually, of course, Ford arrived under more dubious auspices, straight from the hands of Richard M. Nixon himself.

But no one could have invented a better cure for the excesses of the neurotic, vision-driven and fear-haunted men who paced the Oval Office from 1966 to 1974 than the exceptionally ordinary man who inhabits it now.

The voters understand that the Constitution and the country are safe with Ford. He will not bend, stretch or abuse the powers of the presidency, as his two predecessors did.

But, unfortunately, neither will he exercise those powers to lead the nation, as did the Presidents admired by history.

There followed eight paragraphs criticizing Ford's "small-minded" view of the presidency, the quality of his White House staff, and some of his policy judgments. Then I concluded:

And yet, the voters have reason to believe that, just as Ford will do no damage to the presidency, neither will he make the ultimate, irreversible error that spells calamity for the country.

He is stubborn but not arrogant. He can be persuaded by colleagues—and, occasionally, coerced by Congress—to accept decisions that go against his own instincts. As a matter of fact, he did just that on tax policy, Indochina and Angola.

Voters can see no reason to expect much change in Ford's performance if he is given four more years. The management of international and defense policy would remain in competent hands, but, at home, the prospect would be continued stalemate, stagnation and stifled initiatives.

That must concern voters of conscience. The status quo is not uncomfortable for those who already live in comfort. But the burden of governmental impasse would be felt every day by those—the elderly, the unemployed, the poor—who are trapped by circumstances they cannot control.

Many voters have a hard time resigning themselves to four more years of divided government, dispirited leadership and deadening rhetoric. Yet even those voters acknowledge that the presidency would be there, intact and untarnished, for whoever would succeed Ford in 1980.

And that is the dilemma in deciding whether to vote for the Republican. They know that with Ford, they will be both safe—and sorry.

That was certainly not a rave review on his presidency, but it was an effort to deal with both its strengths and weaknesses. For the most part, however, the grip of the caricature we had created was so strong that we could not, or did not, revise it. In that respect, we were, if anything, less flexible than the best of the cartoonists. When Richard Nixon was elected President, Herblock, who had always drawn him as a heavily bearded, sinister figure, ceremonially gave him a clean shave, in a cartoon which carried the unusually personal note, "This shop gives to every new President of the United States a free shave. (Signed) H. Block, Proprietor."

But as reporters, we did not—or could not—erase the picture of stumblebum Ford. We let a television comic, Chevy Chase, and others no better qualified do our work for us, and not until after the election did most of us get around to writing what we really knew.

Two days after the election, Dennis Farney, who covered Ford well for the *Wall Street Journal*, wrote a sensitive piece. "Gerald Ford never did get over his tendency to stumble, both physically and verbally . . . ," Farney said, "but sometime during his presidency, such slipups ceased to bother Mr. Ford. . . . And sometime during his presidency, Gerald Ford grew into his role and became the truly 'presidential' figure his political strategists were always urging him to be." Early in the Carter presidency, John W. Mashek of *U.S. News & World Report* wrote that the "characterization of Ford as a bumbler . . . was a bum rap."

• • •

JUST before Ford left office in January 1977, I attempted another appraisal:

> In an odd, inexplicable way, the truth has begun to dawn on people in the final days of Gerald R. Ford's tenure that he was the kind of President Americans wanted—and didn't know they had.
>
> After a decade of presidential excess, they wanted a man of modesty, good character, honesty and openness. They wanted a President who was humane and prudent, peaceable but firm. Especially, they wanted one uncorrupted by the cynicism and lust for power that they had come to associate with Washington politicians.
>
> Jimmy Carter's campaign was the successful projection of these idealized qualities of the post-Watergate President. It was also a series of promises—to reform the government, end bureaucratic waste, provide an energy policy, curb the nuclear arms race, cure unemployment, etc.
>
> How well President Carter measures up to these character tests and how many of his goals he achieves remains to be seen.
>
> But Gerald Ford—even while acknowledging in his last State of the Union address and in a series of valedictory interviews his disappointments in the fields of economics, energy and governmental reform—gave people a quiet reminder that he had been exactly the kind of personality they prayed to find in the presidency.

I think if we had dug deeper into our own understanding and knowledge of Jerry Ford, we would have come to that conclusion and written it before the election of 1976.

THERE is an even bigger question that ought to bother most of the reporters and editors involved in covering politics in the 1950s and 1960s: How in the world did we succumb to, and spread, the fiction of "the New Nixon"? That was the title that dozens of reporters bestowed on Richard M. Nixon during his second campaign for the presidency in 1968. Its origins went further back. As Stephen Hess and I wrote in our 1967 book, *The Republican Establishment*:

> Those who have puzzled over the essential Nixon character have usually ended by writing about the changes in the man, not the constants. Nixon-watchers tend to see him always evolving from one stage to another. In the

course of a long career he has been called the New Nixon, the old Nixon and the New, New Nixon. A *Baltimore Sun* editorial, viewing Nixon as a 1968 presidential candidate, gave him yet another label: "the Renewed Nixon," suggesting "a certain renewal of spirit and confidence." Rather than any major substantive change, however, the renewed Nixon is a product of changed circumstances and refined techniques.

Only a hundred days after John F. Kennedy moved into the White House [in 1961], the former Republican Vice President went on a national speaking tour and Arthur Edson of the Associated Press reported: "There's a new Richard M. Nixon politicking about the land. It's a Nixon most people never saw, a Nixon who is relaxed and quick with the wisecrack."

According to journalist Earl Mazo's 1959 book, *Richard Nixon: A Political and Personal Portrait*, the first time "the New Nixon" appeared in print was in a July 9, 1953, editorial in the Montgomery, Alabama, *Advertiser*. Referring to the "mawkish ooze" of Nixon's 1952 "Checkers speech," in which he successfully appealed to public opinion to let him stay on the Republican ticket, despite publicity about a private fund that was used to subsidize his Senate office expenses, the editorial said, "We have found ourselves dissolving our previous conception. . . . The New Nixon rejoices us."

The editorialist's judgment that Nixon "is developing into a first-rate man" was based on little more than the impression that in the first five and a half months of the Eisenhower presidency, he "has studiedly shunned the limelight, has worked effectively in solidifying the President's relations with senators and composing differences, and has diligently applied himself to the tasks the President has assigned him to."

As it turned out, the rejoicing was premature. In the 1954 mid-term campaign, when Nixon carried the rhetorical burden for the administration, he stooped about as low as he had in any of his earlier California contests, which also featured implications of softness on communism. Praising John Foster Dulles in that 1954 race, Nixon gratuitously added, "Isn't it wonderful that finally we have a Secretary of State who isn't taken in by the Communists?"

That 1954 campaign was often cited as the base point from which the construction of successive New Nixons could be dated. On October 18, 1955, James Reston wrote an analysis of "The Nixon Reputation," which, while avoiding the phrase, was another landmark of New Nixonism:

Vice President Richard M. Nixon is now making a conscious effort to modify his reputation as a fiercely partisan and highly controversial figure in American politics.

Ever since the illness of President Eisenhower a month ago [Eisenhower had suffered his first heart attack in September], Mr. Nixon's friends have been urging him to couch his public speeches in less extreme terms and to concentrate on themes that will unify rather than divide the country.

His speech in New York tonight illustrates how far he has gone toward adopting this advice. It was moderate in tone, optimistic, carefully balanced, entirely devoid of partisan attacks . . .

Citing the "Isn't it wonderful" line from 1954, Reston said, "There were no such cracks tonight. In fact, he went out of his way to praise the Democratic majority leader, Senator Lyndon B. Johnson of Texas, and the Democratic chairman of the Senate Foreign Relations Committee, Walter F. George of Georgia, for their 'magnificent' support in the foreign policy field during the last session of Congress."

Reston was limiting his point to a shift in tone and rhetoric, occasioned by the change in Nixon's circumstances, and not arguing that he had suddenly assumed a new character. But the theme took hold in journalism, reflecting Reston's reputation as a trendspotter and trendsetter, and a pattern was set.

A *Newsweek* profile in early October 1956 concluded that "Nixon is indeed a different campaigner from '52 and '54, a politician trying desperately to arouse his own party without alienating the independents and Democrats."

That piece, written by Ralph de Toledano, a friendly biographer of Nixon, was an example of the shallowness of analysis that characterized many of these early New Nixon efforts. Because Republicans realized that

Nixon himself will be a major campaign issue . . . , [the Vice President] left Washington under strict and explicit orders from the President to speak and run on the Eisenhower record, and to avoid direct attacks on Democratic individuals. . . . Nobody knows better than Nixon that some people consider him a demagogue. And that others doubt that he possesses the stature, dignity, maturity and judgment to assume the presidency. . . . He is human, and he couldn't possibly ignore what people say and write about him. . . . He realizes that politics is not hospitable to the thin-skinned. If things are going well, he shrugs off criticism. At other times, he can be bitter about it.

Then de Toledano relayed, apparently on the basis of an interview, Nixon's own assessment of the sources of the criticism: the eggheads never forgave him for exposing Alger Hiss. The press did not forgive him for proving so many of them wrong about Hiss and for surviving the "Nixon fund" exposé.

But, de Toledano said, Nixon was carrying out his role. "At his first [campaign] stop, in Indianapolis, he congratulated Adlai Stevenson for a 'forthright' statement about Alger Hiss's guilt, and even had kind words for Mrs. Franklin D. Roosevelt." The "kind words" from Nixon were, "She created great good will abroad."

On the West Coast, de Toledano wrote, Nixon "made a point of reiterating that both presidential candidates were 'men of integrity' and that neither party held a 'monopoly' on loyalty and honesty."

All this seems unexceptional, even minimal, but, de Toledano wrote,

Nixon's admirers, some of whom had journeyed far to see his free-swinging style, were baffled. Republican leaders and some friendly reporters [perhaps de Toledano?] told Nixon that his campaign to stir up the workers was not getting off the ground. Late on the second night out, as he dictated speeches he would make the next day, Nixon brooded over the reports he was getting and finally climbed into bed at midnight. At 5:30 the next morning, after tossing and turning in bed, Nixon got up and, writing in longhand, blocked out new and harder-hitting statements. After handing them over to his secretary for typing, Nixon felt much better and sat down at a piano (at 7:15 A.M.) and played a Brahms rhapsody.

The new statements were not much. He accused Estes Kefauver, the Democratic vice-presidential candidate, of using "low-road tactics," and said the Democrats "talk a good game, but in twenty years, they were never able to produce prosperity except during, or as a result of, war."

What is remarkable about this profile is the skimpiness of the evidence on which the New Nixon proposition rests. The facts cited are these: Recognizing that his old free-swinging campaign tactics are a potentially serious liability, Nixon goes two days—two days!—on the road without impugning the character of his opponents. He even praises them for qualities which everyone else has long acknowledged they possess. But after two days, the strain begins to tell, and, at the end of a sleepless night, he begins to write some routine partisan lines into his speeches.

Looked at thirty years later, the tendency is to say, "Big deal!" The reporters on the trip for the *Post*, the *Times* and the *Star* all noted Nixon's efforts to stay on the high road, but resisted the big conclusions de Toledano reached. William M. Blair of the *Times* wrote at the end of the first week that "He is the same Nixon with a 'new look,'" and suggested that "there are cynics who contend Mr. Nixon is trying to acquire a higher stature, a sort of new identity that will pay off in 1960 when another President is elected."

What does leap out of de Toledano's account—because it anticipates the bizarre behavior in the Watergate period and the unraveling of Nixon's presidency, as described in the Bob Woodward–Carl Bernstein book *The Final Days*, is the weird business of the 5:30 A.M. scribbling and the 7:15 A.M. piano concert. But de Toledano passes that off as if it were the most ordinary behavior in the world.

The emerging 1956 version of the New Nixon was the subject of some scornful remarks from Democratic presidential candidate Adlai E. Stevenson, in a September campaign speech:

No, 1956 is not 1952. Perhaps the most striking change of all is the new face being worn by the Republican vice presidential candidate. I know of no instance in which a man has so energetically tried to convince the electorate that everything he has said and done in past years bears no relation to himself and that, until further notice, he is to be considered a new man. Now you may not agree with him, but you have to be awed by the lack of conviction which makes so swift a transformation possible.

I don't wish for a moment to deprecate the Vice President's new personality. But I do wish that we might hear some word from him repudiating the irresponsible, the vindictive and the malicious words so often spoken by the imposter who has been using his name all these years.

But if Stevenson thought that kind of sarcasm would stop the New Nixon or slow the press's gullibility for that confection, he was wrong.

Nixon was reelected with Eisenhower in 1956, and a year later was once again being celebrated as a New Nixon. The occasion this time was his demeanor in the wake of the stroke President Eisenhower suffered in 1957, and his skillful assumption of the role of spokesman for the administration.

Reston wrote the front-page story and the *Times* carried a full transcript of Nixon's "first formal White House news conference," in which he reported on the President's recovery from the stroke suffered forty-eight hours earlier, and announced that he (Nixon) would preside at the forthcoming cabinet and National Security Council meetings.

Once again, Reston was alert to the changes:

> This was clearly a more assured young man than the Nixon of 26 months ago, who stayed in the background at Denver, while Governor [Sherman] Adams [Eisenhower's chief of staff] presided over the administration during the early weeks of the President's heart attack.
>
> He even looks different. He seems to have lost a little weight. His hair is cut closer on the sides and on top. His speech is more vivid and articulate and his manner more patient and courteous.

Reston was again the style-setter. The following week's issue of *Business Week*, for example, had a profile which began:

> Ever since the presidential campaign of last year, working politicians have been talking about the "new Nixon." Yet they were unprepared for the Nixon who moved confidently into the limelight when the President became ill last week. The "new Nixon" has arrived, and Washington is taking stock of the man afresh. The new appraisal comes to this: More than ever, Nixon is the man to beat for the Republican nomination in 1960.

Not everyone was taken in. Frederic W. Collins, the Washington correspondent of the *Providence Journal*, wrote a savage parody for the liberal magazine *The Nation* in November 1957, which likened the "marketing" of the New Nixon to the annual debut of Detroit's new-model cars. The advertising is equally blatant, he said, "although in one case it is paid, at page rates, and in the other it is free, at column length."

Identifying the changes as tactics aimed at the 1960 election, Collins said:

As a matter of fact, the 1960 Nixon went on the drawing boards soon after November, 1954. It has had several test runs. . . . In keeping with the trend in Detroit, the new Nixon is described as broader but definitely not lower. . . . The power plant develops more horsepower, due to a higher ambition intake attributable to the approach of 1960 rather than to radical innovation in engineering. The steering is more nearly self-contained, depending less and less on the old Eisenhower correction system. It features push-button position selectors, and pneumo-casuist suspension intended to give a smooth ride over the roughest of issues. An advanced differential provides dependable pulling power when traction is poor, as, for example, in mud. The secret is in an added component which permits the Nixon to cover up its own tracks while still digging its treads in.

Since this blast of sarcasm came from the left flank of the journalism profession, it was as futile as Stevenson's partisan shot. Politicians and the press seemed unable to give up the New Nixon game. The Democrats got into it and quarreled among themselves. House Speaker Sam Rayburn in May 1958 said Nixon had been "very cruel" in the tactics he used in 1954, but declared, "I think the medicine he has taken since 1954 has effected a cure on him, and I don't think he'll ever make that kind of campaign again." But John W. McCormack, then the House majority leader, said the New Nixon was simply an invention of "the Madison Avenue [advertising] boys."

The evidence of the 1958 campaign was on McCormack's side. As Nixon battled to put some backbone in the GOP in that year when the recession and Sherman Adams's forced resignation shook the standing of the Eisenhower administration and set the stage for a Democratic landslide, his rhetoric was the rhetoric of old. He spoke of "the Truman-Acheson war in Korea," of the Democrats' unending weakness for "radical, left-wing leadership," and the domination of "left-wing, politico-labor bosses."

Still, journalistically, the game went on. In July 1958, Stewart Alsop wrote a long and brilliant piece for the *Saturday Evening Post*, of which he was then Washington editor, entitled "The Mystery of Richard Nixon." The piece is worth detailed examination, for, in addition to energetic reporting, Alsop also dealt in unusually explicit terms with the internal debate of a journalist who knows he is venturing into dangerous territory by attempting a fundamental character assessment of a controversial public figure. Compared to the columns in the daily papers or the profiles in the weekly news magazines, it is a masterpiece of subtlety. But it also illustrates the inherent danger in that character creation.

Alsop began by describing Nixon as "extraordinary" in at least one respect. Since 1836, when Martin Van Buren won the honor, no Vice President had been nominated as his party's presidential candidate, as Nixon seemed very likely to be nominated in 1960.

"Yet to the vast majority of Americans," Alsop wrote, "this extraordinary man remains a cardboard figure, oddly inhuman and impersonal. To his enemies—and he has, probably, more enemies than any other American—he is a cardboard devil, utterly without scruple or conviction. To his admirers—and they also number in the many millions—he is a cardboard saint, whose strength is as the strength of ten because his heart is pure."

Then Alsop set forth his own biases on the subject, saying Nixon is "one of those men . . . about whom no one can pretend to be wholly objective. Until rather recently," he said,

> . . . Nixon seemed a shrewd, tough, ambitious politician, and not very much more. But especially in the second Eisenhower administration, like many other Washington reporters, I found myself, almost in spite of myself, increasingly impressed by Nixon.
>
> In certain almost impossibly difficult situations—notably President Eisenhower's illnesses—Nixon has handled himself brilliantly. Reporters who have covered him on his trips abroad, some of whom started as strong anti-Nixonites, have come back praising him for his deft sense of personal diplomacy; and, after his trip to South America, for plain physical courage in the face of that most terrifying of phenomena, a mob gone wild.
>
> What is more important, Nixon has repeatedly displayed a knack—useful in a potential President—for being right.

Alsop cited examples of that "rightness," including Nixon's recognition of the importance of the Soviet Sputnik and the space race, and his recognition of the political and economic dangers of the current recession. "And it has been difficult," he added,

> for even the most cynical of the anti-Nixonites to detect a political motivation in some of the positions Nixon has taken, like his strong advocacy of

the politically unpopular foreign-aid program.

I also discovered something else—that Nixon is a most interesting man to talk to. Unlike so many denizens of the Washington zoo, he never wraps himself in the American flag or recites his latest speeches verbatim to a restless audience of one. He talks politics sensibly and well. Indeed, where the subjects of politics and government are concerned, Nixon is something of an intellectual. . . . He has read a great deal, and he has thought a great deal about what he has read.

Nixon also has another quality which is hardly characteristic of most politicians—he listens. An interviewer is apt to find himself suddenly transformed into interviewee, with Nixon taking notes on a large yellow pad. State Department officials who have briefed him before his trips abroad . . . have been amazed by Nixon's incisive questions, his intense determination to master the essentials.

Nixon, in short, is certainly far more than just another tough, shrewd, ambitious politician.

Let us pause for a moment to examine that last proposition and the evidence on which it rests. What Alsop has told us is that Nixon displayed discretion and some courage in sensitive moments when the spotlight was on him; that he was quicker than some others in the Eisenhower administration to recognize the challenges of Sputnik and the recession; that he had advocated at least one politically unpopular cause (foreign aid); that he had read and briefed intensively on questions of immediate concern to him; and that he had spoken sensibly in interviews on those subjects.

Does that prove that he is "far more than just another tough, shrewd, ambitious politician?" Might his support for foreign aid—a staple of American policy for thirteen years when this piece was written—be, in part, not just a recognition of its role in American diplomacy, but of its particular symbolic importance to exactly those establishment journalists, like Alsop and Reston, whose good opinion Nixon is trying to gain? Is it remarkable that a politician aiming for the presidential nomination would be discreet in his dealings with the incumbent President and foreign leaders, or take the opportunity to be briefed intensively by government officials on issues that are sure to arise in public debate? Was there not a touch of shrewdness in Nixon's pulling out the yellow pad and asking Alsop's advice and opinion?

What we have here is a combination of forces producing a preordained result. If Alsop were to conclude, at this point, that Nixon is simply a "tough, shrewd, ambitious politician," indistinguishable from dozens of others of the same breed, then he would have nothing more to write. So, journalistically, he wants to give another answer. And, inasmuch as Nixon is most certainly seeking the presidency and may gain it, there is a certain built-in deference that suggests the writer should not flatly declare that he is without visible qualifications for the post. Far better, paraphrasing Gertrude Stein, to discover and write that there is a "there, there."

For Alsop, the discovery—and the telling—came in stages. He dug into Nixon's boyhood and early political career, gaining flashes of insight from old associates of the Vice President. At Whittier College, a classmate who was often hired to officiate football games told Alsop that whenever the coach cleared the bench and Nixon got into the closing minutes of a game, "I always got out the five-yard penalty marker. Dick was so eager I knew he'd be offside just about every play."

His high school debating coach, Mrs. Norman Vincent, told Alsop, "He was so good it kind of disturbed me. He had this ability to kind of slide round an argument, instead of meeting it head on, and he could take any side of a debate."

But Alsop noted that Mrs. Vincent was "an ardent Democrat" and the tactics she was describing were "those which made Nixon a champion debater." And so he went, carefully balancing the liabilities and peculiarities against the accomplishments in every memorable moment of the Nixon career up to his selection as Republican vice presidential nominee in 1952 and his weathering of the "Nixon fund" crisis that briefly threatened to dump him from the ticket.

Of that crisis, Alsop wrote:

You see a young man of 39, undergoing a terrible personal crisis which could well have destroyed him, and reacting with remarkable toughness and coolness. You also see a young man with only six years in politics behind him, with a sure, instinctive grasp of the political realities, and a bold willingness to act upon them.

Nixon, in short, was already a thoroughgoing professional politician at 39. He is a professional politician still—and proud of it. . . . But there are different kinds of professional politicians; Lincoln was a professional politician, and so were Aaron Burr and Boss Tweed. What kind of politician had the Quaker boy, Richard Nixon, become in 1952, at the age of 39?

To ask that question is to pose the case against Nixon. As this reporter told the Vice President in the interview accompanying this article, I have amassed a vast dossier of anti-Nixon material, courtesy of the Democratic National Committee and Nixon's numerous enemies in California.

Having raised the question, Alsop moved instantly to defuse it. His next sentence reads, "What is striking about this dossier is that it is based, not on the kind of Vice President Nixon now is, but on the kind of professional politician he was; it is based on the past, not the present. Moreover, it is based not on anything Nixon has done, but on the kind of things he has said."

Let us pause to consider that passage. The premise for the article was that a search of his past would reveal clues to the fundamental character of the subject, Nixon. But suddenly the evidence of the past —because it is uncomfortable—is being denigrated as compared to the performance in the present. And if that is not enough, a distinction between words and deeds is introduced, as if words were not the weapons of political warfare, especially for a politician who for six years (as Alsop wrote) had had literally no other forum for action except his speeches.

But Alsop did not allow himself to dismiss the evidence. Instead, he encapsulated the dossier in a single quotation, choosing inevitably the "Isn't it wonderful" line from the 1954 campaign.

In so saying Nixon did not say that Dean G. Acheson and George Marshall, Dulles' predecessors, were "taken in by the Communists." But he implied it, and the implication is grossly misleading and essentially untrue. To make his implication, Nixon used a rhetorical question, which is an old and rather sleazy debater's trick.

Other items from the anti-Nixon dossier might be cited, but that rhetorical question is the most damaging item. It is also the most typical, in its use both of an old debating trick and of an essentially specious "Communist issue."

The essential point of Nixon's critics, at the time Alsop was writing, was that his use of such tactics—his slipperiness, if you will—displayed a fundamental lack of character, which could be dangerous in the presidency. But Alsop did not choose to deal directly with that basic challenge. So he wrote next, "But the purpose of this report is not to make the case for or against Nixon. It is to try to understand the man. And it is not really hard to understand why Nixon, even as late as 1954, was the kind of politician who could ask that rhetorical question."

Now back on the relatively safe ground of explanatory journalism, Alsop wrote with confidence:

Remember that "competitive instinct" which almost always carried Nixon offside in football games. Remember the strong influence of the brilliant Murray Chotiner [Nixon's first campaign manager], to whom the essential function of politics is, quite simply, to win. Remember also, in fairness, Nixon's part in the Hiss case, his first important political experience, which led him to equate the internal Communist danger with the infinitely greater external danger. And remember, perhaps especially, Nixon's years as a champion college debater, which formed his speaking style. The object of college debating, after all, is simply to win the debate, without regard for the merit of the issues, using against the opposition whatever debating points come to hand.

In that paragraph, Alsop has softened an indictment on a fundamental character weakness into the more comfortable notions of competitive instinct, debater tactics, and deeply ingrained anticommunism. From that ground, he is ready to move to his conclusion that there is a New Nixon:

Nixon will remain a bold and brilliant professional politician to the end of his days. But at the same time, he is in certain ways a different kind of politician from what he was eight, or six, or even four years ago. This is not a matter of opinion. At least in a narrow sense, it is a matter of fact, provable on the record.

And what is that "matter of fact"? Alsop answered:

In the anti-Nixon dossier, the case against Nixon ends rather abruptly in about 1954. In 1956, it was an essential part of Adlai Stevenson's campaign strategy to drive Nixon to extremes by brutal attacks on his integrity. The strategy failed. Nixon followed the advice he now gives younger politicians, and built his campaign around the ticket's "positive" asset—President Eisenhower's personal popularity. The change in Nixon's political style has been even more obvious since 1956. And the change is not really at all surprising. Nixon, after all, is a highly intelligent politician, quite intelligent enough to see that the use of specious debating tricks is very bad politics indeed in a potential presidential candidate.

Once again, we see a change in tactics cited as evidence of a change in character. "Does the change go deeper than that?" Alsop asks himself and his readers. And he answers, "The evidence is clear that Nixon has become, rather gradually, a different sort of politician—the sort of politician who regards effective government, capable of facing up to the facts of the national situation, and dealing with those facts, as the best kind of politics in the long run."

In this passage, Alsop harks back to the earlier section where he has said that Nixon had repeatedly displayed "a knack . . .for being right" on such issues as the space race, national defense, the recession, and foreign aid. That his judgment on such questions coincided with the author's is implicit. What is explicit and striking is that on the policy dimension Alsop had no hesitancy in passing judgment—rather final judgment—as contrasted with his caution on the character questions.

That divergence sets the stage for the coda of his piece, where he deals with the question of what a Nixon presidency might be like. Here, too, he is shrewd on the policy questions and blind on the character questions. He writes, for example, that "one can be absolutely certain that in a Nixon presidency, American foreign policy would be bold, perhaps even adventurous; above all, active rather than passive."

"For the rest," Alsop writes, "it is not possible to predict what effect the enormous office of the presidency would have on Nixon, or what effect Nixon would have on that office." And then comes a passage that, read twenty-nine years later, causes the reader to shake his head: "There are those—Nixon's old adversary, Dean Acheson, is one of them—who firmly believe that Nixon, in his ambition, would pervert the great powers of the office to his own political ends."

Alsop brushes right by that and moves on to his upbeat ending:

But those who hold to this extreme view are a dwindling minority. It is true that Nixon, as he himself has said, is a "political animal." It is true that, like Caesar in Mark Anthony's speech, he is ambitious, and always will be. But there is a difference between a President's ambition and that of a lesser politician. For the presidency is the pinnacle of any man's political ambition, and in that office a man's thoughts tend to turn more to the history books than to the next election. And certain qualities Nixon has displayed as a politician—the boldness and decisiveness, the sure instinct for the realities of power, the strong intelligence, the cool toughness in a time of crisis—would also be markedly useful in a President.

What we have here in this peroration is a blend of the enduring myth of the ennobling quality of the White House environment with the emphasis on "cool toughness," especially toward the Russians, that was so characteristic of the thinking of the Cold War period. Indeed, the same adjectives that Alsop applied to Nixon in those closing paragraphs could have been (and were, in other profiles at the time) used for his eventual rival, John F. Kennedy. Yet, obviously, Kennedy and Nixon were men of very different character. And character is the crucial—and missing—dimension of the judgment which Alsop made in this profile.

The judgment was made for him by Dean Acheson. And scattered through his piece are the bits of evidence that went into making it: the relentless ambition, the secretiveness and lack of human warmth that denied him satisfaction from anything other than domination and fulfillment of ambition, the deviousness of his verbal style and the ruthlessness of his tactics toward other politicians who stood in his way.

But those words, which seem appropriate to those of us who lived to see the bitter and tragic ending of the Nixon chronicle, do not appear in the long Alsop piece.

What I conclude from that is that even the best of journalists—and Alsop was certainly that—will likely shrink from making that kind of firm, clear judgment of the character of an important public man, a potential President. And because we shrink from that responsibility, the character we create is likely to be an imposter.

THE New Nixon theme died out a bit in 1960 and 1962, when Nixon lost his presidential contest with Kennedy and his California gubernatorial campaign against Governor Edmund G. (Pat) Brown. In the gubernatorial campaign, Nixon embarrassed those who thought he had changed tactics if not character. He opened the campaign by charging that Brown "is not capable of dealing with the Communist threat within our borders" and stayed on that theme until polls showed that voters were not buying it.

At the end of the race came the bitter outburst, when Nixon let the accumulated venom and frustration of the years pour out in a diatribe against the press, his political opponents, and even his own campaign workers. "You won't have Nixon to kick around any more," he said, "because, gentlemen, this is my last press conference."

As Nixon began the long climb back from that 1962 debacle, the notion of a New Nixon once more resurfaced in newspaper stories and columns and profiles. Once again, naive reporters and politically sympathetic columnists accepted the notion that he had matured into a better person, while the more sensible journalists argued in print with themselves and their readers whether that was likely.

An example of the second category was a piece that Robert B. Semple, Jr., wrote in the *New York Times Magazine* for January 21, 1968. Under the ambivalent headline "It's Time Again for the Nixon Phenomenon," Semple wrestled with the same question that had thrown Stewart Alsop a decade earlier:

The Richard M. Nixon now embarking on his eighth campaign for public office in two decades presents a more serene public image than the "Nixons" of the past . . . the man whom the liberals called the Michelangelo of the smear, the master of corn, a cold fish, "Tricky Dick." Yet that man has vanished—or so it appears. In his place stands a walking monument to reason, civility, frankness.

One says this, of course, with great trepidation. The search for the "real Nixon" has been a popular but often fruitless pastime ever since the Voorhis campaign [Nixon's first race for Congress]. Accordingly, one must move with caution when one talks about changes in Nixon, lest one subject himself to the hoots of those who have done so in the past only to find that the "new Nixon" (benign, relaxed, straightforward) turned out to be the "old Nixon" (furtive, calculating, the "Mr. Mean" of Democratic campaign lore) in disguise.

Yet time moves on. . . .

• • •

Having stated his ambivalence, Semple cited several changes that were evident: Nixon was now older, richer, more willing to use humor in his speeches—even poking fun at himself. "Another and perhaps equally important aspect of the 'new' Nixon is his candor. Both publicly and privately, the former Vice President has been demonstrating over the past year a degree of frankness about his actions, thoughts and plans that pleases his friends and confounds his enemies, to whom he had become the archetype of political furtiveness."

Semple was certainly right on that point. In traveling with Nixon when he was stumping for other Republican candidates during the 1966 mid-term campaign, when there were few reporters around at any given time, I had heard him explain, on background, the dynamics of each district or state where he was heading and even alert us to the ways he would reshape his basic speech to meet the needs of the candidate he was there to help. In 1967, he supplied similarly clear descriptions of some—but not all—aspects of his own strategy for 1968. But dealing with Nixon, one had to be cautious. As Semple wrote:

> So formidable is Nixon's reputation for self-service that many observers simply cannot believe that the shifts in Nixon's outward personality reflect any fundamental change in character. Nixon's candor, for example, is regarded by skeptics as simply another act of political expediency. His use of humor is suspect; since Nixon is not a witty man in private, the argument goes, his platform humor is a mere contrivance. His outward calm is considered to be a seasonal phenomenon that flowers when Nixon is not running for office and withers when he is.
>
> The American voter will have plenty of time to decide whether the "new" Nixon is merely a creature of cosmetics to be unmasked when the going gets tough—or whether, as his friends insist, his years as a private citizen, and the altered circumstances of his life, have in fact wrought meaningful and permanent changes.

But there would be no unmasking, in part because Nixon avoided close scrutiny and questioning by reporters once the campaign actually began. The advertising men in charge of the campaign had figured out that the way for Nixon to win was to avoid debates, avoid press conferences, and take his message—undiluted—to the voters on television and radio. On the first night of his campaign in New Hampshire, Nixon mocked his past. "Gentlemen," he told the gathered reporters, "this is not my last press conference." On the contrary, he promised, to the greatest extent possible, he would be available for interviews and briefings of the kind he had given in 1966, and if he were not immediately accessible, his staff would always know how to get hold of him for us.

The next day, we got a good hint of the seriousness of that pledge. In late morning, we discovered that Nixon had slipped away to the little town of Hillsboro for a question-and-answer session with a carefully screened group of New Hampshire residents that was filmed for use in campaign commercials. When we complained to Nixon aides that the event had not even been listed on the schedule we had been given for Nixon's day, one of them, Robert F. Ellsworth, said the purpose was to keep the exchanges "as free from being examined, inspected, and reported on as possible."

I reported that news—and the criticism it drew from officials of the rival George Romney campaign—on the front page of the *Post*, but subordinated it in the lead and in the body of the story to the kickoff speech of the Nixon campaign—which ironically promised that he would lead America out of "a crisis of the spirit." Despite the anger my colleagues and I felt at being tricked, there was no way that we—as the detached observers we were supposed to be—could present the most important news of the day as anything other than the Nixon speech. I think his managers knew that, and they scheduled another such filming session in New Hampshire later in the week— telling us in advance but once again barring us. That story went onto an inside page in the *Post* and was barely mentioned elsewhere.

Romney soon dropped out of the race, Nelson Rockefeller and Ronald Reagan delayed their challenges, and Nixon had a relatively easy path to the nomination. But the atmosphere of contrivance never left his campaign. As a *Newsweek* cover story on Nixon's capture of the nomination, in August 1968, said, "For Nixon, politics has always been an exercise in technique. . . . Last week, in the sticky, improbable atmosphere of Miami Beach, Nixon laboriously constructed his masterwork. The result was a typically Nixonian technician's triumph—a civics-book example of the politics of accommodation." And *Newsweek* accurately depicted the character of the campaign that Nixon would conduct in the general election: "Nixon's strategy calls for a hermetically packaged, high-road campaign, assaulting the Johnson-Humphrey administration on the issues—mainly law and order and Vietnam."

For all the millions of words that were written and broadcast about that campaign, nothing penetrated the "hermetically packaged" cocoon that had been built around Nixon's vulnerable person. Jules Witcover described "the two-track Nixon strategy" in his book *The Resurrection of Richard Nixon*. On track one, there were the carefully staged crowd events for the television cameras, the ready-in-advance speeches or statements for the newspaper reporters.

The second track focused on the paid television programs, aired on a regional basis, using the same kind of hand-picked questioners his handlers had arranged for Nixon to face in New Hampshire. Most of them were ordinary citizens, but there was always one local reporter or two, just to make it appear to the television audience that Nixon was not stacking the deck. There was an invited studio audience of Nixon supporters, ready to cheer his answer to every question, but the traveling press corps was kept at a distance, watching on monitors.

The real campaign was the television campaign—where viewers saw Nixon standing alone "in the arena," as he liked to say, surrounded by potentially hostile (but carefully screened) questioners and handling everything they could throw at him—as attested by the cheers of his supporters. All the rest—the crowd events, the formal speeches, the travel—was diversion to keep the press busy and create the sense that there was more than an electronic campaign.

We described the elements of the Nixon campaign in our stories, but we did not explore the meaning, the implications of the strategy any more seriously than we probed Nixon's character. When Joe McGinniss's book, *The Selling of the President 1968*, came out after the election, there was embarrassment in the press corps. McGinniss had negotiated insider access with the Nixon media team, and the story he wrote about their manipulation of the candidate, the cameras, and the voters—while flawed by his seeming conviction that this was unique to the Nixon campaign—had the ring of truth to it.

At one point in McGinniss's book, Roger Ailes, the producer of the Nixon television shows, is talking:

Let's face it, a lot of people think Nixon is dull. Think he's a bore, a pain in the ass. They look at him as the kind of kid who always carried a bookbag. Who was 42 years old the day he was born. They figure other kids got footballs for Christmas, Nixon got a briefcase and he loved it. He'd always have his homework done and he'd never let you copy.

Now, you put him on television, you've got a problem right away. He's a funny-looking guy. He looks like somebody hung him in a closet overnight and he jumps out in the morning with his suit all bunched up and starts running around saying, "I want to be President." I mean this is how he strikes some people. That's why these shows are important. To make them forget all that.

The press helped them forget. Why? Some of the reporters were covering Nixon for the first time, and they may have been conned. But most of us had known him in the 1950s and covered his losing campaigns in 1960 and 1962. The history was not only there for us to read; it was history we had written. But just as Stewart Alsop and Bob Semple did in their careful profiles, when it came right down to the judgment, we preferred to discount the history's clear implications.

The closest I had come before 1968 to suggesting that there was something unhealthy and neurotic about Nixon's frantic effort to gain another chance for the presidency came in a piece I wrote for the *Times* in February of 1966. I had traveled with Nixon and described the "backbreaking schedule" he endured in maintaining his law practice while traveling the Republican banquet circuit. I wrote about the reactions in his crowds and the problems he faced in finding a new political base. Toward the end of the story, I said:

> If the tension that drives a man at such a pace is a source of wonder, no less so is the durability of his political appeal. . . .
>
> Two comments are possible. He says of himself, "I think I do better in adversity than when I am living off the fat of the land."
>
> An old friend who has made some of the trips with him remarks, "The man is possessed by a demon."

Once the 1968 campaign began, the Nixon staff made it easy for us to do the job the way they wanted us to do it; there were "events"— however synthetic—every day to write about, and the journalistic and material needs of the press—advance texts, food, laundry—were well provided.

But there was enough grumbling about the cocoon that I'm not sure we had all been tranquilized. Another kind of conformity was probably involved. The conventions of journalism—as practiced on the newspapers and networks—require that you cover the story as it unfolds. We were covering a campaign that, in the end, turned out to be a close contest, and the daily developments—however meager or contrived—were what our organizations wanted most to hear about. As long as other reporters were filing their daily stories about the daily events, that was the expected and the safe thing to do.

Was fear an element? I cannot say that it was not. All through the year, the polls had shown Nixon a good bet to win the presidency, and many of the reporters covering him on the campaign knew or hoped they would follow him to the White House if he won. I don't know that any of them consciously held back for that reason, but it would have taken exceptional courage, in that situation, to have written that, on the basis of his past history and his behavior in this present campaign, there was serious question whether Richard Nixon had the emotional security and integrity of character to be President of the United States.

As professional skeptics, most reporters have deep-seated doubts—and fears—about their ability to pronounce that kind of final judgment. We wonder whether that's our role, or whether that verdict is one for the editorial writers or the voters. We are more comfortable providing the evidence, examining it, but leaving the conclusion to others.

In this case, we did not even do an adequate job of examining the evidence. Frankly, I think we were embarrassed to admit how much we had allowed ourselves to be manipulated, managed, and held at bay by the Nixon campaign. When I had to reread my own reporting and columns on that campaign for this chapter—a painful experience —I found that I was correct in thinking that I had made and kept a vow to myself that I would not write about a New Nixon.

That spared me some embarrassment.

I did not write, as Walter Lippmann did in early October, an endorsement column saying that "I believe that there really is a 'new Nixon,' a maturer and mellower man who is no longer clawing his way to the top, and it is, I think, fair to hope that his dominating ambition will be to become a two-term President. He is bright enough to know that this will be impossible if he remains sunk in the Vietnam quagmire. Ending the war is indispensable if he is to become a successful President." That column is truly cautionary: the best journalist of our century was wrong on every single point he made.

What I did write in a column on October 1, 1968, was a loud protest at the way in which issues, and language and meaning, were being cheapened by the techniques of the campaign—especially Nixon's:

> Certainly, that Nixon commercial—with his voice speaking quietly against the vivid montage of riots at home and warfare in Vietnam—is a classic example of "image" over "meaning." This reporter has yet to meet anyone who can recall what the unseen Nixon is saying; all they know is that conditions look terrible and he seems to promise a change.
>
> It's all very slick and effective, and to disparage it is perhaps to rail against the inevitable. But . . . when words lose their meaning, when the medium overwhelms the message, a system of government like ours may no longer be operable.

But I certainly never sounded a sharp warning that the level of contrivance and manipulation was so great that readers should be concerned about the character of any candidate who resorted to such tactics.

A few journalists, to their credit, did so—and it may be significant that they were writing in magazines, rather than broadcasting or filing for the daily papers. The greater scope and freedom of a magazine article may be the most appropriate place to draw together the evidence and make the judgment.

One man who saw through the Nixon cocoon was Garry Wills, who in a May 1968 profile for *Esquire*, wrote:

> Nixon takes great pride in knowing the nuts and bolts of the electoral game; *he* can be as tough and smart as the next guy. He even hurts his small reputation for candor by boasting to newsmen of the pitch he will give to particular audiences. But he is not really "the old pro." He does not delegate authority; his campaign organization is poor; he does not work well with equals; he drives himself to the edge of fatigue; he seems no more successful than [Woodrow] Wilson in conveying his private vision of

the nation's role. He is not the technician he pretends to be, but a brooding Irish puritan. And a lonely man.

But the best and most honest piece about Nixon and the frustration the most skilled of reporters felt in their dealings with him was written by the *New Republic*'s John Osborne, in his final piece on the 1968 campaign, called "The Summing Up of a Nixon-Watcher." It explains why Martin Schram of the *Washington Post* said in an obituary appreciation of Osborne in 1981 that he "left those of us in journalism with a remarkable model of just how the job should be done." It is worth quoting at some length:

> Like other wearers of the Nixon press badge, pampered and cosseted and served as no campaign reporters have ever been before, I keep waiting for Mr. Nixon to show himself. At this writing, in the fourth week of travel just behind him (not really "with him," as we like to think), I know that I and my companions wait in vain. Richard Milhous Nixon, the Nixon who is certain now that he will be the next President of the United States, is not going to show himself to us and to the electorate in any way that will tell us anywhere near as much as we need to know and are entitled to know about him and the presidency he proposes to give us. . . .
>
> We of the accompanying press, who flatter ourselves with the notion that we never grant to any candidate the degree of faith he demands, debate with boring and incessant fervor the question that Mr. Nixon himself posed to a bunch of high school students the other day. "Is there a New Nixon?" he asked, thanking them with a smile for being too polite to raise the question. "All I can say is this, you've got to look at the man, you've got to answer the question yourself." It was a typical Nixon moment— loaded with frankness, with a readiness to call up and laugh at his controversial past, and totally lacking in clues to the answer that, he tells the American electorate, we have to find for ourselves. After looking at him and listening to him for the better part of a month, the only answer I have to offer is that it is a silly question. There *is* a Nixon, *this* Nixon, the Nixon who is telling me and all Americans that he is going to defeat Hubert Humphrey and George Wallace on November 5 and be our next President, and I am damned if I know who the man is and what kind of President he is likely to be.

Osborne said the "note of complaint" he was sounding was shared by many others in the Nixon press corps, despite the fact that "he and his assistants handle us very well indeed, so well that we as a group supinely submit to evasions and phony spokesmanship by underlings and a show of distant warmth that ought to be, but somehow are not, more offensive than the cold contempt with which he generally treated the 1960 press corps." He added that the reporters "share a sense that Richard Nixon ought to be faulted for a fundamental lack of political honor, for what he is doing to the political process with his tactics of concealment and pseudo-disclosure of himself, and resent our inability to establish a just and factual basis for saying so."

Osborne described the insulated, carefully controlled campaign Nixon was conducting, shielded, so far as was possible, from surprise, challenge, or interrogation, whether from press or public. And he questioned whether that kind of campaign gave any useful clue to the candidate's ability to master the presidency:

> In withholding so much of himself during the campaign, in displaying a public personality so cautious, so carefully molded for appearance and effect, he does convey an impression . . . of a kind of political automaton. He is, one gathers, husbanding his inner self and his real abilities, "the real Nixon," for a supreme effort to earn in the office he seeks the respect of which he speaks. It looks now as if he will be called upon to make the effort, and that we have no choice but to await it and whatever it tells us about Richard Nixon.

That bleak and painfully honest conclusion by one of the most skillful members of the press corps—in effect, a confession that the subject has dodged the effort to report him—writes a suitable finish to this discussion of the whole New Nixon business. It was, as Osborne said, "a silly question" in the first place, seductive to the press because of its alliteration (who ever heard of a "New Reagan"?) and because of its self-flattering implication that we in the press can probe to the heart of that mystery called human character.

QUITE evidently, we cannot. Although we are urged by some political scientists to dig deep into the personality of would-be Presidents, nothing is more terrifying to me than the prospect of a horde of reporters, fancying ourselves as amateur psychiatrists, asking politicians to lie down on our couches and tell our tape recorders how they felt about Daddy and Mommy. What reporters can do is observe the behavior of politicians and describe the way in which they have acted in the past and are behaving in the current campaign. The anecdotes and incidents like those cited in the profiles of Jimmy Carter and Gary Hart can raise important questions for voters—even if they are questions that reporters cannot answer definitively.

If we are looking for ways in which we can come closer to those answers, I think it significant to note that the Oberdorfer and Lardner profiles of Carter and Hart were done very early in the election cycle and by reporters working essentially on their own. By focusing early on the candidates—in these cases, long before they were regarded as likely major contenders—the reporters operated without the burden of undue deference. By moving early, they also found sources more accessible—and less inhibited in what they said. And by reporting on their own, they freed themselves from any of the pressures of the pack and the kind of pernicious group thinking that led to the gross distortions of Ford's character and the suppression of the vital questions about Nixon.

So part of the solution to the problem of improving character studies and profiles lies simply in applying those old-fashioned journalistic virtues—getting to the story early and reporting it independently and well.

In the anecdote Don Oberdorfer told *Washington Post* readers about Carter's lapse of memory on his relationship with George Wallace, he was illustrating the odd combination of self-assurance, self-righteousness, and sudden shifts of position that had made Carter suspect to many fellow politicians in Georgia. These traits ultimately undermined his relationships with Congress, the Washington political community, and finally the public, which lost confidence in him as President.

In Nixon's case, the evidence of what he had done to earn the distrust of other politicians and of the public was overwhelming and of long standing. Even in the 1968 campaign, reporters knew, as Osborne said, that Nixon "ought to be faulted for a fundamental lack of political honor, for what he is doing to the political process with his tactics of concealment . . ." Tactics of concealment and a fundmental lack of political honor are what finally forced Richard Nixon to resign from the presidency.

Not until 1972, when Nixon had been President for four years, did I start whistle-blowing on Nixon's travesty of a campaign in my column. In late August, right after the Republican convention, I complained of the "smugness" in the Nixon camp and the attitude Nixon himself conveyed "that the ritual of renomination and reelection is no more than a necessary nuisance, an interruption in his work, which he bears with minimum patience and on which he will expend minimum energy."

My anger and concern overflowed in an October 1 column, headlined "The President's Shield," which I wrote after I had been on the road with Nixon for several days:

The distance between George McGovern and the reporters covering him is about ten steps on the chartered 727 jet, and the trail is walked several times each day by the candidate making a point to reporters or reporters seeking his response to their questions. Little is secret and nothing sacred on the McGovern plane.

But there is a wall a mile high between Mr. Nixon and the press. Mr. Nixon travels in isolation—in his private compartment on Air Force One, in his helicopter or his limousine.

His major speeches on the trip—to Republican fund-raising dinners— were watched by reporters from separate rooms, via closed-circuit television. In Los Angeles, it took personal intercession by a White House press aide for a few reporters to gain access to the banquet hall—the same room in the same hotel where reporters had freely interviewed guests at a McGovern fund-raiser the night before.

The only sound television cameras in the room when Mr. Nixon spoke were the closed-circuit cameras controlled by the White House itself. The scenes of the dinner you saw on television—and that most of the reporters saw—were exactly what the White House wanted you to see, and nothing more.

Under these circumstances, the press functions more as a propaganda tool for the President than as an independent reporting group. The difference between a journalist and a propagandist is that a journalist can make his own observations and ask his own questions.

I cited Nixon's decision to limit his own availability to the press— he eventually held only two press conferences between the convention and election—and the inaccessibility and guardedness of his staff aides.

In every way possible, then, the Nixon entourage seems to be systematically stifling the kind of dialogue that has in the past been thought to be the heart of a presidential campaign.

That is the source of McGovern's unhappiness, but it's a problem the press must address—directly, even at the risk of being thought partisan.

The press was accused—and I think rightly—of being derelict in 1968 in not pressing Mr. Nixon to expound his strategy for ending the Vietnam war.

How does the press justify itself this year, if the man who is likely to remain President is allowed to go through the whole campaign without answering questions on his plans on taxes, for wage-price controls, for future policy in Vietnam and a dozen other topics?

An election is supposed to be the time a politician—even a President— submits himself to the jury of the American voters. As a lawyer, Richard Nixon knows that if he were as high-handed with a jury as he's being in this campaign, he'd risk being cited for contempt of court.

The press of the country ought to be calling Mr. Nixon on this—not for George McGovern's sake but for the sake of its own tattered reputation and for the public which it presumes to serve.

The editors of the country and the television news chiefs ought to tell Mr. Nixon, in plain terms, that before they spend another nickel to send their reporters and camera crews around the country with him, they want a system set up in which journalists can be journalists again and a President campaigns as a candidate, not a touring emperor.

Those were impassioned words—by my standards—but four years too late. By then, Nixon had been elected President once and was well on his way to reelection. And Watergate had already happened, in part because the press got so bemused by the search for the New Nixon that we could not see the one before our eyes.

The lessons of the 1972 Nixon campaign—in bypassing the press and refusing to talk about the substantive policy choices ahead—were applied by Ronald Reagan in his reelection campaign in 1984, with even more lopsided and politically satisfying results. What was even more remarkable—and disturbing—in the mid-1980s was the spectacle of Nixon once again crawling back into the political dialogue by exploiting the unending fascination and gullibility of the press.

Just as in the mid-1960s we aided and abetted his comeback from the "last press conference" by covering his domestic and foreign travels, seeking him out for interviews, writing profiles that missed the main points about him, and even, so help me, printing him as a monthly guest columnist in the *Washington Post* and other papers, so a new generation of reporters and editors and television producers has been gulled into playing Nixon's game. In 1984, ten years after his forced resignation, he was invited to speak to the American Society of Newspaper Editors and given a standing ovation. Discreet interviews at his home in New Jersey and carefully selected television appearances followed, with journalists vying to get into his date book. In the spring of 1986, he spoke to the American Newspaper Publishers Association, and in May of that year *Newsweek* magazine put Nixon on the cover with a headline proclaiming, "He's Back: The Rehabilitation of Richard Nixon." "The Sage of Saddle River," as *Newsweek* proclaimed him in the eight-page feature, was up to his old tricks, denying his own tactics and simultaneously profiting from them: "The creation of the newest Nixon 'has not been a deliberate program,' he told *Newsweek*, 'and I am frankly surprised at the extent to which there seems to be an audience for what I have to say.'"

But Nixon is only a symptom of the larger problem. Rather than focusing clearly on the characters we are dealing with, we tend to get caught up in the mechanics and the competitive pressures of what we call "the story." Sometimes, as we will see, we make a hash of that as well.

CHAPTER THREE
Plots That Failed

---

*W**E* in the press are on dangerous ground when we indulge in character creation, but we can get into as much trouble when we let our imaginations outpace our reporting and invent a story line. Admittedly, plot creation is an inescapable part of journalism. We are offered, or we dig up, fragments of information, often buried in a mass of irrelevancies, and we have to render a comprehensible, plausible scenario from those fragments.

Journalistic archeology can be valuable. During the 1960s, journalists constructed a picture of Vietnam from the bits of battles and city and village life they observed that contradicted the optimistic official version offered by the United States and South Vietnamese governments. As the Pentagon Papers later revealed, government officials were receiving similar information but withholding it from the public.

But there are times when the journalistic product looks like a mastodon that was assembled from a fossil toenail find. Some plots described in the press don't bear much resemblance to reality. Political conventions are fertile grounds for such speculative journalism. There is an absence of hard news. Every news organization is out to scoop its rivals. The competition can lead to imaginative exercises.

I have played the game along with everyone else and occasionally have scored the momentary triumph. At the 1968 Republican convention, I was credited by a number of people—including Richard Nixon, in a television interview—with being privy to the secret that he would pick Spiro Agnew as his running mate. (How would you like to have on your tombstone, "He knew it would be Agnew"?) I tried to make clear to *Time* and other press section interviewers at the convention that it was an honor I did not deserve.

The previous spring I had reported that Nixon was interested in Agnew—then an unknown freshman governor of Maryland—as a possible running mate and was checking him out with other politicians. I knew that because Nixon had so declared in an interview I had with him aboard his plane on the eve of the Oregon primary. When I wrote the story I thought he was trying to flatter Agnew and speed the progress of this erstwhile Nelson Rockefeller supporter from the uncommitted to the Nixon camp—bringing along the bulk of the Maryland delegation. I thought so little of that angle of the interview that I buried it down in the story. It was the *Post*'s political editor, Mary Lou Beatty, who pulled it up into the lead.

By contrast, in 1972 I sat down, unprompted, and tried to guess George McGovern's choice of a running mate. The name I came up with was Senator Thomas Eagleton of Missouri, and I took the hunch seriously enough to sit down with Eagleton two weeks before the convention for a long, tape-recorded interview, which I told him we would use if he was the choice. It was the only such interview we had in hand when McGovern announced his selection in Miami Beach, and I felt briefly smug. There was no reason to brag, however, because it quickly became known that Eagleton was McGovern's choice for the job after only five others had turned it down.

More frequent than the scoops are the fiascos: stories that should not have been written and guesses that should not have been made. Richard Reeves, the columnist and author, told Lou Cannon of one that embarrassed him during his days at the *New York Times*. As Cannon recounted it in *Reporting: An Inside View*, in 1968 Reeves wrote flatly that Rockefeller would announce his presidential candidacy in four days; Rockefeller announced, instead, that he would not run.

Reeves told Cannon that it was in part the result of "fierce competition" within the *Times* with R. W. (Johnny) Apple, Jr., another top political writer, and in part his buckling to pressure from an editor to "harden up" the story. "I originally went in with a summary saying,

'Rockefeller is expected to announce,' and it was a dope story about what had been discussed in the inner councils. Abe Rosenthal [then the *Times* associate managing editor] told me he had talked to Rockefeller and Rockefeller said he's going to do it. [Reeves told me in 1986 that he was sure Rosenthal had attributed the inside information to "Rocky's people," rather than the governor himself.] I then checked, and people told me as far as they knew, that was true and that the date and time [were] set."

Reeves said, "I would never again write a simple declarative sentence that something is going to happen. I wouldn't write a simple declarative sentence that the sun's going to rise in the east tomorrow. I think it's just a professional error to do that . . . I would never again, I wouldn't care if it was Jesus Christ, I would never again take someone else's word."

But we all do it more often than we should. One of the most embarrassing errors of my working life was one which the readers, thank goodness, never saw. But the incident is well known in the business and I have taken a deserved ribbing on it. It is like the Reeves story in the sense that my boss, Katharine Graham, then publisher of the *Post* and now chairman of the Washington Post Company, was also involved. It happened after Agnew's forced resignation from the vice presidency. The game in town was to figure out whom Nixon would appoint as his successor.

Many names had been bandied about, including that of Virginia Governor A. Linwood Holton, Jr., a moderate conservative with an engaging personality and a record as a longtime Nixon supporter. One day Ben Bradlee waved me into his office, closed the door, and said, "Katharine [Graham] has heard it's definitely going to be Holton. It's set."

A battle plan was quickly devised. Carroll Kilpatrick, the *Post*'s White House correspondent, would be notified, and he would write the main story. I would write a sidebar explaining the politics of the choice—why Holton made sense. Our Richmond correspondent would be told to locate Holton and stay with him but not told why.

Then Kilpatrick called to say that the White House had just announced that the President would go on television that night, presumably to announce his choice. Our scoop was gone, but we could still dazzle the world by having the fullest first-edition package of stories on Holton, thus giving evidence that we must have cracked the mystery in advance. Kilpatrick came back to the newsroom, and both of us started typing furiously. Our certainty was enhanced by a report from Richmond that Holton was going up to Washington; reporters were dispatched to meet his plane at National Airport.

Close to edition time, Kilpatrick started calling his sources at the White House, seeking additional background on the reasons for Holton's choice. He ran into a strangely cold response, with some even suggesting that he might be on a wild goose chase. He asked me how sure we were about this. I asked Bradlee how sure we were about this. He asked Mrs. Graham if she could tell him her source. She decided she could. It was a businessman—an inveterate political gossip, but not anyone in a position to know. I had assumed the information came, if not from Holton himself, at least from someone very close to him—like his pal Nelson Rockefeller, who was also a pal of the publisher's.

By this time, I had a definite sinking feeling about our exclusive, and within a few minutes, Nixon walked into the East Room to introduce Gerald Ford as his choice. Linwood Holton, we noticed, was one of the guests applauding the new Vice President.

There was no harm done. Years later, at a retirement party for Kilpatrick at Mrs. Graham's home, President Ford teased Carroll for writing the story announcing the appointment of Vice President Holton, and later accepted Kilpatrick's gift of a galley proof of the unpublished "exclusive" for inclusion with the papers at the Ford library.

A grimmer example of the dangers of getting ahead of a breaking story came in the spring of 1981, when a would-be assassin wounded President Reagan and three other men outside the Washington Hilton Hotel. James Brady, Reagan's popular press secretary, had been shot in the head and, while he was in surgery at George Washington University Hospital, all three television networks reported that the wounds had been fatal.

The reports that went over the air were not based on any statements by the attending physicians or by a White House spokesman. They did not come through reporters at the hospital or at the White House. Instead, the information was relayed to reporters on Capitol Hill by an aide to Senate Majority Leader Howard H. Baker, Jr., of Tennessee, who had heard it from people on the White House staff.

One network correspondent on Capitol Hill, knowing that this was third-hand information, refused to go on the air himself with the report and warned his network against using it. To his chagrin, the anchorman on the broadcast announced Brady's death, relying on the very information that the correspondent had rejected.

Happily, the news was not true. But when the denials came, a visibly shaken and angry Frank Reynolds, anchoring the broadcast on ABC, exclaimed on the air, "Let's get it nailed down, somebody. Let's find out. Let's get the word here. Let's get it straight so we can report it accurately."

The perils of exaggeration and inaccuracy are greater for live broadcasts of news events than they are for those of us in newspapers, where deadline pressures still allow some opportunity for checking. But the history of print journalism is filled with such incidents as well, from the false armistice story at the end of World War I filed by United Press to the famous *Chicago Tribune* headline, "Dewey Defeats Truman."

Where newspapers most often go off the deep end are on running stories, where the opening chapters may suggest high drama that never materializes. The biggest category of such stories is investigative, where the sniff of scandal, the suspicion of skulduggery in high places, sets reporters and editors salivating. Such stories can take on a life of their own—especially when they become battlegrounds of competition between news organizations. Sometimes they are justified. But when they run amok, they can do tremendous damage to the presumed villains of the piece, who may never recover their reputations. And they are not the only victims. The press's credibility and the public's confidence are also harmed.

CONSIDER "Billygate," the ongoing story of the connection between the President's brother, Billy Carter, and the Libyan government. It dominated the press for part of the summer of 1980, provoking an extraordinary hour-long presidential press conference and a formal Senate investigation that found no illegality. "When we started out,"

Newsweek quoted Democratic Senator Claiborne Pell of Rhode Island, one of the investigators, as saying, "I thought we might very well have had a bear by the tail. At the end of eight weeks, I've come to the conclusion that we really had a mouse."

If so, it was a mouse that roared. Between July 14, when Billy Carter registered with the Justice Department as an agent of the Libyan government, and October 3, when the Senate investigators issued their report, the *Washington Post* published 117 stories on the subject—46 of them on page 1. But the *Post* was not the most aggressive pursuer of that story. Our competitor, the *Washington Star*, averaged better than three stories a day on the subject during the "hot pursuit" period of the summer.

In a postmortem in the *Washington Monthly*, Robert M. Kaus said that the *Star*'s editor, Murray Gart, aggressively pushed his reporters and editors to work on the Billy Carter story, perhaps hoping it would do for the prestige of his paper what the Watergate story had done for his larger crosstown rival, the *Post*.

Billy Carter, the President's younger brother, had been courted by the radical regime of Libyan strongman Moammar Ghadafi, which was seeking some entrée to the United States government to facilitate purchases of aircraft and other equipment in the United States. He made three trips to Libya in 1978 and 1979 and was host to a Libyan delegation visiting this country. The publicity surrounding those events was terrible for the President, as Billy, suffering from the alcoholism that would soon hospitalize him, interspersed his other crudities with frequent anti-Semitic comments. Many published reports indicated that the Justice Department was pressuring him to register as a foreign agent for the Libyans and disclose the terms of his financial arrangements with them.

Thus, it was certainly news on July 14, 1980, when documents filed in the district court in Washington showed Billy had filed a foreign agent registration that day, under threat of a contempt citation; that he had disclosed receipt of $220,000 cash from the Libyans as part of what he termed a half-million-dollar "loan," plus additional, significant amounts in gifts and expenses; and that he had sought to serve as a go-between to increase the Libyan oil allotment of a domestic firm, Charter Oil Company. The Justice Department said it planned no criminal prosecution, now that Billy had registered.

The documents were filed after the final edition deadline for the afternoon *Star*, so the *Post* had the first crack at the story. We ran a single front-page story on July 15. The *Star* produced four stories, including an interview with Billy, in which he said, "All I did was show them some Southern hospitality."

The next day, the *Post* in a page-one story quoted Charter Oil officials on their version of the deal and ran an editorial describing Billy's behavior as "tawdry, shoddy and shabby." But, the editorial said, "it is hard to believe that Billy Carter has had any influence on foreign policy, energy policy or any other policy. . . . His reputation was in decline even before his contacts with the Libyans began, and his brother had done about as much as he could to disassociate himself from a close relative." The editorial called the Justice Department's choice not to prosecute "a close decision," but said it seemed "consistent with its handling of similar cases under this law in recent years, involving people whose name wasn't Carter." In other words, no big deal.

But it was a big deal at the *Star*. Howard Kurtz, one of the key reporters on the story (he shifted to the *Post* after the *Star*'s closing), told me, "This looked like a juicy story at the beginning, and a lot of us thought it would lead somewhere." Gart had a reputation inside his paper for being anti-Carter, but how much of a part that played in his eagerness to hype the story is not clear. "Initially," Kurtz said, "it was the reporters' enthusiasm that pushed the story, but later, Gart just kept pumping it up; it almost became a daily quota of stories."

The July 16 *Star* had five stories, including the disclosure that Billy had "sought and received advice from his brother's legal counsel in the White House." Counsel Lloyd Cutler told Billy, the story revealed, "to get a lawyer immediately." But an editorial said it "looks like crass influence peddling," and it "cries out for illumination."

By July 17, the story had moved inside to page 5 of the *Post*, but the *Star* had three stories, including a front-pager revealing that Phil Wise, the President's appointments secretary, had arranged a National Security Council briefing for Billy before his first trip to Libya. Deep in that story, reporter Lisa Myers noted that the briefing had been mentioned in Billy's foreign agent registration, three days earlier.

On July 18, both papers gave page-one treatment to the President's first comments on the affair, which he termed "regrettable." He said that when he learned of the arrangement, he urged Billy to "make a complete revelation" to the Justice Department. Inside, the *Star* ran a Hearst News Service story about aborted discussions concerning the sale of commercial jets to Libya, discussions that had "no known relationship" to Billy.

On Saturday, July 19, the *Post* came up with three more stories, including our first interview with Billy. But we had shot our wad. There were no further stories in the Sunday and Monday editions. And the *Star* was pouring it on. On Saturday and Sunday, the 19th and 20th, there were seven more stories, and on Monday, the 21st, there was another long recap on the "services and counsel" Billy received from the White House.

The *Post* was getting nervous and restive. George Lardner, Jr., one of the lead reporters in what eventually became a squad of *Post* writers on the case, recalled that "We were slow getting started, but we reacted to what the *Star* was doing. Like Howie [Kurtz], I thought for a long time there was something to it. But it was also a matter of meeting the competition. I remember Howie Simons [then the *Post*'s managing editor] coming out of his office, waving his arms, when he read the first edition of the *Star*, and saying 'We've got to do something.'" Simons recalled his concern that "The *Star* was beating us on it, and it looked like a good scandal. . . . There were whispers of wider implications . . . the White House staff role . . . so we decided we better go after it. Remember, too, it was summer"—a time when the flow of normal governmental news in Washington dries up.

THE stage was set for real competition between the Washington papers. On July 22, the *Post* had two front-page stories—one reporting that intelligence sources apparently had alerted Justice to the Billy Carter payments from the Libyans, as part of an "across-the-board" Libyan effort to secure influence with the Carter Administration, and the other detailing Billy's actions on June 10, the day he apparently learned of the government's renewed interest in him. Both stories hinted at some sort of tip-off.

The same day, the *Star* carried four stories, two texts, a column by William Safire of the *New York Times* News Service, and an editorial. The editorial, called "The High Cost of Influence Peddling," pointed to the Watergate parallels journalists were beginning to see. "Still to be cleared up, furthermore," it said, "is the question we posed here last week: What did President Carter know of his brother's influence-peddling activities, and when did he know it?" Urging a congressional investigation to "fill in some of the missing pieces of the story," the editorial surmised that "those pieces could, of course, be far uglier than anyone now thinks." Game was clearly afoot, Watson.

On July 23, the *Post* off-lead reported that national security adviser Zbigniew Brzezinski had used Billy as an intermediary late in 1979 to set up a meeting with the Libyan chargé d'affaires, seeking Libyan help in the release of the American hostages in Iran. The story said White House officials knew their disclosure "would open a new series of questions." Inside, the *Post* carried a report of Billy's denial of a "tip-off," and a separate story saying Secretary of State Edmund Muskie had told reporters he knew nothing of Billy's dealings with the Libyans. With a four-column headline on that last story, the *Post* was beginning to escalate to *Star* standards.

But the *Star* was up to the challenge. That afternoon it had four stories and a column by Jack Germond and Jules Witcover analyzing "the serious political threat" the scandal posed to Carter.

On July 24, the *Post*'s lead story, under a six-column banner, was a heavy-breathing report headlined, "President Also Met with Libyan Envoy Here." It reported "an undisclosed meeting" with the chargé d'affaires "about three weeks after his brother, Billy, arranged an introductory meeting" with Brzezinski. In the seventh paragraph reporters Walter Pincus and Robert G. Kaiser said, "There was no suggestion that Billy Carter's name or role came up in the President's meeting with [Ali] Houderi in Washington last December, or that Billy Carter helped arrange it." In the twenty-first paragraph the article said Carter saw the Libyan diplomat "to express his own displeasure over the burning of the [American] embassy" in Tripoli a few days earlier. As Kaus said in his dissection of the coverage in the *Washington Monthly*, a "headline 'Carter Rebuked Libyan Envoy for Sacking of Embassy' would have lacked the nostalgic ring of scandal."

The *Post*'s enthusiasm had now reached the point where the paper treated as front-page news the story that the previous April the Internal Revenue Service had put a lien for back taxes on thirty-eight acres of Billy's property, while inside the paper there were separate stories on the plans for the Senate investigation and Ronald Reagan saying an investigation was a good idea. Editorially, the *Post* said the "sympathy" for a President embarrassed by his brother's "truly disgusting conduct" had to be tempered by concern at the White House's failure to close its doors to Billy. "What remains incomprehensible is why Mr. Carter after all the warnings and embarrassments continued to let brother Billy have the run of the official barnyard," it said. Cartoonist Herblock saw it more simply. From the White House, a human chain formed, with Carter holding on to Brzezinski, who gripped Billy by one hand, while Billy handed Ghadafi an envelope stamped "official business" and received, in return, an envelope full of money from the Libyan leader. The title: "The Libyan Connection." The *Star* that afternoon had five stories, an editorial, and a column.

On July 25, the *Post* led with a pair of stories on the formal creation of a Senate investigating committee and Carter telling his staff to "cooperate fully" and suggesting his own readiness to testify. Inside, there were two other news stories and a long Style section profile of a lawyer and Libyan foreign agent who had or had not been enlisted to help in the Carter campaign. The *Star* that day, for the first time, was hard put to win the daily competition for coverage. It had only two stories, a profile, a news analysis, and two columns. The *Star* did come up with a wonderful example of headline simplification on the Germond and Witcover article, which played the Watergate theme, sort of: "No one except the most extreme partisans would suggest that the Libyan connection is in any way comparable to the Watergate scandal. . . . But the Carter White House handling of the episode is reminiscent of the Nixon White House handling of Watergate in one important respect. Once again the full story is being pulled out thread by thread . . . and once again, we have a White House clearly trying to con the voters by putting a veneer of rationality on some essentially bizarre behavior." The headline, naturally, read, "Carter Handles Billy Case As If It Were a Watergate."

• • •

FINALLY, on July 26, there was a real news development. After both the White House and the Justice Department had repeatedly denied that Carter had been involved in the handling of Billy's case, Attorney General Benjamin R. Civiletti disclosed that "in an informal, brief exchange" on June 17, he had told the President that Billy was foolish not to register as an agent and, by departmental precedent, would not be prosecuted if he did so even at this late date. Reading down in the *Post*'s long front-page story, one found that Civiletti's recollection had been triggered by Carter when Carter came across a passage in his notes on their June 17 meeting and that the President said that he had not passed on Civiletti's judgment when he urged Billy, in a July 1 phone call, to make a full disclosure of his activities with the Libyans.

The main point was that the administration had changed its story, and the Watergate parallel leaped once again to mind. The eighth paragraph of the *Post* story said, "Civiletti's revelation is sure to provide more ammunition to administration critics who have been trying to compare the handling of the Billy Carter case to Watergate."

The *Star*, keeping to its pattern, broke the elements of the *Post*'s single story into five separate pieces—one of them a political analysis piece by Germond, hitting the Watergate theme with talk of "the smoking pistol." Germond spotted "a confluence of pressures on the Democratic Party to reassess the inevitability of renominating Jimmy Carter for a second term."

The next day, July 27, was a Sunday—"Billy Sunday" in the Washington papers, as Kaus called it in the *Washington Monthly* article. The *Star* weighed in with eight stories. Its think section reprinted a 1979 *Esquire* article by psycho-journalist Edwin Diamond on the Billy–Jimmy Carter relationship. In separate news section pieces, it reported that Senate Majority Leader Robert C. Byrd of West Virginia told the President to "lay out the facts" before the Democratic convention opened; White House press secretary Jody Powell said Carter would do just that; Billy resurfaced in Plains, Georgia, but would not talk—at least to the *Star*; Billy's friend Randy Coleman also registered as an agent for Libya; the liberal organization Americans for Democratic Action called for Civiletti's resignation, but he said he expected to be exonerated; at the State Department, correspondent Henry Bradsher once again looked into Libya's effort to buy jet transport planes and once again was told Billy had nothing to do with it. But the big story was Lyle Denniston's revelation that when Billy registered, he declined to file a "termination agreement," suggesting that he might have an ongoing relationship with the Libyans.

But the *Star*'s package was modest compared to the *Post*'s. In the comment section, a retired diplomat, working on a book about Libya, wrote a lengthy plea that the Billy case be used to investigate Libya's nefarious role in the world.

In the news section Cairo reporter Edward Cody also reviewed Libya's troubled reputation as a bandit regime and said that for a country ruled by a man called " 'Brother Colonel,' it was perhaps natural to turn for help in America to Brother Billy." In Washington, Justice Department correspondent Charles R. Babcock talked to Joel L. Lisker, the head of the foreign agent registration operation, who said he received no instructions from Civiletti and decided on his own to handle Billy's case by a civil, not criminal, procedure. Nonetheless, White House correspondent Martin Schram led his long front-page piece thus: "Among the President's high command, the realization has slowly set in: they have taken what was a minor irritation and turned it into their own national nightmare." The theme of peril was amplified in columns by Haynes Johnson and Joseph Kraft. But the really titillating news came from the *Post* task force in Americus, Georgia, composed of Peter Elkind, Art Harris, and Sally Quinn. Unlike the *Star*, they had gotten Billy and his wife Sybil to talk. Elkind and Harris spelled out the hard news: "Billy Carter telephones friends and lawyers these days from the lobby of the Best Western Motel here because he believes, rightly or wrongly, that his older brother's government is wiretapping his home and office." Billy claimed in the second paragraph to have been shown transcripts of his own phone conversations, and Sybil was quoted as being "sure it's the Justice Department." (The story included a Justice Department denial, and no evidence ever developed to support the wiretap claim.)

Meantime, Quinn, spinning mood music in her piece, sketched Billy at the motel phone as, "so small, almost frail. He weighs less than 150 pounds now—dieting, golfing, no booze. He smokes five packs of Marlboros a day. He seldom smiles. . . . 'I never knew it would get this bad,' he says."

Eat your heart out, Murray Gart.

On Monday morning, July 28, Quinn was back for round two, a lengthy Style section piece based mostly on conversations with Sybil, with a few asides from Billy, describing "the dark side of the American Dream—the dream that anybody can be elected President. But what if that anybody is your brother? For the Billy Carters, the glory of the voting booth has become the ashes of public scorn . . ." Back in Washington, Edward Walsh, who shared the White House beat with Schram, had his own version of the "national nightmare" story, emphasizing the Carter White House's difficulties in presenting a show of openness that would sharply differentiate it from Nixon's Watergate approach. The difficulty was dramatized by the fact that Walsh's piece shared the front page with one by Walter Pincus, an investigative reporter. The headline over both pieces was "Watergate Memories Shaping Billy Carter Affair."

Clearly in danger of being outdistanced, the *Star* that afternoon offered only three items. Further evidence of the story's temporary exhaustion came in the July 29 *Post*, when the "Personalities" column reported that a worm named Billy Carter won the race at the Hudson, South Dakota, public library and then was crushed accidentally by a judge's boot. Maybe it was meant as a parable.

That day, the *Star* hitched up its belt to produce six stories and a column, and the next day there were five more, but the bologna was being sliced very thin in both papers. On July 31, the *Post* had two stories and the *Star* six. The main news in both papers was that the White House had confirmed that the President had discussed with Billy some "low-classification" cables about his trip to Libya. But the most significant development of the day probably came in two columns that sounded the first clear warning signal of wretched journalistic excess.

In the *Post*, foreign affairs columnist Philip Geyelin said that on the evidence so far, "Billygate . . . may turn out to be something of a bust. . . . The Watergate analogy, so assiduously cultivated by those who would like to make Richard Nixon look better by making Jimmy Carter look worse, simply won't wash. . . . The uproar over the Libyan connection looks all out of proportion to the available evidence."

Even more striking was the column in the *Star* that afternoon by conservative James J. Kilpatrick, who said, "In my own view, Jimmy

Carter is a disaster. I hope to see him dumped in November. But in simple fairness, he deserves something better than the 'drubbing' he had been getting on Billy."

Kilpatrick laid out his argument as if he were addressing his fellow journalists, especially those who "are prowling about the White House like so many hungry catamounts," because "they smell a crippled rabbit inside." Kilpatrick set out to "draw a few distinctions and to fix a fair perspective," something badly in need of doing:

> The business of Billy Carter, the President's black sheep brother, does not yet approach the level of the Watergate scandals of eight years ago. In the Watergate affair, we were dealing with criminal conduct—with breaking and entering, with patent obstruction of justice. In the matter of Billy Carter, we are dealing mostly with misjudgments, with good intentions gone awry.
>
> At the outset, we ought to separate the actions of Billy Carter, private citizen, from the actions of his brother Jimmy, President of the United States. Brother Billy's wrongdoing, by Watergate standards, is trivial. . . . The only allegation of illegal conduct against him is that Billy failed timely to register as an agent of the Libyan government.
>
> Brother Billy is not the issue. . . . The catamounts of the press are after Brother Jimmy, and their self-righteous rectitude is showing. There is a conscious or subconscious desire to demonstrate that the press can be just as rough on Democrat Jimmy Carter as it was rough on Republican Richard Nixon. . . . It is preposterous to equate Billy Carter with Gordon Liddy, Benjamin Civiletti with John Mitchell, and Jimmy Carter with Richard Nixon. The equation will not compute. . . . It was the charge of "cover-up" that felled Nixon in 1974. . . . In the affair of Billy Carter, by contrast, we so far have no reason to believe that anything of significance has been covered up.

After those columns, some of the zest disappeared, but the *Post* of August 1 had five stories and a text. The main news was positive from Carter's point of view. The White House released the text of the State Department cables concerning Billy's trips to Libya and they were bland and approving of his behavior and conduct. The Senate committee agreed to speed up its investigation, shortening the political agony. On the other hand, Lardner and Elkind, in separate stories, detailed the generous terms of Billy's loan from the Libyans and the many contradictions in his past accounts of his actions.

The *Star* that day was less willing to give up the chase. Two of the six stories recapped the developments, mostly favorable to the Carters, of the previous twenty-four hours. Three others picked at various parts of Billy's accounts, looking for contradictions. The lead story said, "The Justice Department weighed this year's political campaign as 'an important factor' in deciding to undertake civil rather than criminal proceedings against Billy Carter, an authoritative department source told the *Washington Star* last night." That sounded like the smoking gun, all right, except that, as the story made clear, the reason the campaign was relevant was that taking the case to a grand jury for criminal proceedings would "lock it up" for six to twelve months and bar any publicity on the matter. "Because a major aim of the law is to get the facts of a foreign agent's activities out in the open, the participants [in the Justice Department decision] were said to have agreed it was better to bring a civil case and get prompt disclosure. One participant said, 'We were concerned that we not lock this up in an election year.'" For leaning over backwards, in other words, the Justice Department got a kick in the pants.

The August 2 *Post* featured a story on the latest turn in the cables business, the disclosure that, despite previous denials, the President had mailed one of the "confidential" and complimentary cables to Billy, on which he had actually scribbled a note of congratulations for "a good job under the 'dry' circumstances," i.e., without liquor, in that Moslem country. The *Post* story, by Babcock and Lardner, characterized it as "the latest flip-flop." That day's *Star* had just one story— on the cable development—and an editorial, reflecting Kilpatrick's admonition to the press. In endorsing "a sober and responsible investigation," the editorial said that "the formation of a select subcommittee" of senatorial investigators "conveys the impression that what some are calling 'Billygate' may be of comparable magnitude [to Watergate]. That must be doubted at this stage."

On August 3, the *Post* had three stories and a pair of columns. The main news piece, by Schram, was a backstage look at the "jolt" the cables' disclosure had been to the White House, but it did not explain how any national interest had been hurt by Billy learning that his conduct had been praised. In another story, Pincus noted that the record seemed to show that Ghadafi had snubbed Billy, rather than treated him as a valued agent, refusing even to see him personally on his visits and blocking his efforts to get more oil for Charter Oil. The Libyan connection was beginning to look thin. But columnist Joseph Kraft hit a new theme which was to become very popular: if the administration wasn't crooked, then it had to be powerfully inept. "As details accumulate," Kraft wrote, "the charges of corruption and cover-up fade away. Into the foreground comes the stark realization that the Carter Administration showed the same ineptitude in handling Billy Carter that it demonstrates in managing great affairs of state. It is a case of Billygoat, not Billygate." One way or another, Carter was going to lose.

In the *Star* that day, Senator Byrd played Kraft's tune, blaming the White House for "bad judgment and some rather amateurish handling" of the case. Four other stories dealt with marginalia, including a sidebar by Phil Gailey on Billy's sidekick Randy Coleman, which noted Jody Powell's comment at a White House briefing that "the idea that we're standing here debating with deep concentration the extent of Randy's influence on American policy towards Libya . . . strikes me as an interesting commentary on the process."

On August 4, the President scheduled an hour-long evening news conference, in an effort to dispose of the questions about Billy before the opening of the Democratic convention, now just a week away. That morning, the *Post* carried a page-one report from our correspondent in Beirut that "Libyan officials in Beirut are promoting a story that their government sent President Carter a $50,000 gift through his brother Billy." The second paragraph was the White House denial that any such gift had been made; the third paragraph said "longtime observers" in Beirut thought it "newsworthy," not that the story had been published there by a minor newspaper, but that there was "definite evidence that Libyan officials, who to date had not commented on the controversy surrounding Billy Carter's Libyan connections, had intentionally sought to leak the story through Beirut's always cooperative media." Working in the office on Sunday night, I expressed my anger that this report—which seemed to be without substance—was being given undue prominence by the *Post* and was told to mind my own business.

But the *Post*'s last shot before the press conference was a popgun compared to the *Star*'s five stories and three columns, including a full-page chronology of "the case so far," and a United Press International pickup of a copyrighted piece from the *San Diego Union*, breathlessly reporting that while the President may have thought Billy was "dry" in Libya, a traveling companion said Billy took vodka in with him and brought no vodka out. Germond and Witcover, in their column, said "there is no comparison between this controversy and the Watergate scandal," but it still raises damaging questions about the President's "judgment," because "the political professionals recognize ... that the facts of a case can be less important than the appearance, at least in political terms."

That evening, the President sent a lengthy report on the case to the Senate committee, which began its hearings that day, and answered questions in an hour-long televised news conference. There was voluminous coverage the next day in both the *Post* and the *Star*, and a general recognition, as Schram put it in the *Post*, that the President "went a long way toward ... defusing the explosiveness of this scandal." Germond, in the *Star*, found the President's account "convincing and credible," suggesting that "there is indeed a path out of at least this element of the political trouble."

There were still the doubters. Pincus and Babcock, in a *Post* news analysis, said the President "failed to address at least one key question" and made "several shifts from previous White House statements." The omitted question, they said, was whether the President had encouraged the payments to Billy "by boosting Billy in the Libyans' eyes. . . . There may be no real bombshells in the report," they conceded, "but it seems certain to leave critics with ammunition to at least question the administration's judgment on the issue."

By August 6, the story was clearly dying. Elkind reported in the *Post* that "despite all the fanfare and theatrics the Billy Carter story is generating in Washington, it appears to be playing to unenthusiastic audiences around the country." A dozen paragraphs of detail confirmed that, in one Peoria businessman's words, "they could care less." In the Senate, Margot Hornblower wrote, investigators were "wondering whether there really is very much to investigate" and were backing away from their plans to take testimony from the President. (He never was called.)

The *Star* editorial said Carter had "succeeded to a remarkable degree" in answering the concerns about his actions, but "it remains difficult to understand how the President could have ignored so many red flags about his rambunctious brother's involvement with a government like Libya's and not have moved quickly to put public distance between his administration and Billy." Decrying Carter's "amateurism," the editorial said "the current White House episodes too often evoke a Beverly Hillbilly style."

So it was Billygoat, not Billygate. Things are never quite that simple, however. Between them, the *Post* and the *Star* published about one hundred more stories, before the Senate investigators wound up work in early October, with a report criticizing Carter, Brzezinski, and Civiletti for errors of judgment, finding no illegalities on anyone's part, and praising the Justice Department for "honestly and conscientiously" investigating Billy's affairs.

Except for one column by the *Star*'s ombudsman, George Beveridge, rejecting a White House complaint of slanted editing and awarding the paper "a strong plus for balance that argues effectively against any charge of deliberate bias," neither paper did a retrospective appraisal of its own coverage of Billy Carter and his Libyan connection —even though it smacked of what some might call amateurism, overenthusiasm, and runaway competitiveness.

There is a responsiblity here for reporters—and even more for editors. Reporters on a story like Billygate have "our foot on the gas pedal," as Kurtz put it in reflecting on the experience. As Lardner stated, "You can't drop a story like that. You have to pursue it to its conclusion." That is correct. Billy Carter's connection with the odious Libyan government was certainly news. Foreign governments, as Pincus pointed out to me, often think they can purchase influence with an administration by hiring a close connection of the President, and the press cannot ignore such practices. Both Kurtz and Lardner made the further point that newspaper investigations may have value in exposing practices and relationships, even if no prosecutions or convictions for illegal activity result. All that is true.

But it does not deal with the question of proportion. Both reporters told me they thought readers tend to provide their own corrective. "I think readers tend to discount a story after they read the same things day after day," Kurtz said. At times, Lardner added, "they call you and say, 'Enough, already.'"

Editors, however, cannot and should not abandon their editing responsibilities to their readers. And in both these cases, the editors failed. Gart, in reflecting on the experience, denied the political motivation suggested by his former reporter, Kurtz, who said, "He got pleasure from sticking it to Carter. . . . We were not allowed to drop the story." Instead, Gart attributed the story's prominence to "eager young reporters . . . a keen sense of competition and heat of a presidential campaign." At the *Post*, Simons, who was running the paper in Bradlee's absence, said, "The thought that you're going to miss something big scares the hell out of you, especially when your competition [the *Star*] is all over the story. So you err on the side of overcovering it."

There is also a managerial problem, Simons said, in turning a team of reporters loose on a story and then reining them in. "It's hard," he said, "when you've got three reporters working on a story to tell them that what they've got today is one story, not three. I'd ask at story conference if we couldn't fold it into one story, and I'd get my head handed to me."

There was, apparently, a failure of communication and perception. Lardner, one of those reporters, said, "There were certainly points where I would willingly have said, 'I've got no story today.' But we were apprehensive about what the *Star* might have, so we played defensively and kept writing."

In retrospect, almost everyone at the *Post* recognizes that Billygate represented a lapse in standards which the paper had established and upheld under the far greater pressures of the Watergate story. In that case, Bob Woodward and Carl Bernstein, like many other investigative reporters before them, uncovered serious wrongdoing without bending or breaking the rules of good journalism. It was Howard Simons in a 1974 speech at the University of Montana who detailed the precautions which were taken on the Watergate story:

Remember, we were dealing with sources who had to remain anonymous, with two young reporters, and with material which, if wrong, could massively damage not just the *Washington Post* but our profession. Accordingly, from the beginning and even today, we, the editors, adopted three rules—they evolved really—to govern the publication of a Watergate story in our newspaper. The first is that any set of significant facts must have come from at least two independent sources. As a result of this rule we never carried some information. This was so simply because we had it from one source only.

The second rule is that one or more of the top editors of the newspaper must read and approve the story before publication. Many was the evening that I or Ben Bradlee decided to hold a story on deadline because we were not satisfied. And the third rule is that a story on Watergate from another publication must be independently verified by our own reporters before we give the story prominence. As a result of these rules, we've been more error-free than even we had a right to expect.

A Watergate "success" does not allow us, however, to ignore the lessons of exaggeration and distortion involved in our too-frequent false-alarm investigations. We need to be especially vigilant at times when the lure of a really big story tempts us to disregard our own standards. Early in Billygate there were abundant signs that would have suggested caution and skepticism. Those signs were noted in the early reports—and then ignored. In the first three days after Billy Carter registered as a Libyan agent, the *Post* quoted Justice Department officials as saying his activities for the Libyans "did not warrant criminal action"; quoted the President as saying he was unaware of Billy's financial arrangements with the Libyans; and quoted Billy as saying he lacked "any influence" with, or on behalf of, the Libyan government. Those three facts—which remained unchallenged throughout—disappeared in the intensity of the Billygate coverage.

In this and other cases, we were all too eager to have the big story pan out, and we brushed aside anything that did not help move the story along to what we thought should be its conclusion. We were not content to report what we knew—and to emphasize what was not known or what had not yet happened. We anticipated events, rather than reporting them. And so we ended up creating a largely false picture in the minds of our readers and viewers. It was not a very substantial creation: the Billygate story was knocked down by a one-hour presidential press conference. The most serious damage, in the end, was to the credibility of the press.

My favorite item, in the vast catalogue of *Star* and *Post* stories about the Billy Carter case, was a paragraph by the *Post*'s astrologer, Svetlana, the day before the President's press conference. Billy is an Aries, she said, and Jimmy a Libra, and "these two signs drive each other batty." Reading the chart, Svetlana also discovered an "eclipse that falls on Jimmy's chart on August 10 and affects his standing. . . . Because of that eclipse on Jimmy's chart [a few hours before the Democratic convention was to open], I have strong doubts that he will emerge as the nominee of the party."

There is a little too much Svetlana in all of us.

IN contrast to stories like Billygate, which draw a volume of coverage that seems inversely related to their intrinsic importance, there are dozens of stories we seem never to notice, or seem to notice belatedly. Our range of vision is limited by the bureaucratic definitions of our beats, by the perceptions of what is news, and by ingrained values and biases that shape the way in which we see the world.

I have had my embarrassing experiences with the parochialism and lack of perspective that beat reporting produces, and have been perhaps more subject to such problems than most reporters, because of the length of time I have remained on a single beat—politics.

As far back as 1967–68, I had an object lesson in the problem of parochialism causing blindness. From the late fall of 1966 onward, there were rumbles of rebellion inside the Democratic Party against the policies of President Lyndon Johnson.

At the end of a closed meeting of Democratic governors following the mid-term election of 1966, which saw the Democrats suffer unexpectedly large losses, Governor Harold R. Hughes of Iowa said they had agreed that an "anti-administration trend" was setting in and predicted that if it continued, Johnson "would have a very tough race" for reelection.

In the summer of 1967, the National Student Association held its annual convention at the University of Maryland, and because it was in our backyard, we sent two summer intern reporters to a convention we rarely cover, where they heard Allard Lowenstein, a former NSA president turned free-lance liberal activist, urge the students to become "the avant-garde in the effort to deny Johnson renomination."

The *Post*, the *Times*, and the *Star* all carried stories in the autumn of 1967 about "dump Johnson" efforts, concentrated on college campuses and among the most left-wing elements and organizations allied with the Democratic Party. Despite such warning signals and the obvious growing public dissent over the Vietnam War, I managed to remain largely oblivious to the possibility of a serious effort to deny Johnson another term.

The fundamental source of this error, I saw in retrospect, was the way in which I defined my beat in my own mind and the way in which the bureaucratic habits of covering that beat reinforced that bias. Covering the Democratic Party meant going to the Democratic National Committee, which John M. Bailey was managing as a wholly owned subsidiary of the Johnson White House. It meant talking to state and local officials of the Democratic Party, whose sense of growing public unease was held in check by their institutional deference to the power of the presidency and their desire to maintain cordial patronage and personal relations with Johnson and his aides. It meant talking with Democratic elected officials, few of whom were as outspoken or independent in their judgments as Harold Hughes had been and most of whom felt very inhibited about criticizing a President of their own party.

In those circles, it was unthinkable that a party would reject a sitting President. In the experience of the people with whom I was talking, there were only two precedents for any such attempt: the effort made by some conservative Democrats to block Franklin D. Roosevelt's bid for a third term in 1940 and the effort led mainly by liberal Democrats to dump Harry S. Truman at the 1948 convention and substitute William O. Douglas or Henry A. Wallace or even Dwight D. Eisenhower at the top of the Democratic ticket. In both precedents, the incumbent had crushed the challenge and then had gone on to prove the doubters wrong by defeating presumably strong Republican opponents in the general election.

Among the people I was interviewing, there was no doubt that if the Allard Lowensteins of this world attempted to dump Johnson, the outcome would be their certain defeat. They understood "power realities," and anyone who denied those realities was stamping himself a hopeless amateur, a dreamer—to be scorned, if not ignored, by those of us who saw ourselves as insiders in that world of power.

Tom Wicker of the *New York Times* expressed that conventional wisdom in an October 1967 column. When asked on a European trip whether "there is a real possibility that the Democratic Party will repudiate President Johnson next year," he answered, he said, that "professional politicians would never do a thing like that." While "the Democratic Party in 1968 conceivably could fall into the hands of impassioned, swarming amateurs, who would do something the professionals would never do," he said, "to believe that this actually will happen remains a plunge that only the wildest hunch bettor would take." As Wicker pointed out to me in 1986, that conventional wisdom was then shared even by Robert F. Kennedy, who did not for another six months grasp how the opposition to the Vietnam War, which he shared, had made 1968 the most unconventional of years.

When a professional defied the conventional wisdom by announcing his readiness to challenge Johnson, a wrenching readjustment of my thinking was required. That, of course, is what I faced when Eugene McCarthy announced on November 30, 1967, that he would run against Johnson in several primaries. McCarthy was no amateur and no political virgin. He was a veteran of the House Ways and Means Committee and a member of the Senate Finance Committee. There are no innocents on those committees. Moreover, while in the House, he had organized the Democratic Study Group, the caucus of liberal members which had grown into one of the real power centers of the House. He had shown himself an adept player at the 1960 Democratic convention, delivering a powerful nominating speech for Adlai E. Stevenson that threatened momentarily to derail John F. Kennedy's nomination drive. Because of his standing in the Democratic Party and in the Senate, Lyndon Johnson had given serious thought to McCarthy as a running mate in 1964, before finally turning to the other Minnesota Senator, Hubert H. Humphrey.

Faced with all that, it was a bit difficult to dismiss the significance of McCarthy's challenge. But I did my best in a column published on Halloween day, 1967:

> The frenzy of the anti-Johnson Democrats has now reached the point where it degrades the Democratic Party and those involved in the mutiny at least

as much as it hurts the President himself.

The scramble to get off the sinking Great Society ship is producing some scenes that would be comic if those involved did not take themselves with such deadly seriousness.

I cited several examples that had offended my sensibilities, among them a speech McCarthy had made the previous week at the University of California at Berkeley. McCarthy had said that unless Johnson fired Secretary of State Dean Rusk and reversed his Vietnam policy, "top Democrats should be prepared to support the men who are willing to carry the flag against the incumbent President of the United States."

McCarthy's effrontery vexed me:

Many will recall that the Eugene McCarthy who last week lent his eloquent voice to the anti-Johnson movement is the very same gentleman who spent the first four days of the 1964 Democratic convention in Atlantic City, in quivering anticipation of a bid to become Mr. Johnson's running-mate.

He did so then in lonely defiance of his old friends from Minnesota and the liberal movement around the country, who were working on behalf of his colleague, Hubert Humphrey.

It is true, of course, as the dissenters maintain, that loyalty to friends and loyalty to Party are less important than duty to conscience. But those Democrats who find it necessary, in conscience, to break with the President now ought at least to have the decency to admit that their judgment may be no more infallible than it was in 1964, when all of them were hailing him as a paragon.

Lyndon Johnson's character, with all its strengths and weaknesses, is no different today than it was in 1964. Those Democrats who rushed to embrace him then, and now so smugly disdain to do so, ought to realize that their own reputations are being affected by their behavior in this difficult time.

The McCarthy story was not the only significant 1968 story I managed to miss until it slapped me in the face. I also gave the third-party movement of Alabama Governor George C. Wallace the back of my hand in my columns. In an August 1968 column, for example, based largely on a Wallace rally in Hammond, Indiana, I described his campaign as "a powerful, impressive and frightening phenomenon," marked by what I characterized as Wallace's "steady and repetitive incitement to violence." These are not ordinary political crowds, I said:

> When Wallace has finished his harangue, the emotion is closer to that of a lynch mob—a pack of angry, frustrated men and women, who see his cause, not just as a chance for victory but as a guarantee of vengeance against all who have affronted them so long.
>
> And who are their targets? Wallace is very shrewd in pinpointing them. "The preachers, the professors, the judges and the newspaper editors who've been looking down their noses at you and telling you they know better than you do how you should run your life."
>
> It is an interesting group. I suppose that if one wanted to name four institutions that are fundamental to the functioning of a free republic, one would think of the institutions of law, of religion, of education and of a free press. These are Wallace's targets in a campaign which, seen close-up, is clearly not a campaign at all, but an incitement of anarchy and violence and thus a clear and present danger to anyone whose liberties depend on the self-restraint of a democratic society.

Rereading that now, I am struck, as the reader must be, by the hyperventilation. With the establishment center of politics under assault from figures as different as McCarthy and Wallace, I was having a hard time maintaining any perspective. By the end of the 1968 campaign year, I was concerned enough about examples of my own political myopia to know I had to do something. Fortuitously, I was offered an opportunity to spend the 1969–70 school year on a fellowship at the Institute of Politics at the John F. Kennedy School of Government at Harvard University. That was hardly a leap into the unknown; Harvard and its Kennedy Institute were even more deeply embedded in the establishment, perhaps, than the newsroom of the *Washington Post*.

But it meant a break in routine, a separation from my regular sources, and a chance to look at Washington from the outside. And 1969–70 turned out to be a year in which much of Harvard (and the rest of academic America) rebelled against the political power structure in Washington. The professors were filing their policy disagreements with the way their former colleague Henry A. Kissinger and his boss, Richard M. Nixon, were handling the Vietnam War. The students did so more loudly, finally shutting down the university after the

U.S. ground forces had gone into Cambodia and campus protesters had been killed at Kent State and Jackson State universities.

It was a year of uproar, led by the young. The main controversy was over Vietnam, but the campus was also being agitated by the early adherents of the women's movement, protesting the treatment of women employees and female students. I was working on a book about the pressures on the party system in the United States and I became increasingly aware that the views and perceptions of a younger generation, moving into the political system, were far different from those I had acquired in college twenty-five years earlier and had reinforced in fourteen years in Washington.

In short, I learned that the surprises of 1968 were not historical oddities, but the kind of thing I could expect to see happening, over and over again, as members of a younger generation challenged past assumptions about the "realities" of politics.

What I learned that year led me to ask for a change of beats when I came back to Washington in September 1970. I asked to cover the House of Representatives, because it is the point of entry to national politics for most newcomers. What I had seen and learned during the sabbatical year had convinced me that the 1970s were bound to be a decade of dramatic change in the House.

My request was rejected, on the sensible grounds that the *Post* had one of the most experienced and competent reporters in the country, Richard L. Lyons, covering the House, and I was needed on my own beat—politics. So I missed the chance to write regularly about the institutional upheaval in the House that began in the early 1970s and accelerated dramatically with the arrival of the "Watergate babies" of 1974, who ended the seniority system and brought previously unimaginable changes to the House.

But the lessons of the sabbatical helped me to write about those changes and left me better prepared, I think, than were those who never left the familiar surroundings of the House press gallery. And the theme of generational change was one I returned to a decade after the Harvard experience in a book, *Changing of the Guard*, describing the emerging networks of young political activists who were coming to play an increasingly important role in the politics of the 1980s.

But there is no sure antidote to the myopia of a Washington political beat. The book, which was published in the autumn of 1980, had good material, I think, on blacks, Hispanics, women, and some of the other new constituencies that were beginning to exercise increasing influence in the political game. It dealt, in one chapter, with the younger conservative thinkers and political activists who, two months after publication, became much more important with the installation of Ronald Reagan's administration and the Republican takeover of the Senate. One of the young "rebels" I had met during that Harvard year was a divinity student named David Stockman. I wrote about him as an example of the emerging leadership among younger-generation conservatives.

But any sense of prescience I might have enjoyed when Stockman was chosen as Reagan's director of the Office of Management and Budget and point man in the conservative counterrevolution was short-lived. The old problem of parochialism was still embarrassingly there.

Describing the changing political landscape and the new leadership cadres, in research that had begun in 1978 and continued until early 1980, I managed largely to miss the religious element of the New Right—the Moral Majority and the other groups that played so prominent a role in the 1980 campaign.

When this obvious gap was pointed out in several reviews of the book, I had to ask myself how it could have happened. And, once again, the answer had to be the peculiarly parochial mind-set induced by the circles in which a reporter operates and lives. I dealt with—and wrote about—New Right politicians like Paul Weyrich and Richard Viguerie, who explained in interviews in the book how they drew the inspiration for their conservative principles from their own religious beliefs. But the tools they were using were conventional ones—grass-roots lobbying, political organizing, direct mail, establishment of caucuses within Congress. The use of churches as centers for political action—either in the flesh or through the electronic ministry—was outside my experience and that of most of the people I talked with on the political beat. Thus, one will search in vain in the index of *Changing of the Guard* for the name of the Reverend Jerry Falwell.

I was not the only one with that difficulty. Falwell got into the *New York Times* as early as March 6, 1972, but the story focused entirely on the growth and size of the Sunday school at his Thomas Road

Baptist Church in Lynchburg, Virginia, and said nothing about the political content of his message.

Seventeen months later, on August 11, 1973, the *Washington Post*'s business page noted briefly that the Securities and Exchange Commission had worked out a settlement with Falwell arising from its challenge to the legality of his issuance of $6.5 million worth of bonds, at a time when the SEC said his church was on the brink of "financial collapse." In lieu of the receivership the SEC had sought, Falwell agreed to submit church affairs to the supervision of a finance committee of five Lynchburg businessmen. Again, nothing was said of his political role.

That subject turned up for the first time that I can find in a couple of brief Associated Press items the *New York Times* ran in October 1976 about Falwell's offering Jimmy Carter four minutes of reply time to answer his criticism on his *Old Time Gospel Hour*, a television program carried by 260 stations. In a preview of what was to become an ongoing dispute, Falwell maintained that when he criticized Carter's famous *Playboy* interview, he was "speaking as a pastor on a moral issue," not engaging in politics.

In May of 1978, the *Wall Street Journal* highlighted Falwell in a piece on the growing scale and revenues of the radio-television ministry. But the first full-scale treatment of Falwell as a political force came in the October 10, 1978, issue of *Esquire*. That piece, by Mary Murphy, was entitled "The Next Billy Graham," and the subhead read, "The name is Jerry Falwell. He may be the first preacher to become a political leader." The article noted that Falwell was the most successful operator in the rapidly expanding field of broadcast evangelism, with twenty-five TV stations and 1,200 radio stations "entirely devoted to religious programming," and a national audience of about two thirds of the population each week.

Obviously, this had not happened overnight. Falwell had his first radio program in 1957. With the expansion of the audience had come an expanded definition of the church's role: in Falwell's case, he had moved from denunciation of homosexual rights ordinances and the Equal Rights Amendment to opposition to the Salt II nuclear arms agreement with the Soviet Union and other defense questions, steadily expanding his list of "moral issues."

Falwell did not directly endorse candidates, but, as a story in the *Washington Post* in· October 1978 pointed out, he encouraged candidates to seek his blessing. Shortly before the 1978 election, both Virginia Senate candidates, Democrat Andrew P. Miller and Republican John W. Warner, attended Sunday services at Falwell's church. As reporter Megan Rosenfeld noted, just "before the final prayer, Falwell said from the pulpit that he had been told Miller had to leave for another engagment. He asked Warner if he, too, would like to leave.

"'No, we'll stay for prayers,' said Warner, who was seated next to his wife, Elizabeth Taylor. Falwell then asked Miller if he wanted to leave. 'No, we'll stay,' Miller replied."

But the full emergence of the evangelicals into a political force was recognized by the media only after a media event, a "Clean Up America" rally on the steps of the Capitol, on April 27, 1979, when Falwell denounced everything from sex education in the schools to the Internal Revenue Service rulings on tax-exempt church schools. On that occasion he was joined by a half dozen of the most prominent conservative Republicans in Congress and eight thousand or so of his church-school pupils, bused to Washington for the rally.

From that point on, the press was on the alert, and the activities of Falwell and his political-action arm, the Moral Majority, drew increasing press coverage in the 1980 campaign, when they claimed credit for registering and indoctrinating hundreds of thousands of new voters. The *New York Times* index for 1980 lists twenty-four entries about Falwell, and by the end of the year he was a familiar and—in some quarters—feared new figure on the political stage.

IF reporters have been out of touch with what has been going on in the churches, we tend to be equally unaware of what is taking place, at any given moment, in the world of ideas. There is less excuse for that, given the extent to which most of us have lingered around places of formal education. Yet reporters rarely note the birth of a politically significant idea—or even its burgeoning. I am not referring here to the coverage of the "pure sciences" or medicine, where journalistic expertise and alertness have improved notably in recent decades, but rather to the policy sciences that directly influence government and politics, such as economics and political science.

Consider journalism's treatment of Arthur B. Laffer, the economist who is generally credited with developing and making popular the version of supply-side economic theory that became the basis of President Reagan's 1981 economic program, with its across-the-board tax cuts.

Laffer broke into the news in the winter of 1970–71, not as an academician but as a thirty-year-old government official, named as senior economic adviser to George Shultz, then Richard Nixon's director of the Office of Management and Budget. His appointment was noted by the *Washington Post*'s Hobart Rowen in November 1970, and two months later he was the center of a lively political-economic debate, when Shultz used Laffer's economic model to buttress his forecast of a $1.065 trillion economy the following year. The forecast was some $20 billion higher than most private predictions, and Laffer was attacked by conventional economists, from both outside government and within. Among them was Arthur F. Burns, chairman of the Federal Reserve Board, and Nobel laureate Paul A. Samuelson. (The GNP turned out to be $1.031 trillion—lower than even the establishment economists had forecast.) The argument over what one critic called "Arthur Laffer's Money Machine" anticipated the debate over supply-side theory by a decade, but it was quite a different model of economic behavior that Laffer was using in 1971.

Laffer was soon back at the University of Chicago and out of the news for the most part during the next seven years. His friendship with journalist Jude Wanniski of the *Wall Street Journal* that had begun during Laffer's brief stay in government kept the blackout from being complete. Wanniski wrote an editorial-page piece for the *Journal* in June 1974, citing Laffer's view on the advantage of fixed exchange rates, and later expanded it into an article for the Spring 1975 issue of *The Public Interest*, a scholarly magazine of small circulation. Fifteen months later, Laffer himself reworked the theme for the *Journal*. Late in 1975, the *New York Times*—in a piece about economic advisers to presidential candidates—noted that Laffer was one of five economists who recently had briefed Ronald Reagan.

On July 28, 1976, the *Wall Street Journal* editorial page carried a twelve-hundred-word article by Laffer (now at the University of Southern California business school) that outlined the basic elements of supply-side theory. "If we are ever to achieve a sustainable high level of output, the tax 'wedge' on producers and workers must be reduced," he wrote. "It is especially important for the reductions to be on the marginal rates of taxation."

While such a piece in such a prominent showcase often triggers a journalistic wave, it did not in this instance. Fortunately for the cause of supply-side economics, Wanniski, who was on the verge of abandoning journalism for direct political and economic advocacy, had been more successful in enlisting the interest of some politicians—notably Representative Jack Kemp, a New York Republican. From 1976 on, the superenergetic Kemp popularized the notion among colleagues in the House and carried it, with their help, onto the Republican banquet and fund-raising circuit.

Occasionally there were pieces in the press. Ronald Reagan, licking his wounds from his 1976 primaries with President Ford, devoted one of his syndicated newspaper columns to the Kemp proposal in October of 1976. In April 1977 Kemp placed a piece on what he then called the Jobs Creation Act in the *Reader's Digest*. In the summer of 1977, when Kemp and Republican Senator William V. Roth of Delaware introduced their updated version of the proposal, there were small stories in a number of papers. But the press did not really catch on to what was happening until June of 1978.

The precipitating event was the passage in early June of Proposition 13, a California initiative rolling back property taxes in that state, and the victory, the same day, of Jeffrey Bell, a young conservative Republican political activist and disciple of Laffer, Kemp, and Wanniski, over veteran Senator Clifford P. Case in the New Jersey Republican senatorial primary.

Suddenly, it seemed, every political reporter in America saw tax cutting as the hottest political movement in years, and Laffer was discovered, as the *New York Times* headlined it on June 17, as the "Tax-Cut Guru." There were profiles and interviews in all the leading newspapers and news magazines, guest appearances on the network interview programs. As Richard Reeves wrote in a July issue of *Esquire* magazine, "The celebrity machine was on automatic pilot." The theory of deep cuts in marginal income tax rates was expounded, examined, and debated vigorously by both proponents and critics, using the media as a forum. The debate expanded into the mid-term election campaign, when the Republican Party adopted Laffer's idea as the theme for its national effort. While it had decidedly mixed results as an issue in that campaign—when Democrats were seemingly successful in ridiculing it—the *Wall Street Journal* was correct in its December 1, 1978, story, headlined, "Arthur Laffer's Influence Climbs on a Rising Curve, Although Many Other Economists Flunk His Ideas." In the 1980 election, with Ronald Reagan as the advocate and the Democrats in disarray, the idea triumphed.

The press was tardy in communicating and analyzing that idea. It was only after the Laffer supply-side theory had shown clear evidence of winning in the political arena that most of the press noticed it or treated it seriously. But that is not unusual. James L. Sundquist, in his book *Politics and Policy*, pointed out that ideas rarely move directly from the academic world to the center of political debate and electoral decision. It takes middlemen, brokers, to bridge the distance. In this instance, one of the middlemen happened to be a man about to leave journalism, Jude Wanniski, and one of the tools he used to promote the policy idea was occasional exposure on the pages of his own paper, the *Wall Street Journal*. The key to its success in the political world was that people like Kemp and Bell were directly persuaded to bring the idea into the heart of the campaigns. Wanniski wrote a book about supply-side economics, *The Way the World Works*, that was published in 1978. But what put the idea on the political map that year was Proposition 13, the Bell campaign, and the Republicans' adoption of tax cuts as the basis for their mid-term campaign.

I wish I could say that we have a better record in spotting other ideas and books that change history, but most of the time we do not. Consider, for example, Betty Friedan and the bible of the women's movement, *The Feminine Mystique*.

Surely there have been few changes more dramatic and far-reaching in their consequences than the redefinition of the role of women in our society. Friedan, a free-lance writer and housewife, was the key figure in that movement, defining its premises in her book and giving it concrete form in the group she founded, the National Organization for Women (NOW).

As she recalled in a ten-years-after piece in the *New York Times Magazine* in March of 1973, her book was published in 1963 only because the women's magazines for which Friedan had been writing regularly—*McCall's, Ladies' Home Journal*, and *Redbook*—at first refused to publish her argument that women had a right to use their talents for their own goals, not just for those purposes imposed on them by their role as wives or mothers. The publisher bravely committed to three thousand copies—underestimating the eventual hardback sale by fifty-four thousand—and most newspapers missed the significance of the book. In the *New York Herald Tribune* book review, journalist Marya Mannes described it as "a damning indictment of the social, educational and commercial pressures . . . which have caused a harmful discrepancy between what women really are and what they are told they should be." She said it was "required reading for . . . those who care about the future development of our society." But the editors of the section coyly headlined the review "Don't Sweep the Ladies Under the Rug."

The *New York Times*, the *Washington Post*, and the *Washington Star* did not consider it required reviewing. Although the *Times*'s education expert, Fred M. Hechinger, wrote a serious and sympathetic piece summarizing Friedan's chapter on "sex-directed educators," neither the *Times* nor the Washington papers ran a review of the book. The magazines were more alert. Though they had rejected her articles, *Mademoiselle*, the *Journal*, and *McCall's* ran prepublication excerpts; *Saturday Review* did a piece shortly after publication; and, at the end of 1963, *Life* magazine devoted four pages to the "overnight best seller" that was "as disruptive of cocktail party conversations and women's clubs' discussions as a tear-gas bomb."

Despite the increasing attention to Friedan and the feminist movement after the book's success, the press was still skeptical—or oblivious. When NOW was formed in 1966, it was not news in the eyes of the *Washington Post*. The *New York Times* reported the fact on its Food, Fashion, Family and Furnishings page— down at the bottom of the page, under the recipes for the "traditional Thanksgiving menu" and the picture of "the culinary star of the day, the turkey, roasted, stuffed and surrounded by other festive Thanksgiving specialties."

The story, by Lisa Hammel, was equally cutesy. Her lead said, "Although no one in the dim ruby and sapphire Victorian parlor actually got up and cried: 'Women of the world, unite! You have nothing to lose but your chains,' that was the prevailing sentiment yesterday morning at the crowded news conference held by the newly formed National Organization for Women."

Two years later, in the spring of 1968, NOW was still on the Food, Fashion, etc. page of the *Times* when Charlotte Curtis reported that six of the eight presidential candidates NOW sought to interview for possible endorsement had ignored the organization's overtures. Once again, attention was drawn to the "blue and red Victorian drawing room," where Friedan declared, "We couldn't be more disappointed."

The women's movement did not hit the front pages of the *Post* or the *Times* until August of 1970, when Friedan organized a strike of women workers (in homes as well as offices and factories) and protest marches in Washington, New York, and other cities around the country. Although the numbers were not large, the tactic worked. The agenda of causes—centering on an end to discrimination in pay and employment opportunities, passage of the Equal Rights Amendment, provision of child-care and abortion facilities—was spelled out in full and, for the first time, fully debated. There was a proclamation from President Nixon on the fiftieth anniversary of the enfranchisement of women and comments, favorable or unfavorable, from other public officials.

In an editorial the day after the strike, the *Times* said:

It is an unfortunate truth that a protest group such as the Women's Liberation Movement can only make itself heard if it speaks at the top of its voice and resorts to publicity-seeking exhibitionism. The suffragettes of a half-century ago, whose great triumph—the Nineteenth Amendment—was commemorated yesterday, were often noisy and obstreperous. Their successors of today go on strike, march down Fifth Avenue and "liberate" the Statue of Liberty. But the attention-getting antics do not detract from the substance of the demand for full equality put forward by modern women.

The question, really, is why such antics seem necessary to attract the attention of the press; why can we not recognize important ideas and movements without the aid of such circus devices? The answer lies not as much in laziness as in our limited range of vision. Most of us cover "official" beats—police, politicians, business, unions, schools, or what have you. Even the sports we cover are organized athletics. Routine happenings on those beats fall within our definition of news.

But when an idea, a concept, or a movement emerges outside those official beats, we do not usually respond unless or until there is an event that compels coverage. The lunch counter sit-ins, the freedom rides and the bus boycotts provided such news pegs for the coverage of civil rights. As Falwell and Friedan discovered from their opposing political perspectives, they had to contrive events on the Capitol steps or at the Statue of Liberty to attract our attention. Arthur Laffer's tax-cut idea was just a laugher—until the voters in California and New Jersey turned it into an event.

Somehow, we in the press have to broaden our perspective and expand our range of vision. We are doing that in some areas, with specialists on many papers combing the sciences, medicine, business, law, and some of the arts for discoveries, ideas, inventions, and creations that may change the way our society thinks and acts. But in our reporting on foreign policy, domestic issues, and national politics, we remain trapped in the assumptions and the parochial limitations of our regular beats and the conventional thinking of the institutions and people we regularly cover.

Fred Barnes of the *New Republic* observed in a February 1983 article for the *Washington Journalism Review* that "right-wingers and left-wingers alike agree that the press focuses on too narrow a slice of events and ideas; it reports the middle-of-the-road viewpoint, often ignoring the view from the fringes." When those fringe views enter the mainstream, we always find ourselves playing catch-up.

As a beat reporter on politics for twenty-five years, I certainly would not advocate that we give up our efforts to cover the day-to-day activities on the beat. But newspapers and television stations need to designate some reporters as outriders and to free them from regular day-to-day assignments at the Commerce Department or the White House or at city hall or the criminal courts, so that they can roam. We need journalistic scout parties out there on the fringes of our society, where the ideas that may ultimately change our politics and government often first appear.

That is a real challenge. The incapacity of the daily press in dealing with ideas of any kind is an institutional defect. But even on the stories we cover assiduously, from the White House to Congress to the campaign trail, we often disappoint our customers. It is time to take a look at the forces that shaped the Washington press corps and the way we do—or don't do—our daily jobs.

2
Covering
the Beats

A Bit of Background

*B*EFORE examining how reporters do their jobs today, a bit of history may be helpful.

The Washington press corps is largely a twentieth-century invention. The National Press Club was formed in 1908 and when Walter Lippmann spoke there in 1959, he could describe himself as a member of the first generation of modern Washington correspondents that "had to find its way through an uncharted wilderness" of journalistic challenges.

As this is written, Richard L. Strout, the grand old man of the *Christian Science Monitor* and the *New Republic* magazine, still regales young reporters with tales of the Washington he first saw in 1923, when he could park his "Model T all day long on the Ellipse behind the White House with plenty of room and no parking ticket." He also remembers there being scarcely enough work to keep either reporters or Presidents occupied.

In his book *TRB*, named for the *New Republic* column he wrote for so many years, Strout remembered walking into the White House for his first press conference. "Warren Harding was President . . . standing in plus fours behind his desk in the Oval Office, so close that I could touch him. . . . 'Gentlemen, gentlemen,' he pleaded at last, 'please go easy on me—I want to get away for some golf.'"

Many of the major Washington stories have occurred during the working lifetime of a single individual like Strout. He covered the Teapot Dome scandal in 1923 and returned half a century later to the same Senate caucus room for the Watergate hearings. The institutional history of Washington journalism is brief because until the two world wars ended America's isolation and the Great Depression gave birth to the welfare state, Washington was not a major center of news, of population, or much of anything else. In his centennial history, *The Washington Post,* Chalmers M. Roberts noted that when the paper was founded in 1877, the city of Washington had a population of 130,000, and there were farms in the District of Columbia. (The *Post* itself was a long way from the paper it became. As late as the 1940s, Roberts's predecessor on the *Post*'s diplomatic beat, Ferdinand Kuhn, complained that "the *Post* will cover any international conference as long as it's in the first taxi zone.")

Of course, reporters had been on the scene long before Lippmann's time. Soon after the seat of government moved to Washington in 1800, President-elect Thomas Jefferson suggested to Samuel Harrison Smith that he bring his printing business to the new capital. Smith's *National Intelligencer* became the organ of the Jefferson administration and the forerunner of a series of papers that enjoyed the patronage of successive administrations. Early Washington correspondence was colorful, individualistic, and partisan—reflecting the newspapers' biases. Douglass Cater's book *The Fourth Branch of Government,* published in 1959 and still a valuable analysis of the press in Washington, cited a dispatch to the *New York Tribune* on a speech made by Senator Robert Toombs of Georgia during one of the bitter pre–Civil War debates:

> It is a sad instance of the wretched effect which the Africanization of the South has had upon even her strongest minds, that a man like Mr. Toombs should feel himself compelled to rise as he did today, in the face of the American Senate and the American people, and debase himself by prostituting his powers of speech and argument to the vain task of proving that to be true which he knows to be false, and that to be sound which he knows to be rotten.

In 1841, James Gordon Bennett, editor of the *New York Herald,* set up the first regular Washington news bureau, and three years later the first telegraphic service connected the capital with leading papers around the country. With the arrival of telegraph, those chatty, personalized "letters from Washington" gave way to a terse style that conveyed the essential information in as few words as possible, thus minimizing the penny-a-character cost to the newspaper. The Associated Press, a cooperative news-gathering network started in 1848, began to enforce impartiality in its dispatches, so that they would be acceptable to publishers and editors of widely contrasting views.

The Civil War increased the focus on Washington, but four years after it ended, only forty-nine correspondents were accredited to the congressional press galleries. In the early years of this century we began to see press conferences and government press agents, and in the 1920s, radio and the news magazines began their coverage of the government.

"Despite all the changes," Cater wrote, "reporting in Washington before the Great Depression and the New Deal had not changed too much in its fundamentals. The Washington correspondent was still a fairly limited political animal. . . . He, like the official, was comparatively unsophisticated. He had few specialties. His understanding was still quite limited. He, even as government itself, was unprepared for —largely unaware of—the vast changes that lay just ahead."

Lippmann, in his Press Club speech the same year that Cater's book was published, agreed that "the modern Washington correspondent, which of course includes news analysts and columnists, is a product of the worldwide Depression and of the social upheaval which followed it, and of the imminence of war during the 1930s." Those events, he said, "have given to what goes on in Washington and in foreign lands an urgent importance. After 1929, the federal government assumed a role in the life of every American and in the destiny of the world, which was radically new. The American people were not prepared for this role. The kind of journalism we practice today was born out of the needs of our age."

In broad terms, Washington reporting since the 1930s falls into three periods. The first, roughly from the start of the New Deal until the mid-1950s, saw the rise of interpretive reporting. The second, which climaxed with Watergate, was the era of investigative reporting. The third, our present time, is hard to characterize with a single word, but an alliterative successor to the eras of interpretation and investigation would be "press-government integration," a time when government manipulation of the news media became troublingly pervasive.

Between the Civil War and the New Deal, American newspapers

stressed "objective" journalism. They emphasized accuracy, direct quotation, and identification of sources. In their book *The News Business,* John Chancellor of NBC News and Walter R. Mears of the Associated Press quoted Lawrence A. Gobright, the AP's first Washington correspondent.

My business is to communicate facts. My instructions do not allow me to make any comment upon the facts which I communicate. My dispatches are sent to papers of all manner of politics, and the editors say they are able to make their own comments upon the facts which are sent to them. I therefore confine myself to what I consider legitimate news. I do not act as a politician belonging to any school, but try to be truthful and impartial. My dispatches are merely dry matters of fact and detail.

Rudyard Kipling saluted the six key elements of this kind of news reporting in a poem published with his *Just So Stories* in 1902:

> I keep six honest serving-men
> (They taught me all I knew);
> Their names are What and Why and When
> And How and Where and Who.
> I send them over land and sea,
> I send them east and west;
> But after they have worked for me,
> I give them all a rest.

Objectivity was an honorable tradition, as Lippmann noted in the 1959 Press Club speech analyzing its eclipse. "Before I criticize this rule [of objectivity]," he said, "I must pay tribute to its enduring importance." He went on:

It contains what we may call the Bill of Rights of the working newspaperman. It encourages not only the energetic reporting of facts, it encourages the honest search for the truth to which those facts belong. It imposes restraints upon owners and editors. It authorizes resistance, indeed in honor it calls for resistance, to the contamination of the news by special prejudices and by special interests. It proclaims the corporate opposition of our whole profession to the prostitution of the press by political parties and by political, economic and ideological pressure groups, and by social climbers and by adventurers on the make.

But while the rule is an indispensable rallying point for maintaining the integrity of the press, the practical application of the rule cannot be carried out in a wooden and literal way. The distinction between reporting and interpreting has to be redefined if it is to fit the conditions of the modern age.

It is all very well to say that a reporter collects the news and that the news consists of facts. The truth is that in our world the facts are infinitely many, and that no reporter can collect them all, and that no newspaper could print them all—even if they were fit to print—and nobody could read them all. We have to select some facts rather than others, and in doing that we are using not only our legs but our selective judgment of what is interesting or important or both.

Interpretive reporting grew out of and was driven by the complexity of the economic, social, and military-diplomatic problems confronting the United States in the 1930s and 1940s. The Depression, Fascism, and Nazism and the policies mounted to counter them needed *explanation* by the press, not simply reporting. But the central lesson was taught not by Franklin D. Roosevelt but by Joseph R. McCarthy. The reporters who covered the Wisconsin senator's 1950–54 "exposés" of Communists in government felt personally and professionally debauched by the experience. Many agreed with Secretary of State Dean Acheson, one of McCarthy's major targets, who told the American Society of Newspaper Editors (as quoted by Cater in his book): "I don't ask for your sympathy. I don't ask for your help. You are in a worse situation than I am. I and my associates are only the intended victims of this mad and vicious operation. But you, unhappily, by reason of your calling, are participants. And your position is far more serious than mine."

During his four-year rampage, McCarthy spread his accusations against a variety of government officials in speeches and hearings. It was all news by any definition—the words and actions of a prominent public official, raising charges of obvious import if they were true. McCarthy, rarely able to substantiate his indictments of Communist sympathizers or "dupes," would move quickly to another individual or agency and begin the cycle of charge-and-denial again.

In his book *Joe McCarthy and the Press,* Edwin R. Bayley, a distinguished journalist turned journalism professor, quotes John L. Steele, then Senate correspondent for United Press and later with *Time* magazine, on the frustrations reporters felt in covering McCarthy: "There was very little opportunity in those days to break out of the role of being a recording device for Joe. I felt trapped. . . . We bear a terrible scar because of that period." William Theis, head of the International News Service Senate staff, said "all three wire services were so goddamn objective that McCarthy got away with everything, bamboozling the editors and the public." George Reedy, another UP Senate correspondent and later Lyndon B. Johnson's press secretary, complained to Bayley, "We had to take what McCarthy said at face value. Joe couldn't find a Communist in Red Square—he didn't know Karl Marx from Groucho—but he was a United States senator."

Charles B. Seib, then with INS in the Capitol and later my boss at the *Washington Star,* said, "We were trapped by our techniques. If he said it, we wrote it." As Bayley recounts, McCarthy understood newspaper deadlines and cycles and would supply fresh (or fresh-sounding) leads just when they were craved—and often when the fear of competition pushed newspapers to transmit and publish them before their accuracy could be checked.

The leading journalists of the time forced themselves and their colleagues to reexamine how they were operating, the code that guided their work. Eric Sevareid wrote that "our rigid formulae of so-called objectivity, beginning with the wire agency bulletins and reports—the warp and woof of what the papers print and the broadcasters voice— our flat, one-dimensional handling of news, have given the lie the same prominence and impact that truth is given; they have elevated the influence of fools to that of wise men; the ignorant to the level of the learned; the evil to the level of the good." Alan Barth, the *Washington Post*'s great editorialist, wrote in a 1951 edition of the *Washington Guild Reporter* that reporters had to consider if "maybe we have a responsibility that goes beyond objectivity."

Going "beyond objectivity" meant going into dangerous, uncharted waters, where the safe and secure (if limiting) rules of the old tradition provided no guidance. For about five years, Bayley wrote, the dangers of "interpretive" reporting were furiously debated at newspaper conventions. But by the time I came to Washington at the end of 1955, it was beginning to be accepted that a reporter's obligation went beyond accuracy of quotation and identification of source. It included some effort to put the raw statement or event into a context where the reader might judge its significance.

As Bayley put it, "There is no question but that McCarthy's exploitation of 'straight' reporting did cause a gradual but fundamental change in American journalism. It probably took a performance as spectacular as his to move the guardians of objectivity to admit that the meaning of an event is as important as the facts of an event."

MCCARTHY taught the Washington press corps another lesson—or reminded us of something we had learned in other places: High officials can bend the truth out of shape. Though his techniques were criticized constantly on some editorial pages and by a number of commentators, the most effective demolition of McCarthy came late in the game, when Edward R. Murrow of CBS, the most eminent broadcaster of his era, devoted a one-hour *See It Now* documentary to the senator. The program mostly consisted of film clips showing McCarthy's bullying tactics and his repeated revisions and retreats from sensational charges. At the end, Murrow editorialized: "This is no time for men who oppose Senator McCarthy's methods to keep silent. . . . We cannot defend freedom abroad by deserting it at home." In the rebuttal time CBS offered him, McCarthy implied that Murrow was part of the Communist conspiracy, but his support never recovered from that blow. As it turned out, this was just a forerunner of twenty years of increasingly serious clashes between the media and government officials.

Such battles had long been part of American journalistic tradition. Lincoln Steffens, Ida Tarbell, and the other muckrakers of the Progressive era had exposed chicanery in city halls and collusion between big business and politicians. During the New Deal years, newspapers investigated and publicized patronage abuses in public welfare and employment programs, and during World War II, there were stories galore about black-market operators, profiteers, and Washington "fixers."

Events in the 1960s and 1970s increased the clashes between journalists and government officials—on issues of greater emotion and of larger consequence, including, finally, the tenure of a President. This period established the investigative role for reporters as clearly as the earlier period had provoked interpretation.

The clashes of this period began in dozens of Southern courthouses, where outside reporters, drawn by the stirrings of the civil rights movement, were stared down by surly sheriffs who advised them to "get out of town." Those reporters learned evasive tactics—Claude Sitton of the *New York Times* popularized the narrow, short notebook that could be kept out of sight in an inside pocket—and their stories helped publicize the black struggle to escape the heritage of slavery. As the protests escalated and the television cameras moved in, the whole nation witnessed the confrontations with police, National Guardsmen, recalcitrant sheriffs, mayors, and governors.

The next major battleground between press and government was in the jungles of Vietnam. As more and more American troops were committed in the 1960s, the press corps in Saigon also grew in size. Almost from the beginning, there was a visible gap between the picture of the war painted by government officials and that recorded by reporters on the scene. John F. Kennedy tried to pressure the *New York Times* to recall David Halberstam from the war zone. Secretary of State Dean Rusk became so exasperated that he asked a group of reporters, "Whose side are you on?"

As domestic controversy grew, an "underground press" sprang up in many cities, focusing not only on the Vietnam War but on local abuses which it said were being covered up by the authorities. The Washington press corps was not immune to that spirit. Some journalists like Joseph Alsop and Robert Novak supported the war in Vietnam to the end, and I was rather late in joining the critics myself. But our colleagues were nearly unanimous in their opposition. When the *Post* was accused of exaggerating the size of some early antiwar marches, executive editor Ben Bradlee ordered Richard Harwood, an ex-Marine and a notably hard-nosed reporter, to cover the next march. He came back a few hours later, shaking his head, and told Bradlee, "Jesus Christ, how am I supposed to write this story? The first goddamn person I ran into in the demonstration was my wife. And the second was yours."

In the early 1970s, not just Vice President Spiro T. Agnew but a number of more sympathetic press observers—Theodore H. White, Daniel Patrick Moynihan, Joseph Kraft—described an "adversary culture" they thought was developing in the press, hostile at least to the government and maybe to much of American society. They exaggerated the danger, for in the same years that the press and television were challenging the government's version of events in Vietnam, we were cheering—perhaps too uncritically—another vast enterprise of the American people and government, the space program. If we denied General William Westmoreland the hero status given commanders of America's earlier overseas armies, we certainly helped make heroes of John Glenn and Gus Grissom and Neil Armstrong.

But the most crucial event in the rise of investigative reporting was the Watergate story. When Bob Woodward and Carl Bernstein of the *Post* started tracing the links from the men who broke into the Democratic National Committee offices back to their sponsors and paymasters in Richard Nixon's campaign committee, they had no idea what they were about to unleash. "We didn't go after the President," Woodward has said. "We went after the story." But before it was finished, the whole world had seen that dogged investigation—pursued in the face of every imaginable kind of official threat and intimidation—could uncover the chicanery and finally force the resignation of the highest elected official in the land. Investigative journalism had scored its most important victory and become an indelible part of Washington reporting.

Woodward and Bernstein became symbols of the new Washington reporters—those who could make things happen by what they wrote. They were unique, in one sense, but in another they typified the media's growing presence and influence in government and national politics. In the post-Watergate period, an era of melding press-government relationships, the media have become a ubiquitous and for many an unsettling presence at the very heart of national political power.

There is no comprehensive directory of all Washington reporters, but in 1982, Dom Bonafede of the *National Journal* estimated in a study of the Washington press that the numbers have tripled since World War II and that "there are roughly 10,000 legitimate journalists who come into the Capitol." The 1985 Congressional Directory listed 1,376 in the congressional press gallery, 287 in the photographers gallery, 1,391 in the radio-television gallery, and 1,219 in the periodical press gallery—a total of 4,273. But there are many more support personnel in news organizations, and the number of journalists who cover specialized beats outside the Capitol is growing.

The growth of the press corps long ago exhausted the office space in the National Press Club building near Pennsylvania Avenue. News bureaus have spread from Capitol Hill to the blocks of office buildings north and west of the White House and even into suburbs like Arlington, where the Gannett newspapers—the largest chain operation— have set up their corporate headquarters.

The *Washington Post,* with 3,000 employees, is one of the largest nongovernmental employers in the city, and there are 1,490 working at the *Washington Times* and *USA Today,* Gannett's national daily, 1,180 more at the Washington bureaus of the American Broadcasting Company, the Columbia Broadcasting System, the National Broadcasting Company, and the Cable News Network, 415 more at the wire services, Associated Press, United Press International, and Reuters, 700 more at the three major news magazines, *Time, Newsweek,* and *U.S. News,* and scores of newspaper and radio bureaus which count their employees in the dozens.

As the numbers have grown, the status and probably the influence of the Washington journalists have also risen spectacularly. Journalists have become as well educated as the people they cover. A 1978 survey by Stephen Hess found that virtually all Washington journalists had college degrees and one third had advanced professional or graduate degrees. More than half had attended private colleges and one third had graduated from the "most selective schools."

From questionnaires answered by about 38 percent of the city's active journalists, Hess drew this picture in *The Washington Reporters:* The press corps was 80 percent male, 96 percent white, 63 percent middle-aged (between thirty and fifty). Geographical backgrounds were definitely skewed, with 38 percent coming from the Northeast, 27 percent from the North Central states, and only 26 percent from the South and 9 percent from the West. Among those news organizations that were rated by reporters as most influential, age and education levels were higher, the percentages of blacks and males higher, and the background even more skewed to the Northeast. In *The American Journalist,* David H. Weaver and G. Cleveland Wilhoit said a 1982–83 survey showed a significant increase in the percentage of women—but not minorities—in news organizations around the country, and I would say that trend is apparent in Washington as well.

Data on incomes is less precise, but with the television correspondents, bylined columnists, and bureau chiefs pulling up the averages, it is probable that the average salary for a Washington journalist in the 1980s was not far behind a member of Congress ($75,100 a year).

The "minimums" for reporters with five or six years' experience on major papers were in the $35,000 range in the mid-1980s, and most Washington correspondents were well above that. Television's pay scale ran about 50 percent higher, and many of the stars drew salaries well into the six figures. Despite the death in 1981 of the *Washington Star,* the capital's longtime afternoon paper, and UPI's struggle for survival, most news organizations represented in Washington were enormously profitable. Some veteran *Washington Post* reporters, who were in its profit-sharing program during its years of rapid growth from the 1950s to the 1980s, retired as millionaires.

The wealthiest, the most visible, and probably the most influential of today's journalists are in television, and I need to say something about this branch of the business at this point.

I had my first encounter with television in 1953. Just out of the Army, I got that job on the *Daily Pantagraph.* The pay was as modest as my talents, but the management allowed me to work a twelve-hour shift on Saturdays, which helped cover the rent.

At about the same time, Bloomington's first television station went on the air. The *Pantagraph* ran the weekly logs of TV programs in the Saturday morning paper and as I arrived for work at 8 A.M., the phone was frequently ringing. An indignant call from the station manager. We had screwed up the listings. I would promise to correct them and assure the manager we would be more careful. After a few times, he exploded. "Don't think I'm being fooled," he shouted. "Your damned paper is deliberately sabotaging me because you think I'm going to take your advertising away. This has to be deliberate. You people aren't that incompetent."

"Oh, yes sir, we are, we are."

That early experience set my pattern with television. I'm not old enough to have reported in the pre-television era, but I have seen television news grow from an awkward infant into a giant. There are communications students, such as Lawrence W. Lichty of the University of Maryland, who contend that TV's impact is exaggerated; two thirds of adult Americans say they read a newspaper every day and only a third watch network or local TV news programs that often. But as someone who appears in a major newspaper almost every day and only intermittently on television, I know what people remember. It pains me to admit that political scientist Austin Ranney was right when he wrote in his 1983 book *Channels of Power* that "television newscasts and public affairs programs unquestionably constitute the major sources of political reality for most Americans."

No print reporter can be indifferent to the change that many of us have resisted. In the innocent days of the 1960 presidential campaign, I joined my share of shoving contests with TV cameramen who muscled their way up front in what we still thought of and called "press conferences." I lost, of course, and those of us in the pencil press have been losing most of the battles ever since, including the battle of language. What we used to call "press conferences" are now "media availabilities."

We have been moved to the back of the campaign press bus, with the front seats reserved for TV correspondents and their crews. We have all seen candidates or other important personages walk past us panting print reporters to station themselves before the cameras. More often than we care to admit, we covered stories by taking notes off the television screen, aware that the networks had access we could not obtain. None of this have we loved.

My experiences as a television "performer" have made me understand what a different world it is. Often, when I thought I had performed well, the letters have persuaded me otherwise. After a dazzling appearance on *Washington Week in Review,* I received a card from Charlottesville: "The next time you appear it would be helpful if you would smile—or at least not frown." Then the viewer decided that was perhaps a bit harsh and added a note to cheer me up: "Your suit and tie were beautifully coordinated."

Next time, I thought, I'll just send my suit and tie.

The differences between television and print news are basic. Television is a picture medium; its strength lies in images. Words and language, the currency of print journalism, and of the informal communication that fills our days, take second place. And television, like radio, is an instant source. When something important happens, television is on the air, often on the scene. That has two effects. It reduces the chance to check and edit information before it goes on the air and increases the risk of error or misinterpretation. It also creates a communications loop that makes the TV coverage part of the story it is covering.

TV news is part of an entertainment medium. Cable channels can resemble newspapers in format; they may present news as their main commodity and sell advertising to those who want access to an audience of news-seekers. But the main television news audiences watch commercial and public networks and stations whose chief commodity is entertainment.

The submergence of news reporting into entertainment companies has limited the share of network budgets and the airtime devoted to news. It has made commercial values—the ratings of the news shows and the attractiveness of their anchormen—at least as important as journalism values in shaping the contents. Newspapers are not charitable institutions, as the late publisher Nelson Poynter remarked. But the "ratings game" is a more compelling force in television.

In the end, television news is a peculiarly personal form of journalism. The television newscast is a direct person-to-person transaction between the journalist, especially the anchorman, and the viewer. Print reporters often play rough to get information—cajoling, berating, threatening, intimidating, bluffing. But, as John Chancellor of NBC News observed, "it gets smoothed over" before it goes into the newspaper. When television comes in, say, at a presidential news conference, the technique of questioning becomes visible, and viewers often complain that reporters have been rude. "I don't think they like what they see," Chancellor said, "because they are not journalists and they don't know that these sometimes very, very hard questions have to be asked."

Television reporting becomes even more controversial when the focus shifts to private citizens who are caught up in a story. Interviews with victims of a tragedy or their survivors have contributed to what George F. Will has called "the pornography of grief." These invasions of privacy are often cited with particular bitterness.

Like most print reporters, I have prejudices about television. But I am also an admirer, especially when it takes me where I most want to be: Wimbledon for tennis, the Super Bowl, the State of the Union address. My admiration extends to the evening news shows and many of the interview and discussion programs. I salute the technical proficiency and economy of words of the best of the television reporters and interviewers. But in this book, which focuses on my own branch of journalism, I have attempted only to discuss how television shapes the way the news is covered and colors the reputation of the news industry.

THIS rapidly growing army of television reporters and technicians has inflated the size and, in turn, has brought with it an expansion in the ranks of government press agents. Everyone in Washington, in a real sense, is now in the communications business. Fights over public policy increasingly have become fights for public opinion—struggles where the battlefields are the printed page and the television screen. As the stakes have increased, media skills have become increasingly important to senior officials, and media management has become a preoccupation, not only for government but for private interests.

From the 1930s onward, and especially since World War II, most if not all the private sector organizations have also become players in this game. Washington has become the major headquarters for the groups and associations representing business and labor, schools and colleges, the sciences and professions—every aspect of our highly pluralistic society. States and cities, corporations and charities, causes of every variety have Washington representatives and Washington offices. They, too, have focused much of their energy on getting their stories and their viewpoints into the press, and like Presidents, cabinet officials, and members of Congress, they scan the newspapers and magazines and monitor the television screens to gauge their own—and their rivals'—success and failure.

In today's America, as we will see in later chapters, social and economic policy debates, political campaign results, congressional actions, and even presidential decisions are all inextricably intermixed with, and influenced by, the news coverage they receive. In recent years, the revolving door between journalism and government has spun so often that the old line of distinction has been blurred, perhaps to the detriment of both institutions. Journalism has recruited well from government and government has taken some of our best people, but the distinction between the two functions is increasingly difficult to maintain. When the President of the United States is known as "The Great Communicator" and White House television correspondents command as large a lecture fee as Henry A. Kissinger, the gap is narrow indeed.

The resulting clique journalism pervades the atmosphere of White House coverage. So we look now at the way the presidential story has been covered.

CHAPTER FOUR

From—and by—the White House

*T*HE White House may seem a strange place to start our examination of the complex but cozy relationship between journalists and public officials. Every recent President has feuded with reporters and fussed about the coverage he has received. And yet there is an intimacy between the press (especially television) and the President. This coziness is symbolized by the location of the White House briefing room and press room in the center of the West Wing working section of the building (over the abandoned indoor swimming pool). It is cozy, in another sense, too. Space is so limited that reporters work at each other's elbows. In that respect, they are like the White House staff members, who—except for the senior six or eight—have less breathing room than the average insurance office clerk. When the Reagan administration remodeled the briefing room in 1981, it installed theater seats with brass plaques on the back, reserved for the forty television, radio, newspaper, and news magazine correspondents considered the regulars. It is like having a family pew in church.

White House reporters think of themselves as an elite group. They cover the top official of the American government and are on the air and the front page more often than other reporters. They are often the best paid and most experienced reporters in their organizations, and as the careers of Tom Brokaw, Dan Rather, and Ben Bradlee all show, covering a President or knowing one is often the way to the highest rungs of television and newspaper success.

For all the intimacy and elitism, White House reporters often seem at odds with the President and his agents. Amost daily, battles erupt between reporters and presidential spokesmen, as each side attempts to do what it considers its job, and objects to the other doing its. The press complains that the President or his agents attempt to manage the news, and the President replies that prying reporters distort or trivialize or simply interfere with important decision making.

Unlike Congress, which has only limited institutional power over how it is covered, the President has political and public relations aides who can lay down rules that work to the President's advantage. They seek to maximize publicity for some of his activities and to keep others secret. They speak volubly at times and attempt to embargo information and comment at other moments. They hoard information and disclose or leak it selectively. Reporters attempt to resist all these tactics and, in doing so, often criticize the President and his agents for being manipulative. As James Deakin, the White House correspondent for the *St. Louis Post-Dispatch* from Dwight Eisenhower through Jimmy Carter, says in his book *Straight Stuff,* "They disagree. They disagree. They disagree."

Given this pattern of disagreement, it may be surprising that, in the relationship, there is a danger of too much coziness. But because of a mutual dependence, many of the forces of antagonism are overwhelmed. For all the fussing and fighting between Presidents and the press, their basic relationship is symbiotic.

Occasionally, we see a clear picture of the cooperative and collaborative relationship between the White House and the press—or, even more, television. Ever since Jacqueline Kennedy led CBS on a backstairs tour of the remodeled White House, every President and/or First Lady has provided cameras and reporters special access, at times of their own choosing and in formats they influence if not control. Richard Nixon arranged for NBC to do the prime-time special *Christmas at the White House* and for CBS to film *A Day in the Presidency,* a day, of course, chosen and arranged by the White House. Jimmy Carter enlisted the television icon Walter Cronkite as host on a call-in program on which Carter answered questions about his energy policy. Ronald Reagan reached back to the medium in which he earlier starred and began a series of weekly five-minute radio broadcasts to the nation.

But much of the interaction takes place behind the scenes and reflects the mutual needs and problems of the two sides. Michael Baruch Grossman and Martha Joynt Kumar in their 1981 book, *Portraying the President,* estimate that at least 30 percent of the White House staff effort is devoted to the public relations aspects of the presidency, and no talent is more vital to a President than being able to handle television and the press. Of the many hats he wears, one of the most important ones, though unlisted in the Constitution, is Communicator-in-Chief. Only the President can make news whenever he wishes, at any hour of day or night. Only the President can command simultaneous live coverage on all the television networks. Only the President can gather the nation at his feet, as if it were a family, and say, "Dear friends, here is how I see things."

The President's power as Communicator-in-Chief is at least as far-reaching, in the real world, as his authority to negotiate treaties, to dispatch troops, to impose his veto on legislation. Had the Founding Fathers foreseen its emergence, my guess is that they would have thought about providing checks and balances for this presidential authority. Since they did not, the press must do much of the balancing.

So in reviewing the relationships that have developed in the White House, we can talk about two dimensions: the President's skill at getting his message across and the press's ability to obtain and to use its access to cover the presidency. In this chapter I want to look at the way those patterns have evolved, and then in the next chapter we will examine how they operate under Ronald Reagan.

I started in Washington in the middle of the Eisenhower presidency. Working at *Congressional Quarterly,* I did not cover Eisenhower. But as a newcomer to town, I was a fascinated spectator at Eisenhower's press conferences, held in the Indian Treaty Room of the Old Executive Office Building, just across from the White House.

Systematic coverage of the White House was about sixty years old at the time. During Grover Cleveland's administration, in 1896, William "Fatty" Price of the *Washington Star* began interviewing visitors on Pennsylvania Avenue as they left their meetings with the President. His scoops drew other reporters. Theodore Roosevelt invited the reporters inside in 1902, providing the first press room in the new West Wing. Woodrow Wilson was the first President to hold regular press conferences. Herbert Hoover had the first press secretary, and Franklin D. Roosevelt brought the press conference to a degree of utility and intimacy it had never known. Roosevelt had the astonishing total of 998 press conferences in his twelve-plus years as President, meeting reporters twice a week before World War II and once a week thereafter. Harry S. Truman, following Roosevelt's pattern, held conferences almost weekly. (The history of presidential coverage is well told in Stephen Hess's book *The Government/Press Connection* and in Deakin's *Straight Stuff.*)

Eisenhower was extremely skillful in managing the press and was more conscientious than any of his successors in providing access to the press at regular news conferences. He was no novice at the game. As a political general, commanding the Allied armies in Europe, dealing with Congress and the Executive as Army chief of staff and then as head of NATO, he had become very sophisticated in using the press to enhance his own reputation and to build support for his policies. He and his supporters played the media game beautifully in overcoming the challenge of Senator Robert A. Taft of Ohio for the Republican nomination in 1952 and in twice defeating Democrat Adlai E. Stevenson for the presidency.

Eisenhower said on becoming President that he had always been treated "fairly and squarely" by reporters and promised to continue being "openhanded and forthright" with them. He was anything but naive, however, about his dealings with the press. When Eisenhower was questioned on a subject he did not like, he would often say things like, "What you are telling me now, I have never heard about this before." When personalities were raised, Eisenhower usually demurred, saying he would not comment on any individual. He was similarly standoffish about what he called "partisan disputes."

Once Merriman Smith, the United Press's White House correspondent, asked Eisenhower, "Mr. President, your speech this last Sunday at Dartmouth was interpreted or accepted by a great many people as being critical of a school of thought represented by Senator [Joseph R.] McCarthy. Is that right or wrong?"

Eisenhower replied, "Now, Merriman, you have been around me

long enough to know I never talk personalities. I think that we will get along faster in most of these conferences if we remember that I do not talk personalities; I refuse to do so."

What Eisenhower could not conceal were his emotions. He had a mobile, expressive face and a fairly hot temper. Two reporters in particular—Raymond P. (Pete) Brandt of the *St. Louis Post-Dispatch* and William McGaffin of the *Chicago Daily News*—fearlessly provoked him. When Brandt asked about the rocky economy or McGaffin questioned Eisenhower about the purchase of a helicopter to "get to the golf course a little faster than you can make it by car," the red would rise from the base of his neck to the top of his bald head. Reporters knew what Eisenhower's mood was. We knew whether he cared about a subject or not and how deeply he felt. There was a recognizable human personality on display.

Some historians have argued that Eisenhower manipulated the news more than we realized. Fred I. Greenstein, in his book *The Hidden-Hand Presidency,* argues that Eisenhower "self-consciously" finessed the inherent contradiction between the conflicting roles of chief of state and of the nation's top political official both assigned to the President by the Constitution. Greenstein writes that "Eisenhower went to great lengths to conceal the political side of his leadership." Deakin and other journalists who covered him insist that concealment often bordered on deceit.

The press conferences were an important part of that strategy. Greenstein cites occasions when Eisenhower, warned that a particular topic might come up, called Secretary of State John Foster Dulles, for example, to be sure he knew exactly what Dulles had said on the matter, then went out and feigned ignorance. On one occasion, Greenstein says, he told his press secretary, "Don't worry, Jim, if that question comes up, I'll just confuse them."

But there was more to it than that. As Greenstein shows, the President artfully framed his "impersonal" responses in such a way that the newspapers shorthanded them into attacks on McCarthy. Greenstein quotes Eisenhower's remark to retired General Lucius Clay: "I put it in talk, principle and idea. They usually put it in headlines, 'The President spanks so and so.'" He understood the process so well that comments he made that never mentioned McCarthy's name would still get headlines like "Ike Lauds Blast at McCarthy" or "President Opposes McCarthy as Judge in His Own Dispute."

While using the press, Eisenhower realized that he had to make himself accessible to reporters. A few years ago Ray Scherer, who covered Eisenhower for NBC, recalled that "he was asked what he thought of news conferences as such several times, and his general answer was that it went with the territory; it was part of being President, and he may not have enjoyed them, but he did them as a duty." At times, Eisenhower sounded enthusiastic about them. In 1956 he called the press conference "a wonderful institution" and went on to say:

> While I have seen all sorts of statements that Presidents have considered it a bore and it is a necessary chore to go through, it does a lot of things for me personally.
>
> For one thing, at least once a week I have to take a half hour to review in my own mind what has happened during that week, so that I don't make errors just through complete inadvertence and failure to look them up.
>
> Moreover, I rather like to get the questions because frequently I think they represent the kind of thinking that is going on.

Except when he was recovering from his illnesses, Eisenhower held press conferences regularly: 193 of them in eight years, an average of more than two a month. The public got to see and hear the Eisenhower press conference more directly than ever before. Transcripts published the next day allowed direct quotations rather than the indirect attribution his predecessors had insisted on using. Radio tapes were made and broadcast for the first time. And well before he left office, Eisenhower allowed television cameras to film his press conferences for later use. White House editing became increasingly relaxed, permitting the networks to run virtually as much of the conference as they wished.

In addition, Eisenhower held occasional private dinners for the White House regulars, where, according to Scherer and Robert J. Donovan, who covered him for the *New York Herald Tribune*, "he would hold forth in a very unrestrained kind of way." No transcripts were made, nor apparently were any notes taken at the session; when the evening was over, the reporters pooled their recollections, and, at an agreed-upon time, a day or so later, wrote unattributed stories, reflecting what they had learned. Eisenhower apparently felt free at such sessions. At one stag dinner, Donovan recalled, "I heard him give one of the best expositions of why we should recognize Red China that I had ever heard: but publicly he would never mention a thing like that, and indeed would have opposed it." (This quotation, like several others cited in this chapter from former White House correspondents, comes from Kenneth W. Thompson's book *Ten Presidents and the Press.*)

Eisenhower, however, never sought or achieved the degree of intimacy and candor with reporters covering him that FDR had enjoyed; memoirs of the Roosevelt era say that he was able, with perfect confidence, to go off the record at his press conferences. Yet Eisenhower enjoyed very good press throughout his two terms. Part of it was, Deakin argues in *Straight Stuff*, "that very little of the atmosphere of Eisenhower's [press conference] confrontations with reporters found its way into their stories."

At the time, I was struck by the difference between the atmosphere in the room and the accounts of the sessions. In those days, before live TV coverage of the news conferences, reporters from the wire services and afternoon newspapers would rush out to phones in the hallway and dictate their stories as the rest of us stood around talking. I remember being awed at the way those wire service reporters—Merriman Smith of UP, Bob Clark of International News Service, and Marvin Arrowsmith of AP—could dictate three or four leads on three or four separate stories on foreign and domestic policy out of the session just ended, and then, without missing a beat, go back and dictate additional segments of six or eight paragraphs on each in turn until they were done.

Deakin is right, however, that their stories had a flat, emotionless tone, lacking the combative flavor they had displayed when trying to pin down the elusive President.

A major reason for Eisenhower's success, all the accounts agree, was his press secretary, James C. Hagerty, a gift to Eisenhower from New York Governor Thomas E. Dewey. Hagerty (a man I regret I never got to know) is remembered as the all-time master of the White

House press room. He invented many of the techniques his successors have happily copied. The growing logistical demands of the television era and its expanding corps of White House reporters and technicians tested his professionalism. In preparing the President's trips, Hagerty anticipated the technical needs of broadcast and newspaper reporters and planned a steady diet of "news" to keep the press occupied and the President's name in the paper.

Hagerty served as *the* press spokesman for the President; reporters who tried to talk to other staff members were routinely sent back to him. But because he was a real White House insider, with the full confidence of the President, reporters raised no objection to his role. One measure of his standing—astonishing in retrospect—was the frequency with which Eisenhower conferred with Hagerty, and even allowed himself to be corrected by Hagerty, during the presidential press conferences.

Deakin suggests that Hagerty was the true inventor of the modern public relations presidency, because he "combined the roles of press officer and public relations expert, and made them one. He serviced the press—no one ever did it more efficiently—but he served the President. All subsequent press secretaries have accepted Hagerty's order of priorities. The President's image comes first."

If the reporters felt they were being manipulated, there were few complaints. They enjoyed their relationship with Hagerty. Scherer recalled in 1981 that before most Eisenhower press conferences, "Hagerty would meet with a few of the press regulars . . . and tell them what was on the President's mind, and we . . . would say what was on our minds, so Hagerty generally had some idea of what was going to come up, so he could brief Eisenhower."

The coziness of this relationship was encouraged by the atmosphere of candor Hagerty created. Although there were some initial delays in the announcement of Eisenhower's first heart attack and some confusion over his stroke (when Hagerty was caught out of town), the medical bulletins were replete with detail, down to the timing and quality of the presidential bowel movements.

Throughout his presidency, Eisenhower maintained the high levels of public affection and trust that he had earned during World War II. It was certainly not irrelevant that he cultivated and enjoyed good personal relations with many of the leading publishers and broadcasting executives of the day. It was an era of good feelings in America—a time of bipartisanship in foreign policy, of cooperative relationships with the Democratic Congress. As Bob Donovan commented, "Ike was not a very good target for reporters; he just wasn't. He rode the punches, he eschewed controversy. There was the obvious probity of the man himself. . . . Even the toughest critics who went after Ike found Ike no great target."

JOHN F. KENNEDY, almost thirty years younger than Eisenhower, made himself the friend and companion of many of the bright men and women who were emerging as the stars of postwar Washington journalism. And he was not reluctant to use his family connections with such aging powers as Arthur Krock of the *New York Times*. Krock, a friend of Kennedy's father, Joseph P. Kennedy, had his agent arrange for publication of Kennedy's first book, *Why England Slept*, and lobbied discreetly to get him a Pulitzer Prize for his pop history, *Profiles in Courage*.

As a junior senator, without much standing as a legislator, Kennedy quickly learned the uses of publicity. He did television with some polish. He was always available to discuss anything from his battles with corrupt union presidents to his life with his beautiful socialite wife, Jacqueline. And beyond the contrivances, Kennedy had a genuine link to journalists. He himself liked to write, he had dabbled in journalism before settling into a political career, and his wife had been an "inquiring photographer" for the *Washington Times-Herald*.

Kennedy could turn an interview into a bull session, artfully picking the reporter's brain for useful items of information or gossip. His own candor in such discussions was breathtaking; the degree of confidentiality they seemed to assume suggested an intimacy that was not really there.

As a very young, totally unknown reporter on the Kennedy campaign, representing the *Washington Star*, I was often drawn into conversations in which Kennedy, with extraordinary detachment, would dissect the vagaries of his and Nixon's campaign; discuss in bawdy, familiar terms the political and personal strengths and weaknesses of important figures in both parties; and in general, carry on very much as if he were one of us covering the campaign.

His style was part a penchant for breaking the rules, part relaxation, and—in large part—a means of learning what he could and gaining what advantage he could from the intimacy he created. As Lewis J. Paper says in his book *The Promise and the Performance*, beyond the genuine friendship he felt for journalists like Joseph Alsop and Ben Bradlee, Kennedy was aware of the press's influence and worked assiduously to be portrayed "in the most favorable light."

So Kennedy converted a portion of the press corps covering him into a cheering section. In the fall of 1960, wherever the Kennedy campaign plane landed, there were late-night arguments over campaign strategy in which it was very difficult to tell some of the reporters from the Kennedy staff members. At times, it was almost impossible not to feel that this was a shared adventure. Peter Lisagor, the great reporter of the *Chicago Daily News*, who was congenitally incapable of being swept off his feet by any politician, remarked on the night that Kennedy had his famous confrontation with the Houston Ministerial Association—a key test of whether the "Catholic issue" would defeat him—that "if the editors of this country had any sense, they'd pull every reporter who covered Kennedy tonight off him the rest of his campaign. You can't have watched him go up against those bigots and still claim to be neutral."

But most of the reporters remained on the campaign, and many followed him to the White House, where some of the camaraderie continued. Rather than channel all dealings through press secretary Pierre Salinger, as Hagerty had done in the Eisenhower White House, reporters had access to the senior White House staff aides—men who had, in most instances, developed their own close relationships with reporters during the long campaign. Kennedy himself signaled his intention to keep direct lines of communication to key reporters by dropping in on Alsop and Bradlee during the first few days of his presidency.

Kennedy's boldest press move was putting the press conferences on live television. Live TV had served him well in the campaign; his debates with Nixon were probably as important to his narrow victory as any other element of the race. He felt comfortable before the cameras, spoke with assurance, and used his quick wit to evade those questions he found troublesome. The live press conferences, held almost twice a month through the thirty-four months of his presidency, suited Kennedy. He once told Bradlee, "I always said that when we don't have to go through you bastards, we can really get our story out to the American people."

But they also served the egos and reputations of the reporters, who flocked to them in greater numbers than ever before. Some of those Kennedy recognized regularly became TV stars themselves, and that status—reinforced by invitations to White House parties and dinners —did nothing to hurt the administration.

Charles W. (Chuck) Roberts, who covered both Eisenhower and Kennedy for *Newsweek*, reflected on the contrast in *Ten Presidents and the Press:*

> Unlike the Eisenhower days—when Ike talked to us like supply troops, a sort of necessary appendage to his command—there was almost a spirit of camaraderie among White House staff and press, particularly during the first-year "honeymoon." This is a dangerous position for journalists to get in; it can numb their critical faculties. However, JFK was our age, knew a lot about our business, and seemed genuinely interested in our work and our families. None of us regarded his friendliness as phony or his hospitality as a mere gambit to get a better press. The first strains in this new relationship occurred a few months into the new administration, when it became apparent to some of us that Kennedy was not only the friendliest, but the most thin-skinned of Presidents. Although JFK and his aides were quick to compliment a reporter on a "good story," i.e., one favorable to the administration, they were intolerant of any criticism. What was worse, reporters who wrote stories that annoyed the White House suddenly found that their sources of information were drying up. Those staffers who had been so accessible were suddenly too busy to talk. Phone calls went unreturned. "You are either for us or against us," is the way Kenny O'Donnell, the President's appointments secretary, put it to me.

Roberts reminds us that a mist of sentimentality has distorted the picture of President Kennedy's relations with the press. They were not, in fact, all sweetness and light. Although Bob Donovan had written an admiring book about Kennedy's wartime heroism, his paper, the *Herald Tribune*, was so critical of Kennedy the White House canceled its twenty-two subscriptions. After the Cuban missile crisis, Kennedy ordered and enforced a government-wide clam-up to prevent reporters from retracing the steps that had led to the confrontation, meantime having his aides and his brother Robert assist his friends Charles Bartlett and Stewart Alsop with their retrospective account for the *Saturday Evening Post*. That brought criticism even from old family friend Arthur Krock, who wrote that "a news management policy not only exists, but in the form of direct and deliberate action, has been enforced more cynically and boldly than by any previous administration in a period when the U.S. was not at war."

Assiduous in courting the press, sensitive to criticism, and aggressive in pushing the press to adhere to his own conception of national security, Kennedy had a love-hate relationship going. Lewis J. Paper quoted George Herman of CBS as saying Kennedy "truly enjoyed" reporters' company, "but he was always trying to manipulate their reporting." When he could not succeed with reporters, he went to editors and publishers. The most famous incident was his intervention with *New York Times* publisher Orvil Dryfoos to get the paper to play down Tad Szulc's story in the spring of 1961 that a CIA-sponsored invasion of Cuba by anti-Castro refugees was imminent. The newspaper ran a front-page story but omitted its information about the invasion's imminence and the CIA involvement and moved it from the lead-story position originally planned. A few days after the invasion ended in disaster, Kennedy told the American Newspaper Publishers Association that they were living in an era of constant danger and they should ask themselves, on every story, "Is it in the interests of the national security?" The publishers did not buy his argument, and Kennedy himself soon whispered to *Times* executives that he wished, in retrospect, they had spotlighted the invasion scheme and "saved us from a colossal mistake."

The tensions continued until Kennedy's death, but overall, Kennedy's reputation was enhanced not only by his own skill in manipulating the press but by the willingness of many in the Washington press corps to be manipulated. Those who swapped partying stories with the President willingly participated in glamorizing and sanitizing the private life of John F. Kennedy. Those granted privileged access to him and his top aides often wrote their stories with the goal of keeping that access intact. Roberts was right when he said that "Most of us now reaffirm what we knew then: that an arms-length relationship (such as we had under Ike) is better for both the journalist and his readers."

LYNDON B. JOHNSON came out of Texas at a time when its battles were fought largely within the Democratic Party, and leading publishers were an important part of the business-political establishment that controlled the state. Conservative papers fought Johnson's rise to power, and some remained enemies to the end, despite his efforts to court their publishers and editors with personal favors. But as Johnson's increased influence became a vital link for the Texas power structure in Washington, it became easier for him to keep his Texas press critics in check. If he learned to deal with the newspapers at home, he never learned to love or respect them.

Still, he had few problems with the press when he was Senate majority leader. He managed the press there very much as he managed the Senate: by respecting the seniority system among reporters; by dispensing information through that system; and by controlling the flow of information, particularly about schedule and tactics, as part of his control of the legislative process.

From these experiences, Johnson derived an essentially manipulative view of press relations: the press was not of prime importance in itself, certainly not in a position to impose its own agenda or demands on an officeholder. It was one of many instruments for achieving the political and governmental objectives of the moment.

Johnson tried to carry this approach to the White House with generally disastrous results. Early in his presidency, he told a small group of reporters, accompanying him on Air Force One that he was going to make them privy to everything that came across his desk. No White House reporters had ever had the kind of access and information he was going to give them. All he wanted in return was their cooperation in his great dream of making this a better America. As Frank Cormier, the AP's White House correspondent, wrote in *LBJ: The Way He Was*, Johnson said:

> "I need your help. I'll tell you everything. You'll know everything I do. You'll be as well-informed as any member of the Cabinet. There won't be any secrets except for where the national security is involved. Of course, I

may go into a strange bedroom every now and then that I won't want you to write about, but otherwise you can write everything. . . . If you want to play it the other way, I know how to play it both ways, too, and I know how to cut off the flow of news except in handouts. . . . There's no reason why the members of the White House press corps shouldn't be the best-informed, most-respected, highest-paid reporters in Washington. If you help me, I'll help you. I'll make you-all big men in your profession."

Put in those crude terms, the invitation lacked the seductive quality of Kennedy's manipulative "openness." Cormier said that his own reaction was to tell Johnson, " 'Mr. President, don't you realize that sooner or later every reporter around this table is going to write something that'll make you mad as hell?' " Besides, it was a false promise; Johnson was too aware of the value of hoarding information, as a leadership tool, willingly to give reporters free access. And he had few personal friendships on which to draw with the White House press corps. These were not the people he had dealt with in Texas or on Capitol Hill. For the most part, they had been covering Kennedy, and, in many instances, they had inhaled the contempt for Johnson that was freely expressed in the Kennedy circle when Johnson was Vice President.

For his first two years in office, from the assassination and the 1964 election through the Great Society Congress of 1965, Johnson dominated the press by his sheer energy and effectiveness as President. He moved so fast, on projects of such scale, that reporters were swept along. He pushed himself, his staff, the Congress, the bureaucracy, and the press relentlessly, overwhelming all of them. Even Cormier confessed that at one point during the 1964 campaign, he was enticed by Johnson's promise to four reporters on Air Force One that he would campaign against any Republican congressman they thought deserved defeat. "I'm ashamed, really, to think how far out of line I got," Cormier said. "I told the President I had been voting for ten years against a very conservative northern Virginia Republican, Joel Broyhill. Johnson promptly announced that he would hold two rallies in Broyhill's district."

As an elemental force and a dominating personality, Johnson was in a league by himself among the Presidents I have covered. Nothing— including the limits of veracity—stood in his way. The first story I wrote about him for the *Star*—an account of the machinations at the

Democratic state convention in Austin that endorsed him for President in the spring of 1960—so aggravated the majority leader that he called my editor and told him he ought to get rid of that incompetent reporter before he embarrassed the paper further. (Editor Benjamin McKelway woke me up down in Texas to tell me of Johnson's call, asked for a memo backing up the story with further details, and, when he read it later in the day, called back to tell this quaking novice, "No problem.")

Later that year, I got a more personal taste of the "Johnson treatment." John B. Connally came to Washington to run a Johnson for President headquarters and answered questions about their plans and strategies. Each time a story appeared, Johnson would call and say, "I don't know where the hell you're getting that b.s., but if you want to know what I'm doing, come see me." So I would go sit in his ornate office, watch him wolf down a hamburger, and be told again that he was "too busy minding the store" in the Senate to be conniving for the Democratic nomination as my story had suggested, and anybody who said otherwise was a damn liar. And I would say, "Yes, sir, Senator," and then go back to Connally, who would say, "Don't worry. He's not sore. He was laughing when he told me about what he had told you."

These habits made it likely that Johnson's early honeymoon with the press could not last. Johnson had a penchant for secrecy and was furious when a planned appointment or action leaked. He sometimes denied the accuracy of the account, occasionally shifted plans, and often later confirmed the report by his own action. Soon there were sufficient denials and subsequent confirmations to prompt reporters to write about a "credibility gap."

And Johnson retaliated. He called impromptu news conferences during lunch hours or on weekends. He ordered aides to leak stories to the competitors of a reporter who had given offense. It became a form of silent warfare, with the President, hovering over the news tickers he had installed in his office or over his three television sets, always ready to pounce.

The pressure on reporters was only a fraction of that he put on his own staff to shut down the leaks, to discipline the information flow. Salinger stayed on for a time after Kennedy's death, then left. George Reedy, who had been Johnson's Senate press secretary, exhausted himself in the job. Bill Moyers tried it for a while, then gave it up. Finally George Christian, an Austin public relations man, took over.

As the first phase of the Johnson presidency ended, the bills for the Great Society legislation began to come due at the same time that the costs, in dollars and lives, of the Vietnam War became so apparent. Both were critically scrutinized by the press, and Johnson could not deal with the criticism.

He could not conceal his rage, so denunciation became the order of the day. It made no difference how minor the offense. Clark Clifford, a friend and counselor of Johnson's before he became his secretary of defense, told me during this period that in White House discussions of the utmost political and diplomatic sensitivity, Johnson was the most detached, skeptical mind in the room, carefully weighing the consequences of alternative courses of action. But when offended by something in the press, he lost all perspective. "I wish I could convince him," Clifford said, "that everyone in the country does not read the jumps [continuations] on stories in the goddamn *New York Times*."

No one could convince Johnson that the tension between the press and the President was inevitable and legitimate. He could not tolerate forces beyond his control. As a throwback to the pre-television era of politics, Johnson especially distrusted the television cameras. He was most effective when nose to nose with a fellow senator or a fellow politican. He could entertain a couple dozen reporters, regaling them with anecdotes of thirty years of Texas and national politics, playing all the parts, imitating voices, mannerisms—an extraordinary, fascinating storyteller, and a powerful advocate of himself and his ideas.

When Johnson spoke on the Senate floor or in a campaign, the distance from the audience put into perspective the sweeping phrases, the big gestures, the force of the big body and the big voice. But put that big face, with its huge features, on television, and he somehow became grotesque. Johnson sought to compensate for the distortion by shrinking himself, closing his throat, aborting his gestures, restraining his richness of both body and verbal language—attempting to make himself what he could never be, conventional. This, too, fed the credibility gap, and contributed to the political destruction of a President whose achievements—and excesses—history has written large.

· · ·

BY the time Richard Nixon became President, he had gone through more ups and downs with the press than a roller coaster. Part of the story I told in Chapter Two with the pursuit of the New Nixon. Part of it is inscribed in "the last press conference," following his defeat for governor of California in 1962, when Nixon left politics (or so he said), saying that if news organizations "are against a candidate [and] give him the shaft," at least they should be responsible enough to "put one lonely reporter on the campaign who will report what the candidate says now and then."

Later the battle-scarred Nixon came to realize that he was not likely to climb back into power by running over the press. So he set out to finesse the press, and he did so quite successfully in the 1968 campaign.

Carroll Kilpatrick, the *Washington Post*'s White House correspondent in the Johnson, Nixon, and Ford administrations, correctly pointed out that Nixon "understood the press better" than Johnson did. As a publicity-hungry member of Congress, he had learned about deadlines and the operational needs of reporters. He knew how to make news. But his distrust of the press had been nurtured for years by the time he became President.

Lou Cannon, who covered the Nixon presidency for the *Post*, remarked in *Reporting: An Inside View* that Nixon had acquired his distaste for journalists from his hard-nosed father. And he cited a speech Nixon gave in high school: "Should the morals of this nation be offended and polluted in the name of freedom of speech or freedom of the press?" Nixon really seemed to believe that, as a group, reporters were out to "shaft" him, for ideological or personal reasons; and he instinctively believed that unless he evaded them, they would find some way to undo him. So his press operations became as manipulative as Johnson's. Nixon's chief of staff. H. R. (Bob) Haldeman, a Los Angeles advertising executive, distrusted reporters at least as much as his boss. Press secretary Ron Ziegler, a former Haldeman employee, lacked independent standing. He was told only what he needed to know and then ordered to relay it without embellishment to the press.

At first Nixon held fairly regular but infrequent news conferences— thirty in the first term, an average of one every seven weeks. His principal messages were delivered through television speeches. When asked about gaps between news conferences, he said, "I think the American people are entitled to see the President and to hear his views directly and not to see him only through the press."

Nixon professed to be detached about criticism. In 1971, he told an interviewer, "I probably follow the press more closely and am less affected by it than any other President. I have a very cool detachment about it. . . . I'm not like Lyndon. . . . The press was like a magnet to him. He'd read every single thing that was critical, he'd watch the news on TV all the time, and then he'd get mad. I never get mad. I expect I have one of the most hostile and unfair presses that any President has ever had, but I've developed a philosophical attitude about it."

Like many other Nixon monologues, this one wandered from the truth. During the Watergate investigation, *Time* magazine reported that White House documents showed that "during one 30-day period [in the fall of 1969], President Nixon had bombarded his aides with 21 separate memos on unfavorable press coverage of his administration. His demands that subordinates somehow quell offending journalists and generate more pleasing reportage and commentary set off a frantic scramble." Much of Nixon's anger had been provoked by some of the television commentary on his Vietnam speeches. Nixon sent Vice President Spiro Agnew out to trash the "tiny and closed fraternity of privileged men, elected by no one," who were clogging his direct channel to the American people. But it didn't stop with words. The Federal Communications Commission, which licenses television stations, asked the networks for transcripts of their analyses and commentaries on Nixon's speeches. In 1972, the Justice Department filed antitrust suits against the three networks, and television stations owned by newspapers regarded as "hostile" to the administration had their license renewals challenged. White House aides admonished network executives to be more prudent.

While conducting this overt and covert campaign of intimidation, the White House devised new ways to get Nixon's message out to the country without the White House press corps interfering. Nixon set up a formal White House office of communications, separate from the press secretary's operation, that distributed the administration's message to editors, reporters, and broadcasters outside of Washington—

through mailings, briefings, and road-show press conferences, where preference in questioning was given to the local journalists.

The first director of communications was Herbert G. Klein, a former Nixon press secretary and editor of the *San Diego Union*, who had a wide circle of personal contacts with editors and broadcasters around the country. Although White House reporters complained at first about Nixon's efforts to "bypass" them and deal directly with news organizations outside Washington, the supplementary system's advantages— to both news organizations and the President—are so obvious that every successor President has maintained and expanded the operation.

Like the press secretary's office, the communications office can be used for whatever purpose the President wishes. Nixon used both essentially as propaganda tools. Nixon himself became increasingly inaccessible to the press, holding only nine news conferences in his last twenty months in office. In mid-1973, when the administration was unraveling and Nixon had isolated himself from reporters for more than three months, I wrote a column arguing that "we have now reached the point that the impairment of the President's credibility must be dealt with before any of the other serious issues facing the country can be addressed. Either he must answer the multitude of questions about what happened in his administration and his re-election campaign, or he ought, in respect for his office and the national interest, to acknowledge that he cannot answer them and step aside in favor of the Vice President."

Two months later, he finally had another news conference. But overall, Nixon's record completely refuted his promise, made in a much-praised 1968 campaign speech written by Raymond K. Price, Jr., a former editorial writer for the *Herald Tribune*, that he would conduct "an open presidency." In mid-June 1973, the professional relations committee of the National Press Club issued an unprecedented report, endorsed by the club's board of directors, calling Nixon's "the most closed administration in recent decades," one which had made "numerous and persistent attempts . . . to restrict the flow of legitimate public information."

By that time, the Watergate disclosures had created the circumstances that would drive Nixon from office. The press's growing recognition of the White House cover-up destroyed whatever relationship there had been between the reporters and the administration's official spokesmen. But during most of his presidency, and especially during his reelection campaign, Nixon's press policy had been very effective. To a very large extent, he controlled the news agenda, denied the press access to news he wanted kept secret (from Kissinger's trip to China to the imposition of wage-price controls), commanded the facilities of television and the press when he wanted them, and evaded our questions by refusing press conferences for up to five months at a time. He also shut down the voices of his critics, to some degree, by Agnew's attacks on the television commentators and by the repeated implication that criticism was an expression of a hostile political-media elite. But for Watergate, it all might have worked.

WATERGATE changed many of the fundamentals in the White House–press relationship. The press came away with an emotional high—but one which was scarcely deserved. As press critic Ben H. Bagdikian noted at the American Society of Newspaper Editors convention in 1973, "no more than 14 reporters" of the several thousand employed in the capital did any substantial early work on the Watergate case. Most publications and most Washington journalists had been skeptical of the investigative work of Bob Woodward and Carl Bernstein. While I was spared from some of the skepticism because of what I learned from the two reporters in office conversations during the fall of 1972, "my own columns" (as I wrote in May 1973), like many other columns that fall, "provide evidence for the observation by the *Washington Post*'s ombudsman, Robert Maynard, that those of us whose supposed insights into the deeper meaning of events gain us editorial-page space in papers around the country did precious little to help readers understand the significance of this political crime."

For the White House reporters, Watergate was a double personal humiliation. Not only were they scooped by two unknown local beat reporters, but they had served as a conduit for what they gradually came to realize was a systematic set of official lies about the case. Their professional fury carried over to the presidencies of Gerald R. Ford, Jimmy Carter, and Ronald Reagan. The style of questioning at the official White House briefings became, after Watergate, almost more prosecutorial than inquisitive. Consider, for example, this exchange between Sam Donaldson of ABC, Helen Thomas of UPI, and

Reagan spokesman Larry Speakes, eleven years after Nixon had left office. The issue was whether Speakes had attempted to conceal the fact that a biopsy had been performed on an irritated patch of skin on Reagan's nose, which later turned out to be a mild form of skin cancer:

Donaldson: Wait a moment. You were asked last Thursday—if you say that your words were, and I accept that—when you were asked whether a biopsy would be performed, and you said, "Sure," well then you were saying one was going to be performed.
Speakes: Well?
Thomas: And on Friday you refused to say one was performed.
Speakes: That's right. But refusal to say does not constitute a lie, Helen.
Thomas: Well, we are questioning your candor.
Speakes: No. No.
Thomas: You were not candid.
Speakes: I was. I told the truth. And I told the truth from the first.
Thomas: Well, on Friday were you candid when—?
Speakes: Do you want to say that I did not tell the truth?
Thomas: Aw, come on, get off of that.
Speakes: No, you come on. You've accused me of something.
Thomas: You pulled an iron curtain down on the truth.
Speakes: Exactly right. But I did not lie. And I told the truth.
Thomas: Is it exactly right that you did?
Speakes: I told the truth. Now, let's get back to yours.
Donaldson: Well, what's the difference between pulling down an iron curtain on the truth, and being completely credible, or not being completely credible? Do you see any difference in those?
Speakes: I'm completely credible. I told the truth from top to bottom. And if you'll look at it, you will see. Now, I think you ought to clarify the record as to what you said here. Would you like to do that? I think you owe an obligation. When you raise an accusation like that. . . .
Donaldson: I'm not withdrawing a thing about questions being raised about your credibility.
Speakes: All right, what are the questions? What are the questions? Raise the questions.

The first two post-Watergate Presidents, Ford and Carter, both recognized that rebuilding public trust in the presidency was essential. Both considerably increased access and availability; while neither was able to build a stable political constituency or to win office as an incumbent, neither failed, in my view, because of his inability to manage the news or because of any hostility in the press.

I have recounted much of the story of Ford's dealings with the press in Chapter Two. For him, offering access to the press was a matter of ingrained habit. A naturally gregarious person, he had both enjoyed and cultivated friendships with reporters during his long years in the House. When he became part of the Republican leadership in Congress, he deliberately set out to overcome the disadvantages of being in the minority party by actively soliciting coverage from reporters. No one had to draw a diagram for President Ford to understand that his best strategy was to be as open as Nixon had been remote.

He did so in large ways and small, and the White House press corps's reaction was one of undisguised delight. John Herbers, who had covered the final, bitter stages of the Nixon's presidency for the *New York Times*, wrote about the contrast in *No Thank You, Mr. President*. When he and his wife were invited to Ford's first state dinner, for King Hussein of Jordan, Herbers reflected:

> For almost two years I had felt like I was entering enemy territory whenever I passed into the White House compound. Now we were being escorted through the great halls and having our names announced by loudspeaker in the East Room. Never mind my objections to the press becoming too cozy with officialdom. It was a time for celebration, and everyone stayed very late, dancing out the deadness of the past.

The smoothness of Ford's relationship with the press was rudely shocked thirty days after his succession when he announced that he had granted Nixon an unconditional pardon. The decision—which I thought justified—aroused suspicions of a political deal between Ford and Nixon, which plagued Ford in the 1976 election and troubles many even today.

The pardon cost Ford his press secretary, Jerald F. terHorst, who resigned because he disagreed in principle with the pardon. TerHorst was the widely respected head of the *Detroit News* Washington bureau before his thirty-day job with Ford, and his own credibility enhanced that of the President. Ron Nessen, the former NBC reporter who succeeded terHorst, never enjoyed the same degree of respect from the White House regulars.

Instead of becoming defensive and neurotic, Ford responded characteristically by redoubling his efforts toward openness. He took the almost unprecedented step of testifying as a witness at a congressional inquiry about the pardon, and he answered reporters' questions on the subject until we could think of no more questions.

Throughout his twenty-nine months in office, Ford continued to meet with reporters—at forty-four press conferences, plus enough small group and individual interviews that the term *exclusive* became almost a laughingstock.

Ford was rarely commanding in these interviews and occasionally verbally awkward, just as he was in many of his speeches. His utterances had a degree of banality and predictability that usually robbed them of any high drama. But that was the man, not the format. He was unfailingly responsive, cordial, and patient with the proceedings; inspiration was simply beyond his reach.

JIMMY CARTER'S ambitions were considerably larger and his view of the press was considerably less charitable and simple than Ford's. Ford liked reporters and was inclined to trust us, unless double-crossed, and then to forgive rather quickly. His trust was rooted in his feeling that he had always gotten "a fair shake," as he would put it, on Capitol Hill. Carter, by contrast, saw himself as an outsider, who had been snubbed and underestimated by the big shots of the press corps from the time, early in his career, when he defeated the candidate favored by the Atlanta newspapers, former Governor Carl Sanders, for the Democratic nomination for governor of Georgia.

As a long-shot candidate for the Democratic presidential nomination, Carter had cultivated the national political press as systematically, relentlessly, and calculatingly as he did everyone else who might help him gain the prize. Hamilton Jordan's initial strategy memo, written on November 4, 1972, advised Carter to "foster relationships with political columnists that you know [and] establish relationships with those you don't know." Carter invited well-known journalists to visit him at the governor's mansion in Atlanta when traveling in the South or just changing planes (as everyone must do) in that city. He sought invitations to visit the editorial boards of newspapers around the country as he stumped for Democratic candidates in the mid-term election of 1974.

Carter was a good host at those back-porch sessions in Atlanta and a voluble guest at the editorial boards. In some cases, his courtship of reporters went well beyond the normal limits, sending Indian arrowheads from his farm to the children of one correspondent, dropping a note to the parents of another one on their fiftieth wedding anniversary.

Nothing was impulsive or spontaneous about these gestures, nor did Carter try to disguise his motivation. He kept careful note of how much success he was having; when he visited the *Post*, for example, after securing the nomination in 1976, he talked with some bitterness of what he considered our slowness in recognizing the importance of his candidacy. As in Georgia, he always suspected that the big-city papers were dismissing him as a country bumpkin or showing favoritism to some more familiar candidate.

But to his credit, Carter and his press secretary, Jody Powell, made little effort to seduce the press in the Kennedy fashion into thinking we were part of the campaign family. Carter knew that to become President he had to deal with the press, so he did so with dogged determination. I saw him repeat, almost word for word, answers to standard questions for relays of reporters at a dozen stops along the campaign trail in Iowa and New Hampshire. He took no joy in the encounters, nor did he complain; it was part of his job.

Reporters quickly learned, however, that although Carter did not mind being questioned, he did resent being challenged. When the first stories appeared questioning his professional background (was he, for example, a nuclear physicist?); his conduct in past campaigns on race-related issues; his relationship with George Wallace, Lester Maddox, and other controversial characters; his accomplishments as governor; or the consistency of his positions, Carter seemed to lose his total self-control. Reporters learned to expect the "icy blues," the stare of contempt, from Carter, and, often, a tongue-lashing from Powell. But neither of them ever severed the relationship. It was too important.

When Carter was elected, he and Powell revived the phrase "an open presidency." Powell told reporters during the transition period that he believed theirs to be "the first administration to have a chance to make a clean break with the Vietnam-Watergate environment and . . . restore relations between press and government to a more even keel." They quickly discovered that some of the ideas they advanced —opening up some cabinet sessions to press coverage, publishing the

President's full daily appointments schedule—were impractical. But the more important promises were kept.

Although Carter observed at his first news conference as President that he expected the "confrontations with the press to kind of balance out the nice and pleasant things that come to me as President," he continued to hold televised news conferences for the Washington reporters twice a month, alternating them with nontelevised sessions for groups of journalists invited from around the country. Carter was responsive and articulate at the news sessions, often sharing with the press and the public his reasoning and evidence, as well as his conclusions. A survey of veteran White House reporters taken by CBS's Robert Pierpoint and published in *Parade* magazine in early 1982 gave Carter the second-highest rating after Kennedy on press conference skills, of the seven Presidents from Eisenhower through Reagan. He was rated as Eisenhower's equal for both "candor" and "informative value" and ahead of everyone else in those categories. Powell's briefings got equally high marks from the press corps because he was close enough to Carter to know what was really going on and quick-witted enough to spar easily with reporters when he wanted to tell them less than he knew.

Although it is hard to remember, in the wake of Carter's later political troubles, in the early months of his presidency he was hailed also for his mastery of the television medium. George Reedy called Carter "our first television President. . . . He uses symbols which convey substantive messages." And in March 1977, I observed that "in his first two months as President, Jimmy Carter has achieved a triumph of communications in the arena of public opinion. . . . He has transformed himself from the very shaky winner of a bungled campaign into a very popular President, whose mastery of the mass media has given him real leverage with which to govern."

The euphoria did not last. Three months after Carter became President, James Wooten, then of the *New York Times*—a reporter who had drawn some of the "steely blue" treatment during the campaign— wrote a story, largely from unattributed sources, saying that Carter was withdrawing into himself, rebuffing or intimidating even longtime associates and "stepping further and further away from the people he gathered together to help him govern."

Wooten had not discussed the story with Jody Powell. He called Wooten at home, told him it was "horseshit," and said that even though it was only 9 A.M. on the day of publication, he (Powell) had talked to twenty-three White House staff members who said that they had not talked to Wooten. Powell spent about half his regular press briefing that day denouncing the story, thus building it up.

A more serious battle came in the summer of 1977, when a Senate committee and the Washington press began investigating the pre-Washington financial transactions of Bert Lance, Carter's close friend and director of the Office of Management and Budget. Powell spearheaded the presidential effort to save Lance, and, in that role, not only mounted a fervent defense but sought to turn the tables on his antagonists. In one instance he called Loye Miller, then head of the *Chicago Sun-Times* Washington bureau, and offered him a tip that Republican Senator Charles H. Percy of Illinois, one of Lance's investigators, had been using corporate aircraft to commute between Illinois and the capital. The *Sun-Times* checked the story, found it was false, and then publicized Powell's effort to smear Percy.

By October 1977, after Lance had been forced to resign and the polls were beginning to sag, Powell told an interviewer he had not given the press and the country, "in an understandable fashion," a sense of what the Carter administration was about. To that end, Gerald Rafshoon, the producer of Carter's campaign spots and his image adviser, was brought onto the White House staff. Rafshoon tried to focus Carter's speeches and appearances on a short agenda of issues, and he set up a series of informal dinners with the President and First Lady for small groups of journalists to improve our understanding of Carter's goals and methods. If the one I attended as part of the *Washington Post* group was typical, these sessions had decidedly mixed results.

Carter was—as I had often seen him on the campaign plane—a man of paradoxes: remarkable in his depth of information on many of the problems facing the country and the world, equally remarkable in the pettiness or obtuseness of his judgment about many of the political figures with whom he dealt, and very touchy about the press he got. The night our group was there, he expressed, more than once, the wish that he had a confidant at the *Post* like the one he said he had in James

Reston at the *New York Times*—someone he could call on the phone and confide in.

Several of my colleagues said they would not be hard to reach if such an impulse struck the President. Others said, rather nobly, that they hoped Carter understood that such confidences could not be allowed to inhibit or color the coverage of the administration. Rosalynn Carter—often more direct than her husband—cut them off: "They don't want to know what you think, Jimmy. They don't care."

There had always been an undertone of that in Carter's own attitude. Before the 1976 election, he had told *Playboy* magazine, "The national news media have absolutely no interest in issues *at all*. . . . There's nobody in the back of this plane [referring to the press seats] who would ask an issue question unless he thought he could trick me into some crazy statement."

That attitude carried over to the White House. Hedley Donovan, the former editor-in-chief of *Time*, was a senior adviser to Carter in 1979 and 1980. In an article in *Fortune* after the 1980 election, Donovan wrote that "the President and his inner circle had a basically low opinion of the quality of the press, a considerable mistrust of its motives, and an incomplete understanding of its role. The mood stopped short of paranoia." That was my impression, too.

Powell, in his book *The Other Side of the Story*, cited other causes of the estrangement: "Carter was different. . . . He was a small-town Southern Baptist with a set of values and beliefs that made many of them [the reporters] decidedly uncomfortable. . . . he was a southerner . . . [who] did not fit the southern-pol stereotype. . . . There was another irritant in the relationship. Carter was smarter than most reporters and clearly knew it. . . . Finally, Carter did not work at being lovable. He did his job and expected everyone else, including journalists, to do theirs, without a great deal of petting and stroking."

When the Iranian hostage situation was added to the sense of domestic deadlock and drift that had grown during Carter's presidency, the aura of futility became too pervasive to be lifted by any communications strategy. The hostage situation interrupted the regularity of the press conference schedule, which had begun to slow down in 1979, adding to the tensions with the press. In 1980, a theme which had been present in the 1976 reporting, but not heavily emphasized, began to emerge clearly. This was the picture of Carter as a manipulative person, cold and even nasty toward his opponents—first Edward M. Kennedy in the primaries and then Ronald Reagan in the general election.

Toward the end, few covering Carter even bothered to disguise their dislike of him. I remember being in the coffee shop of Carter's Cleveland hotel the morning after his debate with Reagan. Election Day was less than a week away. Sam Donaldson, ABC's White House correspondent, spotted Powell at another table and, in a high-decibel voice, shouted over and over, "You're gonna lose, Jody. You're gonna lose."

FROM 1960, when Eisenhower and Kennedy both had a basically comfortable relationship with reporters, to 1980, at the end of Carter's tenure, the course of White House–press relations had gone downhill. And so had the course of the presidency. Kennedy was assassinated, Johnson was driven into political exile by Vietnam, Nixon was forced to resign under threat of impeachment, Ford and then Carter were defeated running as incumbents.

All of these Presidents had attempted to go over the heads of the White House reporters and to establish a direct channel of communication with the voters—via television or personal campaigning—that would provide a stable base from which to govern. Each devoted considerable energy and staff effort to managing the day-to-day coverage of his presidency by the White House correspondents—who, of course, both resisted and protested, even while they acknowledged that they were being used.

It was not good politics or good government or good journalism, and it was a pattern that Ronald Reagan and his advisers were determined to change. Change it they did, but, as we will see in the next chapter, not necessarily for the better.

CHAPTER FIVE

Reagan's Way
—and a Better Way

R ONALD REAGAN'S relationship with the press evolved through almost six years of stunningly successful news management, followed by one of the most embarassing and politically costly blowups in the modern presidency. In the autumn of 1986, the President's credibility was severely damaged by press exposure of secret United States arms shipments to Iran, followed by the even more stunning announcement from the White House that profits from those sales had been transferred—ostensibly without Reagan's knowledge or approval—to support one of his prized projects, the effort to harass and perhaps overthrow the leftist Sandinista government in Nicaragua.

The upheaval in the administration cast into doubt Reagan's political effectiveness in his final two years as President. But even more, it demonstrated once again how the cult of secrecy in the White House —linked to a manipulative view of press relations and rooted in a disdain and distrust of journalists—can easily turn on and victimize the very politician who creates it.

In only a few weeks, a man who seemed the master of presidential public relations saw his image begin to crumble. As an actor and as a politician, Reagan learned that sustaining popularity required cultivating the press. He used his abilities as a talented raconteur and a most engaging companion. With half a dozen other reporters and columnists, I was invited to the White House for cocktails with the President in 1984 (such invitations seem to precede elections) and threw in my share of questions. Though it was all off-the-record, Reagan seemed uncomfortable, until someone asked if he had seen any good movies lately. Well, he had, and he not only told us about *Red Dawn* but about how he thought it could have been improved. I don't know whether his criticism was right, but he certainly enjoyed talking about that picture more than about the budget or the coming campaign.

Charles McDowell, the witty Washington correspondent of the *Richmond Times-Dispatch*, spent five hours as Reagan's head-table companion at the Gridiron Dinner in 1983. All during the various skits and speeches, the President was rapt, and almost everything reminded him of a story. He entertained McDowell with a stream of anecdotes about stars of the past. At the end of the evening Reagan did a surprise turn on stage, singing a satirical chorus of "Mañana," and delivered the closing speech—a graceful, funny, sentimental, and patriotic number of the kind that he seems to toss off at will.

Yet Reagan always was one of the most difficult interviews. He has not been unavailable or unresponsive. But, along with many others, I found it almost impossible to get anything from Reagan except anecdotes and verbatim sections of his standard speeches.

Most politicians' public styles—assertive, declamatory, rhetorical —differ from their private styles, which are more ruminative, questioning, analytical. With Reagan there is almost no difference. My guess is that the President never thinks of himself as being offstage, at least when reporters are around. He is always aware of notebooks and pencils and, certainly, of cameras. He is, as a good actor, constantly aware of the impression he is making. His techniques do not vary, whether the audience is one or one thousand.

Every previous President I have known could stand back from his public positions and talk about the personal, political, and philosophical considerations that led him to take those stands, as well as the forces in the political world that might cause him to have to adjust them. But with Reagan it was particularly fruitless to explore the whys and wherefores, the ambiguities and possible inconsistencies, the derivations and the implications of his positions on issues. He almost invariably ended such discussions by reiterating that he believed exactly what he had said. Nothing more, nothing less. During many interviews between 1966 and 1980 and in several White House sessions, I have closed my notebook, knowing the ever-courteous Reagan had given me exactly what I would have got from reading his most recent speech on the subject.

Speeches were terribly important to Reagan and he did most of them superbly. He made a good living as a speechmaker when his movie and television careers flagged, and speeches were his mainstay as President. The articulation of his beliefs, his goals, and certain of his policies was central to his leadership role. Reagan's reliance on speechmaking and his reluctance to kill his own act by answering questions from the press distinctively shaped the press policies of his administration.

Those policies were based on three principles: limit the direct access to the President, make news management a major priority for trusted White House aides and cabinet secretaries, and shut down the flow of information from lower levels of the administration and the bureaucracy.

REAGAN has been less accessible than his predecessors. He held only thirty-nine news conferences in his first six years in office. (He also had twenty-three of what his aides call "minis," brief exchanges with reporters, usually on a limited set of issues, and two hundred and fifty-eight office interviews, many of which were limited to specific topics or feature stories.) Reagan's news conferences are somewhat more orderly than his predecessors'. Reporters are recognized by raising their hands rather than jumping to their feet. The President keeps a seating chart on the lectern and is able to call by name those he chooses. Most reporters judge the Reagan news conferences to be less informative than Carter's. Robert Pierpoint's survey for *Parade* rated him next lowest to Lyndon Johnson of the last seven presidents for "informative value" but Kennedy's closest challenger in the category of "humor."

More often than not, Reagan seems to obey an injunction he has given to reporters, when evading their questions, ever since his days in Sacramento: "Don't ask me to write your leads for you." The President tries to say as little as possible in news conferences, and the tension he often displays sharply contrasts with his confident assurance when delivering a major speech.

In November 1981, after his fifth press conference, I wrote:

At the last two news conferences, the impression he has created has been one of a man under great strain. The comments on Capitol Hill and in embassies suggest that the tension and anxiety the President displays when answering questions about his policies are beginning to cause concern among those here and abroad who look to the White House for leadership.

The same anxiety is being expressed by members of the White House staff, who have come to view each press conference as a hurdle that must be negotiated with care. They have adopted what my colleague Martin Schram accurately described as a "damage control" philosophy for dealing with the press conferences: scheduling them infrequently, slowing down the pace of questioning by lengthy answers, and hoping that Reagan gets out of them without hurting himself.

He has not always been able to do so. Reagan's responses during news conferences are studded with inaccuracies, and the White House press office regularly issues "clarifications" or simple corrections. After a February 1982 news conference, former *Post* correspondent Lee Lescaze wrote that "President Reagan rewrote the history of early U.S. involvement in Vietnam yesterday," confusing the makeup of the three colonial countries, reversing the blame for the cancellation of their scheduled 1956 elections, and asserting that President Kennedy had sent in "a division of marines," when the first 550 marines were actually dispatched by President Johnson sixteen months after Kennedy's death. Lescaze also wrote that

Reagan opened his news conference with a joke about press reports of his misstatements and he ended with a claim that his Jan. 19 news conference had not been studded with errors. Reagan said "the score was five to one in my favor." His count, however, refers to a White House refutation of a wire-service story on misstatements, not to the errors Reagan made at his Jan. 19 news conference, where every unemployment statistic he used was incorrect.

In the early months of the Reagan presidency, reporters assumed that stories pointing up such misinformation would damage the President's credibility. They did not. Voters seemed to believe his errors were inadvertent, no worse than they—or the reporters—might make. In 1982 Lou Cannon quoted one political aide who described Reagan's misstatements as "part of his charm."

The gaffes have increased the tendency of his staff to shield Reagan from frequent questioning. Although he has improved somewhat, each news conference remains a major risk. In June 1986, for instance, Reagan answered a question about a Supreme Court abortion decision with a comment on an earlier decision on the tangentially related issue of family rights to refuse medical treatment for badly malformed infants; he confused a Warsaw Pact proposal to reduce armies in Central Europe with a Soviet initiative on strategic arms; and he stated his position on the SALT II treaty so awkwardly that the White House had to issue two clarifying statements and answer a host of questions the next day. Faced with this continuing problem from the beginning, senior Reagan aides decided to take over the major information and public relations responsibilities.

At times, their efforts to shield Reagan have become ridiculous. On a 1984 tour of Chesapeake Bay designed to repair Reagan's image as an environmentalist, the President was asked about a controversial appointment he had made in that field. Several White House advance men immediately ordered the television floodlights cut off, press spokesman Larry Speakes jumped in front of him, and Reagan commented, "My guardian says I can't talk."

Such maneuvers did not embarrass Michael K. Deaver, Reagan's deputy chief of staff during his first term. Deaver laid down the doctrine that the White House must set the theme and message for its own coverage. As he once told the *Post*, "The people elected the President to determine the agenda, not the media." Each Friday during the first term, Deaver and then chief of staff James A. Baker III met with the top presidential assistants to plan the next period's communications strategy. The Reagan system built on thirty years of increasingly sophisticated White House news management techniques, going back to Jim Hagerty in the Eisenhower years. The distinction was that managing the news and public opinion was explicitly recognized by the new administration as such a central part of running the presidency that it had to become a major part of the workday of senior policy aides.

With the general outline in place, the daily 8:15 A.M. senior staff meetings nail down each day's White House program, designed to define and dominate primarily that night's network news programs and secondarily the next morning's newspaper headlines. Deaver told Robert Scheer of the *Los Angeles Times* in 1984, "The whole business is now so influenced by network television . . . 100 million people across this country get all of their news from network television. So the visual is extremely important. . . . That visual is as critical as what we're saying.

"If you only get your message across in 30 or 40 seconds on the evening news," Deaver continued, "then it's important that you restate that message in as many ways as you can. . . ." Deaver understood that providing certain pictures of the President—and no others—could largely determine that night's television story. "We try to go with one particular theme," Deaver said. "We don't want to step on our own story. . . . We plot out a decent story or a theme for every day. . . . I explain it to the President and he'll tell me whether he's comfortable with it."

The technique does not please White House television correspondents. Sam Donaldson of ABC has said, with some bitterness, "They [the White House] don't need us as long as they capture our cameras." But as Deaver told Scheer, the correspondents have little choice but to go along. "They've got to get on [the air] in order to keep their jobs," Deaver said. "What good is a TV correspondent who is never on television?"

Often the correspondents attempt to free themselves from White House manipulation by biting back in their stand-ups, the brief summation-commentaries, usually shot with the TV reporter at the scene of the story. But Lesley Stahl, CBS News's White House correspondent during the first five and a half years of Reagan's presidency, learned to her chagrin how pictures can override even the most biting commentary.

During the 1984 campaign, she put together a four-and-a-half-minute piece that showed how far the White House had gone in staging events for Reagan. "It was a very tough piece," Stahl said later, "showing how they were trying to create public amnesia about some of the issues that had turned against Reagan. I was very nervous about going back to the White House the next day. But the show was no more than off the air, when a White House official called me and congratulated me on it and said he'd loved it. I said, 'How could you love it?' And he said, 'Haven't you figured it out yet? The public doesn't pay any attention to what you say. They just look at the pictures.'" Stahl said she looked at the piece again, with the sound off, and realized that what she had shown was a magnificent montage of Reagan in a series of wonderful, upbeat scenes, with flags, balloons, children, and adoring supporters—virtually an unpaid campaign commercial.

I asked whether she agreed with the White House official. "I've come to believe it," she said. Has it changed the way she does stories? "Not really," she said. "I'm still trapped, because my pieces are written to the pictures we have."

Once the story line was settled, little was left to chance. At 9:15 each morning, Speakes would brief about twenty of the White House regulars on what was going to be available for coverage that day. In the afternoon, the White House press office aides would often call around to the three networks to find out what their White House pieces would include, and then lobby to have the tone or focus shift in the direction the White House would like it to go.

Reagan aides also try to capture or steer newspaper coverage, and to do so, they violate the tradition that the President sets the pattern of press relations. In every previous administration, if the President chose to be accessible to the press, others who worked for him were accessible. If he was aloof, so were they. The President always gave the cue. Reagan has operated differently. He has limited access to himself but has allowed, even encouraged, his top aides to be responsive to the press. The effort has involved far more than the press office. Perhaps because press secretary James Brady was critically wounded in the assassination attempt on Reagan in March 1981, and Reagan's long-time spokesman, Lyn Nofziger, declined to serve as White House press secretary, his principal spokesman, Larry Speakes, did not gain the status many of his predecessors enjoyed until after Reagan was well into his second term. (Speakes left in early 1987 to enter private business and was succeeded by Marlin Fitzwater.)

During the first term, the press office was a secondary source of information because higher-ranking officials including Baker, Deaver, deputy chief of staff Richard G. Darman, budget director David A. Stockman, and all three of the national security advisers were more accessible than their predecessors had ever been. Baker consistently gave high priority to influencing press coverage of the White House and the other White House officials took their cues from him.

Until Reagan's reelection was safely in hand, Baker saw to it that no one cut off access to journalists who had criticized the President or administration policies. Throughout the first term, the Reagan White House maintained contact with people in the major news organizations that helped shape Washington and national opinion—no matter what. I tested the policy. Though my columns were often critical, there was never any retaliation. Unlike their predecessors in the Nixon administration, the Reaganites clearly believed that as long as a *Washington Post* writer was asking for their side, they were going to provide it.

The senior staff members were even more responsive to the White House correspondents for our paper and the other major news organizations. During the first term, Lou Cannon, David Hoffman, and others who worked brief shifts at the White House could almost always get their phone calls returned by the officials they needed. Cannon and his colleagues had earned the trust of those sources by their careful, conscientious (but far from uncritical) reporting of the administration. But clearly the administration's policy was to cooperate.

However, much of what these top presidential assistants said was "on background," usable by the reporters but not for direct attribution. What they said appeared most often in the *Post* and other papers as the words or thoughts of those ubiquitous, semianonymous "White House aides" or "administration officials." I want to discuss the broad ramifications of this controversial and troublesome practice in a later chapter, but here I would stress only that the access to senior White House staff was so constant and their responses so full during the first term that—despite Reagan's relative isolation from the press—readers of papers like the *Post* were often better informed about presidential decision making than ever before. For insiders, for those adept at reading the code the "White House officials" used, there were few surprises.

But there were some: In late 1981 and early 1982, the senior White House staff believed almost to a man that the administration should seek tax-law amendments to close some of the loopholes and reclaim some of the revenues Congress had grandly squandered in the orgy of tax cutting Reagan had encouraged in his first year. By talking constantly to reporters about budget deficits and revenue steps, they encouraged a public belief that Reagan was headed in that direction. The sequence of headlines in the *New York Times* tells the story:

December 21: "Reagan Aides Plan to Ask Him to Back Increases in Taxes." January 7: "Reagan's Aides Back Increases in Some Taxes." January 8: "President Studies a $30 Billion Plan for Tax Increases." January 10: "Reagan Expected to Accept Tax Rise." January 12: "Reagan Weighs New Tax-Rise Plan."

The dope stories, quoting no aides by name, did not anticipate the President's reaction correctly. When aides put the proposition to him directly, he said no—and we in the press had egg on our faces.

In retrospect, it was clear that the White House aides had used the press to try to move Reagan to accept tax hikes. When they failed, they shifted to the Republicans in Congress, encouraging them to take the lead in the euphemistic "revenue enhancement." Ultimately, Reagan bowed to the legislative initiative—and to reality—and signed a major tax-hike bill.

Obviously, the Reagan White House aides used the press to accomplish an objective, but that is not wholly bad. Their backgrounding of reporters brought into public view and public discussion a policy question that faced the President and the country. Surely, it would have been better had Reagan himself raised the issue, or responded to it during a press conference or interview, but Reagan had only three news conferences during that three-month period and was asked only five questions about budget-tax policy. He responded in his usual uninformative manner.

But if those aides had not kept White House reporters occupied and informed, there would have been a louder outcry about Reagan's lack of responsiveness. So the trade-off was that reporters got more information, albeit unattributed, and Reagan got a reprieve, in part, from being accused of closing off questioning.

This arrangement had costs both to the public and to the administration, and one compensating advantage. With the backgrounding so constant and each principal policy aide aware that he could not afford to stay out of that press game, Cannon and his colleagues were able to determine the lines of division among the President's aides on major issues—where the fault lines were developing. Dozens of such stories detailed feuds among senior staff members, between them and members of the cabinet, and some even reflected those staff members' occasional frustration with the President himself. The tone is evident in the lead on a Cannon column in the spring of 1983:

Meeting with a core group of longtime Reagan supporters in the White House last week, deputy chief of staff Michael K. Deaver revealed the inside story of why he has been able to lose 40 pounds during the last year.

"The secret of the Deaver Diet," he quipped, "is that you only eat on days when senior staff members are speaking to each other."

When Donald T. Regan replaced Baker at the start of Reagan's second term and Deaver left soon afterward to become a high-priced lobbyist, the pattern of White House news management changed significantly. It became much more a closed shop, at times a hostile one.

Regan, who ran America's biggest brokerage firm before coming to Washington, centralized authority and quickly eliminated any significant competing power centers. Fewer people participated in the policy discussions, so reporters had fewer available sources. The penalties for leaking increased, and Regan lectured on the subject frequently at senior staff meetings. Where Baker had been in communication with key reporters, though largely invisible to the public, Regan was less accessible while more visible. When Regan talked, it was often on the record, but interviews became scarcer. No one really replaced Deaver as an image manager, but Regan's deputy, Dennis Thomas, met at least once a week with people from the major news organizations to guide coverage.

The White House's fundamental attitude changed. Baker and Deaver always had tried to put their "spin" on the depiction of the President and his policies, but they also wanted reporters to understand the whys and wherefores of administration decisions. Regan operated much more on a need-to-know basis, shielding the policy considerations from discussion and concentrating on selling conclusions and rebutting critics. With the evident approval of the President, he closed many of the back channels of information and guidance that in the first term had helped reporters explain the actions of an inaccessible President. When National Security Adviser Robert C. McFarlane left after clashing with Regan, he was replaced by Admiral John M. Poindexter, whose particularly closemouthed approach to reporters weakened explanations of White House foreign policy.

Reagan himself became no more accessible as the second term began, so the flow of information diminished. With no more Reagan elections in the offing, the White House seemed well pleased with the change. Patrick Buchanan, a conservative polemicist who wrote many press-bashing speeches for Vice President Spiro Agnew, came back as White House communications director. Retaliatory policies, shunned before the 1984 election, became acceptable. Reporters deemed too often critical of the administration (like me) were excluded from briefings. And what had been a spluttering effort to shut down leaks became a high-powered offensive.

Bill Kovach, then Washington editor of the *New York Times* and now editor of the *Atlanta Journal and Constitution*, was quoted in a 1985 *Washington Post* story: "There has been a consistent and organized effort on the part of this administration to reduce the flow of government information. . . . There is no area of government where information is not harder to get for us here, harder to get now than it was when I was here in the Nixon and Ford years." Helen Thomas, the UPI White House correspondent, said in the same story, "A lot of events, we're absolutely blacked out, and if you don't like it, too bad. . . . The whole attitude is, 'We will tell you what we think you should know.'"

Anthony Marro, managing editor of *Newsday* and a former Washington correspondent, wrote in a 1985 issue of the *Columbia Journalism Review* that "while it is not clear that the Reagan administration is any more duplicitous than others, it unquestionably has gone well beyond other recent administrations in its attempts to bottle up information, to prevent public access to government officials and records, to threaten and intimidate the bureaucracy in order to dry up sources of information, and to prevent the press and the public from learning how their government is functioning." Marro was reacting to the first-term restrictions, including the decisions to bar reporters from the initial phases of the invasion of Grenada and to seek restrictions on the Freedom of Information Act, and an executive order (later suspended) to use polygraph tests on a wide range of government employees, including senior White House and cabinet officials, and to assert a lifetime censorship on the writings of former officials. But these moves proved to be only a mild prelude to the efforts to shut down leaks in the second term.

The offensive was predicted on December 1, 1984, less than a month after the election, when Undersecretary of Defense Fred C. Ikle

said, "The laws [on unauthorized disclosure of secrets] are not adequate. We have decided to fight it on all fronts." Less than three weeks
later, the *Post* reported that Secretary of Defense Caspar W. Weinberger had urged two television networks and a number of print news
organizations to withhold stories about a secret military cargo on an
about-to-be-launched space shuttle, even though reporters already
knew it was carrying a satellite designed to hover over the Soviet
Union and intercept electronic signals. Weinberger said the story was
"the height of journalistic irresponsibility" and may have given "aid
and comfort to the enemy." But the *Post* maintained that its story
contained only information already in the public record of congressional hearings—a view later confirmed by the Air Force chief of
public information. Nonetheless, the Pentagon ordered a search for the
leakers.

In November 1985, Reagan signed an order authorizing polygraph
testing of thousands of government employees dealing with "sensitive
compartmented information," a broad classification of "secret" documents. When it became clear that the lie-detector program might apply
to cabinet officers, Secretary of State George P. Shultz said publicly
that he would take such a test "once," if ordered, but then resign. "The
minute in this government I am told that I'm not trusted is the day I
leave," he said. Reagan and Shultz then met, and the White House,
suggesting that the President had never intended to put Shultz to the
test, said the issue had been resolved.

In 1986, Shultz and Weinberger each fired a mid-level political ap-
pointee—both were staunch conservatives—for leaking material to
the press critical of administration policies and actions. Central Intelligence Agency director William J. Casey stirred a much larger controversy when he said he was considering asking the Justice Department
to prosecute five news organizations for publishing information about
U.S. intelligence capabilities. Casey's pronouncements were part of an
administration effort to shut down publicity about the damage former
National Security Agency analyst Ronald W. Pelton had done in selling the Soviet Union secrets about electronic interception techniques.
Casey enlisted Poindexter and finally President Reagan in successfully
persuading the *Post* to remove some information from a story on the
subject it had planned to publish.

When Pelton came to trial, Casey and the head of the National

Security Agency publicly "cautioned" news organizations against "speculation and reporting details beyond the information actually released at trial." The White House endorsed the warning, but when news media officials said an implied threat to prosecute "speculation" violated the First Amendment, Casey said he had perhaps used the wrong word. At the same time, it was learned that the White House was considering a recommendation for a special anti-leak "strike force" of FBI agents and the expansion of polygraph testing. But both Baker and Regan reportedly objected to parts of that plan.

Few of the threatened actions were taken, but the impulse to crack down on press leaks has been a powerful one throughout the Reagan years. Lou Cannon, who has covered Reagan longer and studied him more closely than any other reporter, tried to explain the underlying attitude late in 1983. He traced Reagan's desire to limit press access back to several sources: his distaste for the attention his divorce drew from Hollywood gossip columnists in his days as an actor; his association with the conservative movement and his personal belief that most reporters opposed its ideology; and his view, as a World War II veteran, that journalists in Vietnam did not defend the American cause and viewpoint as they had in earlier wars. Still, he quoted Deaver as contending that Reagan values "honestness and openness" in his dealings with the press. Then Cannon wrote:

> The basis of these relations [with the press], however, is a premise that is shared by few members of the media. It is a view that surfaced with rare bluntness at a June 30, 1982, news conference when Reagan was asked whether the American people deserved an explanation for the resignation of Secretary of State Alexander M. Haig, Jr.
>
> "If I thought that there was something involved in this that the American people needed to know with regard to their own welfare, then I would be frank with the American people and tell them," Reagan replied.
>
> It was the answer of a President who believes that it is the responsibility of the government and not the media to determine what the American people should be told.

Despite critical stories such as Cannon's, Reagan stayed above the battle—out of reach of the press, except on rare occasions—and somehow safely removed from the policy and personal conflicts among his senior aides for almost six years. In a sense, the Reagan

arrangement revived the Eisenhower pattern, an effort to focus attention on the President as head of state rather than head of government.
Eisenhower put himself at greater risk than did Reagan by holding
frequent news conferences, but he often obfuscated in his answers.
Reagan, less skillful in the press conference format, stayed away from
it and instead exploited his strengths as a public speaker.

The system was deeply resented by many of the reporters covering
Reagan, even those with long memories. Helen Thomas, in a round-
table reprinted in Kenneth W. Thompson's book *The White House
Press on the Presidency*, remarked that

> ... each President has had his troubles with the press, going back to George
> Washington. We have a photograph of FDR in our press room which is
> inscribed to the White House reporters from their "devoted victim." "When
> the press stops abusing me, I'll know I'm in the wrong pew," said Truman.
> "Reading more and enjoying it less," said Kennedy. What LBJ said is
> unprintable. Nixon had his enemies list, and, once when the press walked
> into the Cabinet room for picture taking, Nixon looked up at the press and
> said, "It's only coincidental that we're talking about pollution when the
> press walks in." Carter always seemed to be saying, "Lord, forgive them,
> for they know not what they do." As for Reagan, well, it's like being in
> those silent movies. He thinks we should be seen and not heard.

Thomas and others on the White House beat have been justifiably
angered by the extremes to which Reagan's staff has gone to hold them
at bay. Referring to the press "pens" that are constructed at every event
to keep reporters at a distance from the President, Thomas observed
that "there would be no covering of the White House if the White
House didn't have a lot of rope. People will never know how physical
is such a job and how demeaning in many ways, because we never
cover a President except when they put a rope around us. We're cor-
ralled like cattle."

During the 1984 presidential campaign, White House reporters
complained about what they felt were excessive "security" precautions
aimed at them. In a rare effort, the White House Correspondents Association issued a report in the spring of 1985 that said there is "little
doubt that the rapidly escalating security restrictions imposed on the
White House press corps are often inconsistent and frequently used by
the White House staff as a form of press management. Secret Service

officials acknowledge that it is not unusual for them to be asked by the White House to perform press management functions that exceed their official duties." The report included a number of recommendations on credentialing, searches, and access, but the practices that were the source of complaint continued.

Democrats complained that Reagan, by avoiding exposure and exploiting state occasions, had created a "Teflon presidency." The charge disturbed many of us journalists, because it underlined our own sense of futility in dealing with Reagan. I must have written a dozen columns a year arguing that Reagan had evaded a significant share of accountability for his own administration's policies and practices, either by not bothering to inform himself of the details or by refusing to consider their implications. One column in the summer of 1986 focused on Reagan's ability to disown responsibility for the unprecedented budget deficits incurred during his years in office. It provoked a protest from a reader named Ronald Reagan, vacationing on his California ranch. In his call he was sad rather than angry, and said he was surprised I did not realize that he was not at fault—that the problem lay in Congress.

"You have no idea, Dave, how frustrating it is to work for months preparing a budget and then just have it tossed aside by those big spenders on Capitol Hill." "Well, Mr. President, I'm sure it is. But the point I was trying to make"—and I read the operative paragraph of the column—"was that you have never in five years proposed to raise enough in taxes to pay for the spending you yourself were recommending."

"Well," the President said, "certainly you know that if Congress had accepted the spending cuts I recommended, the deficits would be billions less." "Yes, Mr. President, but they would still have been far higher than you thought frightening when Democrats were in power." We waltzed each other through three or four more steps, and then he said he wanted to take a canter on his horse, and I said it was time to get back to work, and it sure had been nice . . . and once again I realized that nothing I asked or said would wean Ronald Reagan from the screenplay unreeling in his own mind—a drama in which he was fighting the Big Spenders of the Deficit Gang, all of whom were on Capitol Hill.

• • •

FOR almost six years, voters seemed ready to forgive Reagan any mistake, misstatement, or contradiction in policy. As late as October 1986, when Bob Woodward reported in the *Post* an elaborate administration "disinformation program" designed to unnerve Libyan leader Moammar Ghadafi by planting false stories in American newspapers suggesting that he was about to be the target of a coup or of an American air attack, readers and voters seemed remarkably indifferent.

Woodward cited a memo written the previous August by then head of Reagan's National Security Council staff, Vice Admiral John M. Poindexter, outlining a new strategy that "combines real and illusionary events—through a disinformation program—with the basic goal of making Ghadafi think that there is a high degree of internal opposition to him within Libya, that his key trusted aides are disloyal, that the U.S. is about to move against him militarily."

Ten days after Reagan approved the plan, a Poindexter aide talked to a *Wall Street Journal* reporter, and the result was a front-page story reporting that the Reagan administration was completing planning for "a new and larger bombing of Libya" after finding new evidence that Ghadafi had again "begun plotting terrorist attacks." The day it was published, White House spokesman Larry Speakes told reporters that the *Journal* report was "authoritative," and other publications, including the *Post*, and the major networks carried similar stories.

Reagan later denied that he had authorized the deception of American reporters but said he wanted Ghadafi to "go to bed every night wondering what we might do." Secretary of State George P. Shultz told reporters he knew of "no decision to have people go out and tell lies to the media," but added, "Frankly, I don't have any problems with a little psychological warfare against Ghadafi."

Bill Kovach of the *New York Times* said he was disturbed by the seeming double standard of the administration in sanctioning the Poindexter plan while directing the FBI to set up a special unit to track down leaks of government information. "The position they've taken is that if a journalist gets the truth through unofficial channels, it's a crime," Kovach said, "but if he accepts disinformation through official channels, that's just fine."

Bernard Kalb, a veteran television journalist who had become the chief State Department spokesman under Shultz, resigned from his job in protest, saying that "anything that hurts the credibility of America hurts America." But the controversy barely caused a ripple in the broad lagoon of public support for Reagan.

A month later, however, the Teflon finally cracked and the Reagan presidency's greatest crisis began. On the morning of the mid-term election, a Syrian-backed newspaper in Lebanon reported that the United States had secretly been shipping arms to Iran in an effort to get the Ayatollah Khomeini's help in freeing Americans held hostage in Lebanon.

No American reporter could claim credit for the scoop; it had been leaked by a faction in Iran opposed to the covert dealings with the Americans. But once the story was out, the American press was on it like a horde of hungry locusts, and this time all the administration's press management and damage-control operations, designed to keep the President at a safe distance from any controversy, failed to stem the tide of disclosures—or the consternation of the public. Reagan had renounced dealing with terrorists and had said the United States would not bargain for the release of hostages. He had declared an embargo on military shipments to Iran and had urged other nations to observe it. But now it turned out he had signed off on another Poindexter plan, allowing the arms shipments as an unofficial quid pro quo for Iranian help in gaining freedom for three of the U.S. hostages in Lebanon, whose televised pleas and family petitions had become a matter of personal anguish for Reagan.

Reagan made a televised speech seeking to explain the secret decision—taken over the opposition of Shultz and Secretary of Defense Caspar W. Weinberger, and withheld from Congress despite statutes requiring "timely" disclosure of arms sales and covert activities to appropriate legislative committees. When that failed, he scheduled one of his rare news conferences, and it was worse. The President repeatedly denied that he had sanctioned arms sales by a third party, Israel, even though several high administration officials had already told reporters that the Israelis shipped arms to Iran with our approval and with our assurance that we would replace their stocks from Pentagon supplies. Within an hour of the news conference's end, the White House issued a "clarification" refuting Reagan's version.

But worse was still to come: Attorney General Edwin Meese III began his investigation at the President's direction; he discovered that between $10 million and $30 million of the profits from the arms sales to Iran had been secretly diverted to support the forces fighting the Sandinista government in Nicaragua, ostensibly without the President's knowledge or approval and in apparent violation of other laws banning such aid from the United States.

This time Poindexter was allowed to resign; and a Marine Corps National Security Council aide, Lieutenant Colonel Oliver North, who was charged with managing the funds diversion, was fired. A special prosecutor was named to investigate the whole affair, and two select congressional committees began independent inquiries as demands rose for the firing of other high administration officials who had—or presumably should have—known of the secret operations. Reagan was plainly ambivalent about what had happened. He told Hugh Sidey of *Time* magazine that North was "a national hero," and that he had "bitter bile in my throat," not toward those in the White House who had deceived him or embarrassed him, but toward the press, which had publicized the plan while two hostages he apparently believed the Iranians were on the verge of delivering remained in captivity. It took Reagan a month to say "mistakes were made," and even then he maintained that the basic decision to sell arms to Iran had been correct. By then, his standing with the voters had taken the worst tumble in six years, and doubts were being raised about his ability to function effectively as President until the end of his term.

In my columns about the affair that November, I cited the significance of the shift in information policies from first-term chief of staff, James A. Baker III, to second-term chief of staff, Donald T. Regan:

Baker's view . . . was that no policy of any scope, significance or duration could be maintained unless it could enlist support of sensible people in Congress and be explained and defended to sensible people in the press and public.

Since his departure to the Treasury and the complete takeover of the White House staff by Donald T. Regan, a very different set of assumptions has operated. Regan's belief, as he has stated it, is that he is there to fulfill the wishes of a President who carried 49 states and who therefore has a mandate which overrides any objections that may be raised from any quarter. When the lodging of objections would block the initiation of the policy (as would have been the case had Congress known of the arms shipments to Iran), then this perverse logic suggests that secrecy is not only justified but obligatory.

Ten days later, after the disclosure of the illegal diversion of money to the anti-Sandinista forces, I wrote again about "the cult of secrecy which infected the White House atmosphere in the second term."

It was Reagan who avoided all news conferences during the re-election campaign and made them as scarce as Redskins tickets thereafter. It was Reagan who went on the warpath about "leaks," Reagan who raged about "unauthorized" disclosures of his policies, Reagan who pushed—against the protests of the George Shultzes and Jim Bakers—for widespread wiretapping of government officials.

How often do Presidents have to learn the lesson that in this society the neurotic quest for secrecy undermines effective government? How can they forget so quickly that the only sustainable policy in a nation like ours is one that can be articulated and defended in open debate? What an irony and what a tragedy to see yet another President, who has warned his associates to keep their mouths shut, come before the cameras with the pitiful complaint that those same aides did not tell him what they were up to.

The unhappy fortunes of the Reagan administration at the end of 1986 marked again the costliness of obsessive secretiveness in the White House. Yet, as with the Nixon administration, it must be observed how well and for how long the manipulation of the media worked.

FROM the Eisenhower administration to Ronald Reagan's, the White House propaganda machine has become an increasingly effective instrument of presidential will and presidential purpose. For all the ups and downs over those thirty or so years, the President and his agents have clearly been winning the battle to control the way the most important official of our government is covered and reported most of the time. The White House has learned to keep the President from scrutiny, while projecting his voice and his views far more widely than any other politician's. It has enhanced the power of the Communicator-in-

Chief as against that of other institutions of government, particularly Congress and state and local elective officials. I would not strip any of these tools from the President, for communication is central to his leadership ability, and this system of government does not function well without strong presidential leadership.

But recognizing the White House's communication power—undefined and unlimited by the written Constitution—should clearly focus our attention on how the press can provide an alternative, nonpropagandistic view of the presidency. A major part of every White House reporter's job is simply communicating what the President says and does. He and his aides expound and we report what they say. He travels and we write about where he goes. He acts on legislation, he makes appointments, he confers with other leaders. We report all of that. That is at the heart of the beat, and there is nothing either demeaning or disgraceful about serving that function.

It is, however, a confining task, and the feeling of confinement is reinforced both by the physical arrangements and the routine. In the cramped half-partitioned stalls of the West Wing press room, where the regulars have their desks and phones, any conversation or phone call can be overheard easily by a neighbor. This tends to discourage reporters from pursuing individual story leads while working in the White House press room.

But reporters are pinned down to waiting and watching for briefings, photo opportunities, appearances in the White House driveway of those who have just met with the President—the dozens of daily, often trivial but potentially newsworthy happenings. The nightly television news programs covet film of the President from that day. The television correspondents, many of whom are excellent journalists, often do nothing more than provide lead-ins to and transitions out of what the White House propagandists let the network cameramen shoot. Newspaper correspondents have a bit more freedom, but not a lot.

Clearly reporters must go beyond that "body watch" operation, if they are to be more than auxiliaries to a White House–designed public relations and communications apparatus. Political scientists Michael B. Grossman and Martha J. Kumar studied the White House press corps and noted that the "body watch" was the overriding and almost exclusive preoccupation of the television, radio, and wire service reporters assigned to the White House, as well as many of the newspaper "specials." But they also observed that the *Post*, the *Times*, and the three news weeklies have double-teamed the White House beat, so that one of their reporters (or both, if they divide the "body watch" function between them) can spend all or a part of his time developing analytic stories.

Lou Cannon and David Hoffman, the *Post* team at the White House from 1982 to the present, have made a simple and informal division of labor, with Cannon focusing primarily on diplomatic and national security decision making and Hoffman on domestic and economic matters. By sharing their information and pooling their talents, they have kept *Post* readers current on both the policy and the decision-making process in the top ranks of the Reagan administration.

Other publishers and editors have made or could make a comparable commitment, but at least 90 percent of the papers rely for White House coverage on the AP, UPI, and Reuters. Their reporters are skilled professionals. But because of the relentless time pressures in competing with each other to deliver quick, clear, and accurate summaries of news developments, they barely have a moment to write about how those White House decisions are made. They tend to report discrete actions rather than an unfolding line of policy. Because almost every White House announcement is made in the President's name, they tend to convey a sense that he is omnipotent and omniscient. The picture of a commanding Reagan, ordering this and denying that, which was drawn by the wire services differed greatly from that of an often detached, frequently passive Reagan, being pulled and tugged this way and that by the contending forces on his staff or in his administration, which was drawn by the in-depth coverage of the major papers.

The wire services sometimes pick up the newspaper stories about the White House or report the White House's reaction to them. But, for most of Reagan's tenure, we had a split-screen picture of the President—the one on radio, television, and the news wires, shaped largely by White House communications strategists, and the one in leading newspapers and news magazines, where reporting teams had the freedom to supply a substantial correction of focus.

• • •

THE second path toward improved White House coverage would be improved access to the President. Ignoring the blips of the seven presidents we have covered, the trend is toward increasing insulation of the President. From Roosevelt's 998 news conferences in a bit over twelve years to Reagan's 39 news conferences in the first six years is a quantum leap backward.

Although auxiliary contacts with the ever-growing White House press staff and policy aides are certainly valuable, none of these can substitute for access to the President himself—the opportunity to gauge his mood, his cast of mind, and to hear his own formulations of the policy choices he is making. Nothing but a direct interchange between the President and reporters provides those clues. More than seventy years ago, the institutionalized format for these exchanges became the press conference. Yet the press conference still remains an orphan, left out in the cold whenever it suits a particular President's convenience.

Why? I do not know, but I have some hunches. One relates to the chronic anarchy of the press itself, of which I will have more to say in Chapter Ten. We have been unable ever to organize our own role in the presidential press conference. The members of the White House press corps bridle at the mere suggestion of meeting to discuss press conference scheduling or formats. Not surprisingly, therefore, the press is not organized enough to lobby any President who chooses to "deinstitutionalize" the news conference.

I have thought for a long time that we could get a formal commitment from prospective Presidents for regular and frequent news conferences when they announce their candidacy. Few candidates for the presidency can afford to dismiss the value of press coverage. Each of them could be—should be—asked at his or her first news conference as a declared candidate what press conference practices he or she intends to follow as a candidate and as President.

But some students of the presidency and some journalists consider it a lost cause. In 1986, Larry Speakes said the televised news conference "has really outgrown itself," adding that it no longer satisfies the needs of the President, the press, or the public. In 1984 an editorial in the *Columbia Journalism Review* suggested a boycott of the news conferences, arguing that "in their current form, [they] serve little purpose, at least from the point of view of the journalists who dutifully flock to each session." It said the news conferences were so carefully timed and formatted by the White House that reporters had become "mere extras . . . in the repertory of presidential theater, *An Evening with the Great Communicator.*"

Hugh Sidey, who has written about Presidents for *Time* since John Kennedy, argued that the demands for more press conferences displayed "many of the media problems—arrogance, show business, confusion of the purpose of a Chief Executive, misunderstanding of leadership and the obligations of a President to the people." In a December 1984 speech under the auspices of the Freedoms Foundation and the Center for Responsible Leadership and the Media, Sidey said, "The televised press conference has become a forum in which ambitious correspondents seek confrontation with the President and attempt to show their mastery over him by leading him into mistakes or confusion. . . . The competition among literally hundreds of reporters produces a form of harassment, not news. The President, on the other hand, prepares not to inform the public but to avoid answering certain questions, to dodge the verbal booby traps and appear gracious, to say nothing while appearing knowledgeable."

Sidey and the *Columbia Journalism Review* editors think that because of the infrequency of Reagan's news conferences or his unwillingness to answer substantively the questions, we should abandon the institution for all time. That strikes me as very bad advice. I prefer the view President Eisenhower expressed back in 1958 when Edward T. Folliard, the *Post*'s great White House and political correspondent, asked him a question based on a letter to the editor the *Post* had published that day. A reader had asked, "Why should the President of this country be subjected to personal interviews with the press? Doesn't he have enough serious problems confronting him each day without being heckled by the press?"

When the laughter subsided, Eisenhower said, in part:

This is what I think he forgets: the presidency is not merely an institution. In the minds of the American public, the President is also a personality. They are interested in his thinking. They like the rather informal exchanges that come from the representatives of various types of publications from various geographical areas, and so on. At the same time, they believe that the President, who is the one official with the Vice President that is elected

by the whole country, should be able to speak to the whole country in some
way. . . .

I believe [what] they want to see is the President, probably, capable of
going through the whole range of subjects that can be fired at him and
giving to the average citizen some concept of what he is thinking about the
whole works.

So I say emphatically my view is . . . that the press conference is a very
fine latter-day American institution.

For all its weaknesses, the news conference remains the best available device for what Jim Deakin has called "two-way communication"
between the press and the President. It is an institution worth reviving,
not least for the sake of the presidency itself. Regular news conferences are great devices for letting air and light into the closed atmosphere of the White House. They help break down the "fortress
mentality" bred of secrecy which so often in recent history has led to
lawless acts being performed by men who thought they were serving
the President but forgot they were really working for the citizens of the
United States.

Almost every other elected official accepts the responsibility of
being regularly available to questioning reporters. It is odd and illogi-
cal that the President, who has greater power over public opinion than
any other politician, has been granted a unique exemption, which permits him to schedule news conferences at his own convenience.

It is also dangerous. The President exercises tremendous power
when he takes over the television and radio networks for an address
(and thereby also commandeers the headlines and front pages of the
nation's newspapers). The only check-and-balance on that power is a
President's willingness to subject himself to frequent questioning by
journalists.

It is no accident, in my view, that we have had recurrent secrecy-
caused scandals in the administrations of Presidents who refused to
meet regularly with the press. Frequent news conferences are an antidote to secrecy and an effective deterrent against official misbehavior.
They work in three ways.

First, the knowledge that he will soon be facing reporters' questions
impels a President to ask his associates to update him on what has
been going on in his administration. "I've been preoccupied with

such-and-such," he may say, "but I need to get caught up on what the rest of you have been doing. I don't want to be blind-sided." Eisenhower was, and Reagan is, a great delegator, but Eisenhower, who met the reporters twice a month, was never embarrassed as Reagan was by the Iran-and-Contras scandal at the end of 1986—a period when he was holding one news conference no more than every two months. Four times as often as Reagan, Eisenhower had strong reason to be sure he knew what schemes his aides were hatching.

Second, news conferences enable a President to learn what is going on outside his view. The reporters' questions often short-circuit the official channels, layers of bureaucracy, and tiers of staff advisers that insulate a President from the real world. In Eisenhower's time, it was quite common for an official in some agency or a member of Congress to call a reporter and say: "We're getting odd signals from the White House on such-and-such. We're not sure if that's really Eisenhower's policy or not. If you have a chance tomorrow, would you ask him if he really wants . . . ?" The question would be asked, and not infrequently Eisenhower's statement would be different from what his aides had previously communicated. Or he would say, "I'm not up on that situation. Let me look into it, and I'll have an answer for you next week." In either case, the President was made aware of things he would not have learned otherwise.

Finally, when a President gets into trouble, as inevitably happens, news conferences offer him a quick way out. Eisenhower ended the flap over the Soviets' downing of a U-2 with a news conference. John Kennedy used the same forum to take responsibility for the fiasco at the Bay of Pigs, and found that his ratings soared. As I noted in Chapter Three, Jimmy Carter put the Billygate story to rest with an hour-long news conference. All of them had stayed sharp by meeting frequently with reporters. By contrast, Richard Nixon increasingly hid from the press as the Watergate story unfolded, and his rare news conferences became more and more contentious. The lesson, it seems to me, is obvious. Revival of the presidential news conference can be a boon, not only to the press and public, but to future Presidents.

BACK in 1980, the White Burkett Miller Center of Public Affairs at the University of Virginia showed how it could be done. The panel, headed by former Governor Linwood Holton of Virginia and former NBC White House correspondent Ray Scherer, suggested that the President hold a regular monthly news conference on live television and regular weekly, more informal meetings with White House reporters. They suggested that parts of these informal sessions might be made available for later use on radio or television, but that parts be kept very casual, so the President could talk, without direct quotation, about the decisions he faces and thereby "educate the public indirectly." The main idea, the commission said, is to remove the element of "spectacle" from the news conference and restore more of its original informational function. That report is the right starting point for an effort to revive the news conference.

Most recent Presidents have met reporters, individually or in small groups, without cameras present. But since John Kennedy started the live television news conference, the idea has grown that every one must be live. Clearly this undeclared rule tends to reduce the frequency of news conferences and probably the utility of each individual one. It is a big deal when the President makes a live television appearance, in any format, and it takes a lot of time for him and his aides to prepare for such an appearance. Reagan spent the better part of a day in briefings and rehearsals for each of his prime-time TV news conferences. Taking some of the news conferences off live television would reduce the work and the risk for the President.

It might also reduce the number of reporters who jam into those sessions, hoping by chance to be called on for a question and to be seen on TV. At Reagan's press conferences in the first term the average number of questions was twenty-four; the average number of reporters in attendance, 160. That's absurd. All those hangers-on get in the way of the reporters regularly assigned to cover the President. If those White House regulars are not competent to question the President on the major items on the current news agenda, they ought to be fired or removed from the beat; if they are competent—as they, in fact, are—those of us not assigned to the White House ought to stay the hell out of their way when the President has a news conference.

The smaller the ratio between the number of questioners and the number of questions, the more productive the questioning will be. There can be follow-ups, and follow-ups to the follow-ups. A subject can be pursued until the President's position is as clear as he is prepared to make it.

THE next point may seem paradoxical. While I have been arguing that the press needs more direct access to the President, in some cases we need to back off from the President a certain distance.

There is altogether too much coverage today of the trivial and non-substantive aspects of the President's life. Both television and newspapers—but probably TV more than we—make it too easy for the White House news managers to manipulate us into assuming that whatever the President does is news. Deaver understood this weakness and exploited it constantly on Reagan's behalf. As Lou Cannon reported, at the end of a 1983 Reagan trip to Korea, which featured shots of the President eating hamburgers in a mess hall and attending an open-air chaplain's service, the First Lady was brought forward:

> When the President finally gave in to weariness on the way home, the feature role was taken over by Nancy Reagan, who cuddled two young South Korean children whom the Reagans brought back with them to the United States for heart surgery.
> The videotape shot by a pool NBC camera crew of Mrs. Reagan and the two children . . . was taken off Air Force One at Elmendorf Air Force Base in Anchorage on the return flight and given to the television networks for use on their Monday morning shows. All three of them used the tape.

In the 1980s, the three major networks each assigned four correspondents full-time to the White House, two to Congress, and one to the Supreme Court. In a two-week period in June 1985, the three network evening news shows had eleven stories by White House correspondents, five by congressional correspondents, and three by the Supreme Court reporters. That disparity does not reflect the relative importance of the three institutions; it reflects the priorities that television has attached to the presidency and the skill Presidents have shown in grabbing TV time.

The phenomenon was analyzed in the 1973 Twentieth Century Fund report, *Presidential Television*, written by Newton N. Minow, a former chairman of the Federal Communications Commission, author and former ambassador John Bartlow Martin, and communications lawyer Lee M. Mitchell. They contended that the delicate but vital system of checks and balances established by the Constitution had been tilted in the President's favor by television, which gives the President—as it does no other political leader—free access to massive prime-time audiences on all networks at once. I wrote in an October 1973 column about the report that

> if anything were needed to underscore the report's main point—that the country's prime medium of communication has been converted into a President's personal tool—Mr. Nixon's actions [the previous week] did it.
>
> He decided on Tuesday that he wanted to address the American people on Wednesday evening, and all three networks canceled their programming to accommodate him. He decided on Wednesday that he preferred to hold a televised press conference on Thursday evening, and, once again the eyes and ears of the nation—the television audience—were ready for him. When the Mideast crisis caused the President to change his mind again, the networks adjusted their schedules and awaited the next summons from the Oval Office. It came Friday and once more, the networks cleared their schedules for the President.
>
> This is power. And the burden of the Twentieth Century Fund report ... is that television's unique availability to a President may well be distorting the constitutional system of checks and balances.

The authors of this study proposed a number of steps to improve the access to television for other branches of government and for the opposition political party. But there is hardly a way for any of them to catch up to the President on television.

The President functions both as chief of state and head of government. He can get coverage easily and noncontroversially, lighting the national Christmas tree or laying a wreath at the tomb of the unknown soldier. Those pictures are fine, but we need to focus our coverage on the President as head of government and to treat him similarly to the way we deal with other politicians and officeholders. First, the President should be required to compete for our attention in the way that other politicians do—by making news.

That is no unreasonable burden, for the President is frequently at the very center of major events. But often he gets coverage on the cheap. In 1983 Reagan went on an "education" campaign for several weeks, after a high-level commission had issued a report questioning the quality of American schools. From the outset, Reagan said the states had the primary responsibility for raising the standards of education and supplying the needed money. Then he went around the country visiting schools repeating his exhortations.

The President's "education offensive" got massive coverage. The *Post* carried fifteen stories, totaling 438 column-inches during the nine weeks at the height of his campaign. Almost without exception, the network news shows carried shots of the President at every stop. By contrast, the state governments which were supposed to take the lead in meeting this challenge got short shrift. The *Post* had two stories during this span on state initiatives and four more reflecting the views of other Washington politicians who were arguing for a larger federal response than the President recommended. The upshot of this pattern of coverage—and the exaltation of the presidency that it reflects— was that Reagan was credited with responding to the education issue, while the work was done by others.

From Hagerty's time onward, White House press secretaries have operated on the premise that Presidents have preemptive rights to any story about any administration decision that they want to appropriate for themselves. The press and television almost always go along, even if we know the work has been done elsewhere. The same pattern occurs—as we will see in the next chapter—when Presidents grab credit from Congress for a complex and exacting legislative process by simply holding a bill-signing ceremony. We and our readers would be well served if editors reminded themselves that the President is part of the executive branch, that the executive branch is one third of the federal government, and that the federal government is the top layer of a multilayered federal system.

If we reported the President as one player—an important player, but only one—we might be more prepared to say, "There is no White House story today."

IN my make-believe world, we might do one other thing: we might draw a distinction between the President's public responsibilities and activities and his private life and allow him room to be something of a normal human being. Back in 1973 Daniel J. Evans, the governor of Washington (and now a senator), suggested in a speech at the National Press Club that both the press and the public interest would be served by a simple trade-off: the President would hold a press conference at least once a week (as Evans had done as governor) "in exchange for the privilege of going abroad in the land with relative freedom and flexibility."

"In my view," he said, "there is nothing more essential than that the President of the United States be given the opportunity to see and be seen—personally and informally—by the people. . . . The modern-day tragedy of the presidency is that he is quite literally the prisoner of Pennsylvania Avenue."

I wrote a column endorsing Evans's views and heard from Helen Thomas at UPI, who said that the press should never concede any ground to the White House in the battle for access to the President. She argued forcibly that a President is a President twenty-four hours a day, that at any moment he can do something of importance or (realistically, in this era of violence and terrorism) something of importance may happen to him. Her view is that the press should be there, whenever possible, to report what happens.

That is certainly a view I can respect—but not one I can endorse. First of all, total coverage is impossible. Almost all of the President's most important meetings, utterances, and actions take place outside the purview of the press—in the Oval Office or some other part of the secured perimeter where he does his work. Second, the press cannot keep the President under surveillance even when he leaves the White House. Several times Jimmy Carter slipped away from Camp David to go fishing or jogging. So far as I can judge, no harm resulted to the press or the Republic.

On balance, it seems to me that Evans's trade-off is a sensible one. What is true of Presidents applies even more to the members of their families. Nothing is more distasteful or more distracting than the preoccupation with the mundane doings of the First Family. But every recent President has been subjected to unwanted and unnecessary publicity about his relationships with various siblings, children, and even grandchildren. Those unfortunates, whose only crime lies in having an ambitious and politically successful relative, have lost their own privacy. We learn all about their marriages, their romances, their drinking problems, and their job searches. There is no need for this kind of junk journalism, and no excuse for it. I proposed a remedy in a column written from Plains, Georgia, after the 1976 election. After recalling the chilly reception some of my colleagues gave my earlier plea that the Fords be allowed some privacy for their family life, I said:

> Nonetheless, futile as it may be, there is an impulse here to utter once more a plea that some aspects of the Carters' lives might best be left unreported.
>
> It is going to be difficult—to put it mildly—to shepherd a bright, precocious daughter through her teenage years in the atmosphere of the White House. Amy Carter's happiness is of no greater concern to Carter's constituents than that of any other nine-year-old in the land. But she is of prime importance to the Carters, and a degree of privacy for her and her friends is not an unreasonable request.
>
> As for beer-drinking Billy and his pals at the gas station—well, they can probably take care of themselves.
>
> But for every feature story on Billy, the newspaper or network responsible should be required to run a full-scale analysis of zero-base budgeting and the report of Carter's task force on government reorganization.
>
> That would break them of the habit.

But actually there is a better solution at hand, no farther away than Canada. I was in Canada in 1963 for their national election. The last Liberal Party rally of the campaign was held on a Friday night, and the next morning, Liberal leader Lester Pearson, who was favored in all the polls to become Prime Minister, went off with his wife to their cabin. The reporters made their own travel arrangements to return to Ottawa and await the returns.

At first, I could not believe their nonchalance. I remembered the uproar when Richard Nixon slipped out of Los Angeles for a few hours on Election Day in 1960 and drove down to Tijuana, Mexico, to ease the tension of waiting. "Do you mean you're not going to cover Pearson over the weekend?" I asked. "We have no interest in what he does at the cabin," I was told by a Canadian colleague. "We'll see him when he comes back to Ottawa for the returns." What a reasonable attitude, I thought. What a sensible view of the press's responsibility. I thought about it again when I was on a stakeout of Jimmy Carter's home in Plains, poised to intercept him if he should bolt for a favorite fishing hole or take a stroll through the two-block downtown.

Catching up to the Canadians isn't everything in improving our coverage of the presidency. But it's a start.

CHAPTER SIX
The View from Capitol Hill

A PUZZLE for you: though the Congress offers the best vantage point from which to cover Washington and national politics, the legislative branch is in most respects the worst-reported part of our government. Decode that paradox, and you can draw important lessons about the strengths and weaknesses of political journalism.

To understand why Congress serves reporters so well, you have to understand something about the geography of the beat. Directly off the floor of the House of Representatives, separated by saloon-type swinging doors, is the Speaker's Lobby—a long corridor with portraits of former Speakers on the wall and a lounge library with comfortable chairs, newspapers from across the country, and AP and UPI news tickers.

Signs outside the doors at each end of the Speaker's Lobby announce No Visitors, and House doormen cast a fishy eye at strangers. But the Speaker's Lobby is open, not just to members of the House, but to any of the more than four thousand reporters and photographers accredited to the congressional press, periodical, and radio-television galleries. (Probably not more than one twentieth that number work on Capitol Hill most days, but the congressional press pass is the basic credential in town.)

The Senate is a bit more formal. Its rules require reporters to wait in an ornate antechamber called the President's Room, while Senate doormen inform a senator that such-and-such a reporter would like to speak to him. The Speaker's Lobby, the President's Room, the restaurants, and the corridors of the Capitol are the setting for the exchange of information, judgments, and gossip between legislators and reporters, making Congress the ideal vantage point to keep tabs on the government and national politics.

Because Congress oversees the activities and policies of the executive branch agencies, on almost any given day of the nine months or more it is in session scores of hearings take place in committees charged with writing laws, providing funds, and supervising government activities. No reporter—or news bureau, for that matter—can monitor everything. But hints of lively hearings spread quickly through the Capitol's corridors. Committee press aides alert reporters by press releases and phone calls. If you miss the hearing, the committee will provide the prepared statements of the morning's witnesses or a colleague will fill you in. Within twenty-four hours, a stenographic transcript of the hearing is ready, and committee aides are ready to point out the pertinent passages.

Many reporters find that Congress is the best place to cover the executive branch as well, because the pipelines from Congress into the executive agencies are so useful and the flow of information from "downtown" to Capitol Hill so extensive. To a large extent, the reputations of Presidents and their top political appointees—cabinet members, agency heads, etc.—are made or broken on Capitol Hill. Presidents and their press secretaries seldom understand this. I remember observing to one of President Carter's senior aides, in the fourth year of his term, that the earliest and most serious blow to Carter's credibility as President came from the way Democrats in Congress had described to reporters their early disillusionment with the President.

The assistant seemed surprised. But many more reporters work in the congressional press galleries than in the White House press room. Presidential aides may be guarded in their comments about their boss and loyally defend him, but the members of Congress have no such inhibitions. Their testimony is more plentiful, more uninhibited, and more credible than White House staff members'—and tends far more to define the press image of the President.

This is truer still of those who run the executive departments and agencies. They are called upon incessantly as witnesses in congressional hearings which test their knowledge, skills, and toughness more than the interviews and press conferences they conduct in their own buildings. Committee members and reporters form lasting impressions of cabinet and subcabinet officials. The cabinet member who has to have every response whispered into his ear by an aide, who stumbles or contradicts himself, who antagonizes rather than persuades the members of Congress, is presumed also to be inept in running his department or influencing administration policy. The official who handles his congressional relations and testimony well is immediately judged a power on the inside.

Another reason Congress offers an excellent perch to cover the workings of the government is the back channel of communication from the departments and agencies to congressmen and their staffs. As many students of government have pointed out—and as Presidents learn—there is a real contest of loyalties within the senior career bureaucracy. Career officials have a clear obligation to respond to the policy initiatives of their political supervisors, starting with the general counsels and assistant secretaries and running right up to the President. They also have legal and practical reasons to heed the commands of the lawmakers on Capitol Hill, who write the statutes under which they operate, provide or reduce the funds for their programs, and monitor their performance. To some of the senior bureaucrats, their bosses—the assistant secretaries—are short-timers. Their average tenure is less than two years. By contrast, the chairmen of their legislative and appropriations subcommittees may be around for a long time, and the chiefs of staff of the subcommittees even longer.

The bureaucrats tend to resolve this conflict by giving their allegiance to their executive superiors and their information to their old pals on Capitol Hill. The bureaucrat can say, "Yes, sir," when an assistant secretary directs him to do something dumb, and then make certain that the memorandum he had written protesting the order falls into the hands of the right congressman or staff member. It happens every day. And the congressman or staff member, instead of confronting the assistant secretary, often leaks the memorandum to a Capitol Hill reporter and, when the story is published, declares solemnly that the issue deserves investigation. Capitol Hill reporters have an almost guaranteed supply of scoops, and of the best kind—the ones that are placed in our hands without a lot of effort.

As former House Speaker Thomas P. (Tip) O'Neill, Jr., says, all politics is local, and Congress—particularly the House—is the best listening post in Washington. The 535 senators and representatives must keep on top of any issues, personalities, or problems that command attention in their constituency. Multiply the members by the number of staff in charge of dealing with the press, the party, and the constituencies back home, and you have a formidable army of sources. You can fill your notebook with current political gossip on any afternoon, just by hanging out in the Speaker's Lobby or by walking the corridors of one of the Senate office buildings.

The Congress, after a brief hiatus, is once again an important force in presidential nominating politics as well. For much of the 1970s, the Congress played a diminishing role in choosing the parties' presidential candidates. As the Democrats and (to a lesser extent) the Republicans adopted more open delegate-selection systems, the proportion of delegates drawn from the Congress dwindled. In 1972 Tip O'Neill, then House Majority Leader, complained that he was beaten in his own Cambridge, Massachusetts, district by "the cast of *Hair*"—his description of the young George McGovern delegates. In 1980, only forty-five senators and representatives were delegates to the Democratic convention. But in 1984, the Democrats reenfranchised their congressional contingent. The first presidential primary of 1984 was held on Capitol Hill, when House and Senate Democrats caucused to select the 207 members who would be delegates to the San Francisco convention. Six of the eight candidates for the presidential nomination had served or were serving in Congress. So were three of the four members of the Republican and Democratic tickets. Once again, it was the congressional reporters who knew them best.

For all these reasons, Congress serves the reporter of government and politics wonderfully well. And I have not even mentioned the main reason: the legislative process itself. There is no better arena to test the forces operating in our politics, nor any process more vital to the direction of our government, than the annual congressional battle over the budget and appropriations. All of the central issues of recent years—defense, disarmament, civil rights, the environment—have been fought out and decided on the floor of the House and the Senate, often with dramatic debates and suspenseful roll calls. This is the grist of great newspaper copy, and of good television, too, now that both the House and Senate allow the cameras inside.

WITH all that Congress provides for journalists, it is rank ingratitude that we do not do well by Congress. Through virtually all of the last decade, Congress has rated lower in public approval ratings than the President, the churches, the military, the Supreme Court, banks, public schools, and—most years—even behind the press. It regularly beats out only big business, television, and organized labor.

One of the few times Congress rose in public standing was the Watergate period, when, on television, two of its committees exposed the character and chicanery of the President's aides and ultimately of Richard Nixon himself. First, a special Senate investigating committee under Senator Sam Ervin of North Carolina laid out the doings in the White House and gave a rapt television audience its first view of the Nixon ring.

When it became clear that the evidence was serious enough to invoke the little-known and little-used constitutional mechanism for considering impeachment of a President, the focus shifted to the House Judiciary Committee. In the spring and summer of 1974, the House for the first time enjoyed the full spotlight of television, press, and public attention. Day after day the cameras showed the thirty-eight men and women of the Judiciary Committee, sifting the evidence, weighing their options, and finally voting to bring formal charges against the President of the United States. Nixon's resignation cut short the drama before the full House could vote on the impeachment or the Senate could conduct a trial.

In the weeks of the Judiciary Committee hearings, the public came to know the men and women on that committee as no other House members had ever been known. The three commercial networks alternated in providing live coverage of the committee deliberations, which often ran from early in the morning until late in the evening. Public television taped the daytime proceedings and ran them again at night, with much of America staying up until two or three in the morning to see what they had missed.

The impression was powerful and positive. William Greider wrote in the *Post* that "for the House of Representatives, an assembly where personal glamor is scorned, the impeachment hearings provided an institutional ego trip. For the American public, it was a grand civics lesson in how things work at the other end of Pennsylvania Avenue." Greider quoted Representative Lawrence J. Hogan of Maryland, one of the committee Republicans: "Our colleagues are saying that we have enhanced the prestige of the House. . . ."

But Watergate was an exception. It was one of the few times that Congress as an institution benefited from the coverage it received on television and in the press. Generally, in the battle for influence, Congress loses, although individual members may profit from the way they are covered.

Some of the most thoughtful legislators of our time have been terribly critical of the coverage Congress receives. In 1975 Democratic Senator J. William Fulbright of Arkansas, then chairman of the Senate Foreign Relations Committee, wrote in the *Columbia Journalism Review* that "the national press would do well to reconsider its priorities. It has excelled in exposing . . . the high crimes and peccadilloes of persons in high places. But it has fallen short—far short—in its higher responsibility of public education." Fulbright observed, "A bombastic accusation, a groundless, irresponsible prediction, or, best of all, a 'leak,' will usually gain a Congressman or a Senator his heart's content of publicity; a reasoned discourse, more often than not, is destined for entombment in the Congressional Record."

Decrying "cheap-shot" stories about Congress, Representative David Obey, a Democrat of Wisconsin and one of the most thoughtful members of Congress, said in a 1977 speech, "It has become far easier for working reporters to get the stories aired or printed if they are associated with private scandal than it is if they are about serious legislative struggles. . . ."

Obey's and Fulbright's complaints are mostly justified. They would be echoed by many members of Congress, but most do not speak out publicly because they see no advantage in picking a quarrel with the press and television. Yet individually, most members of Congress do very well under the present system, as do the reporters who cover them. The members tend to have extremely high standing in their states and districts—and comfortingly high success ratios in getting reelected. From 1976 through 1986, 70 percent of the senators and 93 percent of the representatives seeking reelection won their races.

This high rate of reelection serves reporters too, because the relationships they develop with those returning representatives and senators produce a gratifying flow of stories and news tips. Capitol Hill is really a small world within the larger world of Washington government, in which close and cliquish relationships grow up between members of Congress, their staff aides, and reporters. In the time I have spent on Capitol Hill, I have seen the reporters' attitude toward Congress shift from near adulation to near cynicism. It has come to rest, for the time, closer to a healthy medium of care and concern. But throughout, the intimacy of the personal relationships—the cliquishness—has been constant.

One relationship I had about two decades ago was with a young congressman from Illinois named Donald Rumsfeld, later chief of the White House staff and Secretary of Defense in the Ford administration. I cannot recall how we met, but by 1968—his sixth year in the House—we knew each other well enough that he felt free to call me and say, "Next time you're up on the Hill, I wish you'd stop by my office. There's something I want to talk to you about."

When I went in to see Rumsfeld, he had two piles of newspaper clippings on a table. In the very deep pile were stories about the shenanigans of Representative Adam Clayton Powell, Jr., the gaudy Harlem preacher-congressman who was chairman of the Education and Labor Committee. Powell's vacations, his expense accounts, and his habit of filling committee staff jobs with comely young ladies who often turned up as traveling companions on his overseas trips had been extensively covered. The other pile consisted of two or three brief stories about the effort Rumsfeld and a handful of other Republican backbenchers were making to reform the rules of the House.

Rumsfeld, in his earnest manner, interrupted my inspection of the two sets of clips. "Now, you're a newspaperman," he said. "I want you to tell me why Powell is worth this much attention and our effort is worth this."

"You're not as sexy as he is," I replied.

Rumsfeld is not a man to be diverted with a weak joke. "No," he said, "I really want to know why the antics of one damned committee chairman are worth this much press"—and he grabbed the thick pile of Powell clippings—"and our effort to change the system that allows Adam Powell and a lot of others you don't write about to abuse power in ways that are just as bad, why that effort doesn't get any coverage."

Rumsfeld was right that the abuses for which Powell was publicized might be a bit more neon-lit than others, but that many other chairmen were probably doing more damage to the country's interests than was Powell with his playboy life. The trouble was that Rumsfeld and the others were premature revolutionaries. They were part of a Republican minority trying to give the procedural reform issue visibility in the press in order to pressure the Democrats to face up to the systemic problem. But the Democrats were not about to take on a big fight with some of their own committee chairmen, when the White House was trying to get those chairmen to cooperate in passing the President's program.

As a practical matter, nothing was going to come of Rumsfeld's crusade, so reporters didn't write about it. He knew that as well as I did, and it was not really an explanation he wanted from me anyway.

So I said something like, "Congressman, I can't answer your question. But I get your point. I'll write a column about what you're trying to do." I did so, pointing out that the reforms they were seeking were hardly radical: keeping a record of how people voted in committee, limiting the blank-proxy power of the chairman, and allowing the minority party members of each committee to hire two professional staff people and one clerk of their own—without the chairman having veto power over their choices. I quoted Rumsfeld: "Congressional reform is an issue without a constituency," and added my observation that "Even the press, which ought to understand the importance of procedural reforms, seems uninterested."

Afterward, I came to realize that there was another reason the Rumsfeld effort—and most other such reform measures—got short shrift in the press. Rumsfeld was not just bucking our skepticism about the prospects for his reform's success. He was bucking our habit of mind.

Most of us are a lot more comfortable thinking about and writing about individuals than about institutions. "Names make news" is almost the first commandment of journalism, and the gaudier the individual, the better. The Reverend Dr. Adam Clayton Powell, Jr., pastor of the Abyssinian Baptist Church and chairman of the House Committee on Education and Labor ("Just a humble country preacher," he used to call himself, puffing on his big cigar), basking with some beauty on Bimini, while Presidents waited impatiently for him to return their calls and set the price for clearing the Aid to Education bill for floor consideration—that was a story! Rumsfeld and his colleagues' detailed analyses of how the shortchanging of the Republican minority on committee staff assignments diminished their ability to contribute usefully to the legislative process put you to sleep before you got to the typewriter.

A lot of reporters are antiorganization. We have avoided managerial responsibilities and we think and care little about organizational matters. But our aversion to the institutional exposé also reflects the effects of clique journalism, which may be more prevalent on Capitol Hill than in any other Washington precinct. If you expose individual shenanigans, the result is the embarrassment and maybe the removal of that individual. But if you document the failings of an institution, you risk fundamentally changing it. Institutional reform, like that Rumsfeld was advocating, can lead to real power shifts, which can disturb the comfortable relationships reporters have built up with the people in power. They can upset the status quo.

In the mid-1970s, long-building internal pressures, helped along by an influx of reform-minded young members, finally caused the House to curb the arbitrary power of its committee chairmen. Those of us who had covered Congress in the two decades before the reforms of the 1970s knew committee chairmen whose senility, venality, reactionary politics, or simple contrariness had prompted them to pit their will against that of a majority, blocking legislation. These incidents were reported, of course, and often criticized in columns and editorials. But the Capitol Hill reporters tended to accept them as inevitable—a part of Congress's internal system of checks and balances.

An important part of that system was the House Rules Committee. Before a bill could go from a legislative committee to the floor of the House, it had to have a "rule." The rule would set the terms of debate —its length, the amendments that would be in order, the people who would control the time. Although partly custodial, it was fundamentally a political function—deciding what got considered, and when, and under what conditions.

The chairman of the House Rules Committee in those days was "Judge" Howard W. Smith of Virginia, a loyal member of the conservative Democratic Byrd organization, who came to Congress in 1931, when Herbert Hoover was President, and was still there when Lyndon B. Johnson came to office. When a bill that Smith did not like—a civil rights bill or some new social program—reached the Rules Committee, he would sometimes just put it in his pocket and forget about it. If the pressure was too great, he might slip out to his Virginia farm and become unavailable for a time to the press or the Speaker or the President.

Judge Smith was not always so inaccessible, however. He lived in Alexandria, Virginia, where he was chairman of the board of a local bank. As it happened, the head of the Associated Press staff for the House, William F. Arbogast, also lived in Alexandria. Arbogast usually drove Judge Smith to the Capitol each morning. The two men were similar in temperament and political outlook, though Arbogast was some years younger. Both men took a dim view of most of the changes on the horizon.

To some of us in the House press gallery—especially the younger reporters—the commuting arrangement was a matter of envy. By the time Arbogast had deposited Judge Smith at the Capitol, he had a remarkably good idea of what the House would and would not do that day or that week. Arbogast would come up to the third floor and write with considerable confidence for the AP's many clients. And Judge Smith would repair to his office, just across the corridor, assured that the view of the House most Americans would get from their newspapers and radio stations that day was one he liked.

In this cozy, cliquish environment, it was not surprising that the press showed little sympathy for Rumsfeld and company's quixotic crusade to overthrow the powers of the tyrannical committee chairmen. Arbogast may have had a unique advantage, but the other senior reporters in the gallery—most of whom had been in their jobs far longer than most of the members of the House—also had their own special access and sources. A few were occasionally invited to sit with Speaker Sam Rayburn at the late-afternoon "Board of Education" meetings, where the leadership strategy was discussed. Others had home-state ties or long-standing friendships with the majority leader or the Appropriations or Ways and Means Committee chairman.

The delightful thing about this system was that reporters had no need to learn the names or faces of most of the members of the House, let alone worry about what they might have in mind to do. It was a lovely arrangement for the insiders in both the press and the House.

In the Senate, a similar clubbiness and sense of intimacy linked the elders and powers of that body (the two terms being then interchangeable) with the elite of the Senate press corps. Senate reporters, like senators themselves, looked down on the House of Representatives and disdained even to cross the Capitol to visit it. There is a story, perhaps apocryphal, that on the day in 1954 when Puerto Rican terrorists shot up the House, wounding five of its members, a distinguished Senate correspondent, ordered to help out on the coverage, headed out of the Senate press gallery—and promptly got lost.

When I came to Washington in the mid-1950s, the seniority system in the Senate press gallery was almost as rigid as the Senate's. A few minutes before each day's session began, the majority leader, Lyndon B. Johnson, and the minority leader, Everett McKinley Dirksen, held separate press conferences at their desks on the Senate floor. Reporters gathered around them in a semicircle, the senior correspondents in the inner ring, lesser ones to the back. Johnson and Dirksen were two of the great orators of their times, with lungs and throats that could fill an auditorium without a microphone. But at these press conferences, neither raised his voice above the level of the boudoir; it was all whispered intimacies to familiar friends in the front row. The rest of us learned what our elders considered proper to relay to us later.

ONE of the front-row journalists was the gentleman from the *New York Times,* William S. White, who published a much-praised book in 1957, *Citadel: The Story of the U.S. Senate.* There is no better way to recapture what was then the relationship between the press and the Congress than to quote a bit from the book written by the distinguished-looking Texan whose instincts were as conservative as those of most of the men he covered. White venerated the Senate, calling it "the one touch of authentic genius in the American political system . . . a place upon whose vitality and honor will at length rest the whole issue of the kind of society that we are to maintain." He was in love with its intimacy, its eccentricity, its snobbishness, and most of all, its

Southernness. The Senate is, he wrote happily, "the only place in the country where the South did not lose the war."

Elitism dominated the relationship between the Senate and the press, as White saw it. "To it [the Senate], the most influential political writers are almost never those with the greatest circulations, but are rather the truly intellectual journalists of Washington." White offered, as examples, Arthur Krock of the *New York Times* and Walter Lippmann of the *New York Herald Tribune,* who "like Krock, makes not the slightest attempt to converse with vast numbers, though his articles appear in many papers."

"Television . . . is still not really respected in the Senate," White wrote. "For television offers only one-dimensional exposition to the Senator who appears upon it; it has no ideas to put into interplay with his ideas. And then of course it should not be forgotten that television is new; the Senate recognizes its existence, of course, but suspects its *bona fides.*"

In 1972, just fifteen years later, another *New York Times* correspondent, Warren Weaver, Jr., published another book on Congress. The contrast in tone and approach was as dramatic as the difference in their titles. Weaver called his book *Both Your Houses: The Truth About Congress.* The truth, as Weaver saw it, was that "the Capitol is a hall of illusions, peopled by the myths that the legislative branch remains proudly coequal, that Congress continues to serve the nation well, that the old ways are sufficient to the tasks of the new day. None of this is true."

As much as White venerated the Senate, Weaver debunked it—including its moral and sexual hypocrisy. "Senators like to pretend they're never too old," he wrote. "Carl Hayden of Arizona, who was ninety-one when he finally retired, used to shuffle slowly into the Senate each morning, a tall, gaunt figure, barely in motion. Senator Thomas Kuchel of California, the Republican whip, would regularly call over to him, 'Hey, Don Carlos, did you get laid last night?' Hayden would reply with a ponderous wink, so slow and comprehensive that observers swore it put him out of breath for a moment."

How does one explain this remarkable change in tone? For one thing, the Congress itself had changed dramatically. In 1958, a year after *Citadel* appeared, the Senate received an unusually large infusion of new members, eighteen of them. All but three were Democrats, and all but two of the Democrats came from non-Southern states. The Southernness of the Senate began to fade; within three years, no Southerner was left in the Senate Democratic leadership.

Disappearing, too, was the insularity, the clubbiness, the elitism of the Senate that White described. The newcomers beginning with the class of 1958 were increasingly independent political entrepreneurs, schooled and bred in television techniques, impatient to have the public exposure and prominence which White's ideal senators shunned as common.

The same pattern has developed a bit more slowly in the House. The great waves of change in the membership came in the mid-sixties and the mid-seventies, decimating the older generation and reducing the seniority structure to its flattest profile in decades. The newcomers in the House, like their Senate counterparts, were oriented to the larger political world, impatient with the seniority system and other barriers to full participation, and skillful and practiced in using television to advance their own careers and issues.

The House began permitting television coverage on its floor proceedings in 1979, largely as a convenience to its members, who could monitor what was happening on the floor while remaining in their offices to handle appointments, phone calls, or correspondence. A cable television service, which immediately offered the House proceedings to cable systems around the country, found increasing interest. By 1985, the C-SPAN coverage of the House was available on cable systems serving 23 million persons, and the average watcher was spending an extraordinary twelve hours a month with the channel. House members for the first time were developing something of a celebrity status outside their own districts, and envious senators voted in 1986 to bring in the cameras and show themselves on television as well.

VOTERS today can get a TV picture of their individual congressmen and senators, but they rarely have such a clear view of Congress as an institution. It is hard for an institution to speak with a single voice or present a single view. The problem is compounded when three different pictures are drawn: the one a few newspapers offer, the one the wire services transmit, and the one that television presents.

Compared to their colleagues at the White House, reporters working on Capitol Hill have far more choices of how to operate and what to do every day. That makes the congressional beat much more fun, but it also gives it burdens that the White House beat does not have.

One of them is learning the players. With the spread of power from a handful of senior leaders and committee chairmen, it takes reporters time to learn the names, skills, and limitations of a fair proportion of the 535 lawmakers and the 14,000 staff members (who are often as important or more important to the work of Congress and as sources of news). And because the cast of characters is changed somewhat by each election, the learning process is constant.

Even those with years of experience and sharp instincts can have their hands full. In one way, reporting Congress is ridiculously easy; one is saturated with information. Any place with almost fifteen thousand news sources can't be too secretive. But Congress is not one story; it is *Grand Hotel,* in which plots and dramas of some scope and significance are hatched continually behind almost each door, or—to change the metaphor—it's a five-hundred-ring circus. The protracted battles over the annual budget resolutions consume both members and reporters. But there are dozens of sideshows, and if you watch the jockeying of the cotton and the wheat interests in the markup of the agriculture price support bill, you may miss the struggle by a particularly shrewd border-state congressman to save a particularly suspect pork-barrel project from extinction in the Public Works Committee. If you spend the morning watching that, you may miss an important debate on Central American policy in the Foreign Relations Committee.

Those newspapers that have allowed good reporters to settle in on Capitol Hill long enough to build a network of sources provide their readers with some extraordinarily good coverage of the legislative branch. In the past decade, those papers have included the *Wall Street Journal,* the *Baltimore Sun,* the *Boston Globe,* the *Chicago Tribune,* the *Los Angeles Times,* the *New York Times,* and the *Washington Post.* All of them have gone beyond reporting specific bills and have dealt with Congress as an institution of real importance.

Readers of these papers were alerted early, for example, to the emergence of a bloc of conservative Southern Democrats as the swing group in the House in 1981 and to the emergence of a comparable group of moderate Republican senators as the swing group in that chamber in 1983. Those readers were not surprised that Representative Phil Gramm of Texas played a key role in the close roll call by which the Reagan-endorsed budget passed the House in 1981 or that Senator Slade Gorton of Washington played an equally important part in the roll call on which a Reagan-opposed budget passed the Senate in 1983.

Readers of those papers saw early the emergence of a set of junior Democrats on the House Foreign Affairs, Appropriations, and Armed Services committees as important arbiters of national security issues in that chamber. So when the defense and foreign policy debates of the early 1980s were dominated by such men as Representatives Les Aspin of Wisconsin, Albert Gore, Jr., of Tennessee, Michael Barnes of Maryland, and Norman Dicks of Washington, readers had an understanding of the legislative and political context from which these new power brokers had emerged.

Late in 1984, as the Senate's Republican majority prepared to elect new leaders, both Helen Dewar of the *Post* and Martin Tolchin of the *New York Times* wrote front-page stories about the institutional "identity crisis" facing that body and frustrating many of its members. They were authoritative stories because the reporters knew the institution inside out from years of watching it work—and not work. They could produce what I call cornerstone stories, in which reporters on a beat step back from the day-to-day events and tell the readers something so basic that it helps them interpret everything else they will read for weeks or months.

During the many years that he covered Congress, the *Wall Street Journal*'s Albert R. Hunt wrote dozens of those cornerstone stories. It was a Hunt piece on the foibles of the freshman Republican senators at the end of the 1981 session, for example, that largely established the class's reputation as political lightweights. Drawing on historical analogies to big classes of 1946 and 1958, Hunt cited incident after incident to support his thesis that the class of 1980 had "contributed their votes" and very little else to the Reagan legislative victories of 1981. "Among some of their senior colleagues," he wrote, "the new members are called the 'popsicle brigade,' which is a reference not just to their relative youth but also to what is seen as political immaturity." It was a tough piece which only a veteran and well-grounded reporter would write, and which only a newspaper that wanted that kind of reporting would print.

Such coverage is important to give a sense of institutional life and continuity, a feeling for the forces shaping decisions, because so much of what Congress does each day goes essentially uncovered. In the week beginning June 10, 1985, for example, the House and Senate held four days of floor sessions and 115 committee meetings. In that week, the *Post* and the *Times* ran thirty-nine stories off Capitol Hill, an average of almost four a day per paper.

Both papers gave lead-story prominence to the House action renewing American aid to the antigovernment forces in Nicaragua, and there were six other page-one congressional stories in those two papers during the week. But between them, the two papers reported congressional action on only a dozen topics, while Congress itself dealt with at least five times that number of issues. What both the *Times* and the *Post* did do well—particularly in the second-day analysis stories following the Nicaragua aid vote—was to analyze the forces that shaped the outcome of this major issue. They also analyzed the stalemate then prevailing in the House-Senate conference on the budget.

While the best of the Capitol Hill press responded well to the challenge of that week, the coverage seen by much of the rest of the country was more fragmented. The wire services that provide most newspaper and radio stations with their news of Congress actually offered a more comprehensive look at the week. They sent out stories quoting members of Congress on corporate takeovers and reporting the testimony of Indians on the hunting of bald eagles and of experts on child molestation. They reported a Senate amendment calling on Japan to take over more of the costs of its own defense and several other matters that did not make the *Post* or the *Times*.

Although they also offered stories about the pressures on the budget conferees, the changing mood in Congress on tax reform, and other analytical and institutional pieces, these occasional stories were barely distinguishable on the wire from the contrived and routine pieces.

All too typical was this AP story:

The Senate Appropriations Committee on Thursday approved a fiscal 1985 supplemental money bill that includes $38 million in non-military aid for Nicaraguan rebels and $11.8 million for a drug crackdown.

The $13.5 billion measure already has been approved in similar form by the House.

The Senate committee's action was consistent with Senate approval last week of the $38 million to aid Nicaraguan Contras battling the leftist Sandinista government.

Differences between the Contra aid approved by the Senate and the $27 million passed this week by the House will have to be worked out in a conference.

That story tells a reader or editor almost nothing to aid real understanding. It uses congressional jargon like "fiscal 1985 supplemental" and lumps apples and oranges—Contra aid and drug interdiction money—just because that is the way Congress sometimes consolidates spending. Worst of all, it gives no real hint that policy choices were involved—let alone opposing views and compromises.

When I started working on Capitol Hill, the wire services did a lot more of what I would characterize as railroad timetable reporting of Congress, which tells you what train (or bill) has just left what station and what its next stop will be. It tells you a little bit about what's on the train, but almost nothing about how the train was put together and why it is carrying that particular cargo.

The wire services do less of that kind of reporting now, partly because they keep fewer people in the congressional press galleries and partly because they recognize its limits. Their staff members are often among the most knowledgeable and experienced, but they still face enormous demands to produce a volume of routine informational reports to meet the hourly needs of radio clients and the twin news cycles of morning and afternoon newspapers.

In this environment, the analytical piece, dealing with Congress as an institution, understandably takes last place. Nor is there apparently much demand for the stories about Congress's role in shaping foreign policy or budget priorities, stories that emphasize its role in the governmental system. Most local newspapers and all the radio shows want the news from Capitol Hill digested into "Washington shorts." They will take the top two paragraphs of as many stories as they can handle and give the readers or listeners a smattering of what is going on in Congress that day. Their audience gets the impression of Congress as a kind of sausage factory, grinding out separate, discrete items of greater or lesser tastiness, day by day. Contrast this with the importance the White House gives to stressing only one theme each day, and you begin to understand why Congress has a worse public image than the presidency.

Another reason is that television has not figured out how to cover Congress as an institution. In the week we have been examining, the only Capitol Hill story that made it to all the nightly news shows was the President's victory in the House on Nicaragua aid. All three networks allowed either two or four senators to react—one sentence each—to the presidential decision to abide by the terms of the expiring SALT II nuclear arms agreement. CBS looked at the role the Social Security issue played in blocking agreement on a budget, and Senator Ted Stevens of Alaska got one sentence from two of the three networks with a proposal to invoke the death penalty on spies. And that was it.

During this period the commercial networks cut back on their Washington coverage—except of the presidency. Stories on domestic issues that in the past typically were framed around congressional hearings were shot and reported in locations around the country, with brief inserts as needed from congressmen involved in the controversy. Greg Schneiders, in a 1985 *Washington Journalism Review* article, cited figures from the Vanderbilt University television news archives indicating that between 1980 and 1984, fewer than half as many stories about Congress were on the three network news programs as in the period from 1975 through 1979. Schneiders, a former Senate press secretary, said that "almost nobody on Capitol Hill has a good word to say about network coverage of the legislative branch." Programs like PBS's *MacNeil/Lehrer Newshour* and *Capitol Journal* (which has since been canceled) pay closer attention to Congress and focus on the same kind of institutional questions as the best newspapers, but their audiences do not compare with those of the network news shows.

Instead of covering Congress, the network news shows tend to use Congress as a place to frame controversies as simulated combat to fit the time and structure demands of TV news. If the President cuts off aid to Fingoland to express his displeasure for its part in a coup in neighboring Tempusstand, the networks can pick up supporting and opposing views from a House floor debate on the foreign aid bill. If the inflation rate jumps, the secretary of the treasury's appearance before the Senate Finance Committee may provide the snippet of reaction needed to illustrate that story.

If the passage of a piece of legislation occasionally makes the news in more than a one- or two-sentence summary, the process and the institution itself are almost never seriously discussed. The very essence of the legislative process is something that television abhors: the search for compromise and consensus. It is time-consuming. It involves details, not simple-to-describe broad principles. The key negotiators are frequently not widely known. And their negotiating skill may not set the viewer's pulse to racing.

In 1985, there was a vivid example of what television can and cannot do with Congress. Chairman Dan Rostenkowski of the House Ways and Means Committee, a Chicago Democrat who had been a behind-the-scenes powerhouse in Congress for years, was chosen to give the Democratic response to President Reagan's televised call for tax simplification and reform. Rostenkowski was unexpectedly folksy, effective, and attractive, and for the first time he became a public figure. After the tax bill went into Rostenkowski's committee, where the real work of legislation went on, both Rostenkowski and the bill disappeared from the screen. Only when the bill came up for floor debate in the House and Senate did television find the pictures it needed. And the compressed, oversimplified television reports left most of the public uninformed and skeptical about the measure when it became law late in 1986.

For all of these reasons, the picture television gives of Congress is a long way from the one that reporters like the *Post*'s Helen Dewar, Martin Tolchin and Steve Roberts of the *New York Times,* and Albert Hunt and David Rogers of the *Wall Street Journal* have provided their readers. The networks have competent reporters on Capitol Hill but they tend to be frustrated journalists. The television Congress is a highly confrontational body. Any time two members of Congress are on television, the odds are that they will be arguing with each other. The heavier the rhetoric, the better their chance of being on TV. If they are not hollering at each other, chances are they will be picking a fight with somebody else—an executive branch official, a reluctant witness, somebody. That these contentious, ornery characters might actually represent leadership as legitimate as that of the President is almost preposterous.

ONE other kind of story about Congress always gets good play in the newspapers and on TV: congressional scandals and peccadilloes. On the wall of my office, I have the replica of a sign made in the last century that reads, "No man's life, liberty or property is safe while the Legislature is in session." That expresses the American folk wisdom about legislators in general and Congress in particular. Mark Twain summed it up: "It could probably be shown by facts and figures that there is no distinctly native American criminal class except Congress."

Scandals in Congress even of a petty nature are easier to sell to most editors than the stories of larger consequence. Even the *Post,* which deals seriously with Congress in many stories, succumbs to the trivial and demeaning ones. Almost every summer of a nonelection year, we discover the "news" that some members of Congress have left the country during recess. In August of 1981, for example, a sneering four-column headline, "From Hill to Fiji: The Season of 'Fact-Finding Trips,'" surmounted a roundup that began, "Dozens of members of Congress are spending their vacations on taxpayer-paid trips to such destinations as Bermuda, Fiji in the South Seas, Paris and Hong Kong." Two years later, an almost identical AP story was headlined "One-Tenth of Congress Takes to Expenses-Paid Travel Trail."

Some editors may think the junket stories sell papers; more, I suspect, prefer them because they fit their stereotypes of graft and sin on Capitol Hill. Either way, it is bad journalism. The stories don't tell constituents what their member of Congress did with the money or learned from the trip. Many of the members write formal reports when they get back, but those don't make the wires or the papers. It's cheap-shot journalism. At any time during the past twenty years, if anyone had cared to bother, a story could have been written that "Broder makes another expenses-paid trip." My paper judges the trip by the stories it produces; it seems to me we could apply a similar standard to congressional travel.

We do the same thing with the pay and income for members of Congress. The file of stories about the honoraria senators and representatives receive for their speechmaking is one of the thickest under the general heading of Congress. Again, the specialty is the curled-lip headline and lead, like these from the *Post*: "Golden Throats of the Senate Enjoy Speaking Fees to Match," "Lawyer-Legislators Juggle Jobs On, Off Hill," or "The Senators' Dilemma: How to Hide a Pay Raise."

The members' honoraria are public; those that my bosses, my colleagues, and I receive are not. Yet because we in the press and television overemphasize how much money members of Congress can make, their salaries have fallen far below what people of comparable responsibility receive in the private sector. Between 1969 and 1985, for example, the real value of the annual salary of members of Congress was cut almost in half. In 1985, a commission of distinguished citizens reported that the hold-down on congressional and top-level administration salaries (also controlled by statute) meant "we are drifting toward a government led by the wealthy and by those with no current family obligations." That is an important story, but not nearly as sexy as the "golden throats" yarn.

Nor does it fit the notion that Congress is a bunch of greedy bastards. Many stories have dwelt on the financing of congressional campaigns by private contributions, some of which come from business, labor, or other special-interest political action committees, and that the groups which sponsor those committees often have legislative fish to fry with the very members of Congress to whom they contribute.

Like the junket story, which is always available, so is the story which, in one typical *Post* headline, reported, "Congressional Candidates Were Given $104 Million by Special Interests." Congress can blame itself. When it voted to initiate public financing of presidential campaigns after Watergate, it could have and should have voted to subsidize the cost of electing its own membership. It did not because some members feared they would be denounced for "feathering their own nests" and also because some, as incumbents, did not want to put any money in their opponents' coffers.

But however great Congress's guilt on these matters, the press's gullibility is at least as great. As with the junket stories, our reporting stops just where the story may get interesting. That members accept private contributions—special-interest contributions—is nearly as universal as their travel. What is important is what happens next: is there a discernible pattern of behavior explainable by contributions and not by the ideology of the member or the interests of an important group of his constituents? That is the operative question, and it is one rarely addressed in reporting on Congress. Maybe the presumption is that with characters as suspect as congressmen you don't have to prove anything—all you have to do is suggest a crooked connection.

How crooked are they? In 1980, the *Post* and *Congressional Quarterly* counted all those who had "been indicted, convicted, or cleared of criminal charges, or had been subject to disciplinary action by Congress, or had resigned under ethics pressures." Of the 1,978 men and women who served between 1945 and 1980, they found 49, and that included 8 who had been cleared of the accusations. Forty-one miscreants in thirty-five years, including a couple of drunks. A shocking record—especially to journalists!

Nonetheless, in the past five years, dozens of stories ran in the *Post* and other papers about the wayward Congress, about the members from Massachusetts, Mississippi, and New York who had homosexual liaisons, about the members from Illinois, Indiana, and Delaware who went to a house party in Florida with a lady lobbyist who later took off her clothes for *Playboy,* about two congressmen from California and one from Texas who were investigated but never charged with drug abuse, and about the famous Abscam FBI sting operation that ensnared one senator and six House members.

Wilbur Mills, identified for years as "the powerful chairman of the influential tax-writing Ways and Means Committee," made the front page when, drunk and accompanied by his stripper girlfriend, he drove into the Tidal Basin. No question, it was a spectacular story. And as Mills's bout with alcoholism unfolded, the fact emerged that there had been for years sudden, unexplained absences by the chairman that had forced cancellations of Ways and Means Committee meetings and had delayed legislation. It was understandable that reporters (being notorious homebodies) had not run into Mills on what were apparently his frequent visits to Washington dives, but how did we all fail to note Mills's absences from the Ways and Means Committee? Why wasn't that a story long before he drove Fanne Foxe into the Tidal Basin?

I wrote a column that expressed reservations about our coverage of a similar case in 1976, when the *Washington Post* led the press in exposing the shenanigans of Representative Wayne Hays of Ohio and a lady on his committee staff named Elizabeth Ray, who was not paid for her typing skills:

> Just in time for the summer doldrums, there is a genuine sex scandal breaking on Capitol Hill. The newspapers are mobilizing their investigative resources in the greatest display of moral outrage since Watergate. Platoons of top-flight reporters are going down the names in the congressional staff directories of recent years, looking for the former secretary who will spill the beans on her boss. Predictably, they will find her and her sisters, and the resulting exposés will provide enough headlines to compensate for the absence of a contest at the Democratic convention. . . .
>
> A bill will be passed and some scoundrels purged at the polls. Everyone will relax with the warm glow of a moral triumph. And all the serious problems of Congress will still remain. . . .
>
> Of course it is an affront to decency if the hiring policies of some congressional offices reflect the sexual appetites of the boss rather than the competence of the prospective employees.
>
> But one cannot help but being struck by the selectivity of the indignation the press and public display on the question. These scandals, gamy as they may be, are tangential and trivial compared to the real abuses of power on Capitol Hill.
>
> Wayne Hays had been a chronic violator of the standards of political behavior for years before any allegations were raised about his private conduct. . . .
>
> The Democrats in the House had created an obvious conflict of interest situation by allowing Hays to serve simultaneously as the chairman of the House Administration Committee, which writes the election finance laws, and as chairman of the Democratic Congressional Campaign Committee, which raises and spends the funds to keep Democratic congressmen in office.
>
> Hays' flagrant efforts to sabotage and obstruct campaign finance reform legislation over the last five years were documented in this column and in many other places. But the Democratic Party which controls the House did not discipline Hays for that.

I have been tough on my colleagues, and myself, for our coverage of Congress. But one should add that Congress does not begin to do what it could to get a fairer shake from television and the press.

For example, it ignores the fact that its leaders are not just the managers of the Congress's internal business but its spokesmen to the public. The path to leadership within the House and Senate has been based historically on the cultivation of personal relationships inside those bodies. Leadership contests in the House and Senate have been insulated from the press and therefore the public. Reporters covering Congress cannot predict their outcome, much less have any influence in the matter. Occasionally one contestant is said to give his party a better public image than another, but rarely has that influenced the outcome. There were three contests in the 1970s where this might have been a factor, and in none was it significant. Representative Morris K. Udall of Arizona, highly admired by reporters covering the House, was beaten for a leadership post by a man who had cultivated fewer reporters but had built stronger alliances on the House floor. Representative Guy VanderJagt of Michigan, a wizard at generating publicity for himself as chairman of the Republican Congressional Campaign Committee, was no match for Representative Bob Michel of Illinois, a competent floor leader, in the contest for the House GOP leadership. Senator Robert C. Byrd of West Virginia, whose relationships with reporters were tense, ambushed Senator Edward M. Kennedy, proprietor of one of the best publicity machines on Capitol Hill, and defeated him for whip.

As a result the men in the leadership positions in Congress frequently have not been effective spokesmen for their parties outside the caucus room. Speaker Thomas P. (Tip) O'Neill, Jr., of Massachusetts was sensitive enough about his red face, bulbous nose, and occasional fractured grammar to shun the television interview programs. His successor Jim Wright of Texas, had trouble turning down the volume of his florid floor-debate rhetoric to fit the cooler medium of television. Michel, who could be both candid and engaging in discussions with cameras absent, stiffened in a TV studio. Byrd tended to cover his nervousness with pompous solemnities. Of all the recent figures, only Senate Majority Leader Howard H. Baker, Jr., of Tennessee handled both press and television exceptionally well. When Baker retired in 1984, Senate Republicans replaced him with Bob Dole of Kansas, a man who was both a powerhouse inside the Senate and a popular and skillful manipulator of the press. But the Democrats reelected Byrd as minority leader over the challenge of Senators Lawton Chiles of Florida, and J. Bennett Johnston of Louisiana, both younger, more media-minded figures.

That may change in the future. Those in line to succeed Wright and Michel in the House leadership, Representatives Thomas S. Foley of Washington, Tony Coelho of California, Trent Lott of Mississippi, and Richard Cheney of Wyoming, are as good on TV as they are in the House. But for now, Congress is still at a disadvantage.

The lack of media skills in the congressional leadership has cost Congress severely. In Congress's contest with the Executive for control of public policy, casting an inarticulate Speaker against an articulate President (as was the case with O'Neill and Reagan) tipped the scales toward the White House. Presidents have learned the arts of public relations before they get to the White House. They are supported by large press and public relations machines. The Speaker likely has only one or two people handling his press relations.

The President's press conference is elaborately staged, well rehearsed, and held at a time of the President's choosing. The Speaker and majority leader are accessible almost every day, whether or not it is politically convenient.

Even on legislative issues, the President gets the better of it. During congressional debate, there are many and conflicting voices heard from Capitol Hill, while the White House (usually) speaks with one voice. When a bill reaches the White House for signature, the President may organize a bill-signing ceremony. Even when he has opposed important elements of the bill or given his assent late in the game, the President is at the center of the picture as the congressional sponsors who have carried the measure to passage watch him sign.

It has never been clear to me why the leaders of the House and Senate cannot find a way to stage their own ceremony when both chambers dispatch a bill to the President. It is no more contrived to make a fuss over the engrossment of a bill than over the President's signature on it. Both are part of the constitutional process.

Since 1970, the opposition party's congressional leadership has been given the opportunity to respond to the President's annual State of the Union address. It is an unequal struggle. When the President finishes to a predictable standing ovation, the cameras shift to the opposition leaders, gathered in a nearby office to say their piece. Those responses are often awkward, occasionally embarrassing. Since Reagan came to office, the Democrats in Congress have persuaded—or pressured—the networks to allow them to respond to his other televised addresses more often than not. But even with its sessions carried live on cable TV, Congress has hardly established parity with the President on prime-time television.

ALL this said, individual members of Congress have used the media very well indeed. They have done so by exploiting our habits, our weaknesses as well as our tendency toward clique journalism. The skills have been developing for some time; now, they are just about perfected.

About the time White wrote, a different style of senator had begun to emerge. Joseph R. McCarthy of Wisconsin and Estes Kefauver of Tennessee gained power and prominence by staging televised hearings on Communism and crime. They and their successors looked upon the Senate not as a place of special sanctity, to be protected from outside influences, but as a convenient forum for furthering personal ambitions and policy goals in the larger world. While White devoted a chapter to "Why Not Very Many Senators Become President," in nearly every subsequent election the field of candidates has been dominated by senators.

The new senator became skilled in taking an issue from the committee room or Senate floor onto television and into the national political arena—John Kennedy with his labor corruption hearings; Barry Goldwater with his crusade for conservatism; Ed Muskie with his battle for the environment; George McGovern with his effort to end the war in Vietnam; Ted Kennedy with his campaign for national health insurance; Jesse Helms with his fight against abortion and for school prayer.

From 1974 on, House members also have framed the major issue debates and have demonstrated their skills in using the House to play national politics through the mass media. In 1976, for the first time in anyone's memory, a House member, Morris K. Udall, was a major contender for the Democratic presidential nomination, pressing his challenge to the eventual winner, Jimmy Carter, longer than any of the many senators in the field. In 1980, a House Republican, John B. Anderson of Illinois, not only sought the Republican presidential nomination, but when thwarted, ran an independent campaign for the presidency that garnered 5.7 million votes and constant press and television coverage. In 1984, a three-term representative, Geraldine A. Ferraro of New York, became the first woman on a major-party national ticket, serving as the Democratic vice presidential nominee with Walter F. Mondale. As this is written, Representative Jack Kemp of New York and Representative Richard Gephardt of Missouri are regarded as contenders for the 1988 presidential nominations.

Skillful members of Congress have learned to manipulate the media —especially television and radio—almost as well as the President does. They cut audio and video tape recordings in studios in the Capitol complex and send them directly by phone line or satellite to stations in their states and districts. Those shows, in which the member is interviewed or joined by some other government official in a discussion, have become staples of many cable TV systems, and excerpts often show up on commercial TV stations as well.

Both parties maintain media centers on Capitol Hill for their members' use. Steve Lotterer, the spokesman for the Republican Congressional Campaign Committee, explained that the satellite feeds are popular with local TV stations because "it gives the station the appearance of having somebody here in Washington and it gives them the chance to have footage they would not have had otherwise."

These devices supplement the flood of press releases and newsletters coming out of Congress every day. Most members of Congress use their publicity opportunities primarily to build up such high and positive name identification in their home districts that they are virtually invulnerable to defeat and only secondarily, if at all, to enhance their roles inside the Congress. Timothy E. Cook, a Williams College political scientist, found press secretaries in 84 percent of the congressional offices in 1984, compared to only 28 percent in 1970. They were "all but unanimous" in believing that their chief mission was to serve the media in the home district in order to make their member look good to his constituents, Cook said.

It is just as well that they have set their goal, for both Cook and Stephen Hess of the Brookings Institution (in his 1986 book *The Ultimate Insiders: U.S. Senators and the National Media*) found that national coverage is reserved for a few, and those few tend to be the congressional leaders and committee chairmen—the same insiders who have always dominated. Hess wrote, "The overwhelming majority of Senators—between 80 and 90 percent—receive so little attention from the three television networks' nightly news programs, the Sunday interview programs on the networks, major out-of-state newspapers, news magazines and the wire services that the national news media are irrelevant in terms of affecting their elections or promoting their policies."

The rank-and-file members of Congress are far more successful in working their hometown TV, radio, and newspapers, however. Press releases and weekly columns written by the congressman's staff are often printed verbatim in weekly papers and small dailies in the district. Because the number of regional reporters in the AP and UPI bureaus on Capitol Hill has been reduced, members of Congress have been encouraged to phone or telex their routine announcements to the state wire service offices, usually located in the state capitals. The reporters who receive and edit them there, for transmission to papers and radio stations in the state, obviously have fewer resources than their counterparts in Washington to evaluate the newsworthiness, or even the accuracy, of what the member of Congress is putting out. Any member who drops in on a county-seat newspaper while on a "district work period" (and almost all of them do) is virtually guaranteed a story describing his work on an issue of local interest and his viewpoint on any other issues in the news.

There has been a tilt to the incumbent in public opinion because the "regionals," Washington correspondents with a special delegation to cover, have a powerful motivation to stay on the good side of the congressmen they cover. They have no better clearinghouse or source of information than the congressional office. That congressman, if he is sharp, has aides monitoring the legislative proposals of importance to his district, as well as the actions pending in the executive departments and regulatory agencies that can affect his constituents.

Those are, of course, the very stories that the regional reporter wants; so the congressman's staff members become, in effect, legmen for his reporting—as long as he maintains a comfortable relationship with the congressman. As the authors of the 1985 Hastings Center study, "Congress and the Media: The Ethical Connection," politely put it, "It is not surprising that their coverage tends to be supportive of the local congressman, and that the local congressman can often successfully initiate the coverage. Yet these newspapers provide a large portion of the independent information that constituents read about their legislator."

Lou Cannon of the *Post,* who came to Washington as a regional correspondent, wrote in *Reporting: An Inside View* that "between the big story and the local sewer grant lies a vast under-reported landscape of congressional achievements, scandals and intrigue which is almost never seen in the daily paper, let alone on local television. In this wasteland a symbiotic relationship flourishes between congressman and correspondent, a relationship based on mutual need and sometimes on mutual laziness. This relationship permits the typical invisible congressman to become visible in a highly selective way in his home district."

Alan S. Emory, the Washington correspondent for the Watertown, New York, *Daily Times,* recalled that when he had been writing also for the morning paper in Schenectady, the management's hostility to Democratic Representative Sam Stratton was so great that Stratton timed his announcements to meet the opposition afternoon paper's deadline. Eventually, the morning paper ended the feud and Stratton relented. Cooperation was more advantageous to both. Emory added that there are tender feelings when local correspondents write unflatteringly of the local congressman. "They expect you to report their activities in the most favorable light," he said, "and they're shocked when you don't."

There always have been correspondents who maintain a detached and even skeptical view of their congressional delegation. Back when I worked regularly on Capitol Hill, A. Robert Smith, the correspondent for the *Portland Oregonian,* so aggravated the fiery Senator Wayne Morse that Morse barred him from the office and forbade his aides to talk to him. Smith did not back down, and eventually Morse was forced to yield.

Despite the economic and professional pressures, there appears to have been a general improvement in the regional coverage of Congress since, in his 1974 article in the *Columbia Journalism Review,* Ben Bagdikian described members of Congress and their local media as "partners in propaganda." With the acquisition of many small newspapers by publishing giants such as Gannett, Newhouse, Knight-Ridder,

Cox, and Times-Mirror, the previously isolated regional reporters have been able to fall back on the professional standards and power of these parent organizations for increased leverage in dealing with congressional offices. In some cases, papers that had no Washington presence have acquired one after being taken over by a chain, and in other cases, more experienced and senior reporters have become available for regional reporting assignments.

Leland Schwartz, who founded States News Service in 1973 and now runs a bureau that covers Capitol Hill and Washington for forty papers in fifteen states, concedes that there are still "bad apples . . . who enter into unspoken agreements with the congressmen they cover that say, 'Keep me informed and don't let me get egg on my face, and I'll never kick you in the shins.' But there are many more—the vast majority—who are questioning, analytical, and independent in their coverage." For most of the regional reporters, their work remains invisible in Washington. They often experience the disillusionment of seeing a story they reported days or weeks earlier become the subject of discussion when a reporter from the *Post* or the *Times* or some other paper read in Washington gets around to it—and gets the credit for breaking it.

Given the scarcity of their rewards in Washington, the support of their editors at home is vital. And improvement is largely in the hands of those hometown editors who can have just as good Washington and congressional coverage for their region as they are willing to pay for.

Meantime, for those of us in the national press and television, the Capitol dome is a daily reminder of an unpaid debt to the Congress that serves us so well, and which we, in turn, tend to demean or abuse. It is interesting that the public does not criticize us as much for this as it does for our role in covering, or manipulating, campaigns. I now turn to that topic and join my pals, "the boys on the bus."

CHAPTER SEVEN

Campaigns: Horse-race Journalism

TIMOTHY CROUSE has entertained four generations of college students (that's fifteen years' worth) with his description of the shabby denizens of the 1972 campaign press corps, *The Boys on the Bus.* *Rolling Stone* had sent Crouse out to keep an eye on its mad genius author, Hunter S. Thompson, and quickly seeing the futility of that task, Crouse stayed around to gather his impressions of the news contingent on the road:

> The feverish atmosphere was halfway between a high school bus trip to Washington and a gambler's jet junket to Las Vegas. . . . There was giddy camaraderie mixed with fear and low-grade hysteria. To file a story late, or to make one glaring factual error, was to chance losing everything—one's job, one's expense account, one's drinking buddies, one's mad-dash existence, and the Methedrine buzz that comes from knowing stories that the public would not know for hours and secrets that the public would never know.

Crouse spread the word about "the notorious phenomenon called 'pack journalism,'" thereby seeding half the questions we are still asked in college seminars and lecture halls. Pack journalism, as he described it, is the combination of weird and aberrational individual behavior with stifling group-thinking that overcomes reporters when they spend too much time locked up on the candidates' planes and buses.

Crouse didn't invent the phrase, nor did he imagine the ailment. It existed then, and to some extent it still exists. We are still moody, freaky, frivolous, and as fearful as ever of missing the story, the punchline, or the party. The reporters who covered Ted Kennedy's losing campaign in the 1980 primaries were perhaps more ostentatiously giddy than any in recent times. But the tone of that entourage differed only a bit from that of such stately voyages as Ronald Reagan's journey to reelection in 1984. Something about campaigns breeds strange behavior. Reporters are away from home and office, enduring long passages of boring routine broken by moments of high-pressure action and drama. Their intense focus narrows their range of vision and loosens their links to the outside world. Those who ride with the candidates—reporters and staff members—form a close-knit group, rife with loves and hates, rivalries and jealousies, rumors and occasional bouts of remorse.

Crouse described the incestuous nature of the news gathering, the nervous eyeballing of a competitor's contacts, the swiping of each other's leads, and all the forces that produce a groupthink mentality among the reporters who are part of the pack. I escaped relatively unscathed so I was not personally offended that he had told the world not to expect much in the way of judgment from the inmates of my asylum.

Still, Crouse's description would not be wholly accurate today. The group's makeup has changed. More newspapers now have reporters on the bus. But the number of print reporters is dwarfed by the growing ranks of television and radio correspondents and their crews, who operate on different news cycles and in somewhat different fashion.

The more the campaign comes to dominate the national consciousness, the heavier the presence of television. Early on, it is mainly a newspaper story. Television doesn't—and probably can't—give it too much attention. Until the first caucus or primary, most of the relatively small attentive public gets its information from newspapers and magazines. But after the first results in Iowa or New Hampshire, it's increasingly a television story, and by the fall campaign, it's almost entirely a TV tale.

As television moves in, many newspapers deliberately move away. Those newspapers have realized that they must do more than dog the candidates' steps if they are going to capture the dynamic of the campaign. Many reporters stand back, studying the impact of the candidate's visit after he has left town, examining his organization, his media strategy, and talking to enough voters to have some idea of their reactions to all this frantic effort to persuade them.

Perhaps the biggest effect television has had on our politics has been to lessen the substance of the campaign itself. And its consequences are not less serious because they are inadvertent. As late as 1960, when I first went on the road with candidates, the highlight of a typical day was a formal speech to an important audience. These speeches, distributed to the press in advance, provided the copy for most of that day's news coverage, as well as raw material for second-day stories analyzing policy shifts or comparing one candidate's position with his opponent's.

Network television had difficulty covering those speeches because they usually were given too late in the evening for their main evening news shows and were stale news by the next day. Besides, it was hard to compress an eight-point economic program or a discussion of defense issues into the standard ninety-second to two-minute TV news spot. Because these evening news shows are the channel to the largest single audience for news, the candidates changed their approach, scheduling major policy statements earlier in the day. But the TV reporter or producer still made the decision of what portions of the speech were shown to the mass audience.

To control the content of those communications as far as possible, campaigns soon began substituting a very brief statement for the long, formal speech and cast that statement in a way that virtually dictated which key sentences would be on television. Thomas Collins, *Newsday*'s media writer, called it "news straight from the candidate." A candidate decrying unemployment, for example, would go not to a union convention but to a closed-down steel mill. And instead of offering his eight-point program, he would stand in front of the cold blast furnace and say, "This abandoned mill—and the four thousand jobs that no longer exist here—are a monument to the failed policies of the incumbent administration. I say we can do better."

As a final step, the campaign managers learned to lock the candidate up after his TV shot, decreasing the likelihood that that day's message would be supplanted on the evening news by some unprogrammed comment or happening, perhaps even a gaffe. This technique has been so perfected that in 1984 President Reagan avoided all formal news conferences and all but the briefest, shouted exchanges with reporters from late June until Election Day.

This adaptation by the campaigns to the needs and preferences of the dominant news medium has drained content and substance from the typical campaign day. Newspapers like the *Post* still assign reporters to cover the major-party presidential and vice presidential candidates, since our readers want to know what they are doing and saying day by day. But increasingly, our creative and innovative political reporting is done away from the "pack" of which Crouse wrote. This provides better and more balanced coverage, but it has not eliminated the inwardness of our journalistic perspective. It still leaves us victimized by clique journalism. Because as campaign reporters we are a very atypical group—unlike most of our readers and even many of our newsroom colleagues—much of our output has an insider quality.

At a conference held at Harvard's Institute of Politics after the 1980 election, Roger Mudd and Tom Brokaw of NBC both spoke of the dangers of what Brokaw called "the incestuous nature of what we do." As quoted in Martin Linsky's book about the session, *Television and the Presidential Elections,* Brokaw said, "What worries me in a larger sense is the symbiotic relationship that has grown up between the campaigns and our business. . . . We were talking to each other too often during those campaigns."

Mudd, who was on the sidelines in 1980 because of a contract dispute, was a consumer of the news and confessed that "as the campaign went on, as I tried to keep up, I found myself unable to understand half of what I was hearing on the nightly news. . . . There were so many pieces of shorthand built into the switch to Des Moines, the tightly edited clip, the voice left up in the air . . . that when the evening news was over, I felt unsatisfied . . . not very proud, and not very well informed."

The insider or cliquish quality of campaign news coverage helps explain why we get so caught up in minor incidents and disputes that are tangential to the central decisions the voters are making—the arguments over Quemoy and Matsu in 1960 or Jimmy Carter's *Playboy* interview in 1976 or George Bush's "kick ass" comment in 1984.

Every day, the national political reporters are competing with each other. Within the club, we know which reporters are doing well and which ones aren't. And nothing so influences those collective opinions as each individual's skill or lack of skill to gauge the course of the campaign—knowing who is up and who is down.

Our critics love to complain about our tendency to reduce the process of choosing the President to the dimensions of a horse race, with terms like front-runner and long shot. "Horse-race journalism," the critics say, emphasizes strategy and tactics and ignores issues, substance, and serious consideration of candidates' qualifications.

Measuring coverage of the 1976 campaign by network television news shows, news magazines, and a sampling of newspapers, Thomas E. Patterson of Syracuse University reported in *The Mass Media Election* that "the election's substance," which included policy statements, discussions of the traits and records of the candidates, and endorsements, "received only half as much coverage as was accorded the game" aspects of the contest.

James M. Perry of the *Wall Street Journal* was asked by the now-defunct journalism review *MORE*, in 1974, "Why do we do it?" The answers, he said, were all bad: "Tradition. Habit. Laziness. Because, sometimes, our editors want us to do it. Because we see politics as a kind of a game, a race between various performers, and we're the time-keepers. Because it's easy and because, maybe, it's fun."

I think horse-race journalism is all of that. But it is also a genuine and legitimate response to the curiosity about "who's going to win this thing?" It is a reasonable question to try to answer—if we have the skill to do it. If the mission is legitimate, as I believe, two questions still must concern political reporters: Can we judge the race well enough to make the effort worth attempting? And can we do that without losing sight of other aspects of the coverage—especially the issues?

The reporters on the candidates' planes are probably in the worst position to see how the race is going. You can sense the mood of the contender and his attendants and you can establish sources who may be willing to share their insights—and polling information. You can observe the reactions of the crowds. But my experience is that the closer you are to the candidate, the harder it is to judge how he is doing.

"Crowdsmanship" illustrates the problem. Some of the biggest and most fervent crowds turn out for candidates with no hope of winning. The last stages of the Goldwater campaign in 1964, the McGovern campaign in 1972, and the Mondale campaign in 1984 saw magnificent turnouts of adoring supporters. The worse the odds, the more the true believers want to let their man know that they are not wavering. You can also be misled by crowds generated by intensive organization efforts days beforehand, out of your sight. Nixon drew great crowds in Chicago and Atlanta in 1960, but they were dwarfed by the throngs that greeted Kennedy in Cleveland. Yet Nixon carried Ohio and Kennedy carried Georgia and Illinois.

To gauge the course of a campaign you have to move away from the candidate and out among the voters. There are many techniques for doing that. I came to political reporting at about the end of the "horse-back opinion" era, when reporters touched base with county chairmen or cab drivers and presumed that these worthies were in touch with a scientific cross section of the voters. In 1948 the Gallup Poll had been embarrassed when it predicted that Thomas E. Dewey would defeat Harry S. Truman. And Leslie Biffle, the dapper secretary to the Senate Democrats and a longtime adviser of Truman's, had been elevated to the status of seer for simply driving across the country, disguised as a chicken farmer, and finding out that "the people" were with Truman.

Samuel Lubell was the reigning journalistic analyst of voting behavior. He had his own method of sampling grass-roots opinion by knocking on doors in selected precincts. Lubell tested the changing moods of voters against their electoral history and demographic backgrounds; he was able not only to predict elections but to construct original and instructive theories about the underlying changes in American politics, as he did in books like *The Future of American Politics* and *Revolt of the Moderates*.

By 1960, when I started on-the-road campaign coverage, the pollsters had regained their standing with the candidates, if not with the public and the press. Lou Harris worked for John F. Kennedy and Claude Robinson of Opinion Research Corporation for Richard M. Nixon. But the press still employed relatively crude tools. George Gallup and his competitors offered no help in individual presidential primary states. Their early polls tended to reflect name familiarity of the candidates, rather than their potential support.

Leaks of polls from the candidates quickly became a standard form of journalistic and political warfare. The desire to scoop each other made us eager to get the latest private poll numbers before a competitor did. But since we could rarely verify the numbers we were given and since we almost never had independent data against which to measure those reported results, we were easily manipulated.

Early in 1960, for example, the Kennedy forces spread reports that West Virginia would be the toughest primary he would face because its population included fewer than 5 percent Catholics. What they knew —but carefully concealed—was a Lou Harris poll of West Virginia voters (Harris was then a private pollster, not the public pollster he is today) taken in the final weeks of 1959 and the first week of 1960. The survey, now available at the John F. Kennedy Library, showed Kennedy with a 54 to 23 percent lead over Hubert H. Humphrey. With the undecided out, the race was 70 to 30. Later, as Kennedy's religion became more of an issue, there were indications that the early lead had dissipated, but from the very beginning, the press gave Kennedy an underdog position he did not have.

WITHOUT the resources or skills to do our own polling, reporters fell back on the Lubell technique. We substituted door knocking and shoe leather for the random sample and for the number of interviews that a professional pollster would use. Those techniques can work. One of the best ways to report a campaign is to park yourself in a particular community long enough to find out who is for whom—and why. It is reporting, not polling. But when done well—with some luck added— it can tell you as much about the dynamics of a particular election as any poll.

My introduction to the method came in Beckley, West Virginia, and surrounding Raleigh County, during that 1960 Kennedy-Humphrey primary. As a junior reporter for the *Washington Star,* I was an extra in West Virginia. I moved into Beckley, a city of 19,397, and just camped for a week. On May 1, nine days before the primary, the *Star* published a lengthy report under the headline "How a County Decides." It was a straightforward story, which began by showing that "all the factors that make Senator Humphrey's position strong in West

Virginia are present in exaggerated form in Raleigh County." There was high unemployment, a big labor vote, a pro-Humphrey county Democratic organization. It was also 99 percent Protestant and the home county of Senator Robert C. Byrd, the most influential and most anti-Kennedy Democratic politician in the state. But in the fifth paragraph it stated that while "most politicos believe Senator Humphrey will carry Raleigh County—and the state . . . the polling done in Raleigh County by the *Star* shows Senator Kennedy with surprising strength."

Then, carefully, it showed that many nominally pro-Humphrey elements had been neutralized. There was evidence of a clear backlash to Byrd's intervention. The local (and pro-Humphrey) United Mine Workers executive had been called off the campaign by union higher-ups sympathetic to Kennedy. The local sheriff and Democratic Party chairman, Okey A. Mills, preoccupied with a fight over the choice of his successor and a battle over the Democratic gubernatorial nomination, said he had decided on a course of neutrality. Humphrey campaign headquarters was similarly lethargic. Ten days before the primary, only 25 of the 114 precincts in the county had Humphrey workers.

The Kennedy campaign offered a sharp contrast. Edward M. Kennedy, the candidate's youngest brother, was spending half his time in the county, and Ben Smith, a Gloucester, Massachusetts, businessman who would later be appointed to fill John Kennedy's Senate seat until Ted was old enough to run for it, had moved into Beckley for the last several weeks of the campaign, aided by other Kennedy friends from Kentucky, Florida, and Massachusetts.

The local Kennedy committee, headed by a young lawyer named Don Hodson and Mrs. David Kennedy, whose husband was a UMW attorney, had assembled a volunteer phone canvass crew of fifty-one women, drawn from the list of contributors to the only Catholic church in town. Their planned phone canvass of every household would be backed by a drop-off of a Kennedy tabloid at every home in the county by students recruited from Beckley College.

Discussion of the religious issue was everywhere, as I learned from several evenings at the local radio station's call-in show. But apparently a backlash was building to some of the more blatant anti-Catholic expressions. The *Raleigh Register,* the local Democratic paper, accused Byrd of trying "to stir religious hatred against" Kennedy and said "denominational religion has become an issue far beyond its importance in the presidential race."

Having documented the difference in the level of activity in the two campaigns, I ended the article:

> Nonetheless, the universal judgment—of Kennedy managers, of Humphrey managers and of neutrals—is that Senator Humphrey will carry the county. The predictions range from a "very close" race to a 3–2 margin. But no one predicts a Kennedy win.
>
> In the face of that unanimous verdict, it is necessary to report that polling by the *Star* in mining camps, on country roads and in various parts of Beckley gave Senator Kennedy a lead among those Democratic voters who had made up their minds or had a preference.
>
> Some 112 persons were polled. They gave Senator Kennedy 26 sure votes and 16 probable votes. They gave Senator Humphrey 10 sure votes and 8 probable votes. There were 21 undecided Democrats, 27 Republicans . . .

I wish now that I had used "voter interviews" rather than "polling" to describe what I did, for there was nothing scientifically random about the selection of those 112 people. Yet it strikes me still as a careful piece of reporting. My colleagues, who were dealing more intimately with the candidates and managers, told me at the time that it came as a thunderclap to the big shots in Charleston, especially in the Humphrey campaign.

I went back to Washington convinced that Kennedy would win West Virginia. And so he did. He carried Raleigh County with almost 63 percent of the vote and West Virginia by 53 to 47 percent over Humphrey.

THE story helped my stock at the *Star*. But more than that, it convinced me that Lubell was right, that you could learn a great deal about what was going on in an election campaign by absenting yourself from the candidates for a time and doing close-in reporting with the voters.

That judgment has led me to a lot of motels and a lot of fast-food restaurants in small towns across America, to a lot of windswept streets and to as many encounters with watchdogs as your average postman. It has also persuaded me that difficult as it is, there is no more rewarding or instructive area of political reporting than old-fashioned shoe-leather door knocking. It takes work to establish rapport and trust with a succession of people. But once they are convinced that you are genuinely interested in what they think, they open up—often with an eloquence that is extraordinarily moving. The door knocking has given me insights into many campaigns and candidates, and it has been useful in the broader framework pioneered by my friend and colleague Haynes Johnson, who came over from the *Star* to the *Post* in 1970.

At the start of the 1970 campaign, we decided that the key to the election probably lay in areas where George Wallace had run strongly in his 1968 third-party bid. Richard Nixon and the Republicans were trying to convert Wallace's followers to the GOP by emphasizing social issues, particularly the public dislike of campus antiwar protestors and the widespread concern over "crime in the streets." Vice President Spiro T. Agnew was unleashed to attack the Democrats and their "elitist" friends as squishy soft on crime and condoners of protest. The Democrats were trying to highlight the recession and to argue that Wallaceites—as working people—better return to what the Democrats called "the party of the people."

What we learned from precincts where Wallace had received a high share of the vote was that Wallace supporters tended to have National Rifle Association stickers on their front doors, abandoned cars in their yards, lots of dogs, signs saying No Solicitors, and, in many instances, no great liking for interviewers. In city after city, we found that the precincts where they lived were either surrounded by freeways or on the flight paths of airports; they were not paranoid when they concluded that their neighborhoods were the ones that got callous treatment from the egghead planners and the big-shot politicians and power brokers Wallace denounced in his speeches.

We also quickly found that the Republican campaign strategy was not making inroads with the voters. In the story summarizing our findings, we said, "Our impression from what the voters said was that economic concerns—both with inflation and with loss of jobs—are working to the benefit of Democratic senatorial and congressional candidates this year."

Early on, the voter interviewing brought to light the Republicans' strategic misjudgment that was the key to the 1970 campaign. But the exercise found something even more significant: a sense of pessimism about the national future and of cynicism about the leadership of the country that would be the pervasive theme of the decade. That alienation was not something we went out looking for. But having found it so prevalent in the Wallace precincts, we broadened our interviewing to other neighborhoods and confirmed a deep current of disillusionment about the unkept promises of the 1960s and the unpropitious prospects for the 1970s.

In the lead piece of our series, "The Troubled Voters," we quoted some of the voices we had heard:

A housewife in Houston: I don't know about the future, and I'm terrified of bringing my children up in it. I used to feel my son was going to have a future, and now I don't know any more.

A Harvard sociologist: I'm extremely pessimistic. We're even thinking of emigrating to Sweden, but my wife doesn't like Sweden, so we can't agree on where we're going to go. I see no resisting the drift to the right in the United States today, and I despair when the workers are blind to their own economic interests and support demagogues like Agnew who offer nothing for them but . . . feelings of loyalty to some mystic patriotism.

A Baptist minister in Aldine, Texas, a Wallace supporter: Our future's gone. I look for the educational system to fall completely apart. . . . It looks like we're headed for a revolution.

A New Rochelle, New York, housewife in her early twenties, a Nixon supporter, with a youngster in her lap: I don't know if there's going to be a future for him. Everything's coming up all at once all over. Pollution. Too much war. Too much crime. We're in the process of destroying ourselves.

A doctor's widow, living in a gracious home in Richmond, Virginia: You can't tell from day to day, but if it doesn't do better than it is now, it won't be much of a country. This is the saddest situation I've ever seen. I've seen this country go through four wars and a depression and this is the worst.

There were many such statements, reflecting the cumulative concerns of Vietnam, the urban and campus riots, inflation, recession, the fear of crime and drugs—the whole witch's brew that launched the decade of the 1970s. These comments—which made the series one of the most discussed and controversial journalistic projects either of us had ever done—were often triggered by the opening question Haynes Johnson had suggested we use. It was an easy conversation-starter: "What do you think is the biggest problem facing the country; what concerns you personally the most?" People could answer at whatever level they chose, from a threat to close a neighborhood school to world population trends. It let them tell us what was on their minds.

Spending hours and days door knocking became an institutionalized part of the political reporting at the *Post*. In 1972, through this method, Johnson and I determined that nothing George McGovern could do in the two months prior to Election Day would erase the negative impression voters had of him; the presidential election was locked. While continuing to cover Nixon's pseudocampaign from the Rose Garden and watching McGovern try to unimpale himself, the *Post* shifted much of its attention to the question of whether there would be enough ticket splitting for the Democrats to hold their power base in Congress.

In 1974 it took no great skill in door knocking and interviewing, in the period bracketed by Nixon's resignation and President Ford's pardon of his predecessor, to discover that Republican candidates would be punished for the sins of the two Presidents.

But the smugness I felt about my ability to execute this technique under any and all circumstances vanished in Racine, Wisconsin, in the spring of 1976. My confidence had grown so much that shortly before the Wisconsin primary, I suggested to the city editor of the *Racine Journal Times* that he assign a pair of reporters to work with me to sample opinion in the city. The resulting story, published two days before the primary, said, "Jimmy Carter and Gerald R. Ford are headed for comfortable victories in the Wisconsin primary, if voter interviews in barometer wards of Racine and Burlington offer an accurate gauge of this Tuesday's voting."

They did not. While the story referred to leads of two to one for both men among the eighty-five voters in "carefully selected wards of the two cities," statewide Carter finally eked out a 37 to 36 percent win over Representative Morris K. Udall, and Ford had a 55 to 44 percent margin over Ronald Reagan, much smaller than expected. In Racine and Burlington, Udall beat Carter and Reagan beat Ford.

What had gone wrong? Almost everything. The compression of the primary schedule made the project a hasty one. Instead of taking time to understand the historical allegiances that had propelled various people into active roles in the competing campaigns, and then using the voter interviews to flesh out those impressions of how the community was making up its mind, this story was done in a single day and evening. All of the built-in safeguards I had acquired by hanging around Beckley in 1960, or Franklin, New Hampshire, in 1964, or Lafayette, Indiana, in 1968, were missing.

I compounded the error by putting a hard-news lead on the story. With a lot of abracadabra about how the wards had been chosen to mirror the statewide vote results in 1972, I asked readers to believe that a "poll" of eighty-five people could forecast the results in a state with 4.6 million residents. It was preposterous, and I deserved to get burned.

UNFORTUNATELY, that wasn't the end of the Wisconsin humiliations of 1976. Even when the votes were in, I had a hell of a hard time figuring out who had won. I worked out of the NBC affiliate in Milwaukee on primary night, where my friend and mentor Richard Scammon, the elections authority who had regularly helped Johnson and me pick precincts for interviewing, was interpreting the results from the sample precincts and advising the network on its election projections. Scammon is the most experienced elections man in the business, free in sharing his personal opinions but very cautious in his professional judgments, especially when other people are depending on them.

The networks, as everyone knows, are under tremendous competitive pressures to "call" elections. It is their form of scoop journalism, and each "first call" is trumpeted by their advertising and public relations people, in a bid for a bigger audience on the next election night.

Print journalists in 1976 recognized the pressure; we felt smugly superior to it, but not so much so that we were not willing to exploit it.

In 1972 when the primaries first became the dominant arena of presidential nomination politics, print reporters evolved an uneasy compromise. We took advantage of the networks' expensive arrangements to have people phone in quick counts from a random sample of the state's precincts, counts on which to project results. But because we had a little more time than the networks, we would balance one projection against another—and against the actual vote count and the judgments of our sources in the rival campaigns—before making our own election calls.

All of those factors came together that Tuesday night in Milwaukee. The first call on the Democratic primary came from ABC News at 9:27 P.M. Eastern time, naming Udall the winner. Only 2 percent of the raw vote had been counted, and ABC then had a reputation for pushing too hard on occasion in an effort to catch up with its more established rivals. So most of us held off.

NBC made its call, with Udall in the lead, at 10:22 P.M. Eastern time, when seventy-six of the one hundred sample precincts had reported. The raw vote count then showed Udall ahead of Carter by about five thousand votes, a number that had been holding steady for the past hour or more. With a major edition deadline coming up just after 11 P.M., I phoned in a new lead, declaring Udall the winner in Wisconsin.

Soon after the story was filed, edited, and sent down to the composing room, worries began. A researcher in our Washington office called to tell me that CBS was withholding any call because it felt the Udall-Carter race was too close. That sent me padding down the hallway to find Scammon, who assured me—as he did other reporters—that the margin met the statistical tests that NBC had used all year without error.

Then, shortly before midnight, Udall's margin in the raw vote count slowly began to dip. I was getting queasy, and the presses in Washington were running. At last, when the margin in the raw vote got down to two thousand votes and the expressions of the NBC News people indicated some second thoughts, I picked up the phone and made the most difficult call of my professional life. "I think we have a problem," I began.

Indeed we did—about 150,000 newspapers' worth of problem.

More than one quarter of our total press run was beyond recall— printed, loaded onto delivery trucks, and dumped onto curbs for home delivery, with the wrong winner. We were not alone, and we were spared the ignominy of being the most publicized goof-ups when Carter seized a copy of the *Milwaukee Sentinel,* which had headlined his "defeat," and held it up for a news photograph that went around the world. But it was still a very bad night.

SINCE then the networks have expanded their interviewing of voters leaving the polling places during the day and have improved their precinct sampling system. Of all the calls made by the three networks in the primary and general election coverage in 1980, only three had to be changed, and only three in 1984.

Newspapers also have become more sophisticated in measuring changes in public opinion. Thanks to seminars conducted by George Gallup, Jr., and his competitors, we have become more knowledge- able about the techniques of public opinion polling and, I think, smarter consumers of polling information. More of the major newspa- pers now use the standard Gallup and Harris poll results as raw mate- rial for their own stories, rather than printing them verbatim.

That understanding also helps us deal more skeptically and wisely with the private polls leaked from campaigns as part of the gamesman- ship of politics. We have learned to ask how the polling question was phrased, when it was asked, and of whom—all citizens, all voters, or only those most likely to vote. We now understand those factors make a real difference. And because the politicians know that we are better informed and often have data available from our own polls, they are less likely to try to mislead us.

Most important, news organizations have developed their own in- house polling capacity and are using survey research techniques as a form of—in the phrase of Philip Meyer, the former Knight Newspa- pers reporter—"precision journalism." In his book of that title, pub- lished in 1972, Meyer provided the first how-to manual on survey research for journalists. As others followed his lead, newspaper polls have been targeted to topics of interest. In many of the presidential primary states, for example, these polls now offer at least a baseline measurement of the candidates' strength at specific points in the race.

Even more useful have been the exit polls to interpret the meaning of votes in a primary or general election. They eliminate the need to screen the population for likely voters and the possibility that those interviewed will change their minds before they go to the polls. And each voting place offers a convenient polling point, allowing a large number of interviews in a short time. News organizations amass a statistically significant number of interviews early enough to use the data for their election-night and next-morning stories. They can say confidently how various demographic groups differed in their voting and, by asking about the relative importance of certain issues and personal characteristics, can link voting decisions to their probable causes.

Exit polls cannot, of course, be used for preelection predictions. But they are the most useful analytic tool developed in my working life. In 1980, for example, exit polls revealed a fundamental fact which otherwise we could only have dealt with at the level of intuition or opinion: voters in the Democratic presidential primaries agreed with Senator Edward M. Kennedy on many, or most, issues, but were disinclined to trust him because of deep-seated doubts about his personal character. When voters thought Kennedy might wrest the nomination from Jimmy Carter, they voted for Carter to keep Kennedy out of the White House. When they thought Carter would be nominated, they voted for Kennedy to send Carter a message that they wanted his policies to change.

The *Post* began doing systematic polling under Barry Sussman's direction since 1977, and in 1981 was a partner with ABC News in a cooperative arrangement paralleling that of CBS and the *New York Times,* NBC and the *Wall Street Journal,* and CNN and *USA Today.* Sometimes we combine the kind of interviewing Haynes Johnson and I have done with scientific polling, in a way that, I think, gets the most out of both techniques. We have statistics that guard against the sort of error I made in Racine, while preserving the insights that come from interviewing. In the interviews you hear the connections people make spontaneously between issues and personalities, and you sense which feelings are deep and persistent, which are superficial and subject to change. When those insights are put together with the polling data, you know much more than you could learn from either technique alone.

In the spring of 1982, the *Post* used this combination to focus on St. Joseph, Missouri, a conservative community with close ties to the farm economy. We chose St. Joseph because it was exactly average in its unemployment rate and because it was a stable, small city (population 76,000) with a reputation for self-sufficiency.

The key question was how the city and its citizens were faring under the recession and the Reagan administration's budget cutbacks. Schedule conflicts kept me from participating in the project, but Johnson and three other reporters moved into St. Joseph for a week. Before they hit town, Sussman had taken a telephone poll of 609 St. Joseph citizens. Johnson and his colleagues used some of the same questions as the takeoff point for their own extensive interviews with local businessmen, politicians, service agency officials—and unemployed families.

The picture they drew was of a community with a tradition of voluntary help but minimal public services, struggling to cope with the increased responsibilities Washington had thrust upon it, and of a middle class painfully poised between its deep-rooted belief in President Reagan's conservative aims and the shock that its own economic security was threatened by waves of bankruptcies and layoffs. The pressures building in St. Joseph and its citizens were an accurate barometer of the mood of political ambivalence and upheaval we saw across the country—and especially in the Midwest—in that November's congressional elections.

Each campaign year, we have tried to improve our interviewing and polling techniques, building on the experience of the last election and borrowing unashamedly from others.

After learning from Reagan pollster Richard Wirthlin and others in 1980 how rapidly and massively voters' allegiances could shift in the final days before a primary, I suggested to Sussman that the *Post* and ABC do our own tracking poll in New Hampshire in 1984. In that kind of polling, you phone a certain number of prospective voters every night for, say, the last two weeks before the vote, and construct a rolling average of the responses on the most recent three nights of interviewing.

Our New Hampshire poll turned up the first hard evidence of Gary Hart's late spurt of popularity, which carried him to his upset victory over Walter F. Mondale. The first report on Hart's closing rush, appearing twenty-four hours before the polls were to open, caused a sensation. On the morning of the primary, our continuing polling allowed us to say that Hart, "who earlier seemed ready to settle for a strong second, surged into a tie with Mondale. . . . Hart appeared to be growing stronger each day."

What made it all the sweeter was that the *New York Times* the same morning had a front-page poll story with a very different message. Its lead said, "With Senator John Glenn continuing to fade and no new challenger emerging strongly, Walter F. Mondale now holds the most commanding lead ever recorded this early in a presidential nomination campaign by a nonincumbent, according to the latest New York Times/CBS News poll." The polls were quite different: ours was confined to New Hampshire, theirs was national. Ours had fresher data, which anticipated the voting result. Theirs was moot almost before it was published.

Timing is always key in covering the fast-changing primary election picture, which was evident from the different conclusions drawn by two newspapers who used focus groups in New Hampshire in 1980. In a focus group, you interview a number of people together, instead of separately and serially, and the reactions they stimulate from each other often add extra dimensions.

The morning after the first candidates' debate in New Hampshire in 1980, the *Wall Street Journal* published Dennis Farney's focus group story, which found "not a single one of the 14 voters who gathered here, including the six who voted for Mr. Reagan in 1976, intends to vote for him in next Tuesday's New Hampshire primary." The session had taken place several days earlier, before the Manchester debate. Robert Kaiser's story for the *Post* about a similar focus group with seventeen Republicans who had just watched the debate said that though the group had split evenly between Reagan and Ford in 1976, "most will go with Reagan this time." He had it right.

Building on that success, we organized focus groups around many of the key events in the 1984 campaign. One such event came during the Democratic convention in San Francisco. The convention was highly emotional, with dramatic speeches on successive nights by New York Governor Mario Cuomo, defeated challengers Jesse L. Jackson and Gary Hart, and—on the final night—the appearance of the first woman ever selected for a major-party national ticket, Representative Geraldine A. Ferraro. There were tears and a feeling almost of exaltation in San Francisco's Moscone Center, and the reporters on the scene reflected much of this mood in their copy. But all during the week, *Post* reporters Dale Russakoff and Thomas B. Edsall had been with nineteen voters in the St. Louis area, interviewing them jointly as they watched the convention sessions at night and talking with them individually during the day. Their story for the Sunday paper after the convention ended was like a cold shower on the hype of San Francisco. Datelined St. Louis, it began, "Half a continent away from San Francisco, in the Middle America that Walter F. Mondale and his party are struggling to recapture, the triumphal Democratic National Convention lost some of its luster."

They cited the reactions of these Democratic and independent voters that Mondale was "a cold fish" and the Democratic Party a collection of "unfortunate, unhappy people." Reading that dispatch again after the 1984 election, I was struck by how close it came to telling the whole story of the campaign to come:

> For Mondale, the only sure support came from members of the group who represent the party's hard core—blacks, union members and older Democrats—and who said they feel threatened by economic uncertainty. Their lukewarm response to Mondale raises doubts about his strategy of increasing voter turnout by 14 million.
>
> The more independent Democrats whom Mondale seeks to lure to his base—a chemical engineer whose father was a shoe factory laborer, a technical illustrator and a housewife married to an enterprising suburban attorney—expressed discomfort with the party they saw on the screen.

A similar project, conducted by Russakoff and Paul Taylor in Toledo during the August Republican convention, proved equally insightful and confirmed Reagan's appeal to traditional Democrats and the heavy difficulties Mondale faced. But all these polling and interviewing techniques and, more broadly, the whole area of predictive stories—horse-race journalism—are continually criticized. Some of the complaints are that these stories too often are just plain wrong.

At the midpoint of the 1980 primary calendar, for example, *Time* magazine's press section listed a partial catalogue of journalistic errors, ranging from Tom Pettit's pronouncement on the NBC *Today* show that Reagan was politically "dead" the morning after Bush's victory in the Iowa caucus to a UPI story on the afternoon of primary day in New York and Connecticut that began, "Despite a late surge by Senator Edward Kennedy, President Carter was heavily favored" in both states. Kennedy won them both.

I too was embarrassed by that outcome because on the Sunday before those primaries I had written—as my syndicate schedule required —a column for the Wednesday morning papers, with the premise that Kennedy's "campaign is ending with a bang, not a whimper." That judgment was premature by about five months, and it was far from my only gaffe. At the end of 1980, I wrote a tongue-in-cheek column saluting my own perspicacity: "The hint that this would be a vintage year for political punditry was right there in the first week of 1980. 'The safest election bet in America—for the past generation—has been that the Democrats will win Congress,' I wrote on Jan. 6. 'Chances are, the bet will pay off again in 1980.'" Republicans gained control of the Senate for the first time in twenty-six years.

I filled my allotted space with examples of bad guesses and misjudgments. But I was not alone. Every fourth November, a year before the presidential election, Martin Plissner, executive political director for CBS News, and his wife, Susan Morrison, former Washington news manager for CBS, have a party for more than a hundred Washington political junkies—reporters and their favorite sources—and ask them to guess the scenario for the coming election. In November 1979 this group picked Kennedy as the Democratic nominee and said he would beat the Republican ticket of Reagan and Bush. And that was just the beginning of error. Jeff Greenfield, in *The Real Campaign*, commented scathingly that despite "the most intensive polling in the history of politics . . . not one of the preelection polls by any of the news organizations came close to divining the size and nature of Ronald Reagan's [1980] triumph."

WE had that problem at the *Post*. Since I came to the paper in 1966, we have put together a state-by-state rundown of the races on the Sunday before the biennial general election. Our politically hip readers use this twin-page summary as a checklist for the Tuesday night returns. But more than that, they can use all the information we have assembled to try to outguess the experts.

I recognize, as do the editors of the *Post,* the game quality of that preelection piece, and we go at it competitively. For the last week of the campaign, I pump every possible source for the latest information and judgment, drawing on other *Post* reporters, campaign consultants, and media advisers. After we add this mass of information to our own and others' latest polling and up-to-the-minute checks with political reporters in the fifty states, the time comes for judgment—for gut feelings.

From Thursday night until noon Saturday, Maralee Schwartz, our political researcher, and I sit down and call somewhere between 100 and 150 races. We are tough with ourselves. The easy way out—but not as much fun—is to hedge everything doubtful by calling it TCTC, Too Close To Call. Some races really must be put in that category. But if there is any discernible lean, even the slightest, we lean it that way—and take our chances.

For most elections in the late 1960s and the 1970s, the political researcher and I were right on 80 to 90 percent of the calls. (We could boost the percentage cheaply by calling all 435 House races, but we limit the House calls to the fifty or sixty districts with serious races.)

In 1980, when I sat down to write the Sunday preelection survey, two things stood out. The top of the story said, "Ronald Reagan has the pieces in place and the machinery to deliver a Republican presidential victory on Tuesday." Further down, it added, "Equally evident are the possible benefits to the GOP if the Reagan boom that was rolling from Wednesday through Friday should extend to Election Day. The reports to the *Post* indicated brightening Republican prospects in Tuesday's Senate races. There are 10 states where Republicans have a good to excellent chance to take over Democratic seats and only three where they risk losses." Republicans actually made a net gain of twelve seats.

The story felt right to me (and one should not disguise the importance of gut instinct on that kind of question), in part because that is how the campaign had looked when it was just beginning. Immediately after Labor Day, I had gone back to the precincts, trying to test whether the appeal of Reagan to blue-collar voters that we often had seen in the primaries would show again in the general election. In the blue-collar neighborhoods of two states that would be crucial in a close election, Michigan and Texas, I found that, with inflation raging and

Carter seemingly unable to deal with the Iranian hostage situation, a massive shift was in the making. Over and over I heard, "Let's try the other guy. It couldn't be worse."

Now, in the final week of the campaign, with both the economy and the hostages in the headlines, I did not doubt that Reagan would win. But Barry Sussman's scientific polling that week showed a very different picture. He and Robert Kaiser wrote that "just two days before the 1980 election, American voters remain narrowly divided in their choice for President and unusually volatile." Unable to decide between Sussman's too-close-to-call or Broder's Republican-win story, the *Post*'s editors bravely put both stories on page one, in a display of journalistic schizophrenia that must have puzzled a good many of our readers that Sunday morning.

In 1984 we faced no such problem, because both reporting and polling pointed toward the overwhelming Reagan victory. But in any year the serious question is: Why bother? My answer is that readers' curiosity about who is winning is real and we should try to satisfy it.

And I am not convinced that horse-race journalism blinds us—or the voters—to the importance of issues in the election. It is an old charge, one often made by in-house critics of the press. In *The Real Campaign,* Greenfield faulted "the media's fascination with itself as a political force and . . . its fundamental view that politics is more image than substance; that ideas, policies, positions, and intentions are simply the wrappings in which a power struggle takes place." Greenfield's comments were echoed by many others, including Haynes Johnson. But do we "neglect" the issues?

Elections are contests between individuals, not between philosophies. Voters choose between Candidate A and Candidate B, not between liberalism and conservatism, high or low taxes, permissive or restrictive abortion policies. Voters know that history is replete with examples of Presidents who did exactly the opposite of what they had pledged to do in the campaign. Franklin Roosevelt campaigned for a balanced budget and created the welfare state. Lyndon Johnson campaigned against intervention in Vietnam and intervened. Jimmy Carter campaigned for a simplification and decentralization of government and added two new cabinet departments. Ronald Reagan campaigned for fiscal austerity and ran up record deficits.

Still, voters care about issues as they affect their own lives. Inflation, recession, the threat of war or higher taxes or toxic wastes are not abstractions but real concerns to people. Voters use issues to weigh the capabilities of the candidates and to refine their own feelings about the candidates' personalities and character. But the presidency is ultimately a test of character as much or more than a test of policy and management. And we are not mistaken if we focus primarily on the people who are candidates.

In some campaigns issues are of no real importance. In 1976, both Carter and Ford went to the public with one simple proposition: "I am the sort of person you can trust with the power of the presidency." Two years after Watergate, it was not surprising that the trust question dwarfed all other issues. Any reporter who tried to cast Ford and Carter—both essentially men of the middle—as having sharply contrasting philosophies and programs would have distorted reality.

Nonetheless, James McCartney, a veteran correspondent in the Knight-Ridder chain's Washington bureau, said the prevalence of what he called "junk news" was not entirely the candidates' fault. "The media simply never took issues seriously on their own terms," he wrote after the 1976 election in the *Columbia Journalism Review*. "The press in all of its branches—written and electronic—often would fail to report speeches on serious issues at all, or if it did, it would often fail to present them straight: issues, if mentioned at all, would be buried in stories constructed around other subjects—strategy and tactics, evaluations of candidates' momentum, and all of the other kinds of political small talk that arise in any campaign."

Such criticisms had an effect on the 1980 campaign coverage, but the real difference was the candidates' willingness to focus on the issues. Carter was forced, willy-nilly, to defend his record in office. Reagan had always been an issue advocate, almost an ideologue as those things are reckoned in American politics, and he talked regularly, not just about Carter's failings, but about the basic changes he would make: a major, across-the-board tax cut; a sharp slowdown in the growth of domestic programs; a significant shift of resources from the domestic budget to expanded military defense.

And the press did not ignore the issues in the 1980 campaign, or the fundamental party strengths, or the external realities that shaped the outcome to quite the extent Greenfield and other critics suggest. Those were exactly the considerations that went into planning the *Post*'s coverage of the 1980 Republican convention, and I am biased enough to think that our coverage was not only the best in which I have ever been involved, but a model of how the press can deal with these deeper themes.

It all came out of a rather drunken June dinner with Bill Greider, then our national news editor, and Dan Balz, our political editor, and four or five of us involved in political reporting, a dinner to discuss our coverage of the Detroit convention. Reagan's running mate was the only mystery and speculative stories on that were already getting boring. We knew the convention program would be produced and controlled for maximum television impact. So what were we to do with the convention? What could we possibly add to the sights and sounds our readers would have seen on TV?

Over dinner, the answer began to emerge: let's draw back a step or two and look at this convention, not simply in the context of the primaries that preceded it and the campaign that will follow, but as an important moment in the history of this man, this party, and, yes, this country. How did Ronald Reagan, for sixteen years the advocate of losing causes, get one step from the presidency? How did the Republican Party, so battered and discredited a few years before, engineer this recovery? And—the whiskey and wine having undoubtedly freed our imaginations—what if these Republicans and their ideas become the wave of the future in American government?

We came away from the dinner bubbling with enthusiasm. It was one of the few times in my experience when people involved in a story have actually sat down in advance and talked explicitly about the concepts and perspective that we might employ in covering it. The payoff was visible in the contrast between the *Post* and the *New York Times* on the Sunday that began convention week. The *Times* had the conventional "delegates gathered" lead, written by Hedrick Smith:

Detroit, July 12—Riding a tide of optimism, planeloads of delegates converged on Detroit today for the 32nd Republican National Convention since the party's founding in 1856, with Ronald Reagan's choice of a running mate the only real item of suspense.

Mr. Reagan, due to arrive from Los Angeles on Monday for the crowning formality of his nomination, today issued a four-point economic recovery program keyed to the automobile industry and aimed at using recession-bound Detroit to underscore the nation's economic plight under President Carter.

The lead story in the *Post,* which I wrote on the basis of our dinner at Mel Krupin's restaurant, took a different approach.

Detroit, July 12—Ronald Reagan began his political life as a 21-year-old follower of Democrat Franklin Delano Roosevelt. Now there are sober people who think Reagan, at age 69, might become the FDR of a born-again Republican Party.

As delegates gather here for the formal Republican National Convention opening Monday, confidence in Reagan's beating Jimmy Carter has soared to the point that some are beginning to talk of 1980 as a breakthrough year for the GOP—the kind of turning point in American politics that Roosevelt's election in 1932 turned out to be.

Robert Teeter, the Detroit pollster whose recent studies have fueled hopes for a top-to-bottom Republican victory, said Friday, "I think it is possible for Ronald Reagan to build a coalition that would last more than one election and even reshape our politics on a long-term basis."

Throughout the week we continued the theme of a possible shift of historic dimension, examining Reagan, the delegates, the platform, and the party from that perspective. Without neglecting the breaking stories—the choice of Bush for Vice President, for example—that main theme carried through, giving our coverage a coherence and substance it would otherwise have lacked.

Though we continued to deal with the issues and the voters' concerns in every grass-roots reporting story, they often were diffused in the day-to-day coverage of the candidates' tactics, getting lost in the horse-race coverage of the autumn campaign. Tom Brokaw explained that diffusion at the Harvard conference: "The horse race changes all the time, and that's one of the reasons it gets attention. . . . The positions on the issues don't change that much." Thomas Patterson in *The Mass Media Election* criticized the "neglect" of the issues but showed he understood one of the principal reasons for that impression:

Because the news is what is different about events of the past 24 hours, the newsworthiness of what a candidate says about public policies is limited. To be specific, once a candidate makes known his position on an issue, further statements concerning that issue decline in news value. . . . There are not enough major issues for the candidates to keep questions of policy at the top of the news for a full year. . . . Thus the principal effect of a longer campaign is to spread a somewhat fixed amount of substance over a greater period of time.

The problem of diffusion is compounded by the difference between the interest of reporters in a candidate and the curiosity of the public. As both Richard Reeves, the columnist and author, and Stephen Hess, the Brookings Institution student of the press and the presidency, have pointed out, reporters' interest comes early; the public's, late. During the preprimary and primary period, we reporters get our first extended exposure to the candidates and may write in a fresh, insightful way about the contenders and their positions. But the attentive audience for such stories is small.

When the nominees are chosen and the general election campaign begins, the audience expands dramatically, but by this time the reporters have lost a certain amount of curiosity. The habits of journalism discourage repetition. Yet a campaign is largely repetition, designed to increase the odds that a message will reach the less attentive voters, who just start tuning in at the end. These are the less educated voters, for the most part. The elite and the insiders have already acquired the information they need. But the reporters, who are definitely insiders, are reaching out for news, so we tend to focus on tiny shifts in position, on errors and mistakes, on hidden strategies or unplanned distractions.

At the very point when the mass audience is probably most eager for basic information on the policies, programs, and personalities of the presidential candidates, the mass media are least likely to deliver those basics, believing—in accordance with our concept of news—that these are old-hat. It's another example of our serving the clique of insiders rather than the broad mass of our readers and viewers.

• • •

WE did not solve that problem—or many others—in 1984, but we had less egg on our face when the campaign was over. The 1983 Plissner-Morrison party poll picked Walter F. Mondale as the Democratic nominee and had him losing to Reagan. We initially overestimated Senator John Glenn's challenge, but we reported the defects in his campaigning and organization before their effects began to show up in the polls. We may have been a few days late in reacting to the surge for Gary Hart, but we saw him coming—and going. Overall, the horse-race reporting was more excessive than inaccurate, and for once, we did not have to apologize for the polls being wrong. I would like to think that proves we have become more adept, but maybe we were just lucky.

The toughest reporting challenges came in dealing with Jesse L. Jackson as the first serious black presidential candidate and Geraldine A. Ferraro as the first woman nominated for Vice President. We floundered a bit—as we have done with other such exotics as Roman Catholic John Kennedy, Mormon George Romney, born-again Jimmy Carter, and actor Ronald Reagan.

Early in their campaigns, Jackson and Ferraro both received excessively effusive and flattering coverage, and both were later subjects of stories that were excessively critical or unfair. It is tempting—but foolish—to think we should have reported them as we did everyone else. They were not ordinary candidates. Jackson was a black activist who had never held public office but displayed an awesome command of his audiences; Ferraro was a brassy, attractive woman with evident appeal to many other women. Both plainly antagonized many voters. Striking the balance was not easy, and we certainly didn't do it with any consistency.

Exploring their backgrounds was another challenge. Jackson had uneasy relationships with many other civil rights and black leaders, and their comments were often unflattering. How much of this was jealousy and how much signaled serious shortcomings in the candidate? We had trouble deciding.

He also had close ties to some black militants, and one of them, Black Muslim Minister Louis Farrakhan, became a source of major controversy. Jackson felt—perhaps justifiably—that many of us did not have the background to understand Farrakhan and his movement and judged him unfairly. But in my view, it took Jackson a long time

—and much criticism—to distance himself from a man who regularly made racist and anti-Semitic comments.

With Ferraro, the toughest problem stemmed from the family finances and business associations of her husband, John Zaccaro, a New York real estate dealer. For the better part of the summer, all of the press sorted through the Ferraro-Zaccaro financial disclosures and tax payments, with most reporters concluding that though sloppy book-keepers, they probably were not suspect in their intent. Some newspapers—notably *Newsday,* the *Philadelphia Inquirer,* the *Wall Street Journal*—assumed that with so much smoke, there had to be a fire. They pursued the questions of racket connections so far that others in journalism accused them of stirring suspicions and even anti-Italian prejudices. At least one paper, the *New York Post,* pushed the story so hard it seemed a vendetta.

After the long struggle for the Democratic nomination, the press was in a semi-zombie state, which made it easy for Reagan to carry out his election strategy of celebrating the feel-good, patriotic mood of that Olympic summer and saying as little as possible about the tough policy choices in the next four years. Mondale, to his credit, did discuss budget, tax, and defense policy, but he was damaged goods when the fall campaign began.

As always, we covered the campaign as the candidates conducted it. Reporters can complain that a President is ducking press conferences and not talking substantively about issues, but there is no way to do stories about speeches that are not given, press conferences that are not held.

The outcome of the 1984 election was probably sealed well in advance, when Reagan escaped an assassin's bullet in 1981, when he showed his mastery of Congress in that summer's tax and budget fights, when he cut short his mistaken military intervention in Lebanon, and when the economy soared from recession in 1983 without reigniting inflation.

In such a climate, we often succumbed to the temptation to look past the coming election and examine whether this was just a personal triumph for Reagan or the second stage in a rolling realignment that might give the Republican Party long-term ascendancy in politics. It was an intriguing question—but essentially one that interested the insiders in the clique more than the broad public. As Milton Coleman of the *Post* and Jim Lehrer of PBS's *MacNeil/Lehrer Newshour* told an American University forum, there was too much of "our own preoccupation with inside baseball" in the 1984 campaign coverage.

Certainly, 1984 was not a year in which either the politicians or the press distinguished themselves. It left many people—including most of my colleagues and myself—wondering if we had done all that we might to make the election the dialogue about the country's future which it ideally should have been.

THERE are two or three things we might do to improve campaign coverage, particularly during the critical final phase. We in the newspapers need to recognize, explicitly, the different needs of different parts of our audience. Without interrupting the continuity of coverage, around September we need to say, "Okay, for those of you who are just tuning in on the fact that there's an election coming, here is what you need to know about the people running." We could clear the ads from a couple pages and lay out what we think we know about the backgrounds, careers, and views of the candidates.

We have to realize, however, that not every reader who needs that kind of summary will take the time or trouble to read it. One of the inherent weaknesses of journalism is that we cannot reach out, grab the reader by the shoulders, shake him, and command, "Read this. It's important. It tells you what you need to know."

Television, with its "depth" pieces running only five minutes, has an even tougher time being comprehensive and comprehensible. It is always chancy how much closely compacted information, delivered through a picture medium, will remain in a viewer's mind. Perhaps somewhere in our multilayered communications system of radio, television, newspapers, news magazines, monthlies, and even campaign books the voter will find as much information as he really craves—and is ready to absorb.

One device that does get the attention even of inattentive citizens is the campaign debate. I am familiar with all the criticisms of the debate format: that is emphasizes verbal facility and television presence over more important skills; that it can often spotlight secondary or phony issues—the Quemoy-Matsu syndrome. But nothing comes close to televised debates for attracting a mass audience in a format where the candidates must go beyond a five-word slogan in expounding their views. In theory, the press should also refocus its attention on policies and issues, but in fact we tend to concentrate largely on the candidates' performance.

The newspapers' first debate stories tend to summarize exchanges on a variety of issues, but television news shows inevitably take the debate's most dramatic moment, and, by dint of repetition, fix that moment indelibly in the voters' minds. Knowing this, strategists are more determined for their candidate "to take command" of the screen than to score debating points on the issues. In *Wake Us When It's Over,* their book about the 1984 campaign, Jack Germond and Jules Witcover cited a memo in which pollster Patrick Caddell advised Mondale that by unexpectedly turning from his podium and taking one step toward Reagan, he could "in effect 'violate' Reagan's 'space'— an act that on television conveys confidence, strength and domination."

Mondale performed The Pivot as instructed at the Louisville debate, and it was that moment which TV replayed repeatedly, giving him about the only victory he scored over Reagan in the whole campaign.

SUCH theatrics are only one of the reasons journalists should stay out of presidential debates as either sponsors or participants. When the *Des Moines Register* and the *Nashua Telegraph* sponsored candidate debates during the primaries in 1980, who participated and who did not became important news. The editor of the *Register* publicly quarreled with Governor Jerry Brown of California about whether Brown was a serious candidate in the Iowa caucuses and belonged in the *Register*'s debate. You will remember that *Telegraph* editor Jon Breen was literally in a shouting match with Ronald Reagan about the exclusion of other candidates from the Nashua debate. I think those newspapers would have been more comfortable reporting those developments had they not had a conflict of interest as the sponsor and rule setter.

Similarly, reporters should ask questions at news conferences and interviews—but not in debates. Debates, in my view, should be limited to the candidates. Some of the best exchanges came during the primaries in 1980 and 1984, when there was a single moderator and the candidates were free to question and respond directly to each other.

There are other things the press and television can do to deepen the discussion of issues, such as running a substantial chunk of a candidate's speech or a statement dealing substantively with policy and comparing his views with those of his opponent. Lyn Nofziger, Reagan's longtime adviser and former press secretary, complained at an American University forum following the 1984 campaign that we tend to forget this basic obligation, particularly late in the campaign. The *New York Times* periodically runs a long excerpt from the candidate's basic speech, the one he repeats substantially unchanged from rally to rally. It's an idea I would not be ashamed to see the *Post* imitate.

But candidates now tailor their comments for the short sound-bites usable on the nightly television news shows. The pattern of their discourse can be changed by changing or broadening the format. If, during the campaign season, the networks made available a regular ten-minute or fifteen-minute prime-time block for talks by the candidates, it would be an offer no candidate could refuse. The networks ought to specify the topic for the week and retain control of the format. If the candidates knew, for example, that they had ten minutes to outline their views on unemployment in the basic industries, they would very quickly find something substantive to say on the subject. You can convey a great deal in ten minutes—or make it evident that you really have no ideas to offer. The system has worked well in Great Britain and for party spokesmen on public television's *MacNeil/Lehrer Newshour*. Campaign managers also complain that they are forced to use thirty-second ads because the networks and stations are reluctant to disrupt their regular programming to sell them time for five-minute commercials.

So we in the media could make changes to give better structure and definition to the policy side of the campaign. But I would not concede that this is an argument against horse-race coverage. I end, as I began, with the view that the public's interest in who is winning and who is lagging is inevitable and legitimate and human. And, for reasons I have suggested in discussing the use of polls, voter interviews, and focus groups, we are getting better tools and skills with which to predict election outcomes.

But there are other complaints about the way we deal with campaigns. We are charged with setting ourselves up as the new king-makers. The accusation is that from beginning to end—from deciding who is a serious contender and who is not—right up to the election-night voter projections while polls are still open—we are not just reporting the content but manipulating and even controlling it. I turn to those charges next.

CHAPTER EIGHT

Campaigns: Who's in Charge Here?

*T*HE cream of the nation's political press corps descended on a motel between Orlando, Florida, and Walt Disney World in November 1979 for a special Florida Republican Party convention. Ostensibly they were there to gauge the prospects of the field of 1980 presidential hopefuls with the state's GOP activists before the March 11 primary, when the national convention delegates would be elected.

It was a peculiar contest. About one fifth of the 1,326 delegates were party warhorses, being rewarded for their past labors. The others had backed one of the 1980 candidates and won their seats in lotteries at special county conventions. Despite the artificial format, and the fact that nothing was at stake but bragging rights, at least four of the candidates—Ronald Reagan, George Bush, John Connally, and Philip Crane—made major efforts to recruit and influence delegates, Connally doing so lavishly in the hope of denting Reagan's claim to the South.

But their efforts were modest compared to those President Jimmy Carter's operatives launched at a similar state Democratic convention to crush a possible upset by Senator Edward M. Kennedy, who was not yet a candidate. Once again, nothing tangible was involved, but with Kennedy poised to challenge, it became a high priority for the President to avoid a psychological reverse in his home region.

Even before the county caucuses where the delegates to the October state convention were chosen, the Carter campaign had dispatched at least twenty operatives to Florida and had raised a quarter-million dollars. Federal projects had rained down on Florida cities. "It's idiotic," Carter's White House press secretary Jody Powell had complained on the eve of the county caucuses. "It is not democratic, and it's hard to know exactly what it means, and it's a hell of a way to run a railroad."

Nonetheless, Powell was at Carter's Orlando headquarters, so eager to claim victory in time for the first editions of the Sunday papers that even before the results were known in Dade County, the state's largest population center, he announced a two-to-one Carter win. (In a rare twist, that call was conservative; the final margin was three to one.) Reagan's win was smaller, but enough to dampen Connally's hopes.

What was it all about? In one sense, there was no harm in the October and November extravaganzas. They provided pleasant weekends for the delegates and Florida excursions for several dozen reporters who might otherwise have been home raking leaves. Though these straw votes showed the candidates' early if inconclusive standings in that state, the real prize was the headlines and television coverage they commanded. The Carter and Reagan wins were related in page-one stories in the *Washington Post*—the work of five reporters.

One of those reporters, Nicholas Lemann, focused on what he called the "spectacle of symbiosis—the chicken-and-egg game—between politicians and the press." The Florida party chairmen concocted the straw votes specifically to exploit the press's hunger for a scoreable contest, even though nothing tangible was at stake. The candidates, because they knew the press would cover these nonevents, spent time and money out of all proportion to their significance.

Each side blamed the other for the excess. "It's not us who are making a big deal out of it," Henry W. Hubbard, then deputy chief of *Newsweek*'s Washington bureau, told Lemann. "It's the candidates." But Jay Hakes, head of the Carter operation in Florida, disagreed. "The press was heavily involved before I was," he said. "We're just responding to a heavily publicized challenge."

But Jack W. Germond and Jules Witcover wrote a column defending the press and television concentration on the Florida straw vote. "What would the public reaction have been if the press had ignored the Florida caucuses or given them short shrift? . . . Once candidates or their backers choose to make a test of their organizational abilities, as was the case Saturday, the news media's job is to cover it. . . . Undoubtedly a sense of proportion is lost in the process. But that's part of politics as practiced in the era of mass communication."

Whoever was to blame, the Florida straw votes were a classic example of what many critics regard as the press's unhealthy tendency to create campaign news, rather than just reporting or analyzing it. And not only outside critics agree. Charles B. Seib, who became the *Washington Post*'s in-house critic or ombudsman after retiring as managing editor of the *Washington Star*, wrote the week after the caucuses: "Whoever won—if anybody did—one thing is sure: if this sort of thing continues, political news may be hazardous to your mental health."

Ever since Lincoln Steffens acknowledged that he had created a crime wave in New York simply by publicizing each day one or more gaudy examples of the commonplace violence there, press critics have often found evidence that inventive reporters will happily fill any vacuum. Television strictly prohibits staging events for the cameras, but newspapers seem to bear no stigma for inventing plots.

Anticipatory stories are not confined to governmental and political beats. If the sports pages were limited to reporting contests already played, they would be far smaller (and drabber). Anticipation is part of a good journalist's equipment, closely linked to the desire to be first with the news. Except for the obituary pages, where there is a distinct disadvantage in being premature, journalism is heavily oriented to the scoop. If *they* are going to announce it tomorrow, most editors will say, *we* have every reason to break the story today.

The inclination is so deeply embedded that there is no sense complaining about it. In most instances, it serves the public well. When a new President is elected, people *do* want to know who his cabinet members will be, so reporters fiercely compete to smoke out his choices and let the public in on the secret.

But complaints about the press's intrusiveness in campaigns are so loud and come from so many quarters that they cannot be ignored. At every stage, it is said, television and the newspapers do not just report the story but directly influence the dynamics of the campaigns. Reporters blow up an early and essentially inconsequential event like the Florida straw poll into something more significant than it is. Early polls that measure little but name familiarity determine media coverage in ways that cripple less well known candidates in the competition for supporters and financing.

When the voters begin to make their choices, the press interprets the results, sometimes hyping a tiny plurality win and sometimes decreeing that the actual winner was a loser because he fell short of expectations set by the press. Pack journalism inclines reporters to build up a candidate one week and savage him the next—for no other reason than keeping the story alive.

Later, the party convention halls are converted into giant television studios, with cameramen and correspondents elbowing delegates out of the way and hordes of print reporters scouring the aisles and the bars, searching for or promoting fights that keep the party from delivering the message it wants to deliver to the country.

And, it is said, television and the press distort the tone of the general election campaign by focusing on slips and gaffes, by egging the candidates on to attack each other, and by ignoring the policy proposals. Once again, those incessant polls drown out all serious debate and prejudge the voters' decision. Finally, on Election Day, the impatient media snoop out the trends with their exit polls and broadcast those phony, media-made "results" into areas in the West where people have not yet cast their ballots.

In short, what ought to be the supreme exercise of citizen sovereignty in a republic has been twisted by the almighty press and television into a game where they are almost the only winners—and certainly the most important players.

So goes the indictment. And they can summon expert witnesses on their behalf. John E. Merriam, president of a private Washington firm that predicts emerging public policy trends by monitoring the media, wrote in a 1984 monograph that in campaigns, "the media themselves become the major actors, controlling the streams of information among all players. No longer are they observers, but central movers and censors of public knowledge." What Merriam called "the awesome power of the national media" was demonstrated by the week-to-week trackings of favorable and unfavorable stories, which he said "predicted and probably determined the outcomes of major races" in the Democratic nomination contest.

Similarly, William C. Adams of George Washington University wrote in *Public Opinion* magazine that at every stage of the 1984 Democratic nomination race, "media content changes were followed by changes in public opinion." He cited evidence that in the prepresidential year, poll rankings had determined the allocation of coverage on the networks and in the *Post* and the *Times*, and that after each caucus or primary, the press and television reshuffled the coverage deck in a way that determined who did best in the next round.

IF you think I am going to plead guilty to the whole indictment, you are wrong. But neither do I think the press can hope to see the charges dismissed.

In this age of mass democracy and mass media, when millions of people participate directly, not just by voting in the general election but by selecting the candidates for both major parties, it is not surprising that many resent the way reporters intrude on the process. Voters are not dumb. They can see that we are privileged characters. Any voter who goes to a political rally will likely leave hating the press and TV. The voters wait long past the announced starting time. Their first signal that the event is really beginning is a stream of reporters and camera crews marching to their reserved spaces, scrambling for the best vantage points fronting the stage. The voters suddenly realize that all they are going to see are the backs and behinds of some self-important journalists. Do they despise us? Believe it.

It does no good to tell them that their candidates have decreed this arrangement because the national audience for the nightly television news shows is more important than the few thousand gathered in River City. They don't want to blame their candidate. They blame the damned press. But it goes deeper. Most of the campaign is out of the voters' sight. Some voters may glimpse a presidential candidate for a half hour in their hometown, but most will get almost everything they know about those candidates indirectly through the media. Small wonder that they are suspicious — and resentful — of our power.

There is no escape from this situation, unless we return to a system whereby the candidates are selected by a few score bosses, professional politicians, influential givers, or interest-group leaders. That is not likely. In fact, I would guess I am one of the few reporters who even remember that kind of system.

I grew up in Cook County, Illinois, and my earliest knowledge of a nominating system came from the Chicago papers' descriptions of the slating sessions of the Cook County Democratic organization. Whether Mayor Ed Kelly, Col. Jake Arvey, or Boss Dick Daley presided, the procedure was always the same. An aspirant for the Senate or sanitary commissioner presented himself to the assembled party chieftains, offered up his credentials (usually in terms of apprenticeship in lower office and loyal service to the organization), and was judged worthy or unworthy. After that, it was routine. The organization carried the slated candidates through the formality of a primary and did its utmost to elect them in the general election.

I was never bothered by the press sticking its nose into the smoke-filled room where the slating decisions were made. It gave me my only picture of what was going on. The Chicago system seemed perfectly normal to me. But in the postwar United States, big-city machines all but disappeared. The young men who had returned from the war, finished their educations, begun their careers, and moved into local politics were strongly disinclined to bow to the whims and wills of the political bosses.

In the 1950s and 1960s, American politics demanded individual entrepreneurship: you picked the office you wanted, organized your campaign, raised the money, hired your own polling and advertising consultants, recruited your own volunteers—and went for it. John F. Kennedy first brought this new approach to presidential politics. He was a junior (and not terribly distinguished) senator when he set his gaze on the presidency. He traveled the country extensively for four years before he was nominated in 1960, and his operation became the pattern for other ambitious men of his generation.

So many leaped at the opportunity that some weeding out of the presidential field became necessary. With the bosses no longer in charge, that responsibility fell to the voters in the states with presidential primaries. But in the 1960s, there were few primaries: Kennedy competed in only seven in 1960, and in only two—Wisconsin and West Virginia—did he face serious opposition. As the field of aspirants grew larger and they copied Kennedy's tactic of the long preprimary campaign, the small group of reporters from newspapers, magazines, and networks who worked full-time on national politics became, willy-nilly, a sort of informal screening committee.

I wrote about this phenomenon in the first issue of the *Washington Monthly* in 1969:

> At any given time in this country, there are several hundred persons who are potentially candidates for nomination as President or Vice President. They are Senators, Representatives, governors, Administration officials, mayors, military men, scientists, businessmen, educators, astronauts, and other assorted celebrities. Who is it that winnows this field down to manageable size? The press—and particularly that small segment of the press called the national political reporters.
>
> Russell Baker [the *New York Times* columnist] has given us the concept of The Great Mentioner, that mysterious Someone whose existence is implied when we read that so-and-so "is being mentioned for President or Vice President." He works in clandestine ways. The Great Mentioner mentioned George Romney as a presidential possibility before Romney made his first race for governor of Michigan. The Great Mentioner has mentioned Mark Hatfield for Vice President every four years since Hatfield turned 30, and he never seems discouraged by Hatfield's failure to win the job. . . .
>
> The reporter's job makes him a constant traveler in the political community; he is uniquely well positioned to detect the early intimations of greatness, to discover these statesmen in embryo, and bring their rare qualities to the attention of a wider public.
>
> But, alas, it is not quite that simple—or noncontroversial. In his function as a talent scout, the political reporter not only puts some men forward, he rather ruthlessly bars the door to advancement for other men. Martin F. Nolan of the *Boston Globe* has compared the national political reporters to a band of traveling drama critics, covering the new political acts at their out-of-town openings in Sacramento or Lansing or Harrisburg. Their reports, like those in *Variety*, are frequently make-or-break. "No talent," they will say of one man, and his name is forgotten. "Promising," they'll say of another, and he is booked into the Gridiron Dinner [an annual white-tie affair for journalists and politicians which has become an important showcase for ambitious office-seekers] or *Meet the Press*. It's a formidable power, and one that the screening committee of reporters is thoroughly conscious of possessing.
>
> It is important at this point to say something about the members of this

screening committee. . . . The group is small. It probably includes a couple of dozen members, representing news organizations with a commitment to coverage of national politics year in and year out, in dull seasons as well as exciting times. . . .The political reporters for these organizations, plus a few syndicated columnists who cover politics along with other subjects, comprise the screening committee.

Not only is this group small, but its characteristics make it a highly atypical group of Americans. Its members are all Easterners, by residence if not by birth. They are college graduates. They all enjoy, despite the low-paying reputation of newspapers, incomes well over the national median. Not one of them is a Negro. Only two are women. More of them vote Democratic and fewer of them regularly attend church, I would guess, than in a random sample of the population. None is under 30, and few, except for the columnists, are over 45. I am deliberately not commenting on their social, political or ethical views, but I think I have said enough to indicate that they—or we, I should say—represent a narrow and rather peculiar slice of this society. . . .

Nonetheless, the fact is that the reporters do function as a screening committee for aspirants to national office. . . . And whether their standards are good or bad, whether they are characteristic or eccentric so far as the society is concerned, they make their standards stick.

Romney was a notable victim of the system I described. Although he had been a successful executive in both the auto industry and in state government, he was relatively unsophisticated on national and international issues and surprisingly inarticulate in discussing them. The press scrutiny of his views on the Vietnam War in 1966 and 1967 proved excruciatingly difficult. Instinctively he was opposed to the United States intervention, but politically he wanted to avoid being linked to the antiwar demonstrators, so he tried artlessly to hedge. When Romney told a radio interviewer in Detroit in the late summer of 1967 that he had been "brainwashed" by American authorities during a visit to Vietnam, it seemed to epitomize his ineptitude. The ridicule grew so great that Romney—once the front-runner—withdrew from the presidential race on the eve of the 1968 New Hampshire primary.

ALTHOUGH few people in politics realize it, the press's screening power has declined significantly since the 1960s. Two things have reduced it. The number of presidential primaries has multiplied because of the rules changes or "reforms" instituted by the Democratic Party after its tumultuous and crippling convention of 1968. Fifteen states held presidential primaries in 1968, twenty-one in 1972, twenty-seven in 1976, thirty-seven in 1980, twenty-six in 1984, and as many as thirty-one are tentatively scheduled in 1988. The portion of delegates chosen in primaries rose from two fifths to a peak of four fifths.

Secondly, the campaign finance law passed in 1974 largely eliminated the ability of a few fat-cat big givers to launch a presidential candidacy and sustain it through its takeoff period. With individual contributions limited to $1,000 and a Federal matching premium for contributions less than $250, all aspirants were forced early on to seek dollars as well as votes all across the country.

Those two changes began the era of the perpetual presidential campaign, the "marathon" of which Jules Witcover wrote in his book by that name about the 1976 election. In the summers of 1974, 1978, and 1982—two full years before the nominating conventions—anywhere from eight to fifteen "presidential campaigns" existed. No news organization could conceivably monitor all those activities, nor was there any market for them—even among the political news–junkie readers of the *Washington Post*.

While local press and radio and television often covered the candidates, the networks and the national press rarely did. Some candidates were frustrated by this lack of early attention and complained to us. But they began to realize the advantages of the long period of relative obscurity. They could test their themes and practice their speeches without the press's flyspeck scrutiny, which had proved so damaging to Romney and others. I'm sure, in some cases, they were able to fine-tune their messages for the immediate audience, without making them jibe exactly with what they had said a half-continent away. The absence of the pack of accompanying journalists facilitated the kind of person-to-person campaigning critical at that stage, when candidates are seeking not massive numbers of converts but hard-core, committed supporters in key states.

Finally, they could burst upon the national scene, with the primary season drawing near, as candidates with "surprising" campaign skills and organizational support. Jimmy Carter, George Bush, Gary Hart, and others ignored Washington and the other national media centers on their travels. They knew they did not need national coverage or a strong showing in the polls. The dynamic had changed: in the new game, you built your strength quietly, surprised the press in an early caucus or primary in Iowa or New Hampshire, and then sat back and reaped the publicity bonanza. George Bush spoke for many others, in the wake of his Iowa upset, when he said, "I started off as an asterisk in the polls. . . . It was the impossible dream."

People like political consultant John P. Sears have argued in seminars on the nominating process that journalists should more assertively become "the new bosses" by publicizing their recommendations on who has "the right stuff" to be President. But most of us shake our heads, "No, thank you." We are relieved to be rid of our screening committee responsibilities.

But some critics say the press does covertly what Sears urges us to do overtly. One set of complaints comes from the candidates and their managers, who contend that the preoccupation with polling—particularly the very early polls—makes it difficult, if not impossible, for less well known candidates to compete for attention on the basis of their programs, their records, and their personalities.

Not only are such candidates hurt among the voters, but fund-raisers I know attest to the crippling effect of a bad poll in the early stages of a candidacy. Furthermore, there is plenty of reason to distrust early polls: just ask Ed Muskie and Ted Kennedy, who started out ahead and fell behind before they knew what had hit them. Early polls reflect name familiarity and not much more.

Why do we print polls like the ones the Harris and Gallup organizations did in April and July of 1985, showing George Bush leading for the Republican nomination in 1988 and Edward M. Kennedy out in front of the Democratic pack? The answer, once again, is clique journalism. The political junkies can't wait until autumn 1987 to get their first fix on the 1988 presidential race. They need some numbers for their conversations and speculations. And we junkie journalists supply them.

We won't stop, but we could use our early polling more sensibly than for measuring a horse race not yet begun. We could, for example, measure real support against familiarity and thereby distinguish between the widely known candidate with "high negatives" and the lesser-known candidate who might have potentially broader support.

We can frame questions that supply information about lesser-known candidates and report the voters' reaction.

We need to remind readers that experience shows that the standings will change after the early caucuses and primaries. We also need to place circuit breakers in our own minds between the rankings in those early polls and the rationing of space and attention to the various contenders.

That is not easy to do, but we have learned at the *Post* that it can be done. In the last three national elections, we have deliberately not covered the presidential contest until Labor Day of the prepresidential year. Before that date, we have limited the stories to announcements of candidacies, legitimate campaign developments—endorsements, hirings or firings of campaign managers, etc.—and major policy statements. When an issue has popped into the news, we have run solicited comments from all the aspirants side by side.

Our first big effort after Labor Day is the set of candidate profiles, each involving weeks of reporting on the candidate's background, political and governmental history, record and reputation and approach to policy. We do this for all the contenders, long shots as well as front-runners.

We also try to see how the candidates are handling the political challenges coming at them. In 1983, for example, we covered the Democratic contenders at policy forums in New York, Iowa, and New Hampshire and measured their abilities as campaigners, the quality of their local organizations, and the character of their support.

At this point—the autumn and winter before the first caucuses and primaries—it is primarily a newspaper story. The networks and news magazines have not begun to devote as much time and space as we do, and paid television advertising has not started. We rely mainly on old-fashioned techniques, paying much more attention to what we see and hear in interviews with candidates, managers, activist volunteers, and voters than to the intermittent polls. If any candidate has a real advantage, if anyone is moving or stalling, this is when our senses and skills will disclose it.

This is also when our judgments begin to have some impact, in two ways. We begin to sort out the field and to focus on those who seem to have something going. And we begin to share those findings with readers, as I did in the early 1972 stories raising doubts about the effectiveness of Muskie's New Hampshire organization and as so many of us did with similar questions about the John Glenn operation in 1984. At this point the campaign managers start getting miffed with the press. They claim, and rightly so, that most voters have not yet become familiar with the whole field or heard them present all their views, and therefore cannot make an informed judgment.

The candidates would really like us to suspend judgment and let them use the news columns and the precious moments television devotes to the campaign to expound their ideas. Our view—or at least mine—is that we have a responsibility to communicate their views on major issues, as we do by covering the debates and policy forums, but that the job of delivering their message to the voters is primarily theirs, by dint of campaigning, organizing, fund-raising, and advertising.

AFTER the first caucus and the first primary, we are off on a steeplechase in which the best thing candidates or reporters can hope for is to avoid being thrown off into the dirt. The process has a mad momentum beyond anyone's ability to slow it down. Some days we are so wearied by the travel, the deadlines, the flackery, and the pressures that we want to say, "Stop the world. I want to get off." But we can't.

The candidates now complain that our emphasis on the winner in the early contests foreshortens the selection process and denies laggard candidates an opportunity to catch up and voters in the later primary and caucus states a chance to make their judgments have an impact. No question, the early caucuses and primaries get a disproportionate share of coverage and therefore have an exaggerated impact on the whole process. In 1976 and 1980, the New Hampshire primary in late February had much more importance than the California primary in early June, even though California's population is twenty-five times that of New Hampshire.

Michael J. Robinson and Margaret A. Sheehan, in their book *Over the Wire and on TV*, a study of 1980 coverage by CBS News and UPI, reported that "Iowa and New Hampshire on average attracted 74 news stories per election on 'Evening News' and the day [UPI] wire combined. The nine states holding their primaries in June averaged fewer than six stories on CBS and UPI. Iowa caucus voters got sixty times as much news attention per vote as people casting their ballot in the late

California primary. Presidential politics and campaign media are *front-loaded* and grow increasingly more so with each passing election."

This front-loading distortion is partly because we have more time to spend in Iowa and New Hampshire than in almost any other primaries from March until June of the presidential year. But it is also a result of the journalistic desire to get the news first. First events always draw coverage, whether it is the opening of a show or a flight to the moon. R. W. (Johnny) Apple, Jr., a top-notch political reporter on *The New York Times*, won honors for his coverage of the 1976 campaign, in part because of his careful attention to Jimmy Carter's victory in an early straw poll taken at a Democratic fund-raising dinner in Ames, Iowa, on October 27, 1975.

Every four years the Democratic Party debates what it should do to reduce the exaggerated impact of Iowa and New Hampshire and to eliminate the artificial straw polls which come even earlier. So far, states' rights have largely prevailed over the national party's attempts to rationalize its process. Other states, notably in the South, have pushed their 1988 primary dates forward, but a more effective change would be to implement Representative Morris K. Udall's suggestion that primaries be held only on the first Tuesday of March, April, May, and June. With his plan, later states could receive the kind of in-depth coverage that only Iowa and New Hampshire now enjoy.

But the impact of the undoubted media bias for first events should not be exaggerated. In 1972 McGovern lost New Hampshire; in 1980 Reagan lost Iowa; and in 1984 Mondale lost New Hampshire; but all three won their party's nomination. The twists and turns of the competition between Mondale and Gary Hart brought much more press attention to the Illinois, New York, Pennsylvania, and Ohio primaries, and even carried long-denied mass coverage to the closing contests in California and New Jersey.

The focus on firsts also influences who gets covered. Thomas E. Patterson wrote in *The Mass Media Election* that the winner of each week's primary in 1976 drew about 60 percent of the coverage—even if his "victory" was barely visible. In the Iowa precinct caucuses that year, "uncommitted" delegates won 37 percent and Carter finished second with just under 29 percent. But, as Patterson noted, that did not prevent Roger Mudd from saying on CBS that "no amount of bad-mouthing by others can lessen the importance of Jimmy Carter's finish. He was the clear winner in this psychologically crucial test. With thirteen projected national convention delegates [of the 1,505 needed for nomination that year], almost 28 percent of the total, he has opened ground between himself and the rest of the so-called pack."

But that was small potatoes compared to his plurality victory in New Hampshire the next month. Though Carter received just over 28 percent of the vote in a nine-person field, exactly 4,663 more votes than the runner-up, Udall, NBC's Tom Pettit said, "Carter emerges from New Hampshire as the man to beat," and *Newsweek* proclaimed him "the unqualified winner." The New Hampshire victory, Patterson noted, put Carter on all three networks that night and the next morning, and the following week on the covers of *Time* and *Newsweek*, with 2,600 lines of coverage, compared to Udall's 96.

Why the emphasis—the overemphasis—on the winner? Patterson suggested that the answer lies in Walter Lippmann's observation that "the function of news is to signalize an event," to alert the reader to its most obvious aspect, not its complexities. That may be right, but it is not a wholly satisfactory response. The outcomes in Iowa and New Hampshire could have been "signalized" accurately by news leads saying, "Democratic voters were divided in their presidential preferences, with no one approaching majority support." But that is not exciting.

Two experiences in that 1976 campaign led me to think something more powerful was at work. On the night of the Iowa caucuses, Jules Witcover (then with the *Post*) was in Des Moines and I was in Washington. When his story came in, the night national news editor said something like, "Witcover says Carter's winning Iowa. What kind of a head [headline] do you think that deserves?"

I considered the percentages and the number of uncommitted votes compared with those for any candidate, and said, "Don't go overboard." He did not. He put the story at the bottom right-hand corner of the front page with the modest headline "Carter Takes Early Lead in Iowa." But Carter's victory was not only big news on the next morning's TV shows, it was the banner headline in the first edition of the *Washington Star*, an afternoon newspaper, and from that point on, it was off to the races. Witcover's careful second-day story said Carter "has gained early momentum" but called his victory "far from decisive." Our competitors had been far less cautious. Ultimately, the banner headlines and television fanfares drowned out such rare notes of prudence.

The single most troubling letter I received criticizing our coverage of the 1976 campaign came from a Maryland Democratic leader who, after pointing out that his party had barred winner-take-all presidential primaries after 1972, wrote, "You in the press have in effect imposed winner-take-all on us, by the way in which you have chosen to report and interpret the results of our primaries. You have done so to the point that I, as a supporter of Senator Henry Jackson, was put in the ridiculous position of having to vote for Governor Jerry Brown—a man I do not want to see as President—in the Maryland primary, simply in order to deny Jimmy Carter another 'unearned publicity dividend' as the winner of the Maryland primary.

"How do you in the press justify such behavior?"

I could not deny the facts he cited or the effect of the kind of coverage he described. "My only question," I replied, "is whether your argument is with us in the press, or rather with the whole American value system, embodied in Vince Lombardi's famous saying, 'Winning isn't everything. It's the only thing.'"

Because the press is shaped by, and even contributes to the shaping of, the values of society, we cannot report the results of primaries and conventions without emphasizing who won. Does that distort the process? Absolutely. The winner of the early contests gets a big megaphone with which to say, "Look at me, folks. Am I not wonderful? Are you not lucky to have me as your candidate?" Horse-race journalism does everything the critics say. It short-circuits the system, denies voters in the later primary states an equal voice, reduces the chances of detecting a fraud, and lessens the likelihood of pausing for second thoughts before the nomination.

These considerations argue for changing the nominating system and decreasing the number of primaries. But it is important to remember, at this point, that the primaries grew, not from the press, but from rule changes by a group of Democratic Party leaders. Reporters will cover the process any way the parties conduct it—open or closed. Candidly, I prefer, as a print reporter, conventions and caucuses, where a single reporter, with nothing more than a notebook and pencil, can slip in closer to the action than the camera crews and TV correspondents.

Richard L. Rubin in his book *Press, Party and Presidency* argued that while journalists did not promote primaries, television especially has "legitimated" them "as the proper, democratic and 'American way'" to choose nominees. No question, television loves primaries because they provide a real-life Tuesday night serial. Primaries are out in the open, with candidates campaigning in scenic settings, which television values.

Despite the TV preference for primaries, many of us political reporters recognize that the more closed system of the past provided greater suspense and greater rewards for journalistic enterprise. In 1960, for example, I recall no press complaints about the fact that John F. Kennedy did not secure the votes he needed for nomination until Pennsylvania and Illinois delegates caucused in Los Angeles the day before the convention opened. TV folks might grumble in advance, but if the parties went all the way back into the smoke-filled room, when the bosses came out of the hotel suite with the name of the nominee, they would be greeted by a small wall of cameras and a horde of Sam Donaldsons. We would adapt.

THE indictment does not stop with the primaries. According to many politicians, reporters—especially the television stars—have converted the political conventions into showcases for their competitive egos and ambitions.

I suspect I take this complaint more seriously than do some of the people who object to the aisles being cluttered with correspondents and cameras. Many of these delegates enjoy being on camera as much as any other aspect of the convention. Much of their reward comes not from participating in the choice of a possible President but from having folks back home say, "I saw you on TV. You looked great."

It can be argued that the convention's only function is to provide raw material for television because the nominee has been predetermined in the primaries. The platform is written in advance and the floor fights over amending it tend to be forgotten by the next day. The dwindling TV audiences and the networks' decision to cut back their coverage indicate that voters know that nothing much happens.

Persuasive as that may be, I don't buy it. The four-day conventions are the only time a national political party exists. The convention is legally its ruling body, and the convention period defines whether—

and on what terms—the diverse party factions are prepared to work together during the campaign and, if successful, to govern. When the Democratic and Republican parties meet, their surface shenanigans should not disguise the seriousness of their task. That work deserves our respect, and they don't get it today, not with us crawling all over them and doing our damnedest to take over their conventions.

The national party conventions are the greatest clique gatherings the press has. What brings us there in such numbers—twelve thousand accredited journalists at the 1984 Democratic convention in San Francisco—is partly the story but mainly the chance to be part of the scene.

Much that news organizations do at conventions is to impress each other, the politicians, and the officials. The networks are the most ostentatious, with their fancy anchor booths slung from the ceiling, dominating the convention hall. But they are not alone. All the major news organizations throw elaborate parties and entertainments. The schedule is carefully negotiated, so *Time* and *Newsweek*, the *New York Times*, the *Los Angeles Times*, and *USA Today* each has its allotted hours to shine. (The *Post* is invited to *Newsweek*'s function, instead of having its own.) The competition for star guests is fierce, and people keep score.

They also compete in other ways. Newspapers make extraordinary and expensive efforts to deliver each day's edition to the convention hotels and, if possible, to the doors of the delegates and the other journalists. Newspapers report on the network battles for scoops and audience shares and, in recent years, some of the networks have graded the performance of the major newspapers and individual reporters.

Reputations are made or unmade at conventions. No one forgets that the classic Huntley-Brinkley team was forged in the 1956 convention anchor booth, or that both John Chancellor's and Dan Rather's careers were boosted by keeping cool when overzealous security men hassled them on the convention floor. Being assigned to the floor is a career breakthrough for a TV reporter, and those who do well in that elbows-out environment—as Sam Donaldson did in 1976, for example—see their fortunes soar.

●   ●   ●

WHAT gets lost in this superheated, ego-inflating atmosphere is the basic journalistic discipline of delivering news to readers or viewers in a form they can use. Newspaper coverage is excessive. Reporters have to justify their presence and expenses. But television's coverage is worse. It probably puts on more hours of live political "news" during the convention weeks than during the entire fall campaign. Covering the scene live, and trying to keep the audience interested, the networks often create stories or hype them beyond belief. One spectacular example was the Reagan-Ford "dream ticket" fiasco of 1980.

The one thing uncertain as the convention began was the identity of Reagan's running mate. Early on, there had been speculation about a Reagan-Ford ticket, but it had dropped off in early June when Reagan called on Ford in Palm Springs and Ford repeated his view that Reagan should find another running mate.

But the speculation revived on Monday when Ford told the convention, "this Republican would do everything in his power" to elect Reagan, "so when this convention fields the team for Governor Reagan, count me in." Bill Moyers wondered in a CBS commentary what would happen "if Ronald Reagan called up Gerald Ford after the session tonight" and then made a public plea to the convention delegates "to draft him."

Lou Cannon of the *Post* and I learned from people close to Ford that the Reagan side had made fresh overtures but that Ford was determined to resist them—and was so aggravated that the platform had dropped support of the Equal Rights Amendment that he might leave Detroit before Reagan was nominated. Cannon, who had given the Reagan campaign its definitive coverage and who was determined that no one would scoop him in Detroit, wrote Tuesday night that Ford had recommended Bush to Reagan. The story ran Wednesday, the day Reagan would be nominated, and quoted unnamed Reagan aides as saying that the choice was tipping in Bush's direction.

I too expected Bush to be the pick and had said so when Jack Germond, Tom Pettit, and I did our daily NBC *Today* show stint that Wednesday morning. But after the *Today* show, I got a surprise from a chance meeting with a Republican party official who had been in the Ford administration (and who was also an old friend). "I think we're going to get Ford on the ticket," he told me. He said he was serious, and described a late Tuesday night meeting which was now reconvening. A number of top party and congressional officials were lobbying Ford to take the number two slot and were urging Reagan to make the job more attractive to the former President.

I was dumbfounded. But he was a good source and could not be playing games with me. I hurried back to the *Post*'s work space, where Cannon and I got on the phone and soon confirmed that such efforts were under way and that there was a good chance of their succeeding.

As it happened, Ford was scheduled to have lunch that day with *Newsweek* editors and reporters. At lunch, he strongly suggested that he was intrigued by an arrangement in which the President would be the chairman and chief executive of the government and the Vice President the chief operating officer. His description of the role the Vice President would have in appointing other officials, in setting up White House staff procedures and determining the flow of paper to the President showed that these clearly were not idle speculations.

Newsweek and the *Washington Post* are owned by the same corporation, but the relationship is one of intense rivalry, not cooperation. This was a *Newsweek* lunch, to which *Post* reporters were not invited. But there are no secrets in a group of that size, and within an hour, friends at *Newsweek* were telling us—with glee—that we were going to have to "eat" the Bush-for-Vice-President story, because Ford was all but signed on for the job. All afternoon, the "dream ticket" story preoccupied us, and the story Cannon and I wrote for the first edition of the paper said that the speculation was rife but that it was speculation.

The network evening news broadcasts, which went on the air as we were finishing our first-edition story, took the same cautious approach. John Chancellor said on NBC, "a mighty effort is under way tonight" to draft Ford. "The former President is still listening, but his position is that he doesn't want to run." Dan Rather, reporting for CBS at Reagan headquarters, described the negotiations on an enhanced role that Ford might play as Vice President but said, "there is no final answer." He quoted an anonymous congressman: "I'd still be amazed if Ford did it. I personally think it's going to be Bush, but Reagan isn't kidding. He really wants Ford." (These quotations, and others, come from Jeff Greenfield's excellent summary of the evening's television transcripts in his book *The Real Campaign*.)

At this point, the TV news was accurate and restrained. But soon, as the news programs finished and TV began reporting live, the pattern changed. As the live prime-time coverage began at 7 P.M., Ford came to the CBS anchor booth for a long-scheduled interview with Cronkite. (He had already done interviews for the other two networks.) As a lead-in, Cronkite went back to Rather, who reported that there was still skepticism that Ford would accept, but "until he doesn't say a final no [sic], that Ronald Reagan isn't going to consider anybody else."

Cronkite then asked Ford, "Can you verify that Dan's reporting is accurate today? Now, you're not going to go back on Dan?" (The question, though asked in a jocular tone, suggested that already CBS had become proprietary about the story.)

Ford said he could not comment. When Cronkite next asked him about a theoretical convention-floor draft movement, Ford stopped fencing and told the world that his answer would depend "on the arrangements that I would expect as a Vice President in a relationship with the President. I would not go to Washington, Walter, and be a figurehead Vice President," but would insist on "a meaningful role across the board in the basic and the crucial and the important decisions that have to be made."

"It's got to be something like a co-presidency?"

Ford did not demur. "That's something that Governor Reagan really ought to consider."

Everyone in our work booth at Cobo Hall was astonished that Ford had made these discussions public. Reagan, we would learn the next day, had been equally nonplussed. As we scribbled frantic notes, someone phoned Washington to say that the first-edition story would need a quick rewrite.

Meantime, Ford was still rattling on in his cheerful way about other aspects of such an arrangement, even as he cautioned Cronkite, "Don't jump to the wrong conclusion now." "Well," Cronkite replied, "we're going to jump to conclusions all over the place tonight."

And indeed television did. Barbara Walters of ABC intercepted Ford as he was leaving the CBS aerie and, as Jeff Greenfield has reported, "close to tears, begged Ford for several minutes, in near-hysterical terms, to grant her an immediate interview." Ford agreed.

At the same time, every reporter in Detroit was scurrying to find his best sources. As quickly as TV correspondents hunted them down, they were put on the air to broadcast the latest conjectures. The rumors came thicker and faster. The "mays" and "mights" became "wills" and "woulds," until finally, at 10:10 P.M., Cronkite said, "CBS News has learned that there is a definite plan for Ronald Reagan and the former President of the United States, Gerald Ford, who will be his selection as running mate, . . . to come to this convention hall tonight to appear together on the platform for Ronald Reagan to announce that Gerald Ford would run with him."

NBC and ABC stopped a step short, with various correspondents or interviewees saying there was "substance" to the report that Ford was on his way with Reagan, or, in another version, already in the convention building, awaiting Reagan, for their grand entrance, but adding that it was not confirmed. Douglas Kiker, the NBC correspondent with Ford, raised the caution flag so high with his network anchors that NBC contributed relatively little to the hysteria.

For another hour and a half, as the ritual of Reagan's nomination was carried out, there was no confirmation. Print reporters were also nervous because our major edition deadlines were now on us. A number of papers put the "dream ticket" story in the headlines. So did the Associated Press.

Our editors back in Washington were calling us to find out why we were not "hardening up" the story. Cannon and I checked signals again. During the day, each of us had established contact with sources we trusted in the top-floor hotel suite where the discussions had been taking place. They had agreed to call us when they could and to try to keep us from being scooped or suckered. They were our ultimate checkpoints in the rumor-filled madhouse.

Earlier, at about 8:30, my source had given me one crucial bit of information. "There's a deadline on this," he had said. "If it's going to be done at all, it's going to have to be done in the next two hours. We can't let this go on overnight."

So by 11 P.M. I figured the negotiations had probably fallen apart, but I could not be sure, since obviously I could not call my source out of the meetings and he was quite possibly too busy or preoccupied to call me. We decided on a course of caution and avoided error.

What had happened, as we learned the next day, was that once again television's coverage had not only distorted but altered the course of events. The same TV reports that fed the rising speculative fever on the convention floor forced Reagan's hand and possibly changed the outcome of the discussions.

The spectacle of Ford publicly describing to Cronkite the possible division of powers with Reagan forced the presidential nominee to face up to the impossibility of such an arrangement. So long as the discussions had been private, it had been possible to fuzz over the reality— and absurdity—of setting up twin power centers at the top of the government. As the implications of that arrangement became clear, only one of two outcomes was possible: either Ford would go on the ticket, on terms that would be virtually impossible to explain or to live with, or he must refuse, thus disappointing the delegates who had been primed by the TV rumors to believe the Reagan-Ford deal was set.

By about 11 P.M., both Ford and Reagan recognized the impossibility and danger of the situation. Ford finally took himself out of the picture and Reagan made the long-delayed call to Bush. A few minutes before midnight, calls went from the Reagan suite to Joe Louis Arena, saying Reagan was on his way over to tell the delegates he had picked Bush. Those in our work space—unlike those on the convention floor and in the TV anchor booths—were relieved but not surprised. My first reaction to the "dream ticket," fifteen hours earlier, had been "That's crazy." It struck me as an inherently unstable personality mix and as a division of labor that could not work. It also struck me as a political time bomb, which would plunge Reagan into immediate and continuing controversy and would keep him from making his own planned attack on Carter's weaknesses. I remember saying to a political consultant at midday, "That ticket [Reagan-Ford] would blow up as fast as McGovern-Eagleton. It wouldn't last until Labor Day."

Later, having seen how close it came to being, I realized that my initial reaction was dangerously wrong. But not as dangerously wrong as television's riding the rumors it helped spread—riding them right over the cliff.

LIKE a lot of other bad journalistic habits, this kind of convention coverage seems impossible to break, given the competitive pressures. Knowing it would not be accepted, I have nevertheless offered every incoming Republican and Democratic chairman for the last twenty years a suggestion that would move both the parties and the press-TV practices in the right direction. The party chairmen would say in a joint statement: We are holding our conventions next July and August. We invite you ladies and gentlemen to cover us. We will extend every courtesy and help we can, but we think that what we will do in those four days is as important to our party and our country as, say, the Super Bowl or the World Series. Therefore, you will have excellent views of the proceedings, good camera angles and plenty of opportunity to interview the people you want to interview. But, just as in the Super Bowl or the World Series, the playing field should belong to the players. And therefore, you will not be allowed on the floor when the convention is in session.

What would that do? First of all, without all of us in their way, the status of the delegates would change. They could talk with each other more easily—something party leaders from different states rarely have a chance to do, and something that can, in fact, contribute to the health of the parties.

Newspapers and news magazine reporters would be inconvenienced, but not seriously. Our contacts ought to be good enough that we can, from our seats overlooking the convention floor, signal people and ask them to step off the floor for an interview, as we do regularly with House and Senate members.

Without access to the convention floor, television would be less inclined to continue its extensive live coverage. Instead, the networks would treat the convention as a news story, carrying the genuine news live and handling the rest on their regular news shows. C-SPAN could provide gavel-to-gavel coverage for the junkies, but the whole thing would be kept in better proportion.

EVEN that radical a change would not quiet those who argue that during the autumn campaign, the press and TV, with their endless score keeping and obsession with hidden motives, actually interfere with the public's decision making. For instance, they point out that in the presidential debates, no sooner have the candidates completed their closing statements than the airwaves are filled with interpretations and analyses, the pollsters are on their phones, and people like myself are furiously typing our reactions.

Each candidate's "spin patrols" understand that the journalists' verdict can significantly influence who the public perceives as the winner of the debates. Therefore, they hover at our elbows, telling us how successful their man was at achieving his strategic objectives and how flawed his opponent's performance was. Snap judgments, rendered on the scene and with deadline pressures, are often off the mark. In a biting commentary, two days after the Carter-Reagan debate in 1980, Robert Kaiser wrote in the *Post*:

> On the basis of our scant national experience with this art form, instant analysis of it is usually worthless. After the Reagan–John B. Anderson debate [earlier in the autumn of 1980] the analysts said Anderson held his own, but within days the polls showed Anderson sinking like a cold soufflé. The instant analysts missed the significance of Nixon's makeup [in 1960] and misread the electoral consequences of Ford's Polish slip [in 1976].

He's right. Of the three general-election debate "instant analysis" pieces I have written, only the last—after the second Reagan-Mondale debate in 1984—was on target.

A reporter has to jump three hurdles to handle the debate assessment well. We are trained to make a balanced judgment, so we score the debate by rounds, as if it were a prize-fight: we say A did well on Points 1, 4, 6, and 7, but B probably came out ahead on Points 2, 3, 5, and 8. As a result our verdicts tend to be cautious and fuzzy.

Second, being somewhat familiar with the issues, we are inclined to give some weight—perhaps undue weight—to the candidates' accuracy and skill in answering policy questions. Ironically, our performance as instant analysts is handicapped by qualities our critics say we lack: a desire to be fair and an interest in substance.

The third point—which took me a long time to understand—is that our overall assessment of the debate must be based on who seems more in command. That is the test. And if you realize that television news shows will quickly capsulize the whole debate into that moment or two when one candidate or the other takes command, your attention can focus on recognizing that moment and can put it into the context of the campaign situation.

Before each debate I have covered, I have forced myself to write down—based on what I have learned from the two camps and my own sense of the strategic situation—what will constitute success or failure for each of the candidates.

For example, in 1980 Reagan had to do very little to beat Carter; he just had to be a reasonable, nonfrightening alternative to an incumbent whose record appeared so bad that most people wanted a new President. Using that criterion, my lead said that "Jimmy Carter accomplished almost every objective except the most important one: the destruction of Ronald Reagan's credibility as a potential President." But overall the story was so balanced that even the headline writer missed my verdict and wrote, "Carter on Points, but No KO."

In the first 1984 debate, Mondale needed a spectacular showing, and my lead said he "did his part as well as his managers could have hoped." But my reaction to Reagan's unexpected ineptitude was not as sharp—perhaps because it was so unexpected and perhaps because my brain was dulled by just having watched my team, the Chicago Cubs, blow the fifth and final game of the National League playoffs to the San Diego Padres.

Finally, on the second 1984 debate, I got it right. Referring to Reagan's rejoinder on the age question, I said, "There was a huge laugh, in which Mondale joined. But it may well have been that the biggest barrier to Reagan's reelection was swept away in that moment."

I would like to think my on-target analysis of the second Reagan-Mondale debate means I have at last learned this art form. But the serious question, once again, is why we bother calling the debates? Why not just summarize the exchanges and explore the accuracy of the candidates' claims, their competence on the issues, and whatever policy implications emerged?

We do all those things, but we cannot ignore that these debates are major campaign events, not university seminars. They test the candidates' skills, and we must judge how well they meet that test. The campaign organizations do that even during the debate. In 1984 Reagan's pollster, Richard Wirthlin, seated a "focus group" in a television viewing room equipped with simple hand levers linked to a computer, which would indicate their degree of approval, disagreement, or discomfiture as the debate progressed. The group's collective responses were integrated by computer on a running graph, which, when superimposed onto a tape of the debate, let Reagan's managers see, moment by moment, the political-emotional response to the confrontation.

That seems appropriate to 1984 in the Orwellian sense, but news organizations also pursue instant reactions from the public. ABC News was criticized after the 1980 debates for setting up two 900 numbers, where for fifty cents people could call in their verdict. The network flashed running totals of calls that got through on their post-debate broadcast and found Reagan winning two to one. Kaiser in the *Post* said the gimmick "set a new standard for pernicious irrelevance," but the news organizations, including the *Post*, have continued to take and publish post-debate polls as quickly as we can.

WE are, in fact, saturated with polls. At the American University post-election forum, Ann Lewis, the political director of the Democratic National Committee during 1984, described their battering-ram effect:

> Here we have ABC News on September 1—September 1 is relatively early in the campaign; some of us thought we were in there fighting—saying, "There is more bad news today for Mr. Mondale. A new ABC poll published today . . . [shows] President Reagan as of now appears to have a whopping lead in five key states."
>
> Moving right along, here we have the *L.A. Times* on September 3 saying, "A *Los Angeles Times* poll released today"—September 3 is Labor Day; some people think the real campaign begins on Labor Day; the media was telling us it was over—"shows the President 27 points ahead of Mondale, and Reagan's huge lead does more than lift Republican spirits." It certainly does. It wipes us out from trying to talk about the fact that there is a campaign going on.

Certainly the polls have been given exaggerated importance at times. When Nelson Rockefeller belatedly challenged Richard Nixon in 1968, he based his candidacy on the contention that he would be stronger in the general election. But a Gallup poll released just as the delegates were gathering in Miami Beach showed Nixon slightly stronger against Hubert Humphrey. The Nixon camp was jubilant, the Rockefeller camp crushed. Three days later, Lou Harris reported exactly the opposite and the sentiments reversed. Finally, the two pollsters issued a statement saying that both polls showed "a steady gain in public support" for Rockefeller. The delegates nominated Nixon.

This illustrates the danger of journalists' or politicians' believing that the polls have a life of their own. Rockefeller had not run in the primaries. He had relied on a late advertising and speechmaking campaign, hoping to move the polls and sway the delegates. But Nixon had won the primaries and had gained commitments from key party leaders that were far more powerful.

Generally, complaints about polls constitute a classic example of "blaming the messenger." In 1984 the root of the problem for Ann Lewis and other Democrats was not the polls but Ronald Reagan's tremendous political strength and the liabilities Walter Mondale had displayed during the long primary season. But it is always easier to blame the press.

Another, less easily dismissed complaint is that we are so preoccupied with tactics and strategy during the general election campaign that our reporting tells voters, you are being manipulated. At the Harvard conference on television and the election process, campaign consultant John Deardourff said that there is a "constant tension . . . between our interest in having people hear what the candidate has to say and the news media's interest in telling us more about why he or she is saying it at that particular time and place." Several other journalists agreed, including *New Yorker* magazine writer Elizabeth Drew, who said, "I believe very strongly in being skeptical . . . [but] I wonder if sometimes the sum total of the coverage doesn't tip over to the point where the process is robbed of any sense of majesty, inspiration . . ."

The late Frank Reynolds, anchorman for ABC News, said that since a campaign is basically "an attempt to manipulate" the media, "reporters have to inject some reality . . . that may not be at all in conformity with the image that the advisers wish to project." But Robert MacNeil of the *MacNeil/Lehrer Newshour* and Tom Brokaw of NBC both agreed that television has a problem of tone in its treatment of politics. MacNeil said that in a couple of sentences at the end of their pieces, TV reporters seek "to express their detachment and distance" from the story. And in so doing, they "compress into a very few words what, I think, could easily be interpreted as cynicism." Brokaw said that TV correspondents so often feel that the candidate's publicists are dictating scenes and stories and even camera angles that "the way to get back is to go out there and jab him quickly right at the end . . . get one quick shot and go."

The conflict will not likely be resolved. Candidates always want to be taken at face value and to have us report their words just as they deliver them, without interpretation, analysis, or comment, even when they and their agents have obviously glossed their own product and denigrated the opposition. And the press *is* sometimes guilty of seeking secret motives and stratagems even where none exist, and of reporting campaigns as if they were all tactics and no substance. Both sides—the press and the candidates—are too conscious of each other and not mindful enough of the third parties outside our clique— readers, viewers, voters.

THE final indictment concerns the use of exit polls to declare a winner while the polls are still open on Election Day. In 1980, NBC caused a furor when it called the election at 5:15 P.M. Pacific time, almost three hours before the polls closed in California and other Western states. Despite the outcry and congressional hearings and editorials, in 1984 the first network call came in at 5:01 P.M. Pacific time.

The networks cite figures purportedly showing that these early calls did not reduce turnout below expected levels, and therefore cannot have altered the outcome of some close local races—as the politicians in that area contend. They argue that as journalists they have "no right" to withhold news.

I disagree and I am in good company. Eric Sevareid, the distinguished retired CBS commentator and correspondent, said in a 1984 Harvard lecture, "I never could understand the passion to know how people voted before the returns were in. Why can't we wait a couple of hours? I can wait. We've gone through a couple hundred years in this country waiting. It's not a strain on me." Few journalists are so patient, or detached. The public wants to know the winner as soon as possible, and we have the capacity to tell them, based on the exit polls.

The exception, in this case, validates the rule that we report whatever we know. Just as the freedom of the press must yield, in some cases, as when it conflicts with the right to a fair trial, so, in this instance, should the natural journalistic instinct to get the story out fast. The evidence that projections affect turnout and alter election outcomes is very shaky. But that is not the issue. The mystique of the voting act is central to the process of democracy. It is a feeling worthy of protection. Rationally, any individual knows that the likelihood of his vote deciding the election is infinitesimal. But we still believe our individual vote counts. In those few moments we are in the voting booth, we are exercising our sovereignty as citizens over those who seek to govern us; we feel that we hold their fates—and, in a way, the country's fate—in our hands. Yet that feeling is very difficult to maintain when you have been told by your favorite anchorman, "The presidential election has already been decided."

The Canadian solution is appealing. On federal election nights, the broadcast networks are activated by time zones, starting early in the evening with the Maritime Provinces and Quebec, moving westward to pick up audiences in Ontario, the Prairie Provinces, and finally British Columbia. That kind of forbearance would not infringe on the First Amendment rights of our networks any more than their routine delay of the evening news until supper time in the Mountain and Western states, two or three hours after it aired in the East.

But the Canadians enforce their system by law, which I would hate to see our government do. Also, our situation is complicated by time zone lines bisecting some states, by variations in poll closing times within a single time zone, and by satellite Super-Stations and competing news media. As an earnest of good faith, the networks promised after the 1984 election no longer to use their exit polls to *characterize* voting trends across the country or in particular states on their regular evening news shows, while voting is continuing. But they insisted on their journalistic right to *project* results using exit polls once the voting ended in a particular state. They urged Congress to mandate a uniform poll closing time across America, and the House voted such a bill in 1985. Passage by both houses in 1987 would go a long way toward a solution.

WHILE I don't agree with some of the specific criticisms of campaign journalism, I do share many of the misgivings expressed about our modern election process. Communication from the candidates is increasingly controlled by professional campaign consultants—polling and media experts. Sometimes their personal or political bonds to the candidates extend beyond Election Day, but most of the time their responsibility ends when the votes are counted.

Lyn Nofziger, a former newspaperman, a former Reagan press secretary, and now a government relations consultant, explained at the American University forum after the 1984 election why he thought Reagan had been right in 1984 to reject press demands for fresh speeches on substantive issues and press conferences:

> The media would like us to run a campaign . . . that makes it possible for them to write stories and cover things. For example, the media will demand a press conference. . . . They will demand that maybe you have a new speech every week. . . . And they do not understand that they have a job to do, which is to cover a campaign, but the people in the campaign also have a job to do, and that job is to win an election. . . . And winning an election does not mean catering to the press. Winning an election means doing the things and having your candidate do the things that he can do most effectively and that will influence the most votes.

I reject the Nofziger thesis. The campaign is not the candidates' personal property. It is the public's hour of judgment. While I admire the consultants' skills and value them as sources, I worry about their lack of accountability. Some of them have become cynically skillful at manipulating the electorate by exploiting the power of the incumbency or the emotional impact of demagogic appeals while carefully secluding the candidates from reporters and voters. In a column, I once described a consultant in a particular mayoral campaign as a "hired gun." A friend of his reacted with pain and anger to the labeling, and he made a point that struck me very forcibly:

"You, Broder, criticized John for coming in from out of town, running a campaign for a guy he did not really know very well, using some ad themes and suggesting some speech ideas that struck you as inflammatory. You said that he was doing a job, pocketing his money, not worrying whether the guy he was helping really deserved to win this election, and then walking away, knowing that he would not have to live with the consequences, that someone else's city would bear the scars of the campaign and the consequences of this guy's victory."

That was a fair summary of what I had written.

"Well," he continued, "how different is that from what you do? You come in from out of town, representing the *Washington Post*, and write whatever you want about these candidates, the kind of campaign they're waging, and the enmities and divisions you say it is bringing to the surface of the city—all this stuff about how polarized the public is, and all that. You get to know these candidates damn well, but you never say who you think should be mayor, or how the city is going to be put back together again. You just go back to Washington, knowing that you, too, will not have to live with the consequences."

He made me realize that a large percentage of what the public sees and hears in any campaign is generated by people who disavow any personal responsibility for the outcome. The ads, speeches, and letters are composed by people hired to help a candidate win, whether or not they think he deserves the office. The news stories and television pieces are produced by people like myself who are hired to report the campaign without injecting our own views.

As members of the insiders' clique, reporters and consultants have more in common than we like to admit. In the introduction to *Television and the Presidential Elections*, Martin Linsky said that at the Harvard conference,

> for all their quarrels, the politicians and the network people seemed to be more like colleagues and symbionts than opponents. . . . The politicians and the networks need each other, use each other, and are obsessed by each other's businesses. The politicians are media junkies and the network journalists are political junkies. They talk in codes that only fellow insiders— other politicians and their staffs, consultants, and other political reporters—can fully decipher. . . . Viewers and voters are excluded.

I am skeptical about recasting the rules of political journalism and certainly do not welcome any redefinition of my own role. When I am charged, as all journalists are, with "letting so-and-so get away with murder" by not exposing a candidate's alleged hypocrisy, or of "writing off the chances" of someone we know has sterling qualities, I demur. I'm not his advocate, I say. Professionally, I can't give a damn who wins or loses.

I should hold my distance, but I worry that this journalistic detachment can be a crutch for avoiding responsibility. The rules—and our roles—are not quite as clear as we might pretend. Obviously, we know these contenders better than most voters possibly can. Clearly, we have some obligation to share whatever insights we have gained. But what kind of obligation? Jack Germond, one of the best political writers I know, believes that the candidates the reporters most admire rarely get nominated. Is that a sign of our failure to communicate what we know and believe, or a praiseworthy proof that our reporting is not tilted?

I thought two of the men eliminated early from the Democratic field in 1984—Governor Reubin Askew of Florida and Senator Ernest F. Hollings of South Carolina—should have been seriously considered for the presidency. As a columnist, I freely made that point—but not so frequently or insistently that I sounded like Willy Loman's wife, standing on stage, shouting "Attention must be paid" to this man. But as a reporter, I felt obliged to report what I saw—that their campaigns were falling flat—even though such reporting further burdened their candidacies.

Such ambivalence is part of the baggage any journalist takes into the campaign, and acknowledging it is better than trying to conceal it. Cover-ups don't work for journalists any better than they do for Presidents. Our critics will always suspect that we are slanting, in any case, and if we are honest, we have to acknowledge that our values, opinions, and prejudices do have some effect on the way we do our work. It is time to turn to the question of bias in the news.

3
Keeping
the Trust

CHAPTER NINE
Bias—and
Other Sins

*I*N November 1983, a conservative friend from Idaho called to ask if I had noticed that "the first war the United States has won in almost forty years was also the first where the blankety-blank reporters had been kept out of the way." She was referring to the Caribbean island of Grenada, where American forces subdued a small contingent of Cubans and Grenadians, jailed the radical government's leaders, and arranged safe passage home for Americans attending medical school. Reporters and photographers had been barred from the island during the first sixty hours, and those who got there on their own were held incommunicado by the American military. The press squawked, but my friend let me know that "if the crybabies of the press feel unwanted, unappreciated, and unloved because they were not invited ashore at Grenada, the heck with them. Who needs them anyway? If the President or the Pentagon thinks the press gets in the way of something important, then the President or the Pentagon has every right to keep them out."

She was far from alone. Secretary of State George P. Shultz said that during World War II "reporters were involved [in military operations] all along. And on the whole, they were on our side. These days, in the adversary journalism that's been developed, it seems as though the reporters are always against us and so they're always seeking to report something that's going to screw things up. And when you're trying to conduct a military operation, you don't need that."

I wrote a column citing my conservative friend's call. "That view," I said, "is widespread, and it is flat-out wrong. . . . It is wrong because control of information gives a government control over its citizens' minds. That is a power no government should have. It is a power the Constitution of the United States sought to deny our government permanently by the First Amendment. . . . We are asking you to think— from your own self-interest—if you want to live in a society where the government controls, directs and excludes us."

The readers expressed themselves.

From Elk Grove, California: I think that military necessity takes precedence over the people's right to know, as you like to keep putting it.

From Silverton, Oregon: The public does not have much more faith in the media than they have in politicians. . . . Just remember: Those who fail to govern themselves shall be governed. The media has failed.

From a retired Navy captain in Springfield, Virginia: For almost twenty years now, the elite media, both press and electronic . . . has run wild. Its arrogance is overwhelming.

From a physician in Malibu, California: When is the press going to stop whining and go about setting their own house in order?

From Hagerstown, Maryland: Just once, the American people would like to see a major newspaper or network say that their conduct was inappropriate or excessive and they were sorry.

From a Presbyterian minister in Cedar Rapids, Iowa: Frankly, I have told my people that the media as it now operates is not all that necessary.

From Seattle, Washington: The role of judge, jury, witness and prosecutor that the press has assumed in national and international affairs is self-appointed.

From a lawyer in Sherman Oaks, California: There is less danger in government "control" of information than there is in the current media control of it.

From a Findlay, Ohio, insurance man: We the public have recourse against the government. It is called a vote. But what recourse do we have against a press that will only show one side of a story?

And finally, from a retired journalist in Washington, D.C.: If a referendum were held today to restrict press freedom, I would unhesitatingly vote for it, as would thousands of others.

Maybe the mail was unrepresentative, but I was not the only one who got hostile letters. *Time* reported in December 1983 that its "225 letters on the issue ran almost 8 to 1 against the press." When John Chancellor criticized the exclusion of reporters in an NBC commentary, the mail and calls favored the ban five to one. A *Los Angeles Times* national poll in November 1983 found that a 52–41 percent majority supported the ban on reporters in the early stages of the Grenada operation. But, paradoxically, 63 percent said they would oppose a similar restriction in future U.S. combat operations, and by a 75–17 percent margin they said reporters were more useful than harmful in a combat situation. However, almost nine out of ten interviewed by the *Times* said "national security" is proper grounds for censoring the press or withholding information, 76 percent said the government could withhold information that might embarrass it, and two thirds said it could deny information that the press might "twist" to make the government look bad.

With government continuing its efforts to restrict press freedom and access, no journalist can be sanguine or satisfied with the shaky public support we have today. An independent research firm reported in April 1985 that about three quarters of those surveyed have some problem with the media's credibility and one fifth deeply distrust it. "People's impressions of the media often come from television," the American Society of Newspaper Editors report said, "but their doubts about credibility apply just as much to newspapers."

The numbers were better in a January 1986 study conducted by the Gallup organization for the Times-Mirror publishing company. Over 80 percent rated the networks and nationally known news organizations, local papers, radio news, and the Associated Press believable or highly believable (on a four-point scale). These organizations were also considered professional and concerned about quality by more than seven out of ten. However, the scores were only 50 percent on fairness and independence, and most people thought these news organizations covered up their own mistakes, invaded people's privacy, and emphasized bad news over good.

WE must work to establish credibility. As private businesses that also provide an important public service and operate under a unique constitutional protection against government interference, we are, more than most institutions, outside the system of checks and balances. The Founding Fathers thought that informing the public could best be done if we were given a special degree of freedom. We can earn the support we need to maintain that freedom by being as candid as possible about what we do. The more you know about us and how we operate, the more useful the newspaper or news broadcast will be to you. Perhaps then you will be more willing to protest the efforts by government and others to exclude reporters and restrict information.

As communications people, we have done a really rotten job communicating what we think we're doing. In early 1985 the Poynter Foundation sponsored a conference in St. Petersburg, Florida, where top executives and reporters from television and newspapers confirmed and amplified these concerns. The growth of newspaper chains, the decline of local newspaper competition, and the emergence of network television as the main news medium were blamed for making individuals feel more remote from their sources of information.

Marilyn Berger, a veteran newspaper and television reporter, said television has made "the news process" much more visible, by showing reporters questioning officials, interviewing accident or tragedy victims, and—sometimes literally—pursuing the principals in a story. "There are times when to get the news you have to be persistent in ways that are not pretty," she said. "When newspapers do it, no one sees it; when broadcasters do it, everyone does."

While more visible, the news process is no better understood—largely because we do not explain it. I pointed out once that readers often refer to a news story I have written as a column, or call a column an editorial. Judging from those experiences, some of the basic distinctions journalists make—and therefore some of our basic principles and fundamental practices—are simply not understood by our readers.

Why do we not explain? I think the problem is clique journalism again. We know what we're doing; so do our colleagues; and so do the insiders of journalism, politics, and public relations. If others don't understand, tough luck.

David Shaw, the *Los Angeles Times* media reporter, in a 1983 speech at the University of Hawaii said that "arrogance" is "one of the greatest ethical problems we . . . face." Like him, I believe we owe our readers and viewers not only the best job we can do but an answer to their questions about the way we do it. I hope this book gives you a better understanding of what journalists do—and don't do. But journalists, like others, are judged by deeds, not words. And while this book was being written, a run of incidents raised serious doubts about the credibility of the press.

I realize that focusing on these incidents is doing to my own business what critics often accuse journalists of doing to others: emphasizing the negative. But credibility is something we earn or lose every day. Reporters are judged by our demeanor and performance on our beats, and by the fairness and balance of our stories. Every negative impression hurts not just the individual but the organization and the profession. It takes a lot of good journalism to make up for the bad, and unfortunately, there are too many examples of the latter.

THE simplest and most flagrant category of professional sins is consumer fraud—passing off fiction as fact. That is what happened to us a few years ago.

On September 28, 1980, the *Post* published on its front page a story by reporter Janet Cooke about the spread of heroin in the Washington ghetto, dramatized by the scene she said she had witnessed of eight-year-old Jimmy being injected in his mother's home with heroin supplied by her pusher-lover. The story had a sensational impact, triggering a massive and unsuccessful police search for "Jimmy," which the *Post* refused to join or assist, on grounds that Cooke had promised the family confidentiality. The *Post* submitted the story for a Pulitzer Prize and Cooke received the prize for feature writing on April 13, 1981. It was a helluva story. And it was a fraud.

The problems began almost immediately after the Pulitzers were announced. Staff members at the *Toledo Blade*, where Cooke had worked before coming to the *Post*, noticed that her biography listed a master's degree from the University of Toledo. They knew she had only a bachelor's degree from that school and queried the Associated Press about the discrepancy. The AP then checked Vassar College, where Cooke said she had received her baccalaureate, and found that she had dropped out after one year.

When the AP and Vassar College relayed this information to the *Post* on April 14, our editors began quizzing Cooke about her credentials—and about the story, which some people in the newsroom had viewed skeptically from the beginning. After prolonged and emotional questioning, Cooke confessed to the fraud and resigned from the paper. The next day, the *Post* returned the Pulitzer Prize and ran an editorial apologizing to the readers, vowing to examine our internal procedures and declaring that "one of these episodes is one too many."

The debate within journalism about this fraud had only begun. The following Sunday, April 19, the *Post* published an 18,000-word recapitulation, reported and written by Bill Green, a former journalist and Duke University official, who was the newspaper's ombudsman or readers' representative that year. From his opening assertion that "for Cooke, it was a personal tragedy. For the *Post*, it was inexcusable," Green laid out a tale of failures in communication, editing, and checking that allowed the twenty-six-year-old reporter, who had been at the *Post* only nine months, to drag the newspaper into its worst embarrassment.

Green pointed out that neither of her immediate superiors, city editor Milton Coleman or assistant managing editor Bob Woodward, had ever pressed Cooke to identify "Jimmy" or his family; reporters and editors who had doubts about the story did not express them clearly and forcefully; the paper's top editors were largely unaware of the doubts in the newsroom and were vague about how much of the specifics Coleman and Woodward knew; when police and city authorities questioned the story's veracity, the editors went into a protective crouch and simply reasserted their faith in the reporter's integrity.

Green said the failures extended right up the line from Coleman and Woodward to managing editor Howard Simons and executive editor Ben Bradlee. "The system failed because it wasn't used, not because it is faulty. Bradlee and Simons should have asked tough questions, so should Woodward and Coleman and others. And every staffer who had a serious doubt about 'Jimmy' had an unavoidable responsibility to pursue it, hard."

Green also made a larger point. Every reporter has received a tip on a delicious story, one he knows will knock the competition's socks off. And when the reporter starts checking—making calls to elicit further details or confirmation or reaction—the story starts to wither and die. The facts just don't sustain the sweet clarity and punch the original account had, and the moment comes when the disappointed reporter has to tell an editor, "It doesn't check out." Instinctively we want that story to be true—to get it into the paper under our bylines—but we have to yield to the evidence. Because Cooke did not accept this fundamental discipline and her editors did not enforce it, the *Post* was left with egg on its face.

Even Green's lengthy and critical accounting did not still the controversy. The mystery of Cooke's own motivation remained unsolved and there was a fear—even inside the *Post*—that the extreme newsroom competitiveness had contributed to her breach of standards. Bradlee told the American Society of Newspaper Editors convention the next week that no newsroom system will "protect you from a pathological liar." Many journalists did not buy that. The *New York Times* editorialized that the "critical failure occurred the moment Miss Cooke refused to document her story for her editors. . . .Great publications magnify beyond measure the voice of any single writer. Thus, when their editors and publishers want or need to know a source for what they print, they have to know it—and be able to assure the community or the courts that they do."

I agree with that principle and have always tried to operate that way, but it can be difficult because the relationship between reporters and editors has built-in tensions, which you discover in your first six months on a newspaper. I have seen only one side, having always enjoyed a reputation for disorganization and disarray that discouraged anyone from entrusting me with managerial responsibility. But I can sympathize with editors' problems and frustrations. On a paper like the *Post*, the editors who assign and edit stories have the toughest jobs in the building. They are constantly juggling story possibilities, never knowing which ones will collapse and which ones will be added to their list of responsibilities. They are chained to their editing desks and to the telephones linking them to the reporters out on their beats. They operate under the twin tyrants of space and time. There is never enough room to treat all the stories fully, and they must deal with frustrated (and egotistical) reporters who want more space. They also have to whip and goad reporters, who always want to make one more call to check one more source, to get to their word processors and meet the copydesk's nonnegotiable deadline.

Editors are friends and adversaries. They have their own ideas of what makes a good story and try to influence which stories a reporter pursues. Editors on a good paper like the *Post* seldom second-guess reporters, but they test us by asking questions and more questions. And we would rather ask questions than answer them.

Despite the tensions, I think a reporter has an obligation to be open with his editor. Many of my colleagues disagree, preferring to keep their sources, their operations, and their plans for the day's reporting to themselves. But if I want my editor's trust, I have to return that trust. With everything. My appointments or plans for the day are not secret, nor, when I come back, do I try to hide where I learned what I learned. Obviously discretion sometimes requires that you not holler it out to the whole newsroom. But in all the years I have been working, I have never encountered a situation in which I couldn't trust an editor with what I knew and how I had got it.

WHAT perplexed me most about the Janet Cooke case was how a reporter on the *Washington Post* had been allowed to disregard the fundamental distinction between fact and fiction. It was too pat an answer to say that Janet Cooke was unprofessional or unprincipled. I discussed with Bob Woodward whether older reporters, like myself, had failed to pass on to our younger colleagues the same code of professional behavior and reportorial responsibilities that had been drilled into our heads when we came into our first newsrooms.

During the sixties and early seventies, when many young people challenged the social and political status quo in movements for civil rights, feminism, environmentalism, ending the Vietnam War, and curbing nuclear weapons, the "New Journalism" arose. Though never precisely defined, the method emphasized the role of advocacy, personal viewpoint, and personal experience. One school of New Journalism, practiced by such varying personalities as Hunter S. Thompson and Truman Capote, blurred the lines between reporting and creative writing. Thompson's accounts of political campaigns blended real people and incidents indistinguishably with imagined and even hallucinatory episodes. Capote turned the bare facts of a murder case into a book of novelistic perfection. These techniques had never been approved at the *Post* or most other major papers, but I was no longer certain, as I told Woodward, that we had impressed upon our younger colleagues the importance of resisting the temptation to embroider or invent.

The upshot was a series of brown-bag lunches in the *Post* newsroom, where older and younger reporters—many of whom knew each other only slightly—shared experiences and viewpoints. Those discussions were healthy, stimulating, and ultimately reassuring. I came away with a sense that our paper, at least, faced no pervasive generation gap—that the younger reporters were as fully committed to the disciplines of our craft as I could hope, and far more skilled in its practice than I had been at their age. Janet Cooke was the exception, not the rule.

Unfortunately, just a month after the Janet Cooke incident, two other news organizations faced similar problems. A *New York Daily News* columnist had to resign when he was unable to substantiate a piece about atrocities in Belfast, and a bit later, the *New York Times Magazine* admitted that a free-lance writer had duped it with a fabricated story about a trip to Cambodia with Khmer Rouge guerrillas.

Close to home, *Newsweek* magazine, which is owned by the Washington Post Company, ignored abundant warning signs of forgery and did a cover story in May 1983 on Adolf Hitler's "secret diaries." Thirteen pages were devoted to summarizing the diaries and the controversy over their authenticity. The following week, *Newsweek* took four pages to outline the "storm over the diaries," but said *Newsweek*'s own guru, Gerhard L. Weinberg of the University of North Carolina at Chapel Hill, "stuck to his earlier conclusion: that the diaries appeared genuine but still needed closer examination."

Newsweek produced another Hitler diary cover the next week, with "FORGERY" stamped over a page of the document and the subtitle, "Uncovering the Hitler Hoax." It took seven pages to show how West German government experts had uncovered "a grotesque [and crude] forgery." Weinberg was nowhere mentioned in the story. Instead, *Newsweek* introduced its own handwriting consultant, who had "examined the first and last volumes of the actual diaries . . . [and] quickly found them to be forgeries."

Newsweek's follow-up piece was as shabby as the original article, which had concluded with the incredible statement that the "appearance of Hitler's diaries—genuine or not, it almost doesn't matter in the end—reminds us of the horrible reality on which our doubts about ourselves, and each other, are based."

When I read that, I wanted to scream. What the hell do they mean, it doesn't matter? This is a news magazine—not *Popular Romances* —and they write that it doesn't matter whether these papers, on which they have erected this whole construction of pop history and pop psychiatry, all this malarkey about collective guilt and fear and the evil that "lurks somewhere in everyone," are real or fake?

That was grotesque. It contradicted everything I was taught to believe journalism involves. Whatever motivated it—the search for a scoop, the belief that the cover would hype newsstand sales, or just an editor's bad judgment—it was dreadful journalism.

BACK at the *Post*, we were suffering from a second incident, which, though less publicized than "Jimmy's World," in many respects reflected worse on our organization, because it suggested that, like our *Newsweek* cousins, we were more interested in generating comment and perhaps circulation than in being sure of our facts.

It began on October 5, 1981, with an item in "The Ear," a gossip column written by Diana McLellan, who had moved to the *Post* after the demise of the *Washington Star* two months earlier.

Well. Quite a little ripple among White Housers new and old. That tired old tale about Nancy [Reagan] dying for the Carters to blow out of the White House as swiftly as possible is doing a rerun—with a hot new twist. (Remember the uproar? Nancy supposedly moaned that she wished Rosalynn and Jimmy [Carter] would skip out *before* the Inauguration, so she could pitch into her decor chores.) Now, word's around among Rosalynn's close pals about exactly why the Carters were so sure Nancy wanted them Out. They're saying that Blair House, where Nancy was lodging—and chatting up First Decorator Ted Graber—was *bugged*. And at least one tattler in the Carter tribe has described listening in to the Tape Itself. Now, the whole story's been carried back to the present White House inhabitants, by another tattler. Ear is absolutely appalled. Stay tuned, uh, whoever's listening.

Three days after the column appeared, Carter announced that he planned to sue the *Post* for what his former press secretary, Jody Powell, called "a reckless, hurtful lie." "The Ear" column was unpopular with many at the *Post*, but the incident became far more serious to us when an editorial appeared on October 14:

> There are a lot of "we's" at the *Washington Post*, but the one you are about to hear from comes about as close as you can get to being the basic, collective "we"—the voice of the *Washington Post*, speaking for the *Washington Post.* . . .
>
> We are dead serious now. The subject is Jimmy Carter, the Ear column and the *Post*. Mr. Carter and Rosalynn Carter are upset about an item that ran in the Ear column last week. That item, which was accurately sourced, made a relatively modest point that had, nonetheless, a momentous implication for those who read it casually. The point was that *a story was circulating* . . . that Blair House had been "bugged" while the Reagans were staying there during their pre-inaugural/post-election visit to Washington; it was reported to be by virtue of a tape of such eavesdropping that Mrs. Carter learned that Mrs. Reagan wished the Carters would leave the White House sooner than scheduled—a story, incidentally, that we recall Mrs. Reagan herself denying at the time.
>
> It is one thing, however, to read that item to say that such a tale is circulating and being given currency by estimable public figures who repeat it—and quite another to conclude from this that the place was in fact bugged and that the Carters did in fact perpetrate such a scheme. We weren't there. But everything we know about the presidency of Jimmy Carter suggests otherwise, that it was false. . . .
>
> Perhaps it is foolish to expect people to read newspapers with rabbinical or juridical care. . . . The best we can do here . . . is to be as blunt and clear about what that Ear item said as we know how. It said there was a rumor around. There was. Based on everything we know of the Carter instinct and record on this subject, we find that rumor utterly impossible to believe.

That response did not satisfy Carter, nor was he alone. Once again, the *Post* was bombarded with criticism—and this time, many of us on the inside agreed. This looked like a self-inflicted wound or series of wounds. Bradlee had imported "The Ear" and the specific item had been cleared with him. Then, our editorial page editor, Meg Greenfield, had magisterially defended the item as if she were speaking for all of us.

In fact, dissent raged within. Many of us agreed with Jody Powell, who had asked why, if the *Post* thought the bugging story was true, it hadn't been on page one. Those inside the building angrily asked the flip side of the question: if we didn't think the rumor was true, why did we lend it currency and give it enormous circulation by publishing it?

At the regular Monday morning national news staff meeting during the controversy, Murrey Marder, the senior national reporter and probably the most respected, spoke almost in anguish of the breach of faith he thought had occurred. If our standard is simply to report any rumors we hear, leaving the readers to figure out whether they are credible or not, Marder said, then he had spent his life doing the wrong things at the wrong paper.

But Marder was not wrong. On October 23, eighteen days after the item first appeared, the *Post* reported on its front page that its publisher, Donald E. Graham, had apologized to the Carters and retracted the item. In the interim, when Bradlee reinterviewed McLellan's source—a writer named Dotson Rader who had carried the tale from the Carters to the Reagans—Bradlee found that Rader could not verify the rumor either.

In any event, Don Graham wrote Carter apologizing, retracting, and—for the staff's morale, most important—making it clear that the editorial he had approved "did not intend to suggest that the paper prints rumors which it knows to be false, because that is not the policy of the *Washington Post*. Our policy is to print news that is accurate from sources we believe to be reliable."

Carter then withdrew the threat of a libel suit, ending this sorry episode. When Diana McLellan moved her column to the *Washington Times*, most of us heaved a sigh of relief and applauded when Bradlee did not resurrect the gossip column under new authorship. A daily newspaper has many audiences, serves many functions, and ought to make room for many different styles and voices. But for the newspaper's main function—the delivery of news—to be met, basic journalistic standards must be enforced in all its departments and in all its features. Gossip and rumor, untested by rigorous reporting, cannot coexist with news without cheapening the product.

• • •

OUR colleagues in television news have fought a battle to purge their medium of a shoddy perversion of news called "docudramas" and presented by their entertainment divisions. Characteristically prime-time productions, they are based on real people or events but have as many invented bits of dialogue, scenes, and plots as a work of fiction. Between 1982 and 1984, at least twenty docudramas were shown on television, some focusing on historical figures but most on contemporary heroes and villains. Most were criticized for their exaggerations, distortions, and outright historical falsifications, but the networks kept coming up with fresh ones.

All three networks have explicit standards for docudramas, with CBS's code requiring that "fictionalized elements . . . not materially alter or distort history." Nonetheless, news people are plainly uncomfortable with them. Dan Rather made the criticism explicit in the 1985 speech from which I have quoted earlier. "I don't know what to do about the so-called docudramas," he said. "I do think there's a great danger for us in such things. . . . The sophisticated viewers, and I like to think that increasing numbers of viewers are sophisticated, will say to themselves, Okay. This was produced by the entertainment division, and the CBS Evening News is produced by the news division. But on television . . . there's a danger that it all tends to sort of blur into one. . . . That can corrode our credibility pretty quickly."

ASIDE from outright fictions, nothing contributes more to the press's credibility problems than the phrase "sources said." Robert C. Maynard, the former *Washington Post* ombudsman and now publisher of the *Oakland Tribune*, has found readers' confidence in a story "increases exponentially" when the source is named and decreases just as much when the source is concealed.

Ben Bradlee has always crusaded against unattributed information. Although on Watergate and other investigative stories the *Post* got vital information from unidentified sources, Bradlee is enraged by government officials' dispensing news and viewpoints without attribution. In a 1972 article and in dozens of speeches, Bradlee has labeled these events—official "backgrounders"—as "a conspiracy in restraint of truth." His periodic efforts to bar *Post* reporters from any sessions where government officials speak under a cloak of anonymity have failed; competitive pressures prevail in the end. But he still views backgrounders as "a perversion of journalism."

I am not as fervent as Bradlee on the issue. I don't think we can vow to eliminate unattributed information from our pages as flatly as we seek to eradicate fiction and error. But on one occasion I applied his highly principled position—with enjoyable results. In July 1975, I wrote a column tearing into Secretary of State Henry A. Kissinger for advising President Ford not to receive Aleksandr Solzhenitsyn, a refugee from Soviet oppression, at the White House. Kissinger had argued that the "symbolic effect" of a Ford-Solzhenitsyn meeting could "be disadvantageous" to his shaky policy of détente with Soviet leaders. I wrote then (and still believe) that it revealed the flabbiness of Kissinger's policy and betrayed his total lack of understanding of Ford's character. It was a tough column.

A day or two after it appeared, the Secretary's office invited me over. Foreign policy was far from my province, so I knew what it was about. I had misinterpreted his motive, Kissinger said, distorted his rationale, and damaged his relationship with the President. I pulled out my notebook and started writing down his words. "Wait a minute," he said. "What are you doing?"

"Taking notes," I said.

"This is not an interview," he said. "I invited you over here because I respect your work and I want you to understand what really happened."

"That's very flattering, Mr. Secretary," I replied, "but you and I have no private or personal relationship. You invited me over here because of what I wrote about you. You tell me it was wrong. If it was wrong, or if you think it was wrong, I want to share those arguments with the people who read the column."

We sparred for a few minutes, and then Kissinger said, "If I cannot talk to you on background, then this conversation cannot continue."

"I guess it cannot continue," I said, and I left.

Two years later, after Ford's defeat had returned Kissinger to private life, we met in passing. I greeted him and he introduced me to his companion: "This is David Broder of the *Washington Post*. He walked out on me when I stopped his taking notes." I thought, By God, I got to him. It still rankles the so-and-so. That's what I'd like on my tomb-stone: He walked out on Kissinger.

I am not usually so high and mighty with sources on my own politi-cal beat. I take the information any way I can get it, with or without attribution. Yet I know that when many people read that "sources said" something, they think the reporter has made it up, or someone else has, and the reporter was too naive to question it. Mostly, I think they resent not being told. Using the weasel word *sources* advertises that the reporter knows something, the speaker's identity, that he will not share with the reader. The perfectly human response is, You don't trust me. Why the hell should I trust you?

Well, why should you? Because I can tell you things that way, which otherwise I could not. For example, on my own beat, covering politics and elections, I come into a state and, naturally, among the first people I seek out are the rival party chairmen. Tell me, I say to the chairman of the incumbent's party, how is the Senate race going?

He will ask, "Are we on the record, or on what basis are we talk-ing?" If I say he is on the record—that I will attribute quotations to him by name—he will answer: "It will be a difficult fight. Senator Smith's duties in Washington have prevented him from spending nearly as much time here campaigning as he would have liked, but I think the people of this state know how important he has been to us on the Burton-Batten project and many other issues vital to our economic future, and how important his reelection is, also, to the President. So I'm sure that if we do our part in carrying his message while he is in Washington, then he will receive the mandate he deserves for another term."

Thank you, Mr. Chairman.

For the record, his opposite number will answer about the chal-lenger: "Well, you know we are at a tremendous financial handicap, because they have raised six million dollars and are doing saturation television advertising. But the voters I talk to realize that Smith has done nothing but carry the administration's water for the last four years, and I think they're ready to throw him out. It's just a question of whether we can get our man known."

And thank *you*, Mr. Chairman.

Those answers are not terribly helpful to me. But the chairmen are not supposed to help me; they're supposed to use the newspaper to motivate their candidate's supporters and perhaps to generate more votes. Still, I have a story to report. So I am inclined to say, "Okay, Mr. Chairman, now, not for attribution, what is really going on?"

The first chairman might add: "Look, Dave, I won't kid you. Smitty shouldn't lose this race, but if he does, it'll be his own fault, and the President's. The county chairmen are going to give you a lot of gripes about his not being back here. They've had to cancel at least twenty events. We've got the money for TV, and it's running, but I worry whether we're really going to have the grass-roots campaign he needs. I called Marty Jones [the President's top political aide] yesterday and told him that they better find some money to at least start the Burton-Batten project, so he can say he's done something for the state. Just pulling the President's chestnuts out of the fire ain't enough. If they want him back, they've got to come across."

And the second chairman's candid assessment, with a guarantee of anonymity, might produce something like this: "An incumbent like Smith, with his finances and the administration's backing, shouldn't really be vulnerable this year. He hasn't done anything to hurt the people, but I've got to tell you, we have a chance against him because he really hasn't come home to put on any kind of campaign. Our problem is our candidate. He hates fund-raising. He lost a good press secretary because he kept missing payrolls. Despite that, he's still in the race. In our last poll, he was running eight points ahead here in this TV market, where you'd expect him to be best known. Now, he was running further behind than that in Smith's home area, but we are trying to get another $100,000 of TV time bought on those stations, and if we can cut the margin there, he's in the race. I don't want to kid you, but this thing is not locked up yet."

Now, I can do several things with this not-for-attribution information. I can characterize the attitude of "party leaders"—nervousness on the incumbent's side, a mixture of hope and frustration on the challenger's. Any part of these comments I quote directly will be ascribed only to a "party official" or a "senior Republican" or whatever phrase we have agreed upon.

But, more important, I now have leads to further information that I can probably get on the record. Smith's office will tell me—on the record—how many days of the last two months he has spent in Washington and how many at home. It should not be hard to find a county chairman or two who has had to cancel a scheduled Smith event and get him to describe on the record the consequences for the campaign. The White House and the Senate Appropriations Committee can tell me if the administration is pulling any strings to get money flowing for the Burton-Batten Dam project.

I bet I can get the challenger's first press secretary to talk about what has gone wrong in the campaign. Phone calls to TV stations in Smith's home area will tell me—on the record—whether the challenger has come up with money to expand his TV buy. If he hasn't, I pretty much know what that means.

That's the process. You get as much on the record as you can, and then you pump them for more, with a guarantee that it won't be directly attributed. Everything you learn from one person you use to gain more information from the next. And eventually you may have a fairly clear idea of the story. It's not so different in reporting on government decision making, or on any other area where there are built-in differences of views and different objectives among the players. The more you know, the more you can find out.

In your story, you cannot burn your sources by violating the ground rules. And yet you want the readers to know not only as much as possible, but how and from whom you learned it, so they can judge the information's credibility. So what do you do? You don't fudge. If it's marked NFA in your notebook, it is not for attribution. That is a matter of honor—and of professional survival. You live by the conditions you accepted—or forget ever using that source again. But you scour your notebook for that same point made by someone else on the record, and use that quote.

If you can't do that, you can summarize the kind of people you talked to: "the chairmen of the two parties, fund-raisers and strategists in the rival campaigns and elected and party officials in five of the major counties in the state, as well as the candidates themselves and interested observers from the White House on down." When readers see that an unnamed Democratic official has said such-and-such, they at least have an idea what category of person you interviewed.

You are also free to quote the first chairman as saying "if we do our part in carrying his message while he is in Washington . . . then he will receive the mandate he deserves. . . ." And you can write as the next sentence in the story: "Privately, some party officials worry that

Smith's preoccupation with his Senate duties and his role as an administration spokesman on foreign aid have forced him to cancel so many scheduled campaign events that grass-roots workers are losing their enthusiasm for his reelection effort." A discerning reader can pretty well figure out who might have said that.

This process is part of every reporter's repertory of techniques. It's different from the backgrounder, which typically is conducted by a government official, who sets the rules protecting him from accountability. Sometimes backgrounders really do help reporters explain what is going on. Some accounts, for example, say the first backgrounder came when Franklin D. Roosevelt took the United States off the gold standard. White House reporters appealed to Press Secretary Steve Early for help with the decision's implications. Early produced an anonymous Treasury official who gave the journalists a quick economics lesson.

I have relied upon backgrounders on government stories beyond my expertise. Routinely, with a presidential initiative—on taxes, foreign policy or whatever—the White House will wheel in policy experts to brief the reporters. I have no problem with not using their names; what is important is an accurate description of the President's proposal. Similarly on Capitol Hill, when a committee finishes a complex piece of legislation, the chairman and the sponsor may start the press conference, but often they will let the committee counsel answer the detail questions. No problem.

Ultimately, however, every nonattributed source or fact strains the reporter-reader relationship. We have to make certain, case by case, that the gain in readers' understanding is worth the price.

THE final source of distrust toward the press and television is the charge of bias, voiced most vigorously in recent years by our critics on the right. It's not a complaint I take very seriously, but it comes up so often that we have to spend a little time on it.

One reason I am skeptical is that I know how little time reporters spend talking among themselves about ideology or policy. The barroom debates in press pubs are rarely about American policy in the Middle East, supply-side economics, or government's role in our society. We talk about what Clifton Daniel, the former managing editor of the *New York Times*, called "gossip and maneuver," what political people are doing to each other. We rehash the day's events and their possible consequences. Most of all, we love to speculate. "Why did so-and-so do that?" Our preference for gossip and maneuver—for actions over ideas—has survived the upgrading of our formal educations and the shift from the precinct police station of *Front Page* to the Georgetown salons of *Advise and Consent*. I don't know why we journalists have this character failing, but we are not ideologues.

I have been around long enough to recognize that when the press is accused of being part of the liberal establishment, it is just the latest twist to an old conspiracy theory. I first heard the one-party press complaint from Adlai Stevenson and the Democratic National Committee in the mid-1950s. When Richard Nixon and Spiro Agnew took it up fifteen years later, crossed out *Republican* and inserted *Democratic*, they were not only wrong but unoriginal.

Despite the commercial and conservative establishment character of the press, we are criticized these days as being a pervasively leftist counterculture bent on overthrowing the American way. This argument goes back to the Vietnam War period, when it was given flavorful form by Vice President Spiro T. Agnew with his "nattering nabobs of negativism" in "the effete Eastern liberal press." His ghostwriters included a former editorial writer for the *St. Louis Globe-Democrat*, Patrick J. Buchanan, who later returned to journalism as a columnist and broadcast commentator (and is back again in the Reagan White House), and William Safire, who went on from the Nixon staff to become a Pulitzer Prize–winning columnist for the *New York Times*. Buchanan summarized the indictment under his own byline in 1973: "Simply stated, it is that an incumbent elite, with an ideological slant unshared by the nation's majority, has acquired absolute control of the most powerful medium of communications known to man [television]. And that elite is using that media monopoly to discredit those with whom it disagrees, and to advance its own ideological objectives." He said that those who control television news "are taking an increasingly adversary stance toward the social and political values, mores and traditions of the majority of Americans . . . [and] are using that monopoly position to persuade the nation to share their distrust of and hostility toward the elected government."

Others in the journalism world echoed that criticism during the

1970s. Theodore H. White lamented "a strange kind of politicization" of the press, adding in a *Columbia Journalism Review* interview, "The national media have somehow put themselves into the role of the permanent critical opposition to any government which does not instantly clean up the unfinished business of our time." Sociologist-politician Daniel Patrick Moynihan wrote in *Commentary* magazine: "The political consequence of the rising social status of journalism is that the press grows more and more influenced by attitudes genuinely hostile to American society and American government."

Columnists Robert Novak and Joseph Kraft played variations on the same theme, and Michael J. O'Neill, then editor of the *New York Daily News*, pleaded in his 1982 speech as president of the American Society of Newspaper Editors that we journalists "cure ourselves of our adversarial mindset" and "develop a more sensitive value system." O'Neill argued that "we should make peace with the government; we should not be its enemy. . . . Our assignment is to report and explain issues, not decide them. We are supposed to be the observers, not the participants, the neutral party, not the permanent political opposition."

This line of argument ignores the fairly obvious fact that the owners of the mass media, the newspaper publishers, the radio and television station proprietors, are overwhelmingly Republican and conservative in their sentiments. In every presidential campaign but 1964 in the last half century, the great majority of newspapers have supported the Republican nominee. I have not dwelt in this book on the management-generated commercial or circulation or business-side pressures. I know journalists who have quit good jobs because they could not or would not accept the dictates of overbearing publishers or owners. Through good luck, the four dailies on which I have worked—the *Bloomington Pantagraph*, the *Washington Star*, the *New York Times*, and the *Washington Post*—have been singularly free from interference. All were profit-making businesses, with constraints on budgets and tough negotiations on pay. But at no point—literally no point—was any story of mine hyped or censored, nor was coverage tilted, to flatter or appease the publisher or the publisher's friends.

As a hired hand, I am not sure that I can explain this remarkable forbearance. It must be partly the character, the traditions and values of the families who owned those papers: the Stevensons and Merwins

in Bloomington, the Kauffmanns and Noyeses at the *Star*, the Sulz-
bergers at the *Times*, and the Grahams at the *Post* cared about their
papers as more than commercial enterprises. They were actively engaged in running the papers and recognized their role in the community, the region, or the nation. All of them seemed to accept that with
great influence went great responsibility.

But I suspect that something else has inhibited today's publishers
from tampering. The newsroom personnel's increasing professionalism
has probably reduced publisher-imposed bias. When journalists were
itinerant, hard-drinking, but lightly educated and poorly paid
wretches, they were easily replaced by others no worse equipped to
cover a beat or write a headline.

Now, when top-notch editors switch papers far more easily than
publishers switch editors, when bylined reporters develop followings
among their readers who miss them even when they take a vacation,
publishers are less likely to be capricious. I don't want to overstate the
case. A few years ago, during a Newspaper Guild strike against the
Post over a wage dispute, we reporters decided not to ask other unions
to honor our picket lines, but rather to embarrass the paper's owners
by allowing them to publish what would plainly be seen as an inferior
product, a paper without our wonderful work in it. The strategy of
"withholding our excellence," as we arrogantly termed it, was a dud.
The readers went right on reading the *Post* and we eventually came
back to work with meager gains.

However, I do not think it was false modesty that made our principal owner, Katharine Graham, demur when she was praised for standing up to enormous pressure from the Nixon administration during
Watergate. She liked to tell people, "It would have been much harder
to go down to the fifth floor [the newsroom] and tell them to drop the
story than to do what I did and tell Nixon's people we were going to
follow it wherever it led." To call off Woodward and Bernstein and the
others would not only have betrayed her ideals and her family tradition, it would have caused a newsroom rebellion that might have damaged the *Post*'s credibility far more than any political or commercial
pressures from the administration.

Commercial pressures from within a newspaper are something I
have simply never experienced. No story or assignment of mine has

ever been changed for fear it would offend some advertiser. Today's newspapers (many with monopoly positions in their communities) are more important to advertisers than is any one advertiser to that newspaper. Of course, we are aware that advertisers supply the revenues that pay our salaries. But luckily my publishers have allowed me to report as if those advertisers did not exist.

Now, the accounting office affects the whole newspaper. Newspapers are profit-making enterprises, representing large and profitable investments, with a stake in their communities, in the country, in "the system." In every instance, the proprietors have been part of the establishment. Whatever exposés they accept, many of them privately would just as soon that their papers not rock the boat. Most express their preferences where they should, on the editorial and op-ed pages and there, their prevailing conservatism is apparent. Even there, however, the touch is lighter than it used to be. David Shaw of the *Los Angeles Times* surveyed editorial practices around the country in 1985 and wrote that "on matters other than candidate endorsements, the day's editorial positions at the nation's major, big-city newspapers are largely determined at the editorial board's daily meeting, and the publisher frequently doesn't even know what the editorials are going to say until he reads them in the paper."

In the view of our critics, the publishers' forbearance has allowed newsroom leftists to slant coverage against political conservatives, business, and Republicans. Those who argued that there was a liberal bias in the press were able to buttress their case with the findings of several sociological studies, many of which found more Democrats than Republicans, more liberals than conservatives in newsrooms. The most controversial of these studies was a set of 238 interviews conducted in 1979–80 with randomly drawn journalists and broadcasters at "the most influential media outlets" by S. Robert Lichter, Linda S. Lichter, and Stanley Rothman for Columbia University's Research Institute on International Change. The main findings were published in a 1981 issue of *Public Opinion* magazine, with supplements in the *Washington Journalism Review, Public Interest*, and other journals. They found that journalists' voting histories were overwhelmingly Democratic; 81 percent had supported Carter over Ford and an identical percentage, McGovern over Nixon; 87 percent had supported Humphrey over Nixon, and 94 percent, Johnson over Goldwater.

"Over the entire 16-year period, less than one-fifth of the media elite supported any Republican presidential candidate," they said.

Fifty-four percent placed themselves left of center politically and only 19 percent said they were to the right. More detailed questions showed they were particularly liberal on social-cultural and some foreign policy issues, mixed on economic issues, and fairly conservative on basic political-institutional questions.

They strongly opposed government regulation of abortion, homosexuality, or other sexual behavior, and strongly supported affirmative action and environmental controls. In foreign policy, they were opposed to CIA covert operations and inclined to criticize the U.S. role in underdeveloped countries.

Their economic views favored "welfare capitalism," largely rejecting public ownership, endorsing deregulation, and approving business's fairness toward workers. But two thirds wanted a government policy that reduced income gaps (presumably meaning through transfer payments and progressive taxes), and almost half supported government-guaranteed jobs for all.

In institutional terms, while almost half thought the very "structure of [our] society causes alienation," less than one third said the basic institutions need overhaul or judged all political systems "repressive."

Conservative columnists such as Patrick Buchanan and Phyllis Schlafly seized upon the findings of the Lichter-Rothman study as the final, documented proof that Agnew had been right. Another conservative columnist, James J. Kilpatrick, said most journalists "make a conscientious effort in their news coverage to be fair. But there is not the slightest question that their personal liberalism shapes their professional judgments." For examples, he suggested, "read the *Washington Post*'s news stories on the Equal Rights Amendment," or watch the inflections and cadence and eyebrows of TV anchors introducing pieces on El Salvador. "You will catch those subtle bumps that make a pinball machine go tilt. If you think the news is slanted, you're right."

John Chancellor, for many years the anchorman on NBC News and now the network commentator, rejected Kilpatrick's "eyebrow" argument. In the 1983 book *The News Business*, Chancellor recalled that "when Spiro Agnew was Vice President...and was attacking the press and television, our critics were talking about how people like me composed our faces. We were accused of inserting left-wing bias into our reporting by raising our eyebrows, or smirking. I went home one night and tried this in front of the mirror. I got to laughing so hard it was impossible to go on with the exercise."

Chancellor's coauthor, Walter R. Mears, the executive editor of the Associated Press and formerly its top political reporter and Washington bureau chief, wrote, "I've covered five presidential election campaigns, and I'm often asked how it is possible to write about them objectively when, as a citizen, I must have a preference for one candidate over the other. It's possible because I have been trained, and have trained myself, not to let that be a factor in my work. In a campaign, my job is to tell people—voters—everything I can about the candidates who want their support. If I can't do that fairly, I can't buy the groceries or pay the rent."

Mears and Chancellor are certainly influential journalists, but they were not in the Lichter-Rothman sample. Neither was I. In a June 1984 debate with S. Robert Lichter, Ben Bradlee wondered aloud how representative that sample was: "Not one of the twenty-five persons, reporters and editors, who could probably be described by anyone who knew anything about the *Washington Post* as the paper's elite, in terms of decision making and opinion making, was interviewed. And that bothers me."

In a 1985 issue of the *Columbia Journalism Review*, Herbert J. Gans, a Columbia sociologist and author of *Deciding What's News*, charged that in five important respects the Lichter-Rothman study "diverges sharply from scientific methodology," especially in "inferring people's opinions from answers to single questions," and reporting "findings about journalists which do not accurately reflect the answers they gave to the survey questions they were asked." Gans said his own observations and interviews at four news organizations also sampled by the Lichter-Rothman team had very different conclusions. "While I found that journalists, like everyone else, have values, the two that matter most in the newsroom are getting the story and getting it better and faster than their prime competitors—both among their colleagues and at rival news media. Personal political beliefs are left at home, not only because journalists are trained to be objective and detached, but also because their credibility and their paychecks depend on their remaining detached."

The Lichters and Rothman defended their work in a subsequent issue and asserted that "no political agenda underlies our research." Without questioning their motives, it strikes me that their research manages to overlook some fairly obvious evidence against the charge of left-wing press bias. The most influential voices in journalism today—as in the past—are staunchly conservative. Aside from Jack Anderson, whose investigative column seems devoid of ideology, the most widely syndicated columnists today are George Will and James Jackson Kilpatrick, both advocates of Ronald Reagan and of most conservative causes. William Safire, William F. Buckley, Jr., and Robert Novak and Rowland Evans add to the conservative firepower. Most other widely syndicated columns are either middle-road or conservative, and the outspoken liberals like Ellen Goodman, Mary McGrory, Carl T. Rowan, Tom Wicker, Anthony Lewis, and Murray Kempton are outnumbered.

THOSE who think the Washington press corps is part of the proletariat are badly out-of-date. Most of us are well paid and have done very nicely under Reaganomics. We benefited from his tax cuts, reduced inflation, and generous savings incentives. When we question Reaganomics in our reporting, we go against our own interests. But skepticism is something we bring to the job, and it can no more be left at home than our tape recorders. Reaganomics was viewed exactly as the Great Society was viewed sixteen years earlier: it sounds great, but will it work?

That skeptical posture and those professional standards—rather than any ideological bias—really define the attitudes of most working journalists. But what counts finally is not the journalists' attitudes but our work product. In the 1984 debate with Bradlee, Robert Lichter again made the point—as he had in the original article—that the study "does not prove that there is a liberal bias in the news media. It proves that news media people tend to be personally liberal. But you have to look at the coverage. You have to actually see that the proof is in the pudding, before you accuse the media of liberal bias."

The Lichters and Rothman published a book, *The Media Elite*, in 1986 which attempted to establish "linkages" between the journalists' values and ideology, their view of the world, their choice of sources, and the tilt of their stories on nuclear energy, busing, and the oil industry. The most extensive case study, on nuclear power, concluded that "major media coverage highlighted the uncertainties attending nuclear power, even in areas where scientists and engineers felt most secure in their problem-solving abilities." But it cautioned: "None of this proves that journalists consciously set out to slant their reportage against nuclear power. As we have argued throughout this book, the influence of perspectives and paradigms is less direct than conservatives' conspiracy theories often suspect."

At the American Enterprise Institute debate, Lichter said, "There are many areas in which I think there is no media bias," including, he said, "covering presidential elections." He told me, "Everyone assumes that in campaigns, reporters' guards are up" against suspicions of media bias.

The studies that have been made of campaign coverage have generally borne out that view. Michael J. Robinson and Margaret A. Sheehan concluded in their study of CBS and UPI coverage of the 1980 campaign, *Over the Wire and on TV*, that the reporting "was generally balanced and generally fair." Robinson told Lichter at the AEI forum that a four-month study in 1983 of television features and commentaries on public policy questions "found that 77 percent . . . were so ambiguous by quotation or by conclusion that they could not be judged liberal or conservative pieces. Among the remaining 23 percent, 13 percent were liberal by conclusion or by quotation, 10 percent were conservative."

In the January 1985 issue of *Public Opinion* magazine, Robinson and Maura Clancey reported that "quantitative evidence from all three networks indicates that correspondents in the general election campaign of 1984 did, in almost every respect, treat Reagan and Bush much more negatively than Mondale and Ferraro." They speculated that the tilt resulted from the journalists' tendency to promote an underdog in order to spark interest in the campaign; the reporters' irritation at Reagan's exploitation of his incumbency (which also may have tilted them against Carter in 1980); and a sense that this was their last chance to debunk Reagan.

Robinson and Clancey wrote that if there was a tilt in 1984, it had almost no effect. On all the substantive elements of the campaign—the economic issues, the contrast between the candidates, the state of the race— "the network coverage was so 'responsible' that it carried almost no weight." Republicans got equal time with the Democrats, and there was "practically no issue bias" in the policy pieces.

Whatever the social scientists say, conservative partisans keep up their drumfire of criticism. Senator Jesse Helms of North Carolina and his friends have pressured CBS News to alter its policies. Mobil Oil has run a large-scale advertising campaign critical of "bias" in the media. Its vice president for public affairs, Herbert Schmertz, makes speeches and writes columns in which he has said "the public feels that the press is attempting to use its power not to report information but to make policy." But despite efforts to destroy the press's credibility, most of the public seems strangely unconcerned. A 1985 *Los Angeles Times* poll compared the views of three thousand reporters and editors with those of three thousand readers and found that journalists were more liberal than the general public. But those readers said the views of the newspaper they read most often matched their own. By a 59 to 24 percent margin, they said the news they read is impartial rather than slanted, and they ranked the news media ahead of government, business, and labor in honesty and integrity. As William Schneider, the *Times*'s political analyst, wrote, "This poll does not prove or disprove the charge that the media is politically biased, but it does show that if there is any bias, it hasn't crept into the news coverage to the extent that the public feels aggrieved by it."

Interestingly, the *Times* survey also found that while only 24 percent of the journalists polled said they had voted for Ronald Reagan in 1984, more readers thought Reagan had been treated fairly by the press than his Democratic predecessor, Jimmy Carter. Jody Powell, Carter's press secretary, argued in *The Other Side of the Story* that liberal journalists are tougher on Democratic Presidents than on Republicans, holding them to a higher standard and sometimes bending over so far backwards to avoid looking biased that they tilt against those for whom they voted.

Fred Barnes of the *New Republic* noted in a 1983 article for the *Washington Journalism Review* that criticisms of the mainstream press are almost identical, whether from interest groups of the left or right.

We are accused of stereotyping organizations with shorthand labeling, relying on disturbingly casual evaluations of their effectiveness, having a short attention span, and narrowing the issue debate by focusing on mainstream politicians and groups.

I can agree with the first three, which deal with journalistic practices, not ideological bias. The complaint that we focus on the middle of the spectrum also deserves serious consideration, because in reporting for a mass audience, we do tilt toward mass movements, which, most often, are not found at the political extremes. It could as easily be called rampant centrism as leftist or rightist bias. In a 1976 issue of the now defunct journalism review *MORE*, leftist journalist Andrew Kopkind took me to task as a deplorable example of those Washington political reporters who "have had their faces frozen with a permanent hard nose. It is a defensive visage, thought to present the most favorable image in a town where it is far worse to be ingenuous than to be wrong."

In criticizing me for missing the significance of Fred Harris's populist campaign for the Democratic presidential nomination (a campaign which retired Harris to academia), Kopkind wrote:

> Broder's unconcern for the political power of the banks and his overconcern for the role of Congress are biases characteristic of most "serious" Washington columnists. Forgetting for a moment the right-wing cranks (there are no syndicated left-wing cranks) and the gossipers, the opinion-makers of the political mainstream seem scared to death of any notion that is not drenched with "realism," "moderation," soft-core liberalism and pragmatic opportunism. They are forever reiterating the "lesson" of the Goldwater and McGovern campaigns: non-pragmatic conservatism and non-realistic liberalism bring certain defeat in elections. Extremism — defined as ideological integrity — is a cardinal political vice.

I plead guilty and confess that most of us in journalism tend to judge political philosophy by the political marketplace: will it sell? Because we are not ideologues, we do not put great stock — maybe not enough stock — in those politicians who put their ideologies out front. But the evidence I have seen — and the personal experience of thirty years' political talk with other journalists — makes me think the charge of ideological bias in the newsroom laughable. There just isn't enough ideology in the average reporter to fill a thimble.

We are not, however, free of emotions, sentiments, or standards. We may not like discussing them, but we have them. The *Post*'s Richard Harwood once wrote that "our standards are subjective and whimsical. They reflect our taste, values, prejudices, opinions and conveniences." Ben Bradlee agreed with that statement in an *American Heritage* interview in 1982, but when interviewer Michael Gartner, then editor of the *Des Moines Register*, pressed him to identify his, Bradlee threw up a wall: "I don't like bullies. I don't like liars. I'm really prejudiced against them. I don't like people who look me in the eye and tell me a lie and therefore, through me, tell a lie to the world. On the other hand, I'm sort of attracted to rogues. They interest me more than stuffed shirts. I like the Washington Redskins. I don't like phonies. I love the outdoors."

Bradlee said, "I'm not political at all . . . I'm not left or right or Democrat or Republican. . . . The ideology of it doesn't interest me at all." When Gartner asked if that meant he was "skeptical and cynical," Bradlee replied, "I am. And thank God for that."

Few of us would be more forthcoming. But in fact, our values control our most important daily decisions: what to put in and what to leave out. Those judgments are inescapable because of time and space, of which there is never enough to tell the whole story.

Most reporters double-check their stories and ask: Is it a balanced reflection of the variety of views I have heard? Have I given all sides? But even in answering those questions we reflect our prejudices and perceptions.

The same holds for the newspaper's editors. When they determine the space and prominence of the stories cascading onto their desks, they must decide which news to give the readers and which to deny. Again, their own values must shape that decision.

When I worked briefly (for sixteen months) at the *New York Times* in the mid-1960s, I discovered how those organizational values shaped its coverage. My editors were always interested in the John Birch Society. This was shortly after the Barry Goldwater nomination had signaled the beginning of the conservative takeover of the Republican Party. The *Times* editors, who were close to the overthrown Dewey-Rockefeller wing of the GOP, loved stories about the intraparty struggle, particularly those in which Republican Party leaders warned that conservative ideologues could destroy the GOP.

The editors in New York were also excited by the name Kennedy. Robert F. Kennedy was New York's newly elected senator, and they automatically wanted any story that dealt with him possibly restoring the Kennedy era in the White House. In between these two poles of American politics, Kennedy on the left and the Birchers on the right, fell a lot of action that was less than fascinating to them. Stories about Richard Nixon's slow, methodical reclaiming of power were hard to get into the paper. He was neither a right-winger nor a liberal and had few friends among New Yorkers of either party with whom the editors mixed.

Nor are we at the *Post* immune from our own mutually reinforcing value system. The ardent pursuit of Billygate represented, at least in part, the *Post*'s determination that the *Star* would not beat us at our own game—uncovering skulduggery in the White House. With the Watergate story the *Post* became America's preeminent investigative newspaper, with a keen eye for the "big hit" that might change history —or at least the makeup and direction of government. For years before that, it had championed civil liberties, civil rights, social legislation, and political reform. Before the *Post*'s news staff acquired the resources to challenge the *Times*, the *Baltimore Sun*, the late *New York Herald Tribune*, or the *Star*, it had the incomparable Herblock and Alan Barth, Merlo Pusey, Herbert Elliston, and Robert Estabrook on its editorial page. The values of the editorial page drifted into the newsroom. And though the editorial and news sides have always been separate, with no one carrying the title or authority of editor over both, the paper's civil libertarian–social justice–reformist values and its prized self-image as skeptic and perhaps even scourge of governmental secrecy and abuse of power are evident to anyone who works there.

Those values are not unique, of course. Indeed, the "national press" is often criticized for reflecting a shared sense of values. There is some truth to the charge, but our critics often miss the mark.

Secularism, for example, is rarely mentioned as one of our "blinders," but it should be. The Lichter-Rothman survey found that half of those interviewed claimed no religious affiliation and 88 percent seldom or never attended religious services. I think that tilts our coverage. David Shaw of the *Los Angeles Times* wrote in 1983 that "religion coverage is clearly improving in the American press," but he was comparing it to when the only religion stories appeared on the Saturday church pages—"a journalistic ghetto filled with listings of the next day's sermon topics, schedules of church-sponsored rummage sales and potluck dinners and press releases from local ministers," pages that were put together by the "oldest over-the-hill reporters . . . the staff alcoholic or . . . the youngest, least-experienced reporters."

James M. Wall, the editor of the *Christian Century* magazine and a close friend and supporter of Jimmy Carter, wrote in 1985 that he had perceived a bias in the media against religion. Wall and I have had many friendly arguments about why Carter failed, but I do not dismiss his suggestion that "journalists who developed . . . [a] dislike for Carter . . . lived on a different wavelength from the President. From the time he entered the national spotlight, his commitment to service was perceived as self-righteousness."

Wall argued that Carter "happens to be a man with a Christian commitment who was also a good enough politician to win a national election." He said the faithful must be concerned at "the implications of a religious tradition's being so out of sync with the prevailing public consciousness," but equally, I think, journalists need to consider if we are, as Wall contends, "hostile to any genuine religious witness." I am not suggesting that we must "get religion." But we certainly should not let the secularism that pervades the journalistic culture keep us from dealing intelligently and sensitively—without cynicism—with the many leaders and citizens in this nation who draw strength and motivation from their religious beliefs.

Thomas Griffith suggested in his *Time* magazine "Newswatch" column in 1982 that "a tilt called cynicism" was infecting many aspects of journalism. I can see that in mine and my colleagues' campaign coverage. Jeff Greenfield may have exaggerated a bit when he wrote in *The Real Campaign* that we treated all of the issues and arguments in 1980 "with skepticism bordering on cynicism, if not with outright contempt." But our cynicism is evident in our fascination with why and how things are done rather than with what is said.

Sociologist Herbert J. Gans believes we offset that cynicism by a reformist ideology that he identifies in *Deciding What's News* as a latter-day echo of early twentieth-century Progressivism. This reformist progressivism is reflected in the press's suspicions of political chicanery and the influence of money and its sympathy to "responsible capitalism." This may also explain why the press and government are so often seen as adversaries. If that implies a constant tension in the relationship, it is a necessary and proper one because press and government have very different functions. Government often craves secrecy; the press inevitably seeks access. Government depends, ultimately, on consensus; reporters are instinctively fight promoters. Government policy, to be effective, often demands continuity; reporters see and judge events in segments of twenty-four hours or less.

For years, I have accepted the "adversary relationship" concept of press-government relations, by way of analogy to the courtroom. As Tom Wicker has said, lawyers serve the court and the jury by asking the hardest, most skeptical questions, acting as adversaries in order to get at the truth. But because the analogy is imperfect, I lean more to Jim Deakin's description in *Straight Stuff* of a "critical relationship" between press and government. As Deakin said, "The press is the permanent, resident critic of government. A critic, not an adversary. When they do their job well—which is not always the case by any means—the news media draw attention to the mistakes, shortcomings, abuses and corruptions of those in power. And they do this impartially, regardless of which party and which individuals are in office."

Impartially is the key word in that sentence. Impartiality is one of the most important values in a reporter's life. It is part of a code by which we are judged, one that guarantees an absence of partisan or ideological or personal favoritism. Nothing will kill a journalist's reputation faster with his colleagues—whose opinion he values above all others—than breaking that code by currying favor, or conducting a personal vendetta, or condemning particular persons or viewpoints. You could say that it is an informal discipline we exert on each other.

THAT code is our best protection, but it is not enough. Whether by sloppy reporting or other cause, all of us mess up a story from time to time. Fortunately, newspapers are getting better at policing their own faults. Letters to the editor, many bearing corrections or criticisms, have existed almost as long as newspapers, but acknowledging errors came later and has been rarer. In 1967, the *Louisville Courier-Journal* and *Louisville Times* became the first American newspapers to publish corrections regularly. Norman Isaacs, then executive editor of both, said in a memo to his staff, "We can do ourselves and our newspapers more honor and gain more credit and perform a proper journalistic service by wiping out for good all the defensiveness that exists about mistakes and corrections. Let us adopt the principle that the readers are entitled to have the record set straight in every case where the facts have gone astray." The Louisville papers published the day's corrections on the front page of the second section, and the pattern of having a designated location was followed a few years later by the *New York Times*, the *Los Angeles Times*, the *Wall Street Journal*, and hundreds of others.

Each of the television networks has a policy requiring clear and timely corrections, but TV journalists are dissatisfied with its application. ABC News regularly uses its popular *Nightline* program for "viewpoint" discussions in which critics of varying backgrounds and other members of the press discuss how recent stories have been handled. The programs are heated, uninhibited, and diverting—but they rarely include confessions of error from network executives or guests from other news organizations whose coverage is discussed. CBS News's *Sixty Minutes* program, which is often criticized for its reporting and editing techniques, took an on-air look at its own practices in 1981 and allowed its critics their say. But day to day, corrections are largely at the discretion of the anchorman or executive producer of the news program. Dan Rather said in the 1985 lecture cited earlier that "we don't do a very good job" of admitting errors. "We do this on occasion, [but] we don't do it nearly often enough." John Chancellor told the 1985 Poynter Center conference that when he was anchoring NBC News, he pressed for more frequent corrections. But both he and Rather found that the tyranny of time—and the lack of a standardized format—inhibited them.

While newspapers may be better able to correct errors, a number of critics agree with former *Wall Street Journal* editor Vermont Royster that they are more willing to correct simple factual mistakes than to confess having published pieces that are "basically wrong or misleading or unfair." In 1983, *The New York Times* began an "Editors' Note" feature, in which the executive editor A. M. Rosenthal and others could discuss what they considered errors of judgment or balance in previously published stories. Some within the *Times* resented the feature as a device for second-guessing subordinate editors or reporters, and few papers have copied it.

Instead, some papers employ an ombudsman or readers' representative on their staff as a sort of designated hair shirt for the paper's editors and reporters. Again, the Louisville papers led the way. By 1985, thirty-five papers had ombudsmen and the *Post* was on its eighth since the job was created in 1970. The people who have filled the role at our paper have contributed substantially to the paper's credibility in Washington.

Before the ombudsman, there was little recourse at the *Post* for correcting a serious distortion. People could protest to the reporter or the editor, but they were unlikely to judge dispassionately. The ombudsman changed that. He is designated to receive gripes, and his phone number is published daily in the paper. Beyond that, he has a broad charter to be an independent, in-house critic. Our ombudsmen have been chosen largely for their proven independence. Several of our early ombudsmen were recruited from our own ranks of editors, but that wasn't ideal. The ombudsman has to raise tough questions and, when necessary, rap people across the knuckles. The early ones did it, but it is harder when you are just out of the newsroom and think you may go back. More recent ombudsmen, chosen from rival newspapers (Charles B. Seib), from academia (Bill Green), or from government (former State Department spokesman and ambassador to Greece Robert J. McCloskey, former Capitol Hill aide and member of the Consumer Product Safety Commission Sam Zagoria, and former White House and budget bureau spokesman Joseph Laitin), have found this tough job somewhat easier to do.

Clearly, undertaking such an assignment requires a basic love and respect for journalism. Newspaper experience, which all have had, helps. The ombudsman at the *Post* has an office on the newsroom floor but is deliberately kept out of planning the next day's paper. He reads the paper as any other reader does, and he questions dubious or missing items. He also passes on readers' criticisms that come in by phone or letter. Daily or weekly, the ombudsman writes a memo to the top editors and the publisher. Anyone on the staff can read his memo, a procedural safeguard instituted early on in response to reporters' and editors' objections to being second-guessed without their knowledge.

These memos are valuable internally, but I think the *Post* ombudsman's most important weapon for increasing credibility is the uncensored and uninhibited weekly column most of them have written on the editorial page. From experience I know that few things are more painful than being second-guessed on the pages of your own paper, but the lesson sticks in your mind and is not easily dismissed. Dick Cuningham, the first "readers' representative" at the *Minneapolis Tribune*, said, "It's not a comfortable process. It is no more comfortable for a news organization than it is for an individual to face frank feedback. Both would prefer to select what they want to hear and laugh off what is unpleasant. But you can't do that with a good ombudsman."

Richard Harwood was the first of the *Post* ombudsmen, and he set a standard of bluntness in both his memos and his published columns that has been emulated by his successors right down to the present. In February 1977, for example, Charles Seib used his column to question the *Post*'s handling of two sensitive stories, the resignation of the parent company's president and a big increase in the cost of the paper to subscribers and newsstand buyers. On the first, he noted, the twelve-inch story "consisted mostly of prepared statements. . . . That was pretty barebones coverage for the surprise resignation of the president of a national leader in the communications business and a major local enterprise." Readers of the *Post* were told substantially less about the circumstances than the *New York Times* had reported, he noted.

As for the price hike, Seib said, all the *Post* carried were two front-page announcements. "Suppose another major local business with hundreds of thousands of customers—one of the big grocery chains, for example—suddenly raised prices substantially," he said. "Would the *Post* have let it get away with simply posting signs in its store windows?" No indeed. "It would talk to company executives and it would press for figures to justify the increases. It would, in short, treat the story as news."

MORE ombudsmen with Harwood's and Seib's bite on more papers would help solve the credibility problem. But we cannot leave it to them, especially since the papers that most need an ombudsman are least likely to hire one. All of us journalists have to be as tough-minded as they are in separating fact from fiction, in disclosing our sources just as often as we possibly can, in examining our own prejudices and preconceptions, in correcting our errors, in holding our colleagues and ourselves to the strictest professional standards. We need to remind ourselves what it means to be a journalist.

CHAPTER TEN
A Journalist's Values

*M*OST sensible people will avoid journalism as a career. The job's abundant rewards are matched with its costs and risks. At the extreme, you can be shot at and killed, as so many war correspondents have been; you can be threatened and ostracized, as so many reporters were during the civil rights struggle.

Most of us face only an occasional angry citizen, cop, or government official, telling us to get the hell out of his sight—or else. But a journalist's life is inherently disrupted and disorganized. We work too hard and we play too hard. And we tend to die before our time.

The job is tougher on our families than on us. Divorce rates are high, and those who stay married still must contend with missed dinners, missed weekends, missed vacations. The strains arise because as journalists we put the pursuit and publication of news first. We feel the tug of family ties; of friendships; of ethnic, religious, racial, and national loyalties; and of our partisan, political, and social views. But we define ourselves by our calling, and we resolve most of our conflicts by making that goal uppermost.

Often that makes us do things that are less than admirable. In 1972, for example, at a restaurant in New Hampshire, I ran into a man who had been one of my closest friends in college and our early years in Washington. I asked what he was doing there. He was a Washington lawyer who represented Japanese companies. He and several other lawyers and lobbyists had volunteered to help the Democratic presidential primary campaign of House Ways and Means Committee

Chairman Wilbur Mills. As we talked, something in my expression made him stop suddenly and say, "You're not going to write about this, are you?" I recognized the problem. He had greeted me as a friend, not a reporter. He was not a politician and he had imposed no ground rules. He had answered my questions candidly but as a friend. Now he felt entrapped. I suppose I could have said, "Look, if you're uncomfortable about what you're doing, you better clear out. Just pay your check, get on the next plane, and I'll forget we even talked or that I saw you up here."

That's not what I did. "You're not an unknown person," I told him. "You are in a restaurant in Manchester, New Hampshire, the week before the primary, and there are other reporters here. You are taking a role in a campaign I'm covering. The fact that you and your friends are here to help Wilbur Mills is news in my book. It's going to be written about." He said, "You can't do that. The people at my table saw me talking with you. If you write this story, it's going to embarrass me with Mills. It's going to ruin everything." I said, "You should have thought about that before all of you came up here. There's no way you guys are going to be involved without people knowing about it."

I wrote the story and our friendship ended, as I knew it would. I am not sure I did the right thing. I can rationalize the betrayal of friendship on grounds that had I not written the story, another reporter would have. But it still doesn't ease the pinch of conscience.

THE longer you are a journalist, the more such troubling incidents you experience, the more the glamour disappears and the more obvious the limitations of the work become. We journalists always deal with partial information and know less than we should. We never have as much time as we need. And yet we must display our ignorance and haste in the most obvious way—by signing or broadcasting stories read or watched by people who know a hell of a lot more about the subject than we do. And they are not shy about letting us know where we went wrong.

Most important of all, journalists are always inherently outsiders. When an individual or team or nation has a great moment of achievement, we are observers, not celebrants. When tragedies happen, when a child drowns, when a President is killed, when a whole city goes up in flames, instead of sharing the emotions, we record them.

It takes a peculiar and in some respects almost perverse personality to choose a role in life that automatically distances you from the most profound experiences of your friends, your neighbors, your city, or your nation. We are voyeurs, not participants. And the best of us—a Walter Cronkite describing the first manned landing on the moon or a presidential funeral procession, a Frank Johnston photographing Jonestown, a John Hersey writing about Hiroshima—have to be at our most disciplined and dispassionate when almost every human instinct impels us to give way to joy or pain.

Even when reporters have their values before them and their roles thought through, they can land in unexpected controversy, as my colleagues William Greider and Milton Coleman both discovered. Greider, then the *Post*'s assistant managing editor for national news, and David Stockman had struck up a friendship in the late 1970s when Stockman was a representative from Michigan. When President-elect Reagan appointed Stockman director of the Office of Management and Budget, Greider proposed that their regular meetings continue under rules acknowledging Stockman's change of status to one of the administration's three or four central figures.

Greider would tape-record the conversations, which would be off the record for the *Post*'s immediate use. When both agreed, Greider would mine the material for a "full and serious" *Atlantic* magazine account of what promised to be a fateful year of budget policy. The meetings began, over Saturday-morning breakfasts at the Hay-Adams hotel, and by the end of the 1981 session of Congress, the two had met eighteen times.

As Greider wrote in the introduction to the book version of his expanded article, *The Education of David Stockman and Other Americans:*

At the outset, Stockman and I were participating in a fairly routine transaction of Washington, a form of submerged communication which takes place with utter regularity between selected members of the press and the highest officials of government. Our mutual motivation, despite our different interests, was crassly self-serving. It did not need to be spelled out between us. I would use him and he would use me. . . . I had established a valuable peephole on the inner policy debates of the new administration. And the young budget director had established a valuable connection with an important newspaper. I would get a jump on the unfolding strategies and decisions. He would be able to prod and influence the focus of our coverage, to communicate his views and positions under the cover of our "off the record" arrangement, to make known harsh assessments that a public official would not dare to voice in the more formal settings of a press conference, speech, or "on the record" interview. . . . He was using me and I was using him. I did say that it was crass.

The insights Greider gained from Stockman helped steer the *Post*'s coverage of the budget battle. At the breakfasts, he persuaded Stockman to allow some of his statements to be used immediately on a background basis, as the views of "administration officials" or "senior budget officials." Even off-the-record comments helped Greider manage our coverage. Many of us, who had our own back-channel communications with the budget director, knew about Greider's meetings with Stockman.

Stockman's deal with Greider was unique because, at some point, the off-the-record restriction would be erased in the interest of accurate history. Shortly before Labor Day in 1981, after Reagan had signed the first budget and tax bills into law, Greider told Stockman he thought it was time to write. As Greider later told me, "I held my breath, because if he had said, 'No, I've got to go back to these issues in 1982 and I don't want you to write yet,' I would have been bound by our agreement." Instead, Stockman agreed. Greider's only fear as he began to write was that he had no story to tell.

Columnists Joseph Kraft, Robert Novak, and George Will were also meeting regularly with Stockman during the first nine months of 1981, and Greider thought that most informed readers knew what he knew: that "administration officials" and "senior budget officials" were increasingly dismayed by both the President's and Congress's decisions on tax and budget matters. To say that he and Stockman were unprepared for the storm that broke would be an understatement. I remember telling Greider that I had received my copy of the *Atlantic* at home the previous night, had sat up late reading his article, and thought it was "a hell of a piece." He said that he didn't realize that subscribers had received it already, and that he had better let Stockman know. Later, he told me that when Stockman asked him if he thought it would cause any stir, Greider said it would be "a two-day flap at most."

He could not have been more wrong. The inflammatory quotes— "None of us really knows what's going on with all these numbers.... The defense numbers got out of control.... Kemp-Roth was always a Trojan horse to bring down the top rate.... Supply-side is trickle-down theory.... The hogs were really feeding"—read like time bombs set to blow up administration policy from within. The credibility of Reagan's unique policy mixture of deep tax rate cuts, steep defense increases, and reductions in some domestic spending was under increasing attack. Stockman's words to Greider seemed to cut the last thread of plausibility for that policy.

Stockman was summoned to the White House for a session with the President, but he was not fired—an interesting reflection on the nature of the Reagan presidency.

Greider later said two things had disturbed him. The first was that other journalists had sensationalized his careful, balanced account. Greider's story was a subtle tale of the disillusionment of a somewhat naive, perhaps idealistic young public servant, who tried to execute a policy based on consistent principles and found himself, for all his efforts, defending intellectually shabby and morally offensive decisions. Greider's article had been a brilliant case study in the difficulty of governing.

The press and television excerpted from that narrative the sensational quotes and turned Stockman into a heretic blurting inconvenient truths about administration policies. "Thus," Greider wrote months later, "I was confronted with a brief personal glimpse of the qualities in the news media that trouble its more thoughtful critics—the relentless factuality, the haste, the transient attention that obscures meaning even as the media deliver the daily blizzard of startling information."

Second, Greider belatedly discovered the penalties for violating the rules of clique journalism. As I noted, Greider wondered if he had a story, because he already had seen (and in some cases had been a conduit for) many references to the doubts of an official he, as an insider, could clearly identify as Stockman. Greider wrote:

By now, it should be clear why Stockman and I both offended the "rules." The appearance in print of the budget director's candid commentaries shocked sophisticated readers but they were not surprised by the substance of what he was saying. Those who had followed the coded dialogue, who had translated the news stories about "senior budget officials" or perhaps heard Stockman say the same things in private meetings, knew well enough where he stood. Still, it was shocking. The unvarnished private dialogue of government is supposed to remain private—and separate from the bland, reassuring rhetoric of the public discourse. By going public, he violated the privacy and prerogatives of that network and so did I. Publishing the raw version of reality automatically depreciates the value of every insider's knowledge. It also refutes the images of order and progress conveyed by the daily news. These stories of doubts and misgivings and policy battles had, in fact, been printed in the newspapers, but clearly they were not told in a way that made much impression outside the inner circle. As a newspaper editor, thinking my submerged conversations were helping inform general readers, I was most troubled by my belated recognition that the messages were not getting through.

Greider's arrangement with Stockman was criticized by some colleagues at the *Post* and other Washington papers. Howell Raines of the *New York Times* said at a 1983 Poynter Institute conference that he could not "escape the nagging feeling that the real message of this book is that for a time a great newspaper and a group of hardworking journalists got trapped into holding out on their readers, at a critical point in the Reagan administration, information that could have tilted the political balance."

As Greider learned, there are built-in problems when an editor on a daily newspaper takes on a sideline assignment as a magazine writer and uses that assignment for access under special guidelines to an official his paper is covering. The *Post*'s daily coverage of Stockman benefited from Greider's access, and, as Hobart Rowen, the *Post*'s senior economics writer, pointed out at the Poynter conference, other reporters at the *Post* were not inhibited by Greider's "arrangement" from writing, clearly and emphatically, about the contradictions in the Reagan policy mix. Admittedly, those columns and analytical articles lacked the impact of Stockman's confessions to Greider. But I can't see how Stockman could have made such confessions, on the record, while the budget and tax bill were going through Congress in 1981.

Greider got him on the record faster than any other journalist in Washington, and that feat deserved congratulations not censure. At every stage of the interviewing, he bargained with Stockman to modify the ground rules so Greider could share the maximum of what he was learning with readers. At the first opening, he told Stockman he wanted to use the direct quotes in the magazine piece. He did exactly what a responsible journalist must do: put his obligation to the readers first.

THAT responsibility met tougher challenges in the case of Jesse Jackson and Milton Coleman. It began on January 25, 1984, when Coleman and Gerald Boyd of the *New York Times* joined Jackson for coffee at National Airport. Coleman invited Jackson to come to the *Post* sometime soon for an interview on his foreign policy views, including the Middle East and Israel. He accepted, and then, Coleman said, Jackson told the two reporters, "Let's talk black talk." Coleman would later write in a first-person *Post* story about the whole affair:

> I understood that to mean background, and I assumed that Jackson, an experienced national newsmaker now running for President, knew that no amnesia rule would apply. I signaled him to go on.
>
> Jackson then talked about the preoccupation of some with Israel. He said something to the effect of the following: That's all Hymie wants to talk about is Israel; every time you go to Hymietown, that's all they want to talk about.

Coleman conceded the conversation had not been tape-recorded, nor had he taken notes. But he said he was certain about the words he had heard, and in subsequent conversations he had learned that "two or three" other campaign reporters had heard Jackson use them in other situations.

About two weeks after their conversation, *Post* reporter Rick Atkinson was assigned to report on Jackson's history of troubled relations with Jews and its impact on his presidential campaign. Atkinson called Coleman, who was traveling with Jackson, for help in arranging an interview with the candidate and suggestions on the story.

Coleman offered several leads and, because he thought "Jackson's use of 'Hymie' and 'Hymietown' was germane" to such an in-depth story, recounted the incident to Atkinson. He described the context to both Atkinson and then national editor Leonard Downie, and told Atkinson to call Jackson for comment before he used the material.

In the thirty-seventh and thirty-eighth paragraphs of a fifty-two-paragraph story, Atkinson wrote:

> In private conversations with reporters, Jackson has referred to Jews as "Hymie" and New York as "Hymietown."
> "I'm not familiar with that," Jackson said Thursday. "That's not accurate."

Coleman was identified at the bottom of the story as having "contributed to" the report. A few days after its publication, a *Post* editorial that criticized Jackson's language and called for an explanation made the comments an issue in the New Hampshire primary campaign. For more than a week Jackson insisted that he could not recall ever using such words. After he was put on the defensive in the final preprimary debate, he visited a temple in Manchester, where he said he was "shocked and astonished that this ethnic characterization made in a private conversation apparently was overheard by a reporter.... However innocent and unintentional," the comment "was insensitive and it was wrong."

It did not end there, however. A prominent Jackson supporter, Minister Louis Farrakhan, said in a March 11 speech that he was going to "make an example of Milton Coleman," adding, "One day soon we will punish you with death." The *Post* ordered security measures to protect Coleman's family, and he remained in Washington rather than rejoining the campaign reporting team. This roused new demands that Jackson repudiate Farrakhan's remarks, which he did only belatedly and grudgingly, causing new controversy in his campaign.

I was equally disturbed by the angry debate among journalists about the propriety of Coleman's decision. It was complicated—and made infinitely more emotional—by the fact that both men were black. Jackson's campaign had become a symbol of great importance to millions of blacks. But Coleman—operating under incalculable pressure, with his career at the *Post*, his family's safety, and his standing with colleagues of both races all on the line—insisted that the real issue was the reporter's conflicting obligations to his source or subject and to his reader.

Other journalists offered their opinions, with some noted black writers criticizing Coleman and others defending him. Veteran newsmen Carl T. Rowan and Lem Tucker lined up behind him, but when Coleman went before the National Association of Black Journalists in Atlanta, most of the comments indicated skepticism or hostility toward what he had done. The last questioner accused Coleman of being a "Judas Iscariot," and Coleman finally won a wave of applause by saying, "The answer to that is very simple. I ain't Judas. Jesse Jackson ain't Jesus, and I ain't *about* to kill myself."

But before that, in the first-person piece he wrote for the *Post*, he gave as eloquent and clear-minded a definition of the responsibility of a reporter as I have ever read. I quote from his piece with admiration —and even awe that he could distill from his harrowing experience so much wisdom. He marveled that "only 18 words, a single sentence that appeared two-thirds of the way down in a long story," could have caused so much controversy and threats, especially since "the accuracy of that sentence is not in question."

Coleman said that the question he had been asked most often—"Are you a black first or a reporter first?"—was not the real question. "This dilemma was created by the interaction of a presidential candidate, a reporter and a political supporter."

"Do I feel a racial kinship with Jackson and Farrakhan? Of course. Would I call them brother? I would. Do I mean either of them harm or ill will? Certainly not. But this is not about any of that. This is about how a reporter covers a candidate for President of the United States."

He retraced the events summarized earlier, concluding with Jackson's statement at the Manchester synagogue, and then returned to the underlying question of journalistic responsibility and ethics with this strikingly appropriate phrase:

Now let's talk black talk.

The controversy over Jackson's remarks might have been much easier for many blacks to accept had the messenger been white. It certainly would have been neat and easy. But it didn't happen that way. It rarely does.

This is the first time so many blacks have played major roles in such a high-level drama as the presidential campaign and a flawless performance would have been nice. But the glitches here have nothing to do with race. They are part of the process.

When Jackson agreed to run for President, when Farrakhan chose to openly support him and when I agreed to cover the campaign for the *Post*, we all undertook to take the bitter with the sweet.

I am moved by Jackson's campaign. Almost anyone black would be, and it is much easier to be moved by it when you trek across the nation with Jackson, stopping at some of the shrines that were only faraway places of heroic struggle when I was growing up—Selma, Montgomery, Birmingham, Atlanta.

Sometimes, in stories designed to capture mood and color, my heart creeps into print. That is natural and proper. A reporter gauges the mood of the audience from what he hears and sees and how he filters it through the lens of his own experience. No reporter is a robot.

But when it comes to the facts of the campaign, I have to throw personality aside. I cannot openly support any candidate. The others wouldn't stand for it. I cannot covertly support any candidate. My ethics wouldn't stand for it.

At the time Jackson's remarks were inserted into Atkinson's story. I knew they would become controversial—though I couldn't guess how controversial. I continue to think that the controversy caused by their simple publication has been greatly aggravated by the fact that, for 13 days at every opportunity Jackson was given to explain the remarks, he denied them instead. . . .

If I knew that publication of the remarks would cause trouble for Jackson, why did I disclose them? That is simple. It is not my job to avoid controversy for Jackson. His aides have that job. Reporters do not try to help or hurt the candidates they cover. They just cover them.

There are some reporters who pull punches to curry favor with those they cover. Those people should not be categorized as white racist reporters protecting white candidates. Those are bad reporters. They come in all colors.

Though Coleman's view was both courageous and correct, I think he and others covering Jackson made one mistake. Sometime, early on, they should have reached an explicit understanding with Jackson about the rules of discourse. Those are never easily arrived at; candidates are human enough to crave company, and reporters know these informal meetings can produce character insights that they cannot gain any other way. Both sides are served when the talk can flow freely.

But, realistically, in the heat of a presidential campaign, nothing genuinely significant—nothing truly revealing of character, plans, or policy—can remain secret if the candidate utters it in reporters' presence.

I can understand why that ground rule wasn't established with Jackson. Like John F. Kennedy, he likes to create an intimacy which he hopes will bring an obligation of protection. In Kennedy's time, some reporters were willingly co-opted by such confidences. But we are not so innocent these days. Today, whatever the ambivalence about the ground rules, there is no ambivalence about the reporter's responsibility. Coleman did what he had to do.

SOME in journalism believe they can have all of its privileges as well as all the pleasures of actively participating in the political world. The have-it-both-ways clan can cite as an example the most eminent journalist of the last generation, Walter Lippmann. At age twenty-five, while working for the *New Republic*, he drafted labor speeches for Theodore Roosevelt, and later had friendships with almost every President through John F. Kennedy. As Ronald Steel noted in his biography of Lippmann, Kennedy consulted and flattered the old columnist constantly. Ted Sorensen brought a draft of Kennedy's inaugural address to Lippmann's house and accepted some minor changes in the text, which Lippmann praised in his column as "a remarkably successful piece of self-expression." Steel noted that Lippmann hired a new assistant who had worked in the Kennedy campaign and was also well connected at the White House, and, in short time, the columnist "became one of the shining ornaments of the Kennedy Administration." Lippmann's extracurricular activities did not diminish the exceptional quality of his journalism. But now when the journalist's role is more visible and controversial, the eminence some achieve carries with it added responsibilities and ought not act as an excuse for special privilege. At least that's my view, though I readily concede the whole ethical dilemma of outside activities and associations is one each journalist must solve for himself.

I have generally avoided entertaining the politicians I write about or being wined and dined by them. A few years ago, when a Republican I had known for twenty years and become genuinely fond of decided to run for President, I told him, rather pompously, that our custom of

pleasant private lunches and long conversations would have to be sac-
rificed to his ambitions and my job responsibilities. On the other hand,
I participate uninhibitedly in the Gridiron Dinner, cavorting in satirical
skits while my invited guests from the political and journalistic worlds
mingle at an event which many critics consider the ultimate expression
of coziness between Washington reporters and officials.

Still, even by my flexible yardstick, the political involvements of
some journalists raise troubling questions. William F. Buckley, Jr., the
columnist, editor, author, and television personality, founded the
Young Americans for Freedom, which has become a recruiting and
training ground for a whole generation of conservative politicians. He
ran for mayor of New York and has a well-publicized friendship with
President Reagan. Among Democrats, the most notable example may
be Ben Wattenberg, a former Lyndon Johnson speechwriter, who in
recent years has combined his newspaper column with an activist role
as the leader of the Coalition for a Democratic Majority, which has
battled rival factions for control of the party platform and provided
forums and support for favored political candidates.

But the most visible of Lippmann's successors is George F. Will,
probably the most influential journalist today and certainly the most
versatile, with a vast television, magazine, newspaper, and lecture audience. Will has worked vigorously to erase the inhibitions many of us
think go with our jobs. A staff aide for a Republican senator before
taking up journalism, Will has made no secret of his personal relationship with contemporary politicians. After hosting a dinner party for
Ronald Reagan in 1980 which formally introduced the President-elect
to Washington's political and social aristocracy, he laid into the "confused moralists" of Washington, who he said had been spreading a
"silly scrupulosity" about press-government relations. "We all have
our peculiar tastes. Some people like Popsicles. Others like Gothic
novels. I like politicians. . . . A journalist's duty is to see politicians
steadily and see them whole. To have intelligent sympathy for them, it
helps to know a few as friends. Most that I know are overworked and
underpaid persons whose characters can stand comparison with the
characters of the people they represent, and of journalists." Journalists
"have particular professional duties," he said, "but they and politicians
are part of the same process, the quest for the public good."

What he did not mention in that column was that "the quest for the public good" had led him, not just to give dinner to an "overworked and underpaid" politician named Ronald Reagan, but to assist the same Reagan, a couple months earlier, in preparing to debate Jimmy Carter.

Will was one of three conservative journalists invited to Wexford, an estate in Virginia, where Reagan was rehearsing for the most important event in the campaign. One of them, *New York Times* columnist William Safire, had the good sense to say no. Another, Pat Buchanan, Safire's former colleague in the Nixon White House, said yes, which did not surprise me, because he has always put his ideology ahead of anything else.

When Will agreed to prep Reagan for the debate, he made a great mistake and caused many of us who admire him great pain. His work was not secret. As he pointed out, photographers saw him going into Wexford with David Stockman, then a young congressman, who was playing Carter in the rehearsals. But almost three years later, when it developed that Stockman and others on the Reagan team had obtained certain papers prepared for Carter's use in the debate, people took a closer look at who had been doing what.

The *Wall Street Journal* started it with a July 1983 front-page story headlined, "Should a Newsman Be Active Participant in Partisan Politics?"

The story quoted Will's ABC News commentary on the debate: "I think his game plan worked well. I don't think he was particularly surprised." It then disclosed that Reagan aides had had Carter's preparation materials and that, because he had helped rehearse Reagan, Will knew this.

Jack Nelson, the Washington bureau chief of the *Los Angeles Times*, told the *Journal* Will's action was "outrageous." The story pointed out that while "the network mentioned on debate night that Mr. Will had 'met' with candidate Reagan the day before, there wasn't any suggestion that he had participated in the preparations." Will said he went to Wexford because "it's like being invited into the locker room for a sportswriter," but he conceded, "I probably wouldn't go down there again."

The *New York Daily News* dropped his column, saying he had broken faith with his readers, but later reinstated it. Other editors either defended Will or said his column was too valuable to lose—as, indeed, it is. But the furor was large enough that one Sunday in July

Will defended what he had done in a long column in the *Post* and answered his colleagues' questions on ABC-TV's *This Week with David Brinkley*, where he is a panelist.

In addition to his earlier points—that his presence was not secret and that he was of minimal substantive help to Reagan—he argued that as a columnist he had more license than a straight news reporter and that his partisanship toward Reagan was, as he put it, not exactly a "state secret."

So, he concluded his column:

> To those who ask: Should you have accepted access to Wexford?, my reply is: I think so. It was a valuable chance to see certain gears and pulleys of the political backstage.... Would I accept a similar invitation again? Wild horses could not drag me. This, for three reasons. First, some of the questions now being raised seem to me to have merit. Second, it makes so many people anxious. Third, my relationship with ABC is now formal and different. Then I generally appeared in a semi-debate format with a more liberal person.

Will's defense bothered me. First, he said that had he been a regular ABC News employee (as he was by 1983), he would have felt more of a responsibility to stay out of the debate rehearsal. But that reasoning overlooks the readers of his columns for *Washington Post* Writers Group and *Newsweek* magazine. Second, Will is as much of a sports fan as I am—we both have it bad—and he knew full well that sportswriters are invited to the locker room after the game, not before. What Will accepted was an invitation to be with the coaches at the last secret practice before the big game.

Stockman's possession of some of Carter's debate materials almost compromised him. Will said he never wrote about them "because their origin was unknown and their importance was nil." Suppose their origin had been announced at Wexford and their importance recognized by everyone in the room. What would he have done then? Suppose someone had said, "Our Carter sources tell us that he is going to do such-and-such in his closing statement. How do you want to answer him?" Would he have reported that or kept silent?

In his *Post* apologia, Will said, "I did not write about what I saw at Wexford because to have done so would have violated an unspoken but nonetheless important understanding that there are times when a writer is allowed access to things that the writer should not turn into material for his writings."

As far as I could judge, when Will went to Wexford, he was already assigned to comment on the debate for ABC and he would certainly continue to write about the Reagan-Carter campaign. Yet he knowingly entered a situation where no matter what he learned his hands were tied journalistically. That is a pretty dumb position for any journalist to get into. When Milton Coleman sat down for coffee with Jesse Jackson and when Bill Greider had breakfasts with David Stockman, they operated as journalists whose first responsibility is to their readers. As Reagan's invited guest and informal adviser, Will put his readers and listeners in second place.

Mary McGrory and Dick Harwood wrote pieces about the Will affair, and while both concluded that he shouldn't have done it, they also argued that Will was not so different from other journalists. McGrory wrote:

> If you sat all the political reporters in Washington down in a room and told them that only those who had never given advice to a politician should stand up, hardly a soul would dare rise.
>
> Scratch a scribe in this town and you find a campaign manager. The candidate has no more seductive, nay irresistible, gambit in wooing the press than asking, "What do you think I should do?"

Harwood was even more convincing, because he named names, starting with himself.

> In the bad old days when newspaper reporters carried half-pints on the hip instead of tape recorders, we were often expected to be ambidextrous.
>
> One of my early assignments on the *Nashville Tennessean* in the 1940s was to write a speech for one of the publisher's legislative candidates. I then wrote a news story about the speech, which impressed me as dynamic and innovative, and got a third crack at it in an editorial I composed on the brilliance of it all.
>
> That was my introduction to both journalism and politics. On our newspaper they were one and the same. Our mission was to rout the scoundrels and rally the righteous. Whatever it took—fair means or foul—we were prepared to invest.

Although I had been reluctant to write about the Will affair because it might be seen as piling on a colleague I admire, the Harwood and McGrory columns sent me to the keyboard.

I cannot accept—or let my silence seem to lend assent to—what has become the widespread assertion that "everybody does it." There is too much danger in that myth taking hold.

I think most political journalists—reporters or commentators—feel we occupy one of the nation's favored positions. We have access to the minds of many of our fellow citizens, uninhibited by any serious censorship. That is a rare privilege. It is also a form of power. And like any power, it can be exercised justly only with an awareness of the responsibilities and inhibitions that go with it.

As journalists, our responsibility is to the reader. Anything we learn, or think, belongs first to that reader. Not to a politician who happens to be a friend.

As journalists, we owe that reader the fullest and fairest rendition of the facts we can provide and the clearest judgment we can muster, unimpeded by the wish to see some privately recommended strategy fulfilled. That obligation does not change if we call ourselves reporters or commentators.

For the privilege of being political journalists, we accept certain inhibitions. One of them is forsaking the role of political activists—or strategists. It may not be unethical to do both. But it is surely greedy. And that kind of greed properly invites the distrust of the reader who must wonder where our first loyalty lies.

These are the considerations that make it easy for most political journalists to demur when a politician asks the flattering question, "What do you think I should do?"

The answer is simple. "You want to know what I think? Buy the paper. It only costs a quarter. You get all the ball scores and comics—and they toss in my advice for nothing. Which is probably what it's worth."

In fact, turning down a politician's request for advice depends a lot on where he asks, how close you are, and how high his status is. If the request comes up in his office or on the phone, you can easily say, "Hey, wait a minute, I'm supposed to ask you questions." If it's at your dinner table, or his, it's harder.

Lippmann said we should keep "a certain distance" emotionally and socially from our subjects. Presidents and lesser politicians love to tempt us with invitations, appointments, and souvenirs, and each time we swallow one of their lures, we lose a little independence. When I asked Ben Wattenberg to review this section, he said, "I don't think there's a sharp line between activists and vestal virgins in journalism." George Will claims not to be influenced by his dining companions, citing a recent tough column about George Bush, "who has been out for dinner twice." But journalists should be as conscientious as government officials about conflict-of-interest situations. Though he violated it himself, Lippmann laid down the correct standard in a letter to Alexander Woollcott:

> It seems to me that once the columnist thinks of himself as a public somebody over and above the intrinsic value and integrity of what is published under his name, he ceases to think as clearly and disinterestedly as his readers have a right to expect him to think. Like a politician, he acquires a public character, which he comes to admire and to worry about preserving and improving; his personal life, his self-esteem, his allegiances, his interests and ambitions becoming indistinguishable from his judgment of events.

Increasingly, ethical issues, such as conflict of interest, are being addressed in newsrooms across the country. According to a 1983 Ohio State University survey of 902 news organizations, three quarters had written policies on such matters as outside work and the acceptance of gifts by their reporters and editors. The scrutiny is needed because in the television era journalists have far greater opportunities to turn their prominence into money or influence. For instance, those with familiar faces or bylines can get lecture fees that often dwarf what most of us think a good week's pay.

No official rules apply to the profession as a whole. The Society of Professional Journalists, Sigma Delta Chi, adopted a code of ethics in 1926 and updated it in 1973. It says secondary employment and political involvement "should be avoided if it compromises the integrity of journalists and their employers." The code is necessarily general and lacks any enforcement mechanism. Each news organization sets its own standards and each journalist decides how far he will operate within their borders. At the *Post*, the managing editor must be informed in advance and can veto any outside employment, from book contract to teaching invitation. This policy guards against any infringement on the daily demands on a journalist's time and protects against any potential embarrassment the paper could incur from a staff member's inappropriate sideline or free-lance work.

After winning the Pulitzer Prize in 1973 increased my speaking invitations, I set some rules for myself. Colleges, the largest single category of requests, posed no problem. Partisan political groups were out because even if no fee is involved, one's presence is hard to explain. (I have occasionally bent that rule, and have spoken for free to the Women's National Democratic Club and have met with the SOS and the Chowder and Marching Society, groups of House Republicans, where I was clearly a journalist and an outsider.) I also will not accept honoraria or travel expenses from any group of public officials, because I couldn't comfortably take money from anyone I covered.

Business groups are troublesome. Whatever insights I may offer trade associations or companies on election prospects or a tax bill's chances of passing really reprocess material I've already written. I have neither to subscribe to the company's or group's view nor to tailor my speech to them, and most invitations are one-shots or widely spaced appearances, so I'm not dependent on any group for a significant income. Still, the involvement of some groups with the legislative-political process makes them barely distinguishable from a party group. If I speak to one of those groups (like the U.S. Chamber of Commerce or the National Rural Electric Cooperative Association), I ask them to send the honorarium to one of my favorite charities.

But becoming involved in politics is even more tempting and complicated. In a 1984 study for the National News Council (now defunct) titled *Conflicts of Interest: A Matter of Journalistic Ethics*, Charles W. Bailey, former editor of the *Minneapolis Tribune*, cited various newsroom rules barring political candidacies or advocacy—as well as instances when they had been applied or ignored. For example, "a reporter for the *Knoxville News-Sentinel* was ordered not to run for a suburban school board. She ran, won—and got fired. The man who fired her, however, continued to hold both his job as editor of the newspaper and as chairman of the Knoxville Parking Authority."

Bailey pointed out the problems (of which we have many examples at the *Post*) of a reporter's spouse working in government, in politics, or in a political advocacy group or a law firm involved in lobbying. In 1978, he said, his wife made "a substantial contribution" to a Minnesota Senate candidate, which the paper reported along with other major gifts. Bailey sent a memo to his staff, saying: "This contribution may be a matter of some embarrassment to me. I hope it will not be a source of embarrassment for the *Tribune*. It didn't seem to me that I had any business trying to tell my wife what she could do with her money as long as what she proposed to do was legal and would be a matter of public record."

Nonetheless, when it came to newsroom employees themselves, Bailey urged other editors to ignore "those who argue that rules restricting political involvement, community activism, or questionable outside employment are somehow a deprivation of individual rights. Journalists who accept such rules are not forfeiting their rights; they are temporarily suspending their exercise of them. They choose to be less involved in some activities so they can more persuasively be involved with others."

I agree and I think most journalists would too. But, as Bailey pointed out, that rule is harder to apply to the increasing number of people, with increasing prominence, who "go back and forth, sometimes more than once, across the line separating journalism from government and politics." This traffic makes such conflicts much harder to avoid and leads readers or viewers to believe that there isn't really much difference between a journalist and a politician.

Some years back, when the *New Republic* speculated that Walter Cronkite might be drafted as someone's vice presidential running mate, Cronkite responded that "if there were to be a presumption against any profession in politics, it probably should weigh most heavily against journalists, and doubly so for television anchormen." A journalist's credibility, he said, "is something he holds in trust. To turn around and spend that trust on behalf of partisan political campaigns and programs seems somehow to degrade what he has been."

Similarly, journalism's credentials are cheapened when someone basically identified as a partisan assumes the role of a journalist. I had a psychedelic experience on opening day of the 1984 Democratic convention in San Francisco. Peering through the cheap curtains separating our temporary working space from *Newsweek*'s, I saw my old pal Lyn Nofziger sitting at a *Newsweek* desk. My automatic reaction was, "Watch what you say, Nofziger's here." As I mentioned, Nofziger and I were seat-mates on John Kennedy's 1960 campaign plane. But since the mid-1960s, Nofziger has promoted Republican and conservative causes, especially Richard Nixon's and Ronald Reagan's. He has earned a reputation for hard-ball press policies and political tactics in the White House under both Presidents and as the head of a thriving government relations firm. No one doubted that Reagan's interests were still his uppermost concern.

I assumed he was peddling some White House lines on the Democratic proceedings. Wrong. Nofziger had been born again as a journalist for a week, thanks to *Newsweek*, and in the magazine's postconvention issue, a bylined Nofziger piece poked fun at the "new Fritz Mondale . . . a budget-balancer, a pay-as-you-goer and a man who wants a strong national defense." He was identified in italic type as a "private consultant" and "Ronald Reagan's longtime ambassador to the GOP right."

Three weeks later at the Republican convention, Nofziger was once again a Reagan flack. But the surrealism continued. At one of the mass interviews over breakfast, arranged by Godfrey Sperling, Jr., of the *Christian Science Monitor*, Nofziger was the Reagan spokesman being interviewed. David Gergen, who was covering the convention for National Public Radio, was one of the journalists interviewing him. Gergen had resigned only a few months earlier as the Reagan White House communications director—its chief propagandist. And for the first thirteen months of Reagan's first term, when Nofziger had been political director and Gergen's communications director, the two had collaborated on White House strategy. But now born-again journalist Gergen was asking earnest questions of ex-journalist and now spokesman Nofziger. Would everyone please hold up his identity card?

STEPHEN HESS of the Brookings Institution addressed the increasing frequency of these in-and-out and back-and-forth arrangements in a paper he delivered in April 1985:

> The denizens of government's executive suites and the Washington bureaus of the major news organizations are becoming interchangeable. In socioeconomic terms—schools attended, income, spouses' backgrounds, their neighborhoods—they increasingly look alike; in personal terms, some of

them are the same people. At least 11 journalists have served in both the *New York Times'* bureau and in some recent presidential administration. The most fascinating—and commented upon—case is the Gelb-Burt exchange. Leslie Gelb left the *Times* at the beginning of the Carter Administration in 1977 to become director of politico-military affairs at the Department of State, staying into 1979; Richard Burt left the Washington bureau of the *Times* for the same job at the beginning of the Reagan presidency in 1981. Gelb returned to the *Times* in 1981 as its national security correspondent; Burt is presently the assistant secretary of State for European affairs. [He is now ambassador to West Germany.] While once reporters took jobs in government primarily as press secretaries or spokesmen, the Gelb and Burt examples illustrate that ex-reporters are now moving into policy positions.

Government has gotten some very good people this way. Among the other *Times* people who have temporarily served in government are some of the best journalists on their beats: William Beecher and Benjamin Welles on national security, Edwin Dale and Eileen Shanahan on economics, Joseph Loftus on labor. Edward R. Murrow, John Chancellor, and Carl T. Rowan served stints as directors of the U.S. Information Agency or the Voice of America. And in 1968, President Johnson appointed J. Russell Wiggins, the editor of the *Post*, as U.S. ambassador to the United Nations, where he served capably.

Journalism benefits not only from the experience in government but also from the perspective brought by those who first gained renown in governmental roles. A lot of eyebrows were raised when the *Times* hired Bill Safire after his service in the Nixon White House, but he has turned out to be a first-rate columnist, a deserved Pulitzer Prize–winner. Jack Rosenthal and Ed Guthman, now manning the editorial pages of the *Times* and the *Philadephia Inquirer*, are former Justice Department aides. Gerald Warren of the *San Diego Union* became a deputy White House press secretary in 1969 but returned to the paper in 1975 as its editor. James Fallows, President Carter's top speechwriter for a time, became Washington editor for *The Atlantic* magazine; one of his first pieces critically dissected the Carter presidency. Jeremiah A. O'Leary, Jr., reported on the White House and other beats for the *Washington Star*, then joined the White House press staff under Ronald Reagan, and then left to cover Reagan for the

Washington Times. David Gergen went from the Reagan White House to the editorship of *U.S. News & World Reports.* Ben Bradlee once held the dream job of press attaché at the U.S. embassy in Paris, where he probably improved his French and damaged his liver.

I have always pushed for more government internships and fellowships for journalists. The American Political Science Association's annual congressional fellowship program allows a few journalists, political scientists, and executive branch employees to spend a year on Capitol Hill. There should be comparable programs for the executive and judicial branches. I wish that I had just once worked inside a candidate's headquarters, felt the pressures, and learned how people operate when the press is not around.

Still I worry about those who first make their reputations as political spokesmen, then suddenly turn back into journalists, as Nofziger did. The pattern's not limited to conservatives, by the way. Hodding Carter III, the columnist, television host, and reporter, has played on both sides of the street. He started on his father's paper, the Greenville, Mississippi, *Delta Democrat-Times.* His activism carried him into politics, first as a temporary staff member in Lyndon Johnson's 1964 campaign, then as a leader of the "Loyal Democrats" of Mississippi at the 1968 Democratic convention.

He worked actively for Jimmy Carter's campaign in 1976 and became Carter's foreign policy spokesman as assistant secretary of State for public affairs. During the Iranian hostage crisis in 1979–80, Hodding Carter's televised daily briefings from the State Department and his frequent news interview appearances made him a familiar figure.

While Carter was in the State Department, he and his family decided to put the *Delta Democrat-Times* up for sale. The winning bidder was Freedom Newspapers, Inc., a chain better known for the rigidity of its conservative editorial line than for the journalistic quality of its product. The sale grieved Southerners who had esteemed the paper as a voice for social justice during the difficult struggles against segregation. And it made it a bit ironic when Carter began his reconversion to journalism, after the defeat of the Democrats in 1980, as reporter-host for the public television program *Inside Story,* a series examining the performance and responsibility of the press. Television likes to convert into celebrity journalists people who first became famous as White House or State Department operatives. Carter regularly joins George Will on the roundtable discussions that highlight ABC News's *This Week with David Brinkley*. Another regular on that show is Jimmy Carter's former White House press secretary, Jody Powell, who became a syndicated columnist despite his lack of newspaper experience. None of these three "news commentators" tries to hide his partisan or personal leanings. Indeed, the clash of viewpoints is what people tune in to see.

CBS News's principal commentator in recent years was Bill Moyers, a former Lyndon Johnson press secretary. Diane Sawyer was an assistant to Nixon's press secretary, Ron Ziegler, and is now a featured correspondent on CBS's highly popular *Sixty Minutes*. Kennedy press secretary Pierre Salinger is now an ABC news correspondent. When ABC needed someone to help its evening news program compete, it hired, as its commentator, George Will, the man ABC News chief Roone Arledge had described to the *New York Times* as "a known partisan." NBC's *Today* show regularly features John P. Sears, Nixon White House veteran and Ronald Reagan's campaign manager in 1976 and early 1980, along with Robert D. Squier, who produces commercials and formulates political strategy for Democratic candidates and the Democratic Party. Billed as "insiders" in their respective parties, they provide commentary on political developments.

When journalism jobs used to pay much less than they do now, it was assumed that you could "scratch a flack"—a press secretary or public relations person—"and find a former reporter." Nowadays, the quickest path to the top echelons of journalism—particularly television—seems to be flacking for a politician who is or might become President.

John McLaughlin's step up that path is in some ways the most stunning transformation. He was first noticed by political writers in 1970, as a Jesuit priest who was the Republican nominee against veteran Senator John O. Pastore, a Democrat, in Rhode Island. Earlier that year, he had left his position as associate editor of the Jesuit magazine, *America*.

After losing to Pastore, McLaughlin was hired as a White House speechwriter. During Watergate, McLaughlin proved useful to the White House propaganda machine. In May 1974, after the release of damning White House tapes, Carroll Kilpatrick reported in the *Post* that McLaughlin "defended the President as a moral man who was 'thirsting for the truth.'" The story continued:

> McLaughlin, who no longer wears clerical garb and is now deputy assistant to the President working on various assignments, said accusations of immorality against Mr. Nixon are "erroneous, unjust and contain elements of hypocrisy."
> The President has "acquitted himself with honor," McLaughlin said. . . .
> The President's use of profanity is "a form of emotional drainage," he said, "a form of therapy, a form of release."

After Nixon's resignation, McLaughlin left the priesthood, married an attractive Nixon administration colleague, became a radio talk-show host and the Washington editor of William F. Buckley, Jr.'s *National Review*, and eventually started his own television talk show, *The McLaughlin Group*.

A number of these Washington TV talk shows feature journalists discussing the week's events. The best of the lot, public television's *Washington Week in Review*, is run by a veteran print and television journalist, Paul Duke. The exchange among the four reporters and Duke is the closest simulation television offers of the valuable newsroom bull sessions. When I am on the road, *Washington Week* is almost as good as being around the *Post*'s watercooler. The journalists on the show respect each other's reporting and opinions as much as the audience values them.

McLaughlin's Group is different. The tone is acerbic, and whoever yells loudest gets the floor. McLaughlin's questions invariably call for value judgments or predictions. Analysis of what has happened — let alone reporting — is not on the menu. I went on the program once and found it as bad in person as it is on the screen. It is really awful, and also widely popular among people who apparently think reporters deal with issues by snapping insults at each other. Many of Washington's best print reporters and columnists go on the show. They love the celebrity and the resultant lecture dates, even though some of them derogate the program as "mud wrestling." They haven't asked my advice, but I'd tell them the same thing I tell aspiring young journalists: Don't work anywhere where you don't respect the product or the values of the people in charge. You damage your credentials and the credibility of the press when you work below your own standards.

WELL, it is a long climb up from the McLaughlin Group to the soaring, trumpets-blaring conclusion expected from a book on the press. So I will spare you the standard "Free Press, Guardian of a Nation's Liberty" coda. My former publisher and ultimate boss, Katharine Graham, said it best in her remarks to the Duke University graduates in 1984:

> Today we enjoy more freedom than any people of any nation. And our country has a press that is more free, more diverse and of higher quality than anywhere in the world. This is not a coincidence.

She spoke from experience. During the Watergate crisis, when a President tried by threat, intimidation, and disinformation to stop the *Washington Post*'s efforts to expose the crime, Katharine Graham proved her mettle and thereby helped preserve a vital portion of the nation's liberty and law. She helped write a proud moment in the history of American journalism.

In many less dramatic circumstances, a good newspaper or a good television news show can be of substantial value to you—but only if we earn your trust by our daily work.

There are no safe shortcuts. In my more than thirty years as a reporter, for five different organizations, I have learned that the only way to cover a story is to cover it: to spend as much time with the people as humanly possible, to ask as many questions as they will tolerate, and never to assume I know what is going on without asking.

For all the reasons I have described, we often fall short of the truth. Whether covering the campaign trail, the Congress, or the White House, defining a public figure's character or tracing a complex plot, we sometimes miss the mark—by some distance. The news we present is distorted by the limits of our skills, the principals' reluctance to share all they know, and the pressures of time and space.

Still, a good newspaper is a citizen's best resource for exercising his rights and responsibilities in this Republic. It provides the broadest and, on occasion, deepest look into the affairs of the society and its government. Books and magazines can provide more concepts, perspectives, and history, and television and radio can bring you closer to the actual event. But a good newspaper has both immediacy and perspective that foster the discussion and judgment so essential to the dialogue of democracy.

Dialogue is the key word because neither our government nor our press functions well without public involvement. Voters and newspaper readers—the same people, really—are ultimately as well served by their government and their press as they demand to be.

Walter Lippmann wrote, "The theory of a free press is that the truth will *emerge* from free reporting and free discussion, not that it will be presented perfectly and instantly in any one account." Eric Sevareid quoted those words in a 1967 address to the Massachusetts legislature, and added, "The ultimate burden must fall upon the individual citizen. If he wishs to be well informed he must read widely in the press and listen widely to the broadcasts. No one example of either can serve him more than very partially."

You cannot be passive about citizenship or about journalism. A good newspaper will reward you only so far as you are devoted to reading it critically.

The paper you read is shaped by unstated, implicit values and biases which you must recognize. I admit that the mirrors we use to reflect reality are inevitably flawed by our own presuppositions and prejudices. You must correct the "spin" those twists impart to what you read. The clues are there in all the subjective elements—phrasing, word selection, story placement, sourcing—that shape a particular reporter's or paper's version of the news.

With these worthwhile efforts, the half hour you spend with the paper will give you more than a new set of facts and opinions; it will open a new set of your own questions. Every good journalist reads the paper or watches television news with this in mind: Where does the story go next? What questions remain unanswered? What new puzzles are there now to be solved?

So should you. And when your paper fails to answer your questions, let them—or us—know. At its best, a newspaper is in constant conversation with its readers, and you have to hold up your end of the dialogue.

I just can't accept those who deal with criticism of the press by saying, "If people don't like it, they can stop buying it." The conversation between newspapers and readers doesn't end at the coin box or subscription counter any more than voters end their dialogue with elected officials at the ballot box. Representative government is a 365-day-a-year give-and-take proposition. So it must be between newspapers and our readers.

We need to hear more about what we do that leaves you unsatisfied, your curiosity unfulfilled. We need to know when you think our values and prejudices bend the news out of shape. We also need your support when you agree with our side in one of our inevitable clashes with those we are covering—especially government officials. The press's freedom ultimately depends on how important our work is to you.

The last words in this book are not the last word. I am going back to my newspaper to cover my beat and to write my column, but I may return to this subject. So I ask you now, as I have asked so many politicians and voters over the years, "What do you think?"

Acknowledgments

This book, like the others I have written, would not have been possible without the tolerance and support of the members of my family and my colleagues and editors at the *Washington Post*. In the former category, Ann, George, Josh, Matt, and Mike Broder all put up with the grumpiness and distractedness of having an author in the family, and all made helpful suggestions on parts of the manuscript.

At the *Post*, Ben Bradlee, Howard Simons, Len Downie, Bob Kaiser, and Dan Balz, my editors, generously allowed me time to work on the project and persuaded me, at the times I was in doubt, to keep at it.

Esther Newberg, an indefatigable agent and enthusiast, helped greatly with her reactions. Many friends and colleagues contributed ideas and read portions of the book, correcting errors of fact and interpretation and suggesting improvements. They bear no responsibility for the mistakes and misjudgments that remain, but I want to acknowledge the assistance of, among others:

Joseph Alsop, R. W. Apple, Jr., Charles R. Babcock, Ben Bagdikian, Charles Bailey, Russell Baker, James David Barber, Fred Barnes, Charles Bartlett, Edwin R. Bayley, Marilyn Berger, Creed C. Black, Herbert Block, Peter Braestrup, Tom Brokaw, Lou Cannon, Hodding Carter III, John J. Casserly, Douglass Cater, John Chancellor, Milton Coleman, Frederic W. Collins, Frank Cormier, John Corry, Walter Cronkite, James Deakin, Ann Devroy, Helen Dewar, Sam Donaldson, Robert J. Donovan, Thomas B. Edsall, Alan S. Emory, Dennis Farney, Reuven Frank, Mary Beth Franklin, Herbert J. Gans, Murray Gart, David R. Gergen, Jack W. Germond, Philip Geyelin, Stanhope Gould, Donald E. Graham, Bill Green, Jeff Greenfield, Meg Greenfield, William Greider, Thomas Griffith, Richard Harwood, John Herbers, George Herman, Stephen Hess, Don Hewitt, David Hoffman, Margot Hornblower, Albert R. Hunt, Michael Isikoff, Peter Jennings, Haynes Johnson, Robert M. Kaus, Murray Kempton, James J. Kilpatrick, Herbert Klein, Morton M. Kondracke, Nick Kotz, Bill Kovach, Howard Kurtz, Joseph Laitin, George Lardner, Jr., Jim Lehrer, S. Robert Lichter, Martin Linsky, Robert MacNeil, Myra MacPherson, Murrey Marder, Anthony Marro, John W. Mashek, Barbara Matusow, Robert C. Maynard, Richard D.

McCarthy, Charles McDowell, Mary McGrory, John McLaughlin, Walter R. Mears, Peter Milius, Loye Miller, Morton Mintz, Andrea Mitchell, Bill Moyers, Roger Mudd, Reg Murphy, James M. Naughton, Ron Nessen, Lyn Nofziger, Robert Novak, David Nyhan, Don Oberdorfer, Michael J. O'Neill, Robert Pierpoint, Walter Pincus, Bill Plante, Martin Plissner, Jody Powell, Sally Quinn, Howell Raines, Eleanor Randolph, Austin Ranney, Dan Rather, George Reedy, Richard Reeves, James Reston, Chalmers M. Roberts, Charles W. Roberts, Michael J. Robinson, Howard Rosenberg, Hobart Rowen, Vermont Royster, Dale Russakoff, Van Gordon Sauter, Richard M. Scammon, Martin Schram, Leland Schwartz, Mitzi Scott, Charles B. Seib, Robert B. Semple, Jr., Eric Sevareid, Tom Shales, David Shaw, Ray Scherer, Mark Shields, Hugh Sidey, Carole Simpson, Hedrick Smith, Susan Spencer, Lesley Stahl, James L. Sundquist, Barry Sussman, Jerry terHorst, Helen Thomas, Martin Tolchin, Richard Wald, James M. Wall, Edward Walsh, Ben J. Wattenberg, Warren Weaver, Jr., Tom Wicker, George Will, Thomas Winship, Bob Woodward, and James Wooten.

Most of all, I want to thank those people whose dedication and intelligence made the book possible: Amy Rosenfeld, the researcher who began collecting and organizing material; Lee Kennedy, who took over that task when Amy went off to law school and carried through to publication; and Alice Mayhew and her assistant, Henry Ferris, who edited it into something leaner and better than the manuscript they received.

Suggested Reading

Bayley, Edwin R. *Joe McCarthy and the Press*. Madison, Wisconsin: University of Wisconsin Press, 1981.

Bradlee, Benjamin C. *Conversations with Kennedy*. New York: W. W. Norton, 1975.

Broder, David S. *Changing of the Guard*. New York: Simon and Schuster, 1980.

Cannon, Lou. *Reagan*. New York: G. P. Putnam's Sons, 1982.

————. *Reporting: An Inside View*. Sacramento: California Journal Press, 1977.

Cater, Douglass. *The Fourth Branch of Government*. Boston: Houghton Mifflin, 1959.

Chancellor, John, and Mears, Walter R. *The News Business*. New York: Harper & Row, 1983.

Cormier, Frank. *LBJ: The Way He Was. A Personal Memoir of the Man and His Presidency*. Garden City, N. Y.: Doubleday, 1977.

Crouse, Timothy. *The Boys on the Bus*. New York: Random House, 1973.

Deakin, James. *Straight Stuff*. New York: William Morrow, 1984.

Germond, Jack W., and Witcover, Jules. *Blue Smoke and Mirrors*. New York: Viking Press, 1981.

————. *Wake Us When It's Over*. New York: MacMillan, 1985.

Greenfield, Jeff. *The Real Campaign*. New York: Summit Books, 1982.

Greenstein, Fred I. *The Hidden-Hand Presidency: Eisenhower as Leader*. New York: Basic Books, 1982.

Greider, William. *The Education of David Stockman and Other Americans*. New York: E. P. Dutton, 1982.

Grossman, Michael Baruch, and Kumar, Martha Joynt. *Portraying the President*. Baltimore: Johns Hopkins University Press, 1981.

Herbers, John. *No Thank You, Mr. President*. New York: W. W. Norton, 1976.

Hess, Stephen. *The Ultimate Insiders: U.S. Senators and the National Media*. Washington, D.C.: The Brookings Institution, 1986.

————. *The Government/Press Connection*. Washington, D.C.: The Brookings Institution, 1984.

————. *The Washington Reporters*. Washington, D.C.: The Brookings Institution, 1981.

Lichter, S. Robert; Rothman, Stanley; and Lichter, Linda S. *The Media Elite*. Bethesda, Md.: Adler & Adler, 1986.

Liebling, A. J. *The Press*. New York: Pantheon Books, 1961, 1981.

Linsky, Martin. *Impact: How the Press Affects Federal Policymaking*. New York: W. W. Norton, 1986.

————, ed. *Television and the Presidential Elections*. Lexington, Mass.: D. C. Heath, 1983.

Lippmann, Walter. *Public Opinion*. New York: The Free Press, 1922.

McGinniss, Joe. *The Selling of the President 1968*. New York: Trident Press, 1968.

Making Sense of the News. The Poynter Institute for Media Studies. St. Petersburg: 1983.

Matusow, Barbara. *The Evening Stars: The Making of the Network News Anchor*. Boston: Houghton Mifflin, 1983.

Minow, Newton; Martin, John Bartlow; and Mitchell, Lee M. *Presidential Television*. New York: Basic Books, 1973.

Nessen, Ron. *It Sure Looks Different from the Inside*. New York: Playboy Press, 1978.

Patterson, Thomas E. *The Mass Media Election: How Americans Choose Their President*. New York: Praeger Publishers, 1980.

The People and the Press. The Gallup Organization. Los Angeles: Times-Mirror, 1986.

Perry, James M. *Us and Them*. New York: Clarkson N. Potter, 1973.

Peters, Charles, and Rothchild, John. *Inside the System: A Washington Monthly Book*. New York: Praeger Publishers, 1970.

Powell, Jody. *The Other Side of the Story*. New York: William Morrow, 1984.

Ranney, Austin. *Channels of Power: The Impact of Television on American Politics*. New York: Basic Books, 1983.

Rivers, William L. *The Other Government: Power and the Washington Media*. New York: Universe Books, 1982.

Roberts, Chalmers M. *The Washington Post: The First Hundred Years*. Boston: Houghton Mifflin, 1977.

Robinson, Michael J., and Sheehan, Margaret A. *Over the Wire and on TV: CBS and UPI in Campaign '80*. New York: Russell Sage Foundation, 1983.

Shaw, David. *Journalism Today: A Changing Press for a Changing America*. New York: Harper's College Press, 1977.

Strout, Richard L. *TRB: Views and Perspectives on the Presidency*. New York: Macmillan, 1979.

Thompson, Kenneth W., ed. *Ten Presidents and the Press*, Lanham, Md.: University Press of America, 1983.

————, ed. *The White House Press on the Presidency*. Lanham, Md.: University Press of America, 1983.

Weaver, David H., and Wilhoit, G. Cleveland. *The American Journalist: A Portrait of U.S. News People and Their Work*. Bloomington, Ind.: Indiana University Press, 1986

Weaver, Warren, Jr. *Both Your Houses: The Truth About Congress*. New York: Praeger Publishers, 1972.

White, Theodore H. *The Making of the President, 1960*. New York: Atheneum, 1961.

———. *The Making of the President 1964*. New York: Atheneum, 1965.

———. *The Making of the President 1968*. New York: Atheneum, 1969.

———. *The Making of the President 1972*. New York: Atheneum, 1973.

White, William S. *Citadel: The Story of the U.S. Senate*. New York: Harper & Bros., 1957.

Wicker, Tom. *On Press: A Top Reporter's Life in, and Reflections on, American Journalism*. New York: Viking Press, 1978.

Witcover, Jules. *The Resurrection of Richard Nixon*. New York: G. P. Putnam's Sons, 1970.

Wolfson, Lewis W. *The Untapped Power of the Press: Explaining Government to the People*. New York: Praeger Publishers, 1985.

Woodward, Bob, and Bernstein, Carl. *The Final Days*. New York: Simon and Schuster, 1976.

———. *All the President's Men*. New York: Simon and Schuster, 1974.

Index

Frankel, Max, 63
fraud, 309–15
  Cooke's ghetto drug story as, 309–11
  Hitler diaries and, 313–14
Freedom Newspapers, Inc., 362
Freedom of Information Act, 186
Friedan, Betty, 125–26, 127, 128
Fulbright, J. William, 213
Future of American Politics, The (Lubell),
  243

Gailey, Phil, 109
Gallup, George, Jr., 252
Gallup Poll:
  on election of 1968, 295
  on press credibility, 307
  Truman's defeat predicted by, 243
Gannett newspapers, 142
Gans, Herbert J., 328, 335
Gart, Murray, 99,100, 112
Gartner, Michael, 333
Gelb, Leslie, 361
George, Walter F., 69
Gephardt, Richard, 234
Gergen, David, 360, 362
Germond, Jack W.:
  on Billy Carter-Libya connection, 102,
    103, 104, 110
  on candidates' press coverage, 301
  on election campaign of 1980, 42,
    271–72, 287
  on election campaign of 1984, 267
  on Muskie, 25, 31
  on Reagan-Bush debate (1980), 27, 42,
    43, 44, 47–48
Geyelin, Philip, 106
Ghadafi, Moammar, 99, 103, 109, 191
Glenn, John:
  in elections of 1984, 255, 264, 281
  hero status of, 50, 141
Gobright, Lawrence A., 136
Goldwater, Barry, 233, 243, 332, 333
Goodman, Ellen, 329
Gore, Albert, Jr., 222
Gorton, Slade, 222
government officials:
  former journalists as, 147, 359–64
  press clashes with, 139–41
government-press connection:

career changes and, 360–64
clique journalism and, 16–17, 146–47
journalists' friendships and, 351–53
symbiosis of, 271, 300
Government/Press Connection, The (Hess),
  151
Graber, Ted, 314
Graham, Donald E., 316
Graham, Katharine:
  Nixon's vice presidential appointment
    and, 96–97
  Watergate reporting and, 325, 365
Gramm, Phil, 222
Great Britain, television news coverage in,
  268
Green, Bill, 310–11, 338
Greenfield, Jeff, 257, 259, 261, 288, 335
Greenfield, Meg, 57–58, 315–16
Greenstein, Fred I., 152
Greider, William, 213, 261, 343–47, 355
Grenada, U.S. invasion of, 186, 305, 307
Gridiron Dinner, 276, 352
Griffith, Thomas, 335
Grissom, Virgil (Gus), 141
Grossman, Michael Baruch, 150, 195–96
gross national product (GNP), U.S., 123
Guthman, Ed, 361

Hagerty, James C., 154–55, 157
Haig, Alexander M., Jr., 188
Hakes, Jay, 271
Halberstam, David, 140
Haldeman, H. R. (Bob), 164
Hammel, Lisa, 126–27
Harding, Warren, 133
Harris, Art, 40, 105
Harris, Fred, 332
Harris, Lou, 243, 244, 295
Hart, Gary:
  in elections of 1984, 254–55, 264, 282
  Lardner's profile of, 53–54, 90
Hartke, Vance, 29, 30
Hartpence, George, 53
Harvard University, 118–19
Harwood, Richard, 140, 333, 339, 355–56
Hatfield, Mark, 276
Hayakawa, S. I., 63
Hayden, Carl, 219
Hays, Charlotte, 16

170–75, 178, 189, 200
in Eisenhower administration, 150,
151–56, 157, 158, 172, 189, 200
in Ford administration, 167, 168–70
history of, 150–51
in Johnson administration, 160–63,
178, 189
in Kennedy administration, 157–60,
161, 171, 172, 178, 189, 200
news conferences and, 197–202
in Nixon administration, 164–67, 169,
189, 194, 200
in Reagan administration, 167, 176–94
retaliatory efforts in, 158–59, 162,
165–66, 186, 188
Why England Slept (Kennedy), 156
Wicker, Tom, 17, 116, 329, 336
Wiggins, J. Russell, 361
Wilhoit, G. Cleveland, 142–43
Will, George F.:
conservatism of, 329
on Ford, 56
Reagan aided by, 352–57
Stockman and, 344
as television commentator, 363
on television reporting, 145
Wills, Garry, 87–88
Wilson, Woodrow, 87–88, 151
wire services:
informational vs. analytical journalism
and, 196, 223–24
pre-television reporting by, 154
regional reporting by, 235
size of, 142

Wirthlin, Richard B., 45–46, 254, 294
Wisconsin, primary elections (1976) in,
249–51
Wise, Phil, 100
Witcover, Jules:
on Billy Carter-Libya connection, 102,
103, 110
on elections of 1976, 283
on elections of 1980, 42, 271–72
on elections of 1984, 267
on Nixon, 84
on presidency, 278
on Reagan-Bush debate (1980), 27, 42,
43, 44, 47–48
Woodward, Bob:
Cooke ghetto-drug story and, 310,
312, 313
on disinformation program, 191
on political sabotage of Muskie, 38
Watergate story reported by, 71, 112,
141, 167
women's movement, 125–27
Woollcott, Alexander, 357
Wooten, James, 172–73
World War I, 98
World War II, 305
Wright, Jim, 231, 232

Yorty, Sam, 29, 30, 32
Young Americans for Freedom, 352

Zaccaro, John, 265
Zagoria, Sam, 338
Ziegler, Ron, 164, 363

About the Author

David S. Broder is the National Political Correspondent and an associate editor of the *Washington Post*. His twice-weekly syndicated column appears in more than 260 newspapers across America and abroad, and in 1973 he won the Pulitzer Prize for Distinguished Commentary.

Mr. Broder was born in 1929 in Chicago Heights, Illinois, and received his B.A. and M.A. from the University of Chicago. He began his newspaper career on the Bloomington (Illinois) *Daily Pentagraph*, came to Washington in 1955 to work for *Congressional Quarterly*, and later worked for the *Washington Star* and the *New York Times* before joining the *Post*'s reporting staff in 1966. He is the author of *Changing of the Guard: Power and Leadership in America* (1980), *The Party's Over: The Failure of Politics in America* (1972), and coauthor with Stephen Hess of *The Republican Establishment: The Present and Future of the G.O.P.* (1967). In addition, he contributes articles to many magazines, appears frequently on such television shows as *Today, Meet the Press*, and *Washington Week in Review*, and regularly gives talks to various college and civic groups around the country.

Mr. Broder and his wife, Ann, have four sons and live in Arlington, Virginia.